D0128834

C#

FOR JAVA DEVELOPERS

Microsoft
.net

Allen Jones
Adam Freeman

PUBLISHED BY
Microsoft Press
A Division of Microsoft Corporation
One Microsoft Way
Redmond, Washington 98052-6399

Library of Congress Cataloging-in-Publication Data
Jones, Allen, 1970-
        C# for Java Developers / Allen Jones, Adam Freeman.
            p. cm.
        Includes index.
        ISBN 0-7356-1779-1
        1. C# (Computer program language)   2. Java (Computer program language)   3.
    Computer software--Development.   I. Freeman, Adam.   II. Title.

    QA76.73.C154 J66 2002
    005.13'3--dc21   2002075302

Printed and bound in the United States of America.

1 2 3 4 5 6 7 8 9   QWE   7 6 5 4 3 2

Distributed in Canada by H.B. Fenn and Company Ltd.

A CIP catalogue record for this book is available from the British Library.

Microsoft Press books are available through booksellers and distributors worldwide. For further information about international editions, contact your local Microsoft Corporation office or contact Microsoft Press International directly at fax (425) 936-7329. Visit our Web site at www.microsoft.com/mspress. Send comments to *mspinput@microsoft.com*.

Acquisitions Editor: Danielle Bird
Project Editor: Devon Musgrave
Technical Editor: Robert Brunner

Body Part No. X08-81843

All credit goes to my wife, Elena, whose love, support, and tolerance are the only things that have made this book possible.

—Allen Jones

I would like to thank Jacqui Griffyth, who suggested writing another book. After seven years together, it is a testament to her humor and forbearance that she still smiles at me when we meet.

I would also like to make special mention of my father, Tony Freeman, who always brings me a Mars bar when he visits and still buys me an Easter egg every year.

—Adam Freeman

Contents at a Glance

Part I   Introducing .NET

   1   **Introduction to Microsoft .NET**   3
   2   **Comparing Java and .NET Technologies**   17

Part II   The C# Language

   3   **Creating Assemblies**   25
   4   **Language Syntax and Features**   37
   5   **Data Types**   65
   6   **Advanced Language Features**   121

Part III   Programming .NET with C#

   7   **Strings and Regular Expressions**   147
   8   **Numbers and Dates**   173
   9   **Collections**   187
   10   **Streams, Files, and I/O**   207
   11   **XML Processing**   239

Part IV   Advanced Topics

   12   **Reflection**   275
   13   **Threading and Synchronizations**   289
   14   **Networking**   311
   15   **Remoting**   341
   16   **Database Connectivity**   365
   17   **Security and Cryptography**   397
   18   **Graphics and UI**   419
   19   **Introduction to XML Web Services**   435

A   Platform Integration   **447**

B   Shared Assemblies   **473**

C   Configuring Applications   **481**

D   Garbage Collection   **489**

E   Cross-Language Code Interoperability   **495**

F   Java to .NET API Reference   **501**

Table of Contents

Introduction   xxi

Part I   Introducing .NET

  1   **Introduction to Microsoft .NET**   **3**

     Background   3

     Goals of .NET   5

       System Integration Using XML   5

       Platform Neutrality   5

       Language Neutrality   6

       Technology Consolidation   7

     Overview of .NET   7

       The .NET Framework   7

       Development Tools   9

       Server Products   12

       Devices and Clients   13

       Building Block Services   13

     Platform Migration and Integration   14

       Web Services and Open Standards   14

       Java User Migration Path to Microsoft .NET   15

       Third-Party Products   15

       Skills Transfer   16

  2   **Comparing Java and .NET Technologies**   **17**

     Java 2 Platform, Standard Edition   18

     Java 2 Platform, Enterprise Edition   20

Part II   The C# Language

  3   **Creating Assemblies**   **25**

     Using the C# Compiler   25

     Other .NET Framework Tools   28

     Assemblies   29

	Contents of an Assembly	29
	Single-File and Multifile Assemblies	31
4	**Language Syntax and Features**	**37**
	General Program Structure	37
	The *Main* Method	38
	Comments	39
	Documentation Comments	39
	Case Sensitivity	39
	Naming Conventions	40
	Source Code Character Sets and Unicode	40
	Identifiers	41
	Source File Names and Contents	41
	Keywords	41
	Package and Namespace Keywords	41
	Simple Type and Constant Keywords	42
	Type Declaration, Access, and Manipulation Keywords	43
	Modifier Keywords	45
	Flow Control Keywords	46
	Exception Handling Keywords	47
	Unmanaged Code Keywords	48
	Keywords as Identifiers	48
	Operators	49
	Precedence and Associativity	50
	Literals	51
	Modifiers	52
	Access Modifiers	52
	Inheritance Modifiers	53
	Other Modifiers	54
	Namespaces	56
	Declaring Namespaces	56
	Using Namespaces	57
	Statements	58
	Labeled Statements	59
	Selection and Iteration Statements	59
	Jump Statements	61
	Other Statements	62

5   Data Types   65

Types   65
    Unified Type System   66
    Value Types   68
    Reference Types   76
    Conversion   85
Members   88
    Member Types and Declaration Context   88
    Versioning and Inheritance of Members   89
    Static Members   91
    Member Attributes   91
    Member Modifiers   91
    Constants   91
    Fields   92
    Static and Instance Constructors   95
    Destructors   97
    Methods   98
    Events   100
    Properties   105
    Indexers   108
    Operators   111
    Nested Types   116
Variables   116
    Value Parameters   117
    Reference Parameters   118
    Output Parameters   119

6   Advanced Language Features   121

Threading and Synchronization   121
Exceptions and Exception Handling   122
    Declaring Exceptions   122
    Catching Exceptions   122
    Throwing Exceptions   123
    The Exception Hierarchy   124
    The *System.Exception* Class   124

Attributes 126
    Attribute Names 127
    Attribute Specification 127
    Custom Attributes 129
    Compile-Time Attributes 131
Assertions 133
Preprocessor Directives 133
    #define and *#undef* 134
    #if, *#elif*, *#else*, and *#endif* 134
    #region and *#endregion* 136
    #warning and *#error* 136
    #line 137
Unsafe Code 137
    The *unsafe* Modifier 137
    The */unsafe* Compiler Flag 138
    Managed and Unmanaged Types 138
    The *sizeof* Operator 139
    Pointers 139
    The *fixed* Statement 142
    The *stackalloc* Command 143

Part III **Programming .NET with C#**

7 **Strings and Regular Expressions** **147**
Strings 147
    Creating Strings 148
    Comparing Strings 149
    Copying Strings 150
    String Length 150
    String Concatenation 150
    Changing Case 151
    Working with Characters 151
    Working with Substrings 152
    Splitting Strings 153
    Strings as Keys 153

Parsing Strings 153
Formatting Strings 154
Encoding Strings 157
Dynamically Building Strings 162
Regular Expressions 164
Compiling Regular Expressions 164
Manipulating Text 166
Ad Hoc Regular Expressions 171

8 Numbers and Dates **173**

Numbers 173
Numbers as Objects 173
Converting Numbers 177
Formatting Numbers 177
Mathematical Functions 181
Random Numbers 182
Dates and Times 183
Creating Dates 184
Manipulating Dates 185
Formatting Dates 186
Parsing Strings 186

9 Collections **187**

Indexers 187
Collection Interfaces 189
ICollection 190
IEnumerable, *IEnumerator*, and the *foreach* Keyword 190
IComparer and *IComparable* 193
Other Collection Interfaces 194
Basic Collections 194
Arrays 194
Hashtable 196
ArrayList 198
Queue 199
Stack 200
SortedList 201

Specialized Collections	202
Strongly Typed Collections	202
Unusual Collections	203
The *CollectionsUtil* Class	203
Synchronization	204
Custom Collections	205

10   Streams, Files, and I/O   207

Working with the Console	207
Writing to the Console	208
Reading from the Console	209
Changing the Console Streams	209
Console Summary	209
The File System	210
Paths	210
Files and Directories	212
Streams	218
The Foundation of Streams	218
Base Streams	219
Pass-Through Streams	222
Readers and Writers	222
Synchronizing Streams	225
Streams Summary	225
Asynchronous I/O	225
Asynchronous I/O Summary	228
Isolated Storage	228
Obtaining and Managing the Isolated Stores	229
Reading and Writing Isolated Data	231
Isolated Storage Summary	232
Object Serialization	232
Simple Serialization	233
Selective Serialization	235
Custom Serialization	235

11   XML Processing   **239**

XmlNameTable   240
XmlReader   241
   XmlTextReader   241
   XmlValidatingReader   251
   XmlNodeReader   255
XmlWriter   255
   XmlTextWriter   256
Document Object Model   260
   Key Classes   260
   Document Creation   261
   Other Key Differences   262
XPath   262
   IXPathNavigable   262
   XPathDocument   263
   XPathNavigator   263
XSL Transformations   269
   Creating a Transformer   269
   Loading a Style Sheet   270
   Transforming XML Data   270
Extensibility   271

Part IV   Advanced Topics

12   Reflection   **275**

Dealing with Types   275
   Local Types   275
   Foreign Types   276
Inspecting Types   277
   Inspecting Constructors and Methods 280
   Inspecting Properties   282
   Inspecting Events   283
   Inspecting Parameters   283

Inspecting Fields   284

Inspecting Attributes   285

Late Binding   285

Instantiation   286

Manipulation   286

13   Threading and Synchronization   289

Threads   290

Creating and Starting Threads   290

Suspending and Resuming Threads   291

Stopping Threads   292

Setting Thread Priorities   294

Thread States   294

Interrupting a Thread   296

Local Thread Data   297

Timers   298

Basic Threading Summary   301

The *ThreadPool* Class   302

Explicit Thread Alternative   302

Waiting for an Event   303

Synchronization   304

Basic Locking   305

Waiting and Notifying   306

ReaderWriterLock   307

WaitHandle   308

14   Networking   311

Accessing the Internet   312

URLs and URIs   312

The *WebClient* Class   315

WebRequest and *WebResponse*   318

HTTP Connection Features   323

Names and Addresses   325

Sockets   329

Creating a TCP Client   329

Creating a TCP Server   332

Using UDP   334

Programming with Native Sockets 335
    Creating Sockets 335
    Client Sockets 335
    Server Sockets 336
    Configuring Sockets 337
    Asynchronous Sockets 338

15   Remoting   341

First Steps 341
    Creating the Server 342
    Creating the Client 344
    Building and Testing the Example 346
Copies and References 347
Channels 348
    Creating a Channel 349
    Registering a Channel 351
    Using More than One Channel 351
Publishing and Activation 353
    Client Activation 354
    Server Activation 354
    Using Configuration Files 356
    Publishing Limitations and Scope 360
Lifetime Leases 360
    Configuring a Lease 361
    Renewing a Lease 362
    Setting Lease Defaults 364

16   Database Connectivity   365

Data Providers 366
    Interfaces and Implementations 366
    Data Provider Sample Code 368
    Connections 372
    Transactions 374
    Commands 376

DataSet	386
DataSet Component Classes	387
Creating a *DataSet*	388
Managing a *DataSet* with a Data Adapter	389
Manually Managing a *DataSet*	391
XML Support	392

17   Security and Cryptography   397

Code Access Security	397
Programming for CAS	398
Declarative CAS Statements	399
Imperative Security Demands	404
CAS Policies	405
Role-Based Security	406
Cryptography	409
Encrypting and Decrypting Data	409
Hash Codes	413
Digital Signatures	415

18   Graphics and UI   419

Windows Forms	419
Using Windows Forms	420
Control Overview	421
Docking and Anchoring	424
Handling Events	426
Drawing with GDI+	427
Obtaining a *Graphics* Instance	427
Lines, Shapes, and Curves	428
Drawing Strings	431
Drawing Images	432
Double Buffering	433

19   Introduction to XML Web Services   435

Creating XML Web Services	436
Building and Deploying XML Web Services	438
Deployment Directory	438
Compiling	438

Creating the Directive   439
Configuring XML Web Services   439
Testing XML Web Services   441
Summary   441
State Management   441
Application State Management   442
Session State Management   442
XML Web Service Clients   443
Creating a Proxy Class   443
Using a Proxy Class   444
Asynchronous Programming   445

A   Platform Integration   447

Runtime Environment   447
Command-Line Arguments   448
Environment Variables   448
Drives and Directories   448
Machine and Operating System Information   449
Process Control   450
Creating New Processes   450
Obtaining a Reference to an Existing Process   451
Terminating Processes   452
Information About Existing Processes   452
Process Synchronization and Events   453
Windows Registry   454
The *Registry* Class   454
The *RegistryKey* Class   455
Remote Registry Access   456
Windows Event Log   456
Writing to the Event Log   456
Reading from the Event Log   458
Creating and Deleting Custom Logs   460
Event Log Notifications   460
Windows Services   462
The Service Application   462
Service Installer   466
Service Controller   469

B   **Shared Assemblies**   **473**

    Creating a Shared Assembly   473

    The Global Assembly Cache   474

        Assembly Versions   475

    Assembly Probing   478

    Codebase Probing   479

C   **Configuring Applications**   **481**

    Application Configuration Files   481

        Specifying a CLR Version   482

        Using Concurrent Garbage Collection   482

        Managing Assembly Versions and Locations   483

        Registering Remote Objects   483

    Application Settings   483

        Simple Settings   483

        Complex Settings   484

D   **Garbage Collection**   **489**

    Controlling the Garbage Collector   489

        Forcing a Collection   489

        Generations   490

        Concurrent Collection   491

    Finalizing and Disposing   491

        Destructors   492

        Resurrection   493

    Weak References   494

E   **Cross-Language Code Interoperability**   **495**

    The Common Type System   496

    The Common Language Specification   496

    Writing CLS-Compliant Code in C#   496

    The *CLSCompliant* Attribute   497

F   Java to .NET API Reference   **501**

The *java.awt* Package   501

The *java.awt.color* Package   504

The *java.awt.datatransfer* Package   504

The *java.awt.dnd* Package   504

The *java.awt.event* Package   504

The *java.awt.font* Package   505

The *java.awt.geom* Package   506

The *java.awt.im* Package   506

The *java.awt.im.spi* Package   506

The *java.awt.image* Package   506

The *java.awt.image.renderable* Package   506

The *java.awt.print* Package   506

The *java.io* Package   507

The *java.lang* Package   508

The *java.lang.ref* Package   510

The *java.lang.reflect* Package   510

The *java.math* Package   510

The *java.net* Package   511

The *java.nio* Package   512

The *java.rmi* Package   512

The *java.security* Package   512

The *java.sql* Package   512

The *java.text* Package   515

The *java.util* Package   515

The *java.util.jar* Package   517

The *java.util.logging* Package   517

The *java.util.prefs* Package   517

The *java.util.regex* Package   517

The *java.util.zip* Package   518

The *javax.swing* Package   518

The *javax.swing.border* Package 522

The *javax.swing.colorchooser* Package 522

The *javax.swing.event* Package 522

The *javax.swing.filechooser* Package 523

The *javax.swing.plaf* Package 523

The *javax.swing.table* Package 523

The *javax.swing.text* Package 523

The *javax.swing.tree* Package 524

The *javax.swing.undo* Package 524

The *javax.sql* Package 524

The *javax.xml.parsers* Package 524

The *javax.xml.transform* Package 524

The *org.w3c.dom* Package 525

The *org.xml.sax* Package 526

Index 527

Introduction

We are both twelve-year veterans of the technology treadmill. Having reinvented ourselves numerous times during our careers, we have always stayed towards the leading edge of the technology curve. It is this desire to stay ahead that drove us to seek a deep understanding of first Java, and now C# and .NET.

Why We Wrote This Book

As Java programmers, we would have found this book useful when starting out with Microsoft .NET and C#. The similarities between C# and Java are immediate and obvious, but there are many challenges to be overcome before a competent Java programmer can become effective with C#. Having faced these challenges, we saw the opportunity to use the similarities and our experience to guide prospective C# developers past the pitfalls and provide a quick route to making effective use of C# and .NET.

Who Should Read This Book

To get the most from this book, the reader should be a Java developer who wants or needs to develop using C# and the Microsoft .NET Framework. Throughout this book, we rely on knowledge of Java to provide an easy path to understanding C# and .NET.

Organization of This Book

We looked around at the C# books in print when we started developing .NET applications and found that most spend a lot of time introducing concepts that are already known to the Java programmer.

Throughout this book we have tried to be concise, comprehensive, and accurate. We have not spent time explaining the basics of programming, detailing the evolution of programming languages, or expounding our favored methodologies. We concentrate on C# and .NET, using Java as the basis for comparison, and provide frequent examples and details of how Java and .NET differ.

Part I: Introducing .NET

The first part of this book provides a brief overview of the .NET platform and includes a comparison between .NET and Java to provide a context for the later chapters.

Part II: The C# Language

The second part of this book consists of a detailed explanation of the syntax and features of the C# language. Java programmers will be comfortable with the majority of the C# syntax and keywords. Part II provides an exhaustive reference for each language feature and explains the differences from Java as required.

Part III: Programming .NET with C#

Part III discusses how to use C# and the .NET Framework to accomplish common programming tasks, including string and number manipulation, Input/Output, using collections, and dealing with XML. The contents of these chapters will provide the reader with an understanding of the basic .NET facilities and demonstrate how the C# language is applied to program the .NET Framework. After reading Part III, readers should be able to write simple C# applications.

Part IV: Advanced Topics

Part IV builds on the previous chapters to introduce more advanced programming areas, such as threading, networking, and accessing databases.

Appendices

Appendices A through E contain information that will be of use to the advanced developer, but which will not be essential for most development projects. Topics include configuring applications, controlling the garbage collection process, and integration with the Microsoft Windows operating system.

The Java to .NET API Reference contained in Appendix F provides mappings between the key classes of the Java 2 Standard Edition (J2SE) and the .NET Framework, broken down by Java package. Developers who need to know whether there is a .NET substitute for a Java class should refer to this appendix.

System Requirements

The best way to learn is to try out the examples in this book as you encounter them. To get the maximal benefit, we recommend using a PC that is running either Windows 2000 or Windows XP operating systems, with a complete .NET

Framework installation. This can be easily achieved by installing Microsoft Visual Studio .NET.

The system requirements for running the .NET Framework SDK, which can be freely downloaded from Microsoft's Web site, are

■ Microsoft Windows NT 4.0 (SP 6a required)

■ Microsoft Windows 2000 (SP 2 recommended)

■ Microsoft Windows XP Professional

and

■ Microsoft Internet Explorer 5.01 or later

The complete requirements for running Visual Studio .NET can be found at *http://msdn.microsoft.com/vstudio/productinfo/sysreq.asp.*

Support

Every effort has been made to ensure the accuracy of this book. Microsoft Press provides corrections for books through the World Wide Web at the following address:

http://www.microsoft.com/mspress/support/

To connect directly to the Microsoft Press KnowledgeBase and enter a query regarding a question or an issue that you may have, go to

http://www.microsoft.com/mspress/support/search.asp

If you have comments, questions, or ideas regarding this book, please send them to Microsoft Press vial postal mail to

Microsoft Press
Attn: C# for Java Developers Editor
One Microsoft Way
Redmond, WA 98052-6399

or via e-mail to

MSPINPUT@MICROSOFT.COM

Note that product support is not offered through the above mail addresses. For support information regarding C# or the .NET Framework, visit the Microsoft Product Standard Support Web site at

http://support.microsoft.com/directory

Part I

Introducing .NET

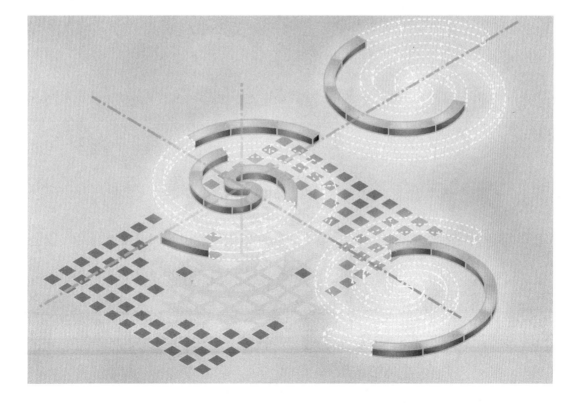

1

Introduction to Microsoft .NET

This book focuses on providing Java programmers with the information they need to write applications for the Microsoft .NET platform using C#. The first hurdle in becoming proficient with the .NET platform is to understand the basics of the .NET initiative. Understanding the goals, structure, and capabilities of .NET provides programmers with a context through which they can better understand the detailed technological discussions presented in later chapters of this book.

We start this chapter by providing background information that has driven and shaped the .NET initiative. We then discuss the goals, scope, and structure of .NET. Finally we give a summary of the migration and integration options when dealing with Java and .NET.

Background

Since the release of Java 1.0 in 1996, dramatic changes in the use and capabilities of information technology (IT) have occurred, including

- The explosive growth in the use of the Internet and the increase in the availability of high-bandwidth connections to both corporations and individual users

- A major change in the design of enterprise systems to using thin clients to access n tier back-end systems

- The major development and broad adoption of many open standards supporting systems integration, including the widespread adoption of XML-based technologies for the representation, manipulation, and exchange of data

- The proliferation of intelligent devices such as mobile phones, PDAs, set-top boxes, and game consoles

- An increase in the availability of free software alternatives to commercial products developed under a variety of licensing and development models but commonly categorized as *open source* software

- Increased emphasis on the adoption of technology by companies to improve the interaction with their customers and partners

- Most recently, explosive growth in the interest in adopting Web services as a means to revolutionize the way that businesses and consumers communicate

Although not directly responsible for any of these changes, Java holds a prominent position as a technological enabler and has often been at the forefront of making these changes become reality.

The Java platform is the result of six years of evolution, driven by the fastest-changing IT market ever. This has resulted in changes to Java at the most fundamental levels; principally, Java has undergone a transformation as it has expanded into new application domains. Originally aimed at consumer devices and the development of applets for providing rich Internet content, Java and more precisely Java 2 Enterprise Edition (J2EE) have become the enterprise and Internet systems development platform of choice for many organizations.

As Java has evolved and been applied to more problems, the API has grown many times. The Java class libraries and optional packages now support all aspects of contemporary business computing.

There is no denying that Java has been a great success. Java is a major platform for the development of both stand-alone and distributed systems and has evolved into a proven, stable, and robust technology. Java offers a wide range of legacy integration capabilities and has the active backing and support of most large software vendors and system integration companies.

Goals of .NET

Microsoft has been successful in the desktop operating systems and applications market for many years but has yet to achieve similar success in the areas of large-scale enterprise and Internet systems, highly distributed systems, and devices. The .NET initiative is Microsoft's attempt to make greater inroads into these markets.

Microsoft .NET is an ambitious initiative with the goal of providing an integrated platform for the creation, distribution, and execution of applications. While Microsoft .NET is a general-purpose development platform, it has been designed from inception to use many open Internet standards and offers strong support for highly scalable distributed applications, in particular XML Web services.

Comparisons of Java and .NET are common. Although it is undeniable that the Java platform provides the foundation for the primary competition .NET will face, the scope of the .NET initiative is much greater. Not only does .NET provide a framework in which applications can be developed and run, it also encompasses the development tools and a broad range of server products used by the applications.

System Integration Using XML

The XML standard was not formalized when Java was first released; nonetheless, Java has been able to offer XML support through third-party solutions for many years. However, it is only with the JAX series of APIs that broad Java support for XML is being standardized; the first component, JAXP, is now part of the standard distribution as of Java 2 Standard Edition (J2SE) version 1.4.

Microsoft recognizes the importance of XML and has built strong XML support deeply into the .NET platform. The use of XML and related technologies is critical to the .NET strategy for systems integration and realizing Microsoft's vision of .NET being the platform of choice for the development and delivery of XML Web services.

Platform Neutrality

Java has always been platform neutral and has embraced the slogan *write once, run anywhere*. Implementations of the Java Virtual Machine (JVM) and the Java 2 software development kit (J2SDK) are available for most existing platforms, and it's common for developers to write applications on one platform and deploy to another—for example, developing on low-cost Microsoft Windows or

Linux machines but deploying to higher-cost server farms and clusters running a variant of UNIX.

Unfortunately, the consistency that the Java platform provides can also be a limitation; Java programmers are often unable to take advantage of specialized hardware and operating system features without making use of the clumsy Java Native Interface (JNI). As an example, features such as asynchronous I/O have become available to Java programmers only with J2SE version 1.4 but have been available in mainstream operating systems for many years.

These limitations aside, the ability to target a range of platforms has been incredibly successful and is one of the reasons behind the widespread adoption of Java. Sun Microsystems has made significant marketing mileage from this ability, and rightly so, since the advantages to developers and companies alike are obvious and immediate.

Microsoft has taken a different approach to platform support. The .NET Framework is built around the features of the Windows operating system and relies on many of the features of the Win32 API.

However, Microsoft has defined the platform adaptation layer (PAL), which defines the Win32 API calls that are used by the .NET Framework, and a *shared source* implementation (known as *Rotor*) of the European Computer Manufacturers Association (ECMA) common language infrastructure (CLI), which is built on the PAL. In principle, porting the PAL to a new platform (that is, mapping the Win32 API calls to native calls) should allow Rotor to run on the new platform.

The catch is that the ECMA CLI standard contains a subset of the .NET Framework features and excludes key elements such as database access (ADO.NET), GUI toolkits (Windows Forms), and server-side applications (ASP.NET). The Rotor implementation is available for noncommercial use and cannot be used to build competing products. Rotor is not based on the source code behind the commercial .NET Framework and is currently available for Windows and FreeBSD.

Language Neutrality

The Java language specification is at the heart of the Java platform. Attempts have been made to port other languages to the platform—most notably Jython, a version of the Python language that generates Java byte code for execution in a JVM—but there has been little adoption of these alternatives to this point, and for the most part applications that run on the Java platform are written in the Java language.

Microsoft has stated that the .NET platform is *language-neutral* and that .NET applications and components can be written in any language. Like a lot of marketing information, there is an element of truth in this statement, but it's not entirely correct.

.NET does support multiple languages, but it isn't the case that any arbitrary language can be used. Only languages that conform to the common type system (CTS) are supported, and, as a result, .NET-supported languages tend to have slightly modified syntax. For example, Microsoft Visual Basic and Visual Basic .NET are not the same language. Likewise, an experienced C++ programmer will have to understand the changes in Managed Extensions to C++ before being able to write a .NET application. The .NET Framework is biased toward object-oriented languages, so procedural languages such as C are unlikely to be introduced, and if they are, they will still be subject to syntax changes.

Technology Consolidation

Although not a stated goal of .NET, it is very much in the interests of Microsoft and its customers for many of Microsoft's overlapping and competing products and technologies to be rationalized and consolidated. The .NET platform presents the ideal scenario for such an exercise, making it more palatable to the user community because the new technology will offer greater integration with the .NET platform.

Overview of .NET

The *.NET* label is frequently applied to a broad range of technologies, products, and marketing initiatives, much the same as the *Java* label. Specifically, the scope of the .NET initiative can be broken down into the following five areas:

- The .NET Framework
- Development tools
- Server products
- Devices and clients
- Building block services

The .NET Framework

The .NET Framework is roughly equivalent to the Java platform, consisting of a set of class libraries and a run-time execution environment, not unlike the Java Virtual Machine. Java binds these two items together with the Java Language Specification, whereas the .NET Framework is designed to support multiple languages, including C# and modified forms of Visual Basic and C++, and so does not include a single language specification.

Microsoft Intermediate Language

The Microsoft intermediate language (MSIL) is the equivalent of the Java byte code system. When compiling a Java source file, the compiler generates a class file that contains Java byte codes representing instructions for the virtual machine. Because these instructions will be interpreted at run time and are not the native instructions of a processor, byte codes are known as an *intermediate* representation of the application logic.

When a C# source file (or a source file containing any other .NET-compatible language) is compiled, the output consists of MSIL instructions. Like Java byte codes, MSIL is an intermediate representation and must be compiled to native instructions in order to be executed; this task is delegated to the common language runtime, discussed next.

The Common Language Runtime

The common language runtime (CLR) is responsible for managing the execution of code and providing core services such as automatic memory management, threading, security, and integration with the underlying operating system—responsibilities similar to those of the Java Virtual Machine.

Before MSIL can be executed, it must be translated into native code, which is specific to a particular CPU. This process is called just-in-time (JIT) compiling and is a core feature of the CLR. MSIL cannot be interpreted like Java byte codes; the JIT cannot be disabled.

The tight integration between the Windows operating system and the format of a .NET application means that the CLR is invoked automatically when a .NET application is started.

The Common Type System   The CTS defines how types are declared, used, and managed at run time. The CTS is an important part of the .NET cross-language support and provides the basis for types written in one language to be used in another.

The Common Language Specification   The Common Language Specification (CLS) is a subset of the CTS. Components that conform to the CLS are guaranteed to be usable by any other component that conforms to the specification. For more information, see Appendix E, "Cross-Language Code Interoperability."

Base Class Libraries

Like Java, the .NET Framework includes a rich set of libraries that a programmer can use and extend during the development process. All of the types contained in the class libraries are CLS-compliant and can be used from any language whose compiler conforms to the CLS, including the C# compiler.

The scope of the .NET class libraries is similar to that of the Java libraries and includes types that

- Represent basic data types and exception

- Support I/O and networking

- Support reflection of types

- Support platform and application security

- Integrate with the underlying operating system

- Provide services for constructing GUI applications

- Provide access to databases

- Support the development of XML Web services

> **More Info**   Chapter 2, "Comparing Java and .NET Technologies," provides a high-level comparison of the Java and .NET class libraries. Part III, "Programming .NET with C#," and Part IV, "Advanced Topics," demonstrate how to program the .NET class libraries with C#.

Development Tools

A computing platform is of little use without the tools and languages necessary to develop applications for it. .NET provides a larger, more sophisticated set of development tools than the standard Java software development kit. The J2SDK provides the minimal set of tools that are required to compile and run Java applications, which leaves the development of more advanced tools to third parties. Microsoft, on the other hand, with a long history in the development tool market and a large established developer community, has updated and expanded its existing range of tools and languages to support the .NET environment.

Command-Line Tools

The J2SDK ships with a set of command-line tools necessary to compile and run Java applications; the same is true of the .NET SDK. Both are freely available and can be used to develop commercial applications for their respective platforms.

Integrated Development Environment

Many programmers prefer to work with a graphical *integrated development environment* (IDE) instead of the command-line tools. A good IDE can dramatically increase the productivity of a developer and make development a more pleasant experience, especially when designing user interfaces.

There is no standard IDE for the Java platform. Many third-party organizations offer both free and commercial IDEs; the quality and utility of these products vary greatly.

As part of .NET, Microsoft has released Visual Studio .NET, the latest version of the popular Visual Studio development environment. Visual Studio .NET is a common development platform for all .NET technologies, comes with support for developing applications in all Microsoft .NET languages, and offers all the features expected of a modern IDE.

The strength of Visual Studio .NET lies in its deep integration with the .NET platform, offering development time integration with some of the .NET servers such as Microsoft SQL Server and Microsoft Internet Information Services.

Languages

Multilanguage support and integration is a fundamental design goal of the CLR and is critical to promoting adoption of the .NET platform from all areas of the development community. The strength of the .NET language support is that components produced in one language can be consumed by another; for example, a managed C++ application can make use of a C# library. The requirement is that components must conform to the CLS; it is possible to develop components with one .NET language that cannot be consumed by another. Consult Appendix E for more information about complying with the CLS.

Microsoft currently provides three languages as part of .NET: Visual Basic .NET, Microsoft Visual C++ .NET, and Microsoft Visual C# .NET. In addition, Microsoft Visual J# .NET is currently in beta.

Visual C# .NET   Unlike the other .NET languages, C# has been designed from the ground up to support the .NET Framework. The design of a programming language is shaped by the success and failure of earlier designs. The Java language includes many elements from C and C++ but excludes many more that were considered unsafe or difficult to use.

The designers of the C# language and the .NET Framework have clearly been influenced by Java, C, and C++ but have taken a fundamentally different approach to resolving conflicts in safe design. A great deal of effort has been made to ensure that the developer can easily write safe and robust code, but features that are considered to be dangerous are still available to the advanced or legacy programmer who can explicitly indicate the need to step outside the limitations of *safe* code.

Although the .NET platform has only recently been released, comparisons between Java and C# are natural because of the many similarities. Generally, these comparisons tend to focus solely on the obvious structural and syntactic similarities, whereas a deeper exploration reveals fundamental differences and a wealth of new features available to the C# programmer.

Fortunately, the strong influence of the Java language allows experienced Java programmers to learn the basic C# language quickly, and with less diffi-culty than a C/C++ programmer. However, some C# features are derived from elements of C or C++ that were excluded from Java and that may be difficult to appreciate from a pure Java perspective.

Visual Basic .NET   Visual Basic .NET is the latest release of the popular Visual Basic language. While still maintaining many similarities with previous versions, Visual Basic .NET has undergone significant change and expansion to provide support for the .NET platform.

Visual C++ .NET   Visual C++ .NET provides nonstandard extensions to the C++ language that allow developers to create C++ applications that take advantage of the .NET platform.

Visual J# .NET   Visual J# .NET is a language compatible with Microsoft Visual J++. We discuss J# in the "Platform Migration and Integration" section later in this chapter.

JScript .NET   JScript .NET is an implementation of the ECMA 262 language specification, which is a standardized language that derives from JavaScript. JScript .NET is an object-oriented scripting language that can use the underlying features provided by the .NET Framework.

Other languages   Third parties have already implemented .NET versions of more than twenty familiar languages. Many of these languages have been extended to meet the requirements of .NET and offer new features provided by the .NET platform. Table 1-1 contains some of the more prominent languages implemented for the .NET platform and provides a link to where additional information can be found. A search on *.NET languages* at *www.microsoft.com* will lead you to a more complete list.

Table 1-1   Third-Party .NET Languages

Language	Link
COBOL	*www.adtools.com/dotnet/index.html*
Component Pascal	*www2.fit.qut.edu.au/CompSci/PLAS/ComponentPascal/*
Delta Forth	*www.dataman.ro/dforth/*
Eiffel	*www.eiffel.com/doc/manuals/technology/dotnet/eiffelsharp/*
Fortran	*www.lahey.com/dotnet.htm*
Perl	*aspn.activestate.com/ASPN/NET/*
Python	*aspn.activestate.com/ASPN/NET/*
SmallScript	*www.smallscript.net/*
Standard ML	*www.research.microsoft.com/Projects/SML.NET/index.htm*

Server Products

The .NET server range consists of a set of rebranded and updated versions of existing Microsoft server products. The .NET server functionality covers everything from operating systems and relational databases to process integration and communications. The range currently includes the following products:

- Microsoft Application Center 2000

- Microsoft BizTalk Server 2000

- Microsoft Commerce Server 2000

- Microsoft Content Management Server 2001

- Microsoft Exchange Server 2000

- Microsoft Host Integration Server 2000

- Microsoft Internet Security and Acceleration Server 2000

- Microsoft Mobile Information Server 2001

- Microsoft SharePoint Portal Server 2001

- Microsoft SQL Server 2000

The integration of Microsoft server products into the .NET platform is still in its earliest stages. To date, most efforts have been focused on adding support for the XML Web services application model to existing products, reflecting the importance Microsoft places on this technology. Over the coming years, this situation will improve: integration will deepen and functionality will increase with the release of new products.

The inclusion of Microsoft server products into .NET highlights one of the primary differences between .NET and Java. The Java platform is vendor independent and provides no products, relying on third parties to provide them.

A Java application server provides a J2EE-compliant environment in which to run enterprise Java applications. Many vendors provide application servers, sometimes with their own set of functionality and extensions to the J2EE specification. Because many of these servers provide similar functionality to the .NET servers, the .NET server market is an area where Microsoft is expected to face intense competition.

Devices and Clients

The .NET Framework runs on a broad range of Windows versions, including Windows 98, Windows Me, Microsoft Windows NT 4.0, Windows 2000, and Windows XP. .NET also targets a new category of client called *smart devices*; Microsoft considers smart devices to be clients that can consume XML Web services. The list of Microsoft devices that are classified in this manner includes

- Pocket PC 2002 PDAs
- The Microsoft Smartphone Platform
- Microsoft Xbox

Microsoft also provides a limited version of the .NET Framework for use on devices, known as the .NET Compact Framework, which is a direct competitor of the Java 2 Micro Edition (J2ME) platform.

Building Block Services

The .NET building block services are a set of XML Web services that provide globally accessible functionality commonly required in distributed systems development. Microsoft has begun a process of making some of its product offerings available via XML Web services and developing new services to drive the adoption of the .NET product set.

Early offerings from this process include Microsoft Passport (a single point of authentication) and MapPoint .NET (which offers map generation and location services). The attraction of XML Web services to Microsoft (and to other companies) is that the revenue model tends to be *per-user*, offering a recurring revenue stream that is not reliant on users purchasing upgrades.

Although the business model behind XML Web services is unproven, many companies are developing tools and services to exploit this technology. XML Web services have clear benefits in simplifying existing business processes and allowing systems from different vendors to operate, but the value of XML Web services as consumer service offerings will not be clear until a critical mass of quality services is available.

> **More Info**   See Chapter 19, "Introduction to XML Web Services," for more information on using the .NET Framework and the C# language to develop XML Web services.

Platform Migration and Integration

The strength of a technology is rarely the deciding factor in a strategic IT decision of a large organization. There are companies that will never use a Microsoft product as a matter of principle, just as there are companies that will never use anything but Microsoft products. Most companies are more pragmatic and make their strategic IT decisions based on a more complex set of criteria.

Many organizations will choose either .NET or Java as their standard enterprise platform. However, through either good or bad planning, some organizations will end up with both .NET and Java platforms. This could be to harness the power of the best technologies from each platform, or simply because too little control is exercised over the individual departments of an organization. Often companies will want to integrate their IT infrastructures and systems closely with their partners, suppliers, and customers who use a different platform.

Whatever the situation, various options exist for integrating the Java and .NET platforms, and some for performing Java to .NET migration. While we have not seen any .NET-to-Java migration tools, we are sure they will appear over the next few years.

Web Services and Open Standards

A current focus of both Java and .NET is the use of open communication standards, XML for data representation, and XML Web services as a means of system integration. This loosely coupled integration capability provides promising, yet unproven, capabilities to bridge the gap between the two competing platforms.

Java User Migration Path to Microsoft .NET

The *Java User Migration Path to Microsoft.NET* (JUMP to .NET) is a set of technologies designed to simplify the short-term integration and long-term migration of Java applications and skills to the .NET platform.

JUMP to .NET currently contains two components, Microsoft Visual J# .NET and the Microsoft Java Language Conversion Assistant (JCA). Both tools are currently in beta release and are freely available for download from the Microsoft Web site.

Visual J# .NET

Visual J# .NET is an implementation of Java language syntax, corresponding to the Java Development Kit (JDK) 1.1.4, that targets the .NET Framework. Visual J# .NET is fully integrated with the Visual Studio .NET IDE and provides complete access to the features of the .NET Framework, including cross-language integration.

Visual J# .NET enables customers with applications written in Microsoft Visual J++ to migrate them to .NET as painlessly as possible. Although Java programmers can use Visual J# .NET to develop new applications, it isn't compatible with J2SE and lacks many of the features a Java programmer would expect.

Java Language Conversion Assistant

The purpose of the JCA is to convert applications developed using Microsoft Visual J++ to C# and so only works against JDK 1.1.4–level code. Currently the JCA will convert most Java language constructs but only about 20 percent of the class library.

It's expected that future releases of the JCA will increase the class library coverage, but no indication has been made of updating the JCA to convert Java code developed based on later versions of Java.

Third-Party Products

Other alternatives for cross-platform integration include third-party middleware products that span both platforms—for example, messaging systems. In addition, there have been numerous announcements about new products designed to execute components from both platforms. We anticipate that many of the predominant J2EE application servers will eventually provide .NET integration capabilities.

Skills Transfer

Java programmers will have little trouble learning the C# language. The difficulty in learning to develop for the .NET platform is in learning the APIs contained in the .NET class libraries. The quickest way for Java programmers to become proficient in C# and .NET is to read this book and write code, code, and more code.

Summary

Both Java and .NET address many of the same issues and offer similar features; after all, they are both platforms attempting to address contemporary IT issues. However, different ideologies lie at their hearts, and different organizations guide their future.

There is undeniable strength in a single, well-executed vision backed by substantial money and resources. Microsoft has hit the road running with the first release of .NET. Time will see more legacy Microsoft products and technologies either replaced by or integrated into the .NET platform. Still, at this point, we're not predicting anything other than an even share of the enterprise market going to Java and .NET in the coming years.

Whatever the outcome, both Java and .NET will be important platforms in the years to come. We have been happy and successful Java developers for many years, but primarily we are technologists. We looked at .NET and liked what we saw; we would suggest all Java programmers do the same and make an informed decision for themselves.

2

Comparing Java and .NET Technologies

Chapter 1, "Introduction to Microsoft .NET," presented a high-level introduction to Microsoft .NET, comparing it both conceptually and technologically with Java. This chapter extends that discussion but focuses more deeply on the technology provided by the two platforms.

> **Note** Although this book focuses predominantly on the .NET functionality that is directly comparable to that of Java 2 Standard Edition (J2SE) version 1.4, this chapter also covers functionality provided by Java 2 Enterprise Edition (J2EE) version 1.3.1. Many Java programmers work with both J2SE and J2EE, and although .NET has a ways to go before it competes with J2EE, it's useful to demonstrate the current features that are comparable and the alternative technologies to use where there are gaps. We don't discuss APIs that aren't part of J2SE and J2EE: they provide compelling and interesting functionality, but it's simply not possible to cover every Java API, and it's often difficult to make substantive comparisons. This is true even for the new Java XML APIs. Although they will help to address the imbalance between the XML capabilities of Java and those of .NET, at the time of this writing they are still in early access release. Also, we haven't included a comparison of Java 2 Micro Edition (J2ME) and the Microsoft .NET Compact Framework. Each is important to the Sun and Microsoft consumer device strategies, but they are topics deserving of their own books.

When viewed holistically, the Java and .NET platforms are comparable: both provide solutions to most contemporary business computing issues. However, when the platforms are broken down into functional components, mapping between the constituent parts is often very loose.

The .NET class library doesn't yet encompass all the functionality found in the J2EE class libraries and often needs to utilize other Microsoft technologies to provide a complete solution; we expect that these technologies will become more tightly integrated as the .NET platform matures.

Despite these inconsistencies, we proceed with a liberal attitude, presenting technology alternatives that are accessible from the .NET platform even though they are not explicitly part of it.

> **Note**   Namespaces are the mechanism used to provide categorization and structure in the .NET class libraries. We discuss namespaces in Chapter 4, "Language Syntax and Features," but for now it's enough to understand that namespaces are analogous to Java packages.

Java 2 Platform, Standard Edition

Table 2-1 shows .NET technology alternatives to the major components of the J2SE platform as broken down within the J2SE platform documentation.

Table 2-1   Comparison of Java 2 Standard Edition and .NET

Java	.NET
Core APIs	
Lang and Util	The .NET class libraries contain functionality that is broadly comparable to the Java Lang and Util APIs. However, the diverse nature of the functionality in these two APIs makes it impossible to provide a useful high-level functionality mapping. For more information, see Appendix F, "Java to .NET API Reference", which provides a class-level mapping between the Java and .NET class libraries.
New I/O	The New I/O API is a collection of features and performance improvements new to J2SE version 1.4. Many of these features provide functionality that is already available in .NET, including regular expressions, asynchronous I/O, and character encoding. In .NET, asynchronous I/O capabilities are incorporated directly into the standard networking and Stream classes. Both Chapter 10, "Streams, Files, and I/O," and Chapter 14, "Networking," provide details of the asynchronous I/O capabilities provided by the .NET classes. Regular expressions and character encoding are both covered in Chapter 7, "Strings and Regular Expressions."

Table 2-1   Comparison of Java 2 Standard Edition and .NET   *(continued)*

Java	.NET
Networking	The *System.Net* namespace of the .NET class library contains functionality comparable to that of the Java networking classes. Consult Chapter 14 for complete details.
Preferences	Along with the Microsoft Windows registry, .NET provides a mechanism called *isolated storage*. Together, these features provide the technology that is most comparable to the Java Preferences API. We discuss isolated storage in Chapter 10 and discuss the Windows registry in Appendix A, "Platform Integration."
Collections Framework	The *System.Collections* namespace of the .NET class library includes functionality comparable to the Java Collections Framework. Chapter 9, "Collections," provides a detailed discussion of .NET collections.
Java Native Interface (JNI)	JNI provides access to platform-specific functionality from the platform-neutral environment provided by Java. As a Windows-based environment, .NET doesn't face these issues. However, .NET does provide the *Platform Invocation Service* (PInvoke), which allows calls to functions contained in unmanaged libraries. .NET also includes extensive capabilities for interoperability with COM components.
Security	The .NET Framework provides a comprehensive security system, which can be used to grant or deny platform features to applications. Chapter 17, "Security and Cryptography," provides a discussion of the .NET security system.
Java API for XML Processing (JAXP)	XML processing capabilities are built deeply into the .NET class libraries, and many individual classes are XML-aware. The functionality that compares most directly with JAXP is contained in the *System.Xml* and *System.Xml.Xsl* namespaces. Chapter 11, "XML Processing," contains a detailed description of these facilities.
Logging	The .NET Framework doesn't provide a generic logging mechanism equivalent to the Java Logging API. Instead, Logging in .NET uses the Windows Event Log, which we discuss in Appendix A.
JavaBeans	.NET doesn't provide a technology that is directly comparable to JavaBeans. Some of the property and introspection capabilities of JavaBeans are built directly into the .NET languages and the class library. From a visual component perspective, .NET includes a component model based on implementation of the *System.ComponentModel.IComponent* interface.
Locale Support	.NET provides extensive support for localization of applications. Much of this functionality is contained in the *System.Globalization* namespace.

(continued)

Table 2-1   **Comparison of Java 2 Standard Edition and .NET**   *(continued)*

Java	.NET
Integration APIs	
Remote Method Invocation (RMI)	The .NET Framework includes the *remoting* system, which is a functional equivalent of RMI. Chapter 15, "Remoting," details the remoting system.
JDBC	A subsection of the .NET class library below the *System.Data* namespace and commonly referred to as ADO.NET provides functionality comparable to that of JDBC. Chapter 16, "Database Connectivity," provides a complete description.
Java Naming and Directory Interface (JNDI)	Classes contained in the *System.DirectoryServices* namespace provide access to Active Directory, NDS, and LDAP directory servers.
CORBA	The .NET platform does not provide support for CORBA integration.
UI Toolkits	
Abstract Windows Toolkit (AWT) and Swing	The .NET Framework includes a UI toolkit known as Windows Forms. Although less flexible and less complete than the Java alternatives, Windows Forms allow the programmer to develop applications for the Windows platform. Chapter 18, "Graphics and UI," contains an overview of the Windows Forms toolkit.
Java 2D	Windows GDI+, exposed through classes in the .NET class library, is the functional equivalent of the Java 2D API. Chapter 18 contains an overview of GDI+.

Java 2 Platform, Enterprise Edition

J2EE is a set of programming interfaces that allow programmers to build server-side applications. Unlike J2SE, J2EE doesn't contain operational implementations of the APIs it defines; this is left to third parties.

Few .NET technologies compare directly to the J2EE APIs, although in most cases other Microsoft products exist to fill the gaps. Table 2-2 lists the J2EE APIs and the equivalent technology provided by or accessible through .NET.

Table 2-2   Comparison of Java 2 Enterprise Edition and .NET

Java	.NET
Enterprise Java Beans (EJB)	The .NET Framework can provide a mechanism that is similar to the Session Bean model via interoperability with COM+, but it has no equivalent of the Message and Entity bean models; this is a surprising omission, given the broad and rapid adoption of EJBs.
	Microsoft has indicated that an equivalent of Entity beans will be included in a future release of the .NET Framework, but for the moment .NET doesn't offer a complete alternative to the EJB model.
JavaMail	The *System.Web.Mail* namespace contains functionality for creating and sending e-mail from .NET applications.
Java Connector Architecture (JCA)	.NET provides integration with legacy systems through Microsoft Host Integration Server.
Java Message Service (JMS)	.NET provides messaging capabilities through Microsoft Message Queuing (MSMQ).
Java Server Pages (JSP)	Microsoft ASP.NET provides functionality similar to that of JavaServer pages.
Java Transaction API (JTA)	.NET provides transactional support for enterprise applications through Microsoft Transaction Server (MTS).
Servlet API	Microsoft ASP.NET can be used to process HTTP requests, providing functionality comparable to that of Java Servlets.

Summary

Microsoft has included a huge amount of functionality for the first release of a platform and product set, and the .NET Framework can be readily used to develop client and server applications.

.NET provides functionality equivalent to that of the J2SE platform but doesn't yet contain all of the features available with J2EE. The most obvious omission is an equivalent of the full EJB model. This should be addressed with future versions of the .NET software.

Part II
The C# Language

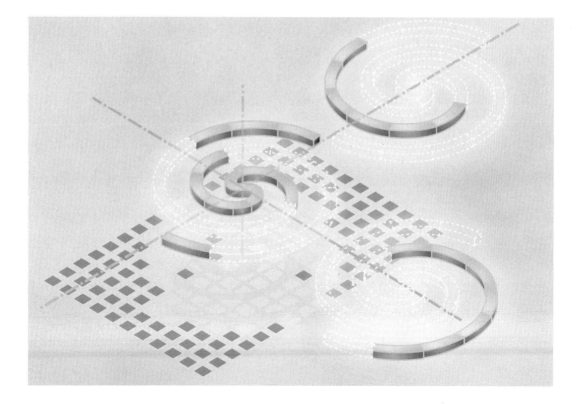

3

Creating Assemblies

This chapter introduces assemblies, which are the .NET unit of deployment, reuse, versioning, and security. Assemblies are a logical rather than a physical structure and include one or more modules and resources. Assemblies are self-describing, containing metadata in a manifest that describes the contents and dependencies of the assembly.

The *assembly manifest* is the link between the data types contained in an assembly and the common language runtime (CLR). The CLR relies on the metadata in the assembly to load the assembly and required libraries, enforce security policies, handle version support, and perform type validation.

Using the C# Compiler

This section demonstrates how to compile C# source files by using the C# compiler, csc.exe. This is a simple process, similar to using the javac compiler. The significant difference is the result of the compilation process, which we'll discuss in the "Assemblies" section later in this chapter.

The csc.exe application can be found in the main directory of the .NET Framework installation, typically C:\<*windows directory*>\Microsoft.NET\Framework\v<*version number*>. As is the case with the other .NET command-line tools, csc.exe will not be added to your *PATH* environment variable during the installation process, so you'll need to do it manually.

The following code represents the C# Hello World! application:

```
class MyApplication {
    static void Main(string[] args) {
        System.Console.WriteLine("Hello World!");
    }
}
```

The syntax and keywords of the C# language are described in Chapter 4, "Language Syntax and Features." For the moment it's not important to understand the meaning of the C# keywords but simply to accept that this small program will print the *Hello World!* string when executed.

We save this code in a source file named MyApplication.cs by using a standard text editor; both ASCII and UTF-8 formats are supported. The .cs extension is the standard for C# files. The source file is compiled using the C# compiler (csc.exe) as follows:

```
csc MyApplication.cs
```

The compiler produces an executable file named MyApplication.exe that prints *Hello World!* when executed. There's no need to invoke the runtime explicitly as you do with Java; Microsoft Windows understands that this is a compiled Microsoft intermediate language (MSIL) application and implicitly invokes the common language runtime.

The general usage form for the C# compiler is

```
csc [compiler options] [list of source files to compile]
```

Table 3-1 lists the most important options that can be used with the C# compiler. Note that many of the compiler options have abbreviated forms; see the online documentation for more details.

Table 3-1   The Most Commonly Used C# Compiler Options

Option	Description
Input Files	
/addmodule:<file list>	Specifies a list of modules to be linked. See the "Assemblies" section for more information.
/reference:<file list>	Specifies a list of assemblies to be referenced. See Appendix B, "Shared Assemblies," for more information on using references.
/recurse:<wildcard>	Searches the current directory and all subdirectories for files to compile that match the specified wildcard.
/nostdlib	Doesn't reference the standard library (mscorlib.dll).
Output Files	
/out:<file>	Specifies the name of the output file.
/target:exe */target:library* */target:module* */target:winexe*	Specifies the format of the output file. See the "Assemblies" section for more information.
/define:<symbol list>	Defines conditional compilation symbols. See Chapter 6, "Advanced Language Features," for more information.

Table 3-1   The Most Commonly Used C# Compiler Options   *(continued)*

Option	Description
*/optimize[+	-]*	Enable code optimization.
/doc:<file>	Generate XML class documentation to the specified file.
Debugging	
/bugreport:<file>	Creates a file containing information that can be used to report a bug with the C# compiler.
*/checked[+	-]*	Specifies whether integer arithmetic overflows are checked. See Chapter 6 for more information.
*/debug[+	-]*	Specifies whether debugging information should be included in the output.
/debug:full |pdbonly	Specifies the type of debugging information that is generated. The *full* option allows a debugger to be attached to a running application, and the *pdbonly* option requires the application to be started by the debugger for MSIL statements to be viewed.
/fullpaths	References to files in the output files will be fully qualified.
/nowarn:<warning list>	Suppresses specified warnings from the compiler.
/warn:<n>	Specifies a warning level (0 to 4).
	Level 0 disables all warnings.
	Level 1 displays only severe warnings.
	Level 2 displays level 1 warnings plus certain less severe warnings, such as warnings about hiding class members.
	Level 3 displays level 2 warnings plus certain less severe warnings, such as warnings about expressions that always evaluate to true or false.
	Level 4 displays all level 3 warnings plus informational warnings.
*/warnaserror[+	-]*	Specifies whether warnings should be promoted to errors.
Resources	
/linkresource:<resinfo>	Links a .NET managed resource.
/resource:<resinfo>	Embeds a .NET resource in the output file.
/win32icon:<file>	Inserts an .ico file into the output.
/win32res:<file>	Inserts a Win32 resource into the output.
Miscellaneous	
/main:<type>	Specifies the application entry point. See the "Assemblies" section for more information.
/lib:<file list>	Specifies a list of directories to search for assemblies specified using the */reference* option.

Table 3-1   The Most Commonly Used C# Compiler Options   *(continued)*

Option	Description
/? /help	Prints a usage guide that contains a complete listing of all compiler options.
/incremental[+ |-]	Enables incremental compilation of source files.
/unsafe[+ |-]	Permits compilation of code that contains the *unsafe* keyword. See Chapter 6 for more information.

Other .NET Framework Tools

Table 3-2 lists some of the more useful tools that are included with the .NET Framework. As mentioned earlier, be forewarned that these tools are not automatically added to your *PATH* environment variable during the .NET installation process. The default installation directories for these executables are *C:\Program Files\Microsoft Visual Studio .NET\FrameworkSDK\Bin* for all but dbgclr.exe, which is installed in *C:\Program Files\Microsoft Visual Studio .NET\FrameworkSDK\GUIDebug*.

Table 3-2   Useful .NET Framework Tools

Tool	Description
Assembly Linker (al.exe)	Generates metadata for one or more files that are combined into an assembly.
Microsoft .NET Global Assembly Cache Utility (gacutil.exe)	Lists and manipulates the global assembly cache (GAC) and the download cache. See Appendix B for more information.
.NET Framework Configuration Tool (mscorcfg.msc)	GUI tool for managing and configuring the .NET Framework using the Windows Management Interface (WMI).
Microsoft CLR Debugger (dbgclr.exe)	Graphical debugging tool.
Microsoft CLR Runtime Test Debugger Shell (cordbg.exe)	Command-line debugging tool.
Microsoft .NET Framework Strong Name Utility (sn.exe)	Assists in creating assemblies with strong names. See Appendix B for more information.
Code Access Security Policy Tool (caspol.exe)	Security policy management for machine, user, and enterprise security policies.
Resource File Generator (resgen.exe)	Creates CLR binary resource files from existing native formats.
Microsoft .NET IL Disassembler (ildasm.exe)	Graphical tool to disassemble MSIL files.

Assemblies

Assemblies are usually created using the C# compiler; however, Assembly Linker (al.exe) might be required under certain circumstances. We demonstrate one area where the assembly linker is required later in this chapter in "Creating a Multifile Assembly."

The format of an assembly governs how it can be used; for example, the exe and winexe formats are executable but cannot be imported as references to other assemblies. The format of an assembly is specified using the */target:<format>* switch on the C# compiler and the assembly linker. Table 3-3 details the four assembly formats.

Table 3-3   The Four Formats for an Assembly

Assembly Format	Description
exe	A console executable. The assembly must contain one entry point, which is defined as a valid *Main* method.
library	A type library that can be used by other assemblies.
module	A nonexecutable collection of compiled code for use in other assemblies. See the "Modules" section later in this chapter for details.
winexe	A graphical Windows executable. The assembly must contain one entry point, which is defined as a valid *Main* method.

Contents of an Assembly

An assembly comprises the following elements:

■   An assembly manifest that contains metadata.

■   One or more modules.

■   Resource files, such as icons for Windows applications.

The Manifest

Every assembly contains a manifest consisting of metadata describing the assembly and the types contained within the assembly. The manifest contains the information described in Table 3-4.

Table 3-4   Information Defined in a Manifest

Information	Description
Name	The name of the assembly.
Version	A major and minor version number, and a revision and build number. The common language runtime uses these numbers to enforce version policy.
Culture	Information about the culture or language that the assembly supports, similar to the Internationalization and Localization concepts in Java. This is required only for assemblies that contain solely localized resources, such as culture-specific strings, known as "satellite" assemblies.
Strong name	Strong names are discussed in detail in Appendix B.
Assembly contents	A list of files that make up the assembly. See the "Creating a Multifile Assembly" section later in this chapter for more information.
Type information	Details of types exported by the assembly.
References	Details of assemblies required to support the types contained in the assembly.
General information	General details, such as the company that produced the assembly, a description string, and copyright information.

The first four items (name, version, culture, and strong name) are used to identify an assembly. Most of the information in the manifest is generated automatically when the assembly is created. The general information can be specified by the programmer. See the sections on single-file and multifile assemblies for more information.

Modules

As detailed in the following list, an appreciation of modules is important in understanding assemblies.

- Modules contain one or more .NET types described in MSIL.

- Modules can contain types from more than one namespace, and namespaces can span more than one module. Namespaces are discussed in Chapter 4.

- Modules can be compiled from one or more source files.

- Modules cannot be used directly by the common language runtime.

Modules are designed to ease the development process by allowing independent development of modules, which can be written in different .NET-supported languages. These modules are later combined into a single assembly.

Modules are created with the C# compiler using the option */target:module*, for example:

```
csc /target:module /out:MyModule.netmodule
    FirstSourceFile.cs SecondSourceFile.cs
```

The output of this command will be a file named MyModule.netmodule containing MSIL representations of the types defined in the source files; the .netmodule extension is the default for modules. The module file contains the following information:

- A manifest listing the assemblies that the types in the module rely on and a declaration of the module name.

- The types compiled from the source files, grouped by namespace.

Modules can rely on the types contained in other modules. This is achieved by using the */addmodule* compiler switch. The following command demonstrates how to compile a source file that relies on types defined in *MyModule.netmodule*:

```
csc /addmodule:MyModule.netmodule /target:module SourceFile.cs
```

Using the */addmodule* switch allows the compiler to load the types contained in the original module and to correctly compile the types contained in the source file.

Resources

As well as a manifest and modules, assemblies can contain resources. Resources enable text and images to be separated from the logic of the application, thereby easing the tasks of maintenance and localization of applications.

Single-File and Multifile Assemblies

Assemblies can comprise either a single file (a *single-file assembly*) or a set of files (a *multifile assembly*). A single-file assembly combines one module with metadata into a single disk file. The C# compiler creates single-file assemblies by default.

Multifile assemblies consist of one or more modules and a separate file containing the assembly manifest. Multifile manifests would be used for the following reasons:

- To combine modules written in different languages. For example, the C# compiler, by default, creates a single-file assembly containing MSIL generated only from C# code. To include a module written in

Microsoft Visual Basic .NET, or any other supported .NET programming language, in an assembly, a multifile assembly is used.

■   To minimize the consumption of system resources by including rarely used types in a separate module. The common language runtime will load modules as required.

■   To support the independent development of application components, which is commonly known as component programming.

The manifest file and the module files form a single unit and cannot be separated; these files must be deployed together. The manifest file does not directly incorporate any of the types included in the modules.

Creating a Single-File Assembly

The following statement compiles two source files into a single-file assembly:

```
csc /target:exe /out:Application.exe
    MyApplication.cs MySupportClass.cs
```

This command creates a new assembly named Application.exe using the exe format. Exe and winexe assembly formats must have an entry point, typically a *Main* method. If more than one component defines a *Main* method, the compiler relies on the */main* switch to indicate which should be used. Unlike Java applications, .NET assemblies are not started by specifying a class; the identity of the application entry point is included in the assembly.

Setting metadata for a single-file assembly   For single-file assemblies, metadata can be defined in a C# source file. Microsoft Visual Studio .NET automatically creates a file named AssemblyInfo.cs, which contains placeholder definitions. If this source file is included in a compilation, the statements are used to construct the assembly manifest.

To demonstrate your ability to purposefully define the informational elements of the manifest, we'll create a file named AssemblyInfo.cs, which contains the following statements:

```
using System.Reflection;
using System.Runtime.CompilerServices;

[assembly: AssemblyTitle("MyAssembly")]
[assembly: AssemblyDescription("This is a single-file assembly")]
[assembly: AssemblyCompany("MyCompany")]
[assembly: AssemblyProduct("MyProduct")]
[assembly: AssemblyCopyright("2002, My Company")]
```

This file contains statements that are interpreted by the C# compiler when creating an assembly. We define our programming logic in the MyApplication.cs file, as shown here:

```
class MyApplication  {
    static void Main(string[] args) {
        System.Console.WriteLine("Hello World!");
    }
}
```

To create a single-file assembly incorporating the manifest information and the code file, use the following command:

```
csc /target:exe /out:Application.exe MyApplication.cs AssemblyInfo.cs
```

The information supplied in the AssemblyInfo.cs file can be seen on the Version tab in the Windows Explorer properties window for the Application.exe file. Metadata is also available through runtime reflection. Figure 3-1 shows the metadata for the sample assembly viewed via the Windows Explorer "Version" tab.

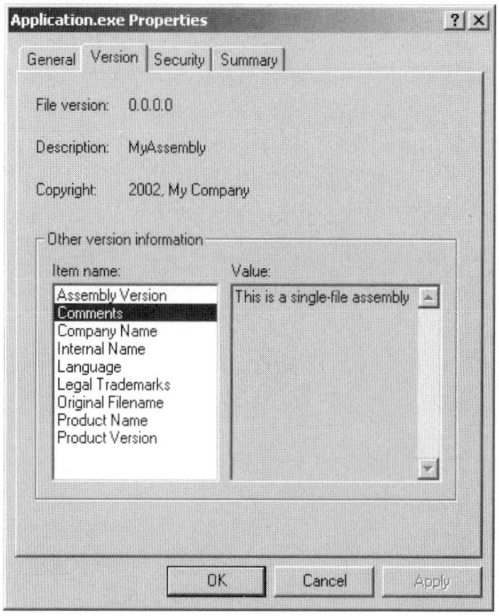

Figure 3-1   Metadata for a single-file assembly

More Info   For details of reflection, see Chapter 12, "Reflection."

Creating a Multifile Assembly

Multifile assemblies are created using the assembly linker (al.exe). The linker takes a number of modules and generates a file that contains the assembly manifest data. To demonstrate creating a multifile assembly, we'll create two classes and compile each into a separate module. The first class is shown here and should be stored in a file named StringPrinter.cs:

```
public class StringPrinter {
    public void printString(string messageString) {
        System.Console.WriteLine("Message: " + messageString);
    }
}
```

This class contains a single method that accepts a string argument and prints a message to the console.

The second class should be stored in a file named HelloWorld.cs, shown here:

```
class HelloWorld {
    public static void Main(string[] args) {
        StringPrinter myPrinter = new StringPrinter();
        myPrinter.printString("Hello World!");
    }
}
```

The *HelloWorld* class contains a *Main* method that creates a new instance of the *StringPrinter* class and invokes the *printString* method with the string *Hello World* as an argument. We compile each class into a module using the following statements. Note that because the *HelloWorld* class relies on the *StringPrinter* class, we need to add an */addmodule* switch to ensure that the types can be resolved correctly:

```
csc /target:module StringPrinter.cs
csc /addmodule:StringPrinter.netmodule /target:module HelloWorld.cs
```

These statements create two modules, named HelloWorld.netmodule and StringPrinter.netmodule. We combine these into an assembly by using the assembly linker as in the following statement:

```
al /out:App.exe /target:exe /main:HelloWorld.Main
    HelloWorld.netmodule StringPrinter.netmodule
```

Here are the details:

■   The */out* switch specifies the name of the manifest file.

- The */target* switch specifies the format for the assembly.

- The */main* switch specifies the application entry point, in this case the *Main* method contained in the *HelloWorld* class.

- The remaining arguments are the file names of the modules that should be included in the assembly.

Executing the App.exe file results in "Message: Hello World!" being printed on the console. If any of the module files are missing, the CLR will report an error indicating that a dependency cannot be resolved.

Setting metadata for a multifile assembly The statements used to set the assembly metadata for a single-file assembly are interpreted by the C# compiler. When using the assembly linker to create a multifile assembly, the metadata can be specified using command-line switches. The following command illustrates setting metadata via the command line; the switches that were used to set metadata appear in boldface:

```
al /out:App.exe /target:exe /main:HelloWorld.Main
   /title:MyAssembly
   /description:"This is a multifile assembly"
   /company:MyCompany
   /product:MyProduct
   HelloWorld.netmodule StringPrinter.netmodule
```

Summary

This chapter has provided a working knowledge of the key tools necessary to build applications for the .NET Framework. We also provided a detailed description of assemblies. Assemblies are one of the most significant differences introduced by the .NET Framework. Assemblies have an impact on almost every aspect of .NET and provide some sophisticated features to aid the packaging and deployment of applications. More advanced information about assemblies, including how to create an assembly that can be shared between applications, can be found in Appendix B.

Language Syntax and Features

This chapter details the basic syntax, structure, and features of the C# language. We expect the reader to be familiar with the Java language, and we concentrate on C# features that are new or different.

General Program Structure

We begin with a simple program example to demonstrate the basic points that must be understood when writing C# code. The following Java code should be familiar:

```java
public class Hello {
    public static void main(String[] args) {
        System.out.println("Hello World!");
    }
}
```

Contrast it with the following C# code:

```csharp
using System;

public class Hello {
    public static void Main(String[] args) {
        Console.WriteLine("Hello World!");
    }
}
```

Although obvious similarities exist, the following points should be noted:

- The *java.lang* package is implicitly imported to all Java programs. C# does not implicitly import any classes. The `using System;` statement makes the classes required for this program available. Note that *System* in the C# code refers to a namespace from the .NET class libraries, not a specific class as it does in Java. Importing classes into C# programs is covered in the "Using Namespaces" section later in this chapter.

- The classes and methods used to write to the console are different. The .NET class libraries are covered in Part III of this book; console output is covered in Chapter 10, "Streams, Files, and I/O."

- The *application entry point*—or main method—uses different capitalization; it's *Main* in C#. See the next section for more information about the *Main* method.

The *Main* Method

The capitalization of the method name is not the only difference between the two *Main* methods. The Java *main* method has the following signature:

```
public static void main(String[] args)
```

The *Main* method in C# can return either an *int* or a *void* and can take either an array of *string* arguments or nothing as its parameters, resulting in the following four possible signatures:

```
static void Main()
static void Main(String[] args)
static int  Main()
static int  Main(String[] args)
```

Points to note:

- The *public* access modifier is not required for the C# *Main* method. The application entry point is always accessible to the runtime regardless of its declared accessibility.

- The *int* returned by the third and fourth signatures serves as the *termination status code* that is returned to the execution environment on termination of the program. This is equivalent to the use of *Runtime.getRuntime.exit(int)* or *System.exit(int)* in Java. The *Main* method signatures that return *void* will always return 0 as the termination status code.

Comments

C# supports both the single-line (*//*) and multiline (*/*...*/*) comment syntaxes.

Documentation Comments

C# implements a code documentation tool similar to the *javadoc* utility. Like *javadoc*, this works only if the developer places markup in appropriately formatted code comments. Unlike *javadoc*, this markup is extracted at compile time and is output to a separate file as XML. Being XML, this information can be easily processed to produce documentation in different formats—not just HTML, but any format that is supported by a valid XSL transformation. The most common approach, however, is to utilize an XSL transformation to generate HTML pages.

Code documentation comments are preceded by three forward slashes, as shown here:

```
/// A single line documentation comment
```

The C# specification also recommends use of the familiar */*** token to identify multiline documentation comments. However, version 7.00 of the C# compiler does not support this syntax.

> **More Info**   To produce code documentation output, use the */doc* flag when compiling. Full coverage of compiler options is contained in Chapter 3, "Creating Assemblies."

> **More Info**   Refer to the .NET documentation for complete coverage of the tags supported by the documentation comment tool.

Case Sensitivity

Like Java, C# is a case-sensitive language. However, case sensitivity shouldn't be used to differentiate program elements. The multilanguage support in the .NET runtime means that components developed in C# can be called from components written in other .NET languages that might not be able to differentiate on the basis of case.

Naming Conventions

The C# specification advises a combination of Pascal and camel case conventions for the names of various programming identifiers. Pascal casing capitalizes the first character of each word—for example, *MyMethod* or *SomeIntegerVariable*. Camel case convention capitalizes the first character of each word except the first one—for example, *myMethod* or *someIntegerVariable*.

The .NET class libraries implement these guidelines. This guideline has the commendable goal of making all C# code and class libraries more readable, consistent, and predictable. In many cases, developers will continue using conventions that they are comfortable with, or that their organization dictates, but familiarity with these conventions will help to navigate and understand the .NET class libraries. Refer to the C# Language Specification for full details.

Warning   One result of these naming conventions is the difference in capitalization of method names between the Java and .NET class libraries. .NET uses Pascal convention for method names:

```
SomeObject.ToString();
```

Java uses camel convention:

```
SomeObject.toString();
```

This subtle difference is certain to cause frustration for Java developers when they first begin the transition to C# development.

Source Code Character Sets and Unicode

C#, .NET, and Java all support the use of Unicode internally and provide extensive Unicode support to the developer through their class libraries. However, there is some difference in the support for Unicode in source files. By default, all Java tools, including the Java compiler, can process only LATIN-1 and Unicode encoded characters in a source file. The Unicode characters in the source file must be encoded using Unicode escape sequences. For other character encodings, the *–encoding* compiler flag must be used, which forces the Java compiler to translate source files in different encoding formats into the default format before compiling the source code.

The C# compiler, on the other hand, will accept characters in the default code page (LATIN-1) or Unicode (UTF-8-encoded) files by default, conveniently allowing the programmer to use and view Unicode characters in source files. C# also supports the use of Unicode escape sequences.

Identifiers

The naming of C# program elements follows rules that are broadly similar to Java:

- Both languages support Unicode characters in identifier names.

- C# identifiers must begin with a letter or underscore, but the $ symbol permitted by Java is not valid in C#.

- The remainder of the identifier is made up of letters and numbers.

- C# allows the use of keywords as identifiers by preceding the identifier with the @ symbol. Refer to the "Keywords as Identifiers" section coming up for full details.

Source File Names and Contents

Java requires a single *public* class definition per source file but allows any number of nonpublic classes. The file name must match the public class name with the .java extension. C# permits any number of public and nonpublic classes to be contained in a single source file. The source file can have any valid operating system name independent of the classes it contains.

If more than one class contains a *Main* method, the application entry point must be specified at compile time by using the */main* flag. Compiler options are discussed in Chapter 3.

Keywords

C# has more keywords than Java. When both languages define the same keyword, they typically have the same function, although some equivalent features are available through different keywords. Each keyword will be discussed in detail in the appropriate section of this chapter, but we'll begin by presenting a high-level comparison of the keywords available in both languages.

Package and Namespace Keywords

Although Java packages and C# namespaces are significantly different in their implementation and capabilities, both languages provide keywords for their use and declaration. Table 4-1 contrasts these keywords.

Table 4-1   Comparison of Package and Namespace Keywords

Java	C#	Comments
import	*using*	Makes the elements of a package/namespace accessible without the need to use fully qualified names
package	*namespace*	Declares program elements to be members of a named package/namespace

> **More Info**   For details of packages and namespaces, refer to the "Namespaces" section later in this chapter.

Simple Type and Constant Keywords

Table 4-2 contrasts the Java and C# keywords associated with

- Built-in constant values required by the languages: *null*, *void*, *true*, and *false*.

- Built-in simple data types: *char*, *int*, *byte*, and so forth.

In this category, C# provides a superset of the keywords provided in Java. Because the Java Virtual Machine supports a restricted range of data types that doesn't include unsigned integer types, Java does not have keywords to represent them. Java also doesn't have the *decimal* type, although the *BigDecimal* class provides similar functionality.

> **More Info**   For a comprehensive coverage of each keyword in Table 4-2, refer to the "Types" section in Chapter 5, "Data Types."

Table 4-2   Simple Type Comparison

Java	C#	Comments
boolean	*bool*	True or false values.
char	*char*	16-bit Unicode character.
byte	*sbyte*	8-bit signed integer (-128 to 127).

Table 4-2   Simple Type Comparison   *(continued)*

Java	C#	Comments
N/A	*byte*	8-bit unsigned integer (0 to 255).
short	*short*	16-bit signed integer (-32768 to 32767).
N/A	*ushort*	16-bit unsigned integer (0 to 65535).
int	*int*	32-bit signed integer (-2147483648 to 2147483647).
N/A	*uint*	32-bit unsigned integer (0 to 4294967295).
long	*long*	64-bit signed integer (-9223372036854775808 to 9223372036854775807).
N/A	*ulong*	64-bit unsigned integer (0 to 18446744073709551615).
float	*float*	32-bit double-precision floating point.
double	*double*	64-bit double-precision floating point.
N/A	*decimal*	128-bit high-precision decimal number with 28 significant digits. Intended for precise financial calculations.
true	*true*	Technically, *true* is not a Java keyword but a Boolean literal.
false	*false*	Technically, *false* is not a Java keyword but a Boolean literal.
null	*null*	Technically, *null* is not a Java keyword but a literal.
void	*void*	Identify a functional member as not returning a value.

Type Declaration, Access, and Manipulation Keywords

Table 4-3 contrasts the Java and C# keywords associated with declaring, accessing, and manipulating complex types and their members.

> **More Info**   These keywords are covered in detail in the "Modifiers" section later in this chapter and in the "Types" and "Members" sections in Chapter 5.

Table 4-3   Complex Type Keyword Comparison

Java	C#	Comments
class	*class*	Declares a new class type.
const	*const*	Java reserves but does not implement the keyword *const*.
N/A	*delegate*	Declares a reference type that defines a method signature.

(continued)

Table 4-3 Complex Type Keyword Comparison   *(continued)*

Java	C#	Comments
N/A	*enum*	Declares a value type defining a set of named constants.
N/A	*event*	Declares an *event* member in a class or struct.
N/A	*this*	Declares an indexer member in a class or struct. Duplicate use of the *this* keyword here is a syntax decision by the C# designers bound to cause confusion.
interface	*interface*	Declares a new interface type.
Object	*object*	*Object* is not a Java keyword but a class name. C# defines the *object* keyword, which is an alias for the *System.Object* class.
N/A	*operator*	Declares an *operator* member in a class or struct.
String	*string*	Unicode String values. *String* is not a Java keyword but a class name. C# defines the *string* keyword, which is an alias for the *System.String* class.
N/A	*struct*	Declares a new struct type, a complex C# type that has no Java equivalent.
extends	*:*	No keyword used in C#. Syntax is `class : super_class {…}`
implements	*:*	No keyword used in C#. Syntax is `class : interface {…}`
N/A	*params*	Used to identify a parameter array in a method call.
N/A	*out*	Identifies a variable as not needing initialization prior to being passed to a method where its value will be set. Note that unlike the case with Java, the use of *out* in C# has nothing to do with I/O.
N/A	*ref*	Identifies a variable that is to be passed by reference instead of by value.
N/A	*as*	Performs a cast but returns *null* if the cast fails instead of throwing an exception.
instanceof	*is*	Determines whether an object is an instance of a specified type.
new	*new*	Creates an instance of a type.
N/A	*typeof*	Returns an instance of *System.Type* for the specified type.
super	*base*	Used to reference superclass members.
this	*this*	Self-reference for use within object instances.
N/A	*explicit*	Declares an explicit type conversion operator.
N/A	*implicit*	Declares an implicit type conversion operator.

Modifier Keywords

Tables 4-4, 4-5, and 4-6 contrast the keywords used as modifiers for program elements. We have broken this category down into three topic areas: access modifiers, inheritance-related modifiers, and others.

> **More Info**   For comprehensive coverage of each keyword, refer to the "Modifiers" section later in this chapter.

Table 4-4   Access Modifier Keyword Comparison

Java	C#	Comments
public	*public*	Identifies a public program element.
private	*private*	Identifies a private program element.
protected	*protected*	Identifies a protected program element. The *protected* keyword provides different accessibility in C# than Java.
N/A	*internal*	Identifies an internal program element providing access to all members of the containing assembly.

Table 4-5   Inheritance Modifier Keyword Comparison

Java	C#	Comments
abstract	*abstract*	Identifies an incomplete implementation of a program element.
final	*sealed*	Identifies an element that cannot be derived from.
N/A	*new*	Identifies an element that hides an inherited member.
N/A	*override*	Identifies an element that overrides an inherited virtual member.
N/A	*virtual*	Identifies a member that can be overridden by a derived class.

Table 4-6   Other Modifier Keyword Comparison

Java	C#	Comments
final	*readonly*	Identifies a field that can be assigned to only once.
native	*extern*	Identifies an externally implemented member.
static	*static*	Identifies a static program element.

(continued)

Table 4-6   Other Modifier Keyword Comparison   *(continued)*

Java	C#	Comments
strictfp	N/A	C# has no equivalent for the *strictfp* keyword.
synchronized	*lock*	Synchronizes access to a statement block.
transient	N/A	C# does not provide a language equivalent of *transient*; however, the *NonSerialized* attribute provides comparable functionality. See Chapter 10 for full details.
volatile	*volatile*	Ensures synchronized and ordered access to a field.

Flow Control Keywords

Table 4-7 contrasts the Java and C# keywords used to provide conditional and flow control capabilities.

> **More Info**   See the "Statements" section later in this chapter for a full description of the keywords in Table 4-7.

Table 4-7   Conditional and Flow Control Keyword Comparison

Java	C#	Comments
assert	N/A	C# alternatives are implemented through static members of the *Trace* and *Debug* classes in the .NET class libraries.
if	*if*	Conditional statement.
else	*else*	Optional component of the *if* statement.
switch	*switch*	Conditional statement.
case	*case*	Component of the *switch* statement.
default	*default*	Optional component of the *switch* statement.
for	*for*	Determinant loop.
do	*do*	Postloop conditional.
while	*while*	Preloop conditional.
N/A	*foreach*	Collection-specific enumerator.
N/A	*in*	Part of the *foreach* statement.
goto	*goto*	Java reserved keyword (unused). Provides unconditional branching support in C#.

Table 4-7   Conditional and Flow Control Keyword Comparison   *(continued)*

Java	C#	Comments
continue	*continue*	Start a new iteration of a loop.
break	*break*	Terminate a loop.
return	*return*	Return from a functional member.

Exception Handling Keywords

Exception handling is predominantly the same in C# and Java, although declaring exceptions is not required in C#. C# adds keywords used to control how integral arithmetic overflow is handled at compile time and run time. Table 4-8 describes the C# keywords related to exception handling.

> **More Info**   For comprehensive coverage of the keywords in Table 4-8, see the "Statements" section later in this chapter and the "Exceptions and Exception Handling" section in Chapter 6, "Advanced Language Features."

Table 4-8   Exception Handling Keyword Comparison

Java	C#	Comments
try	*try*	Encloses a block of code statements. If an exception is thrown by one of these statements, program execution will be transferred to the statements enclosed by a suitable catch block or to the statement immediately following the enclosed statement block.
catch	*catch*	C# also supports general and anonymous catch clauses.
finally	*finally*	Code to execute regardless of whether a *try...catch* statement block exits normally or via an exception.
throw	*throw*	Throw or rethrow an exception.
throws	N/A	Not supported in C#.
N/A	*checked*	Turns on integral arithmetic overflow checking.
N/A	*unchecked*	Turns off integral arithmetic overflow checking.

Unmanaged Code Keywords

C# introduces four keywords specifically related to the use of unmanaged code, a feature not available in Java. Table 4-9 summarizes these keywords.

> **More Info**   Refer to the "Unsafe Code" section in Chapter 6 for comprehensive coverage of the keywords in Table 4-9.

Table 4-9   Unmanaged Code Keywords

Java	C#	Comments
N/A	*fixed*	Allows a pointer to reference a managed variable, ensuring that the garbage collector does not relocate or deallocate the variable while it's still referenced.
N/A	*sizeof*	Gets the size in bytes of the memory occupied by a value type instance. See the section "Unsafe Code" in Chapter 6 for details.
N/A	*stackalloc*	Allocates memory blocks on the stack for the storage of local variables.
N/A	*unsafe*	Identifies unsafe types, members, statements, or code blocks.

Keywords as Identifiers

It's possible to use keywords as identifiers in C#. The compiler will not interpret an identifier as a keyword if it's prefixed with the @ symbol. For example:

```
public class @class {
    public string @public(string @string) {
        string @return = @string + @string;
        return @return;
    }
    public static void Main() {
        System.Console.WriteLine(
            new @class().@public("A silly test"));
    }
}
```

Because the common language runtime (CLR) is designed to run components developed in different languages, the @ prefix is required to allow methods to be called in components that have used identifiers that are also C# keywords.

Operators

With few exceptions, the operators available in C# are syntactically and operationally the same as those in Java. Table 4-10 summarizes the operators available in both languages and highlights the differences in bold.

Table 4-10 Operator Comparison

Category	Java	C#
Arithmetic	+ - * / %	+ - * / %
Logical	&& ||	&& || ***true false***
Bitwise	& | ^ ! ~	& | ^ ! ~
String concatenation	+ +=	+ +=
Increment and decrement	++ --	++ --
Bitwise shift	<< >> **>>>**	<< >>
Relational	== != < > <= >=	== != < > <= >=
Assignment	= += -= *= /= %= &= |= ^= <<= >>= **>>>=**	= += -= *= /= %= &= |= ^= <<= >>=
Member access	.	.
Indexing	[]	[]
Cast	()	()
Conditional	?:	?:
Delegate concatenation and removal	N/A	**+ -**
Object creation	*new*	*new*
Type information	***instanceof***	***is sizeof typeof***
Overflow exception control	N/A	***checked unchecked***
Indirection and address	N/A	**** -> [] &***

The following list summarizes the differences between the Java and C# operators:

- **Logical (*true* and *false*)**   C# considers *true* and *false* to be operators as well as literals. C# allows the *true* and *false* operators for a class or struct to be overridden. Operator overloading is discussed in the "Members" section in Chapter 5.

- **Bitwise shift (>>>)**   There is no equivalent in C# of Java's zero-fill right-shift operator.

- **Delegate operations (+ and -)** The delegate concatenation and removal operators are new to C#, as are delegates.

- **Type information (is, sizeof, and typeof)**

  ❑ The C# *is* operator is the equivalent of the Java *instanceof* operator.

  ❑ The *sizeof* operator returns the bytes occupied by a value type in memory. It has no equivalent in Java and can be used only in an *unsafe* code block. See the "Unsafe Code" section in Chapter 6 for details.

- The *typeof* operator is a useful way to get a *System.Type* object for the class name specified as the operand. The Java equivalent is the static method *Class.forName* or the *public static Class* field that is inherited by every type.

- **Overflow exception control** The overflow exception control operators (*checked* and *unchecked*) have no equivalent in Java. They control how overflow is handled when carrying out numeric operations, and they're discussed in the "Statements" section later in this chapter.

- **Pointer operators** Indirection and address operators are related to pointer operation and have no equivalents in Java. See "Unsafe Code" in Chapter 6 for details.

Precedence and Associativity

There are some subtle differences in the precedence and associativity of operators in C#. These differences have been highlighted in bold in Table 4-11.

Table 4-11 **Operator Precedence and Associativity**

Java	C#	Associativity
[] . ()	[] . () **x++ x-- new typeof checked unchecked**	left to right
(unary)+ (unary)- ! ~ ++ -- (cast) **new**	(unary)+ (unary)- ! ~ **++x --x** (cast)	right to left
* / %	* / %	left to right
+ -	+ -	left to right
<< >> **>>>**	<< >>	left to right
< <= > => **instanceof**	< > <= => **is as**	left to right

Table 4-11 Operator Precedence and Associativity *(continued)*

Java	C#	Associativity
== !=	== !=	left to right
&	&	left to right
^	^	left to right
|	|	left to right
&&	&&	left to right
||	||	left to right
?:	?:	**Java: left to right** **C#: right to left**
= += -= *= /= %= &=	= += -= *= /= %= &=	right to left
|= ^= <<= >>= **>>>=**	|= ^= <<= >>=	

Literals

C# and Java both support the same categories of literal values. No differences exist between the Boolean and Null literals in either language. Table 4-12 summarizes the key differences between Integer, Real, Character, and String literals.

Table 4-12 Literal Values

Category	Comments
Integer	C# adds support for unsigned integer and unsigned long literals.
	C# does not support octal representations of integer literals.
Real	C# adds support for *decimal* literals. Use the M or m suffix to specify a *decimal* literal.
Character	C# does not support octal escape sequences to represent characters.
	In C#, the escape sequence \0 represents *null*.
String	C# supports verbatim string literals. Preceding the string with the @ symbol causes the compiler not to interpret simple, hexadecimal, or Unicode escape sequences within the string. This is useful when working with directory and file names and regular expressions.

Modifiers

C# and Java both use modifiers to specify the accessibility and behavior of program elements. Much commonality exists between Java and C# modifiers, but many differences and inconsistencies exist as well. The differences in usage and effect are often subtle and difficult to understand and remember when coming to C# from a Java background. In this section, we contrast the Java and C# modifiers. We group these modifiers into three categories: access, inheritance, and other.

Access Modifiers

C# includes all of the access modifiers available in Java and provides additional flexibility with the introduction of two new modifiers. However, accessibility based on package membership in Java doesn't translate to the equivalent accessibility based on namespace membership in C#. In Java, a program element with no access modifier is accessible to all members of the same package. C# has no direct equivalent; the closest match is the *internal* modifier. Table 4-13 contrasts the Java and C# access modifiers.

Table 4-13 Access Modifiers

Java	C#	Accessibility of Program Element
public	*public*	No access restrictions are enforced. Any code can access a *public* element.
protected	*protected*	Accessible only to members of the containing class and members of derived classes.
		This is notably different from the meaning of *protected* in Java, which permits access by all members of the containing package and only those members outside the package that are derived from the containing class.
private	*private*	Accessible only to members of the containing class or struct.
N/A	*internal*	Accessible only to program elements contained within the same assembly.
N/A	*protected internal*	The *protected internal* combination is the only valid combination of access modifiers.
		Accessibility is equivalent to that granted by the *protected* or *internal* modifier (in other words, it is the union of the two, not the intersection), resulting in the element being accessible to any code within the containing assembly as well as any members of the containing class or classes derived from the containing class.

Inheritance Modifiers

C# provides more inheritance modifiers than Java to accommodate the additional control over member inheritance provided by C#. See the "Versioning and Inheritance of Members" section in Chapter 5 for more details of inheritance in C#. Table 4-14 contrasts the Java and C# inheritance modifiers.

Table 4-14   Inheritance Modifiers

Java	C#	Effect on Modified Member
abstract	*abstract*	The *abstract* modifier is applicable to both classes and members of classes.
		Use of the *abstract* modifier on a class declaration identifies that the class cannot be directly instantiated. Abstract classes have a potentially incomplete implementation and are intended for use as base classes from which other classes will be derived.
		Use of the *abstract* modifier on a class declaration identifies that the class cannot be directly instantiated. Abstract classes have a potentially incomplete implementation and are intended for use as base classes from which other classes will be derived.
		■ The *abstract* and *sealed* modifiers are mutually exclusive.
		■ Structs are not valid targets of the *abstract* modifier because they do not support inheritance.
		■ When applied to members of *abstract* classes, *abstract* identifies an incomplete member implementation that must be provided by a derived class.
		■ All *abstract* members are implicitly *virtual*.
		■ The *abstract* modifier is mutually exclusive with the *static*, *virtual*, and *override* modifiers. A member marked as *abstract* cannot contain implementation code; an empty statement must follow the declaration.
		■ The member in the derived class that provides the implementation of the *abstract* member must have the *override* modifier.
N/A	*new*	Explicitly confirms the intention to hide an inherited member of the same name. This behavior is not available in Java but is the default behavior applied to members in C#. Despite being the default behavior, the compiler will raise warnings if the *new* keyword is not used. Note that this should not be confused with the word *new* used in the context of object instantiation.
		■ If the *new* modifier is used on a member that is not hiding an inherited member, the compiler will generate a warning.
		■ The *new* and *override* modifiers are mutually exclusive.
		■ The combination of the *new* and *virtual* keywords creates a new point of specialization.

(continued)

Table 4-14 Inheritance Modifiers *(continued)*

Java	C#	Effect on Modified Member
N/A	*override*	Specifies that the member is overriding an inherited virtual member with the same signature. Only *virtual* inherited members can be overridden, including those with the *virtual, abstract,* or *override* modifier.
		■ The overriding member must be declared with the same accessibility modifiers as the member being overridden.
		■ The *override* modifier is mutually exclusive with the *new, static, virtual,* and *abstract* modifiers.
		■ The member being overridden must be accessible to the overriding member.
		■ A compiler warning is raised if a member attempts to override a non-virtual member. The *new* modifier should be used to hide the nonvirtual member.
final	*sealed*	The *sealed* modifier can be applied to both class and member declarations with slightly different results.
		Using the *sealed* modifier on a class declaration states that the class cannot be used as a base class for a derived class. A compile-time error will occur if this is attempted.
		■ The *sealed* and *abstract* modifiers are mutually exclusive.
		■ Structs are implicitly sealed and do not support inheritance.
		■ The *sealed* modifier can be applied in conjunction with the *override* modifier on an inherited *virtual* method to ensure that the method cannot be overridden by derived classes.
		■ A base class cannot simply define a method as sealed as with the *final* keyword in Java.
		■ The *sealed* and *abstract* modifiers are mutually exclusive.
N/A	*virtual*	Identifies members as virtual and allows derived classes to override, as opposed to hide, inherited members. This is the default behavior in Java.
		■ Derived classes use the *override* modifier to specialize the implementation of a *virtual* member.
		■ The *virtual* modifier is mutually exclusive with *static, abstract,* and *override.*

Other Modifiers

Table 4-15 contrasts other modifiers available in Java and C# that are unrelated to program element accessibility and inheritance.

Table 4-15 **Other Modifiers**

Java	C#	Effect on Modified Member
native	*extern*	Indicates that the implementation of a member is external to the C# code. This usually means that the implementation is contained in a pre-.NET Microsoft Windows dynamic-link library (DLL).
		■ If the external implementation is contained in a Windows DLL, members must be *static* and decorated with the *DLLImport* attribute. See "Attributes" in Chapter 6 for details.
		■ The *extern* modifier is mutually exclusive with *abstract*.
		■ The body of a member modified with *extern* must always be an empty statement.
final	*readonly*	Identifies a field as being read-only. Read-only fields are more flexible than constants because they can be initialized at declaration or within an instance constructor. Static read-only fields can be initialized at declaration or within a static constructor.
		The *ref* and *out* parameter modifiers can be used only on *readonly* fields within the context of an instance constructor.
static	*static*	The modified member exists within the context of the type in which it's declared, independently of a specific *class* or *struct* instance.
		Significantly, C# static members cannot be referenced through an instance of the type, only through a reference to the containing type.
		Static function members have no access to the operator *this*.
strictfp	N/A	C# has no equivalent for the *strictfp* modifier.
synchronized	N/A	The C# equivalent, *lock*, is not used as a member modifier. See the "Statements" section later in this chapter and Chapter 13, "Threading and Synchronization," for complete details.
transient	N/A	C# does not provide a language equivalent of *transient*; however, the *NonSerialized* attribute provides comparable functionality. See Chapter 10 for full details.
volatile	*volatile*	Forces synchronization and ordering of access to a field without resorting to the explicit use of *lock*. The field modified with the *volatile* modifier must be one of the following types:
		■ A reference type
		■ A pointer type
		■ One of *byte*, *sbyte*, *short*, *ushort*, *int*, *uint*, *char*, *float*, or *bool*
		■ An enumeration with a base type of *byte*, *sbyte*, *short*, *ushort*, *int*, or *uint*.

Namespaces

Namespaces are a flexible alternative to Java packages, providing a mechanism to organize types into a logical hierarchical structure and ensuring globally unique type names.

Declaring Namespaces

Java classes and interfaces are allocated to a *package* by using the *package* statement at the start of a source file. All types declared in that file become members of the specified package. In C#, membership of a *namespace* is specified by declaring types within the body of a *namespace* statement. This enables C# to support multiple namespaces in a single file, eliminating the Java requirement for namespace hierarchies to map to file system directory structures. In the following example, both *MyClass* and *MyInterface* are members of the namespace *Com.MyCompany*:

```
namespace Com.MyCompany {
    // Namespace member declarations
    public class MyClass{
        // Implementation code for MyClass
    }

    public interface MyInterface{
        // Implementation code for MyInterface
    }

    // A nested namespace declaration
    namespace Tools {
        // Namespace member declaration
        public class MyClass{
            // Implementation code for MyClass
        }
    } // End of Tools namespace
} // End of Com.MyCompany namespace
```

Notice that we declare a nested namespace named *Tools* (which has the fully qualified name *Com.Namespace.Tools*) and two class definitions for *MyClass*. This is permitted because each *MyClass* declaration is contained within distinct namespaces, giving them the following fully qualified names:

```
Com.MyCompany.MyClass
Com.MyCompany.Tools.MyClass
```

When you declare a nested namespace, you cannot use a hierarchical name in a single declaration. You must declare multiple single-level nested declarations. For example, instead of this,

```
namespace TopLevel {
    namespace SecondLevel.ThirdLevel {

    }
}
```

the appropriate technique is this:

```
namespace TopLevel {
    namespace SecondLevel {
        namespace ThirdLevel {

        }
    }
}
```

The following program elements can be members of a namespace: class, struct, interface, enum, delegate, and namespace. If no namespace is specified, any declared members will be members of the default global namespace. Members of the global namespace are accessible without using any namespace; see the next section for more information.

Namespaces implicitly have public accessibility; they are not valid targets for access modifiers. The accessibility of namespace members is determined independently based on the access modifiers applied to them. See the "Types" section in Chapter 5 for details.

Using Namespaces

The C# *using* statement is the equivalent of the Java *import* statement, and it makes members of the specified namespace available for use without requiring a fully qualified name. When a namespace is imported, all of the members in that namespace are made available; unlike the Java *import* statement, *using* does not allow the programmer to specify an individual member to be imported.

If two imported namespaces contain members with the same name, the fully qualified names are used to differentiate between the members. C# also provides a mechanism for defining an alias that can be used to represent the namespace portion of the fully qualified member name. However, if an alias is declared for a namespace, members of the namespace cannot be accessed directly using their name and must always be prefixed with the alias.

The *using* statement operates at the namespace level; different namespaces in the same source file can import unique sets of namespaces. Each namespace is free to assign any aliases to the namespaces it imports, irrespective of those declared by other namespaces. An example of namespace usage follows:

```
namespace MyNamespace {
    using company = Com.MyCompany;
    using tools = Com.MyCompany.Tools;

    public class AClass : tools.MyClass, MyInterface {
        company.MyClass x = new company.MyClass();
    }
}

namespace MyOtherNamespace {
    using mycompany = Com.MyCompany;
    using utils = Com.MyCompany.Tools;

    public class BClass : utils.MyClass, MyInterface {
        mycompany.MyClass x = new mycompany.MyClass();
    }
}
```

In this example, the namespace *Com.MyCompany* is imported for use in the *MyNamespace* namespace and is assigned the alias *company*. The ambiguous class name *MyClass* is qualified using this alias.

Statements

Extensive commonality exists in the syntax and functionality of statements in C# and Java:

- All statements must end with a semicolon.

- Block statements are formed using braces.

- An empty statement is represented by a single semicolon. In both languages, it's considered a good idea to comment the existence of any empty statement.

Labeled Statements

Labeled statements are implemented by C# and Java in the same way, differing only in how jumps are performed. In Java, jumps are made to a labeled statement using the *continue* or *break* statement, as shown in the following example:

```
mylabel:
// statements
while (/* some condition */) {
    break mylabel;
}
```

In C#, the *break* and *continue* statements do not take targets. To jump to a labeled statement, use the *goto* statement:

```
mylabel:
//statements
while (/* some condition */) {
    goto mylabel;
}
```

The *break*, *continue*, and *goto* statements are discussed in detail later in the "Jump Statements" section.

Selection and Iteration Statements

The following selection and iteration statements are the same in syntax and function:

- The *if...else if...else* statement
- The *while* statement
- The *do* statement
- The *for* statement

The following sections discuss the difference between the Java and C# *switch* statement and introduce a new C# iterator, the *foreach* statement.

The *switch* Statement

The *switch* statement in C# differs from Java in three ways:

- C# supports a broader range of data types for the *switch* expression, including enumerations, chars, and built in integer types. Most usefully, C# supports the use of strings as *switch* expressions.

■   C# does not support falling through *case* clauses. A compile-time error occurs if a case clause is not terminated with a *break* or *goto* statement. C# does allow multiple case expressions on a single statement block.

■   C# supports *goto* statements to jump from one case clause to another. Following a *goto* statement with a *break* statement results in a compiler warning.

The example below demonstrates these differences:

```
public void MyMethod(string color) {

    switch (color.ToLower()) {    // Note - using a string

        case "orange":
        case "red":
            SomeMethod();
            goto default;    // Note - jump to default clause

        case "aqua":
        case "blue":
            SomeOtherMethod();
            break;

        case "green":
            SomeThirdMethod();
            goto case "red";    // Note - jump to "red" clause

        default:
            SomeDefaultMethod();
            break;
    }
}
```

The *foreach* Statement

The C# *foreach* statement iterates through the elements of a collection. For the purpose of the *foreach* statement, a collection is

■   Any type that implements the *System.IEnumerable* interface.

■   Any array (because *System.Array* implements *IEnumerable*).

■   Any type that implements a pattern equivalent to *IEnumerable*.

The syntax of a *foreach* statement is

foreach (type identifier in collection) statement

The *type* and *identifier* declare a read-only local iteration variable that's available within the scope of the statement.

The following example of the *foreach* statement iterates through the contents of a string array and prints out each element:

```
string[] days = new string[] {"Monday", "Tuesday", "Wednesday"};
foreach (string myString in days) {
    System.Console.WriteLine(myString);
}
```

■   The type of the iteration variable must be the same as the collection element type, or an explicit conversion must exist between the two.

■   A compiler error occurs if an attempt is made to assign a value to the read-only iteration variable inside the statement.

> **More Info**   For more detail about the *foreach* keyword, see Chapter 9, "Collections."

Jump Statements

C# provides equivalents for all of the Java statements used to transfer processing control, but functional differences exist between most of them. In addition, C# also defines the *goto* statement.

The *return* Statement

The *return* statement has the same function and syntax in both C# and Java.

The *throw* Statement

See the section "Exceptions and Exception Handling" in Chapter 6 for details of the *throw* statement.

The *break* and *continue* Statements

C# supports both the *break* and *continue* statements but does not support the use of label identifiers as targets of these statements.

■   The *break* statement exits the nearest enclosing *switch, while, do, for* or *foreach* statement.

■   The *continue* statement starts a new iteration of the nearest enclosing *while, do, for,* or *foreach* statement.

■   Use the *goto* statement, discussed in the next section, to jump to a labeled statement in C#.

The *goto* Statement

The C# *goto* statement allows an unconditional jump to a labeled statement. The *goto* might cause execution to jump either forward or backward in the code, but the *goto* statement must be within the scope of the target labeled statement. Because Java doesn't currently implement the *goto* keyword, the nearest equivalent of the C# *goto* statement in Java is targeted *break* or *continue* statements, although these do not provide the same levels of flexibility. Note the following:

- Using *goto* to jump out of a *try* or *catch* block will cause the *finally* block to execute.

- A compile-time error occurs if the *goto* statement is used to jump out of a *finally* block.

Other Statements

This section discusses statements not related to selection, iteration, and the transfer of processing control. The *try* and *fixed* statements are listed here for completeness; a detailed description of each statement is included in Chapter 6.

The *try* Statement

See "Exceptions and Exception Handling" in Chapter 6 for details of the *try* statement.

The *lock* Statement

The C# keyword *lock* is nearly equivalent to the Java keyword *synchronized*. The principle difference is that the *lock* keyword cannot be used as a modifier to synchronize access to an entire method. It's applicable only to statement blocks, as in the following example:

```
public void SampleMethod() {
    lock(SomeObject) {
        // statements needing synchronized access
    }
    return;
}
```

> **More Info**   Use of the *lock* statement is covered in detail in Chapter 13.

The *checked* and *unchecked* Keywords

Arithmetic overflow occurs when the result of an integer type mathematical operation or conversion is greater or smaller than can be represented by the defined data type. For example, in Java and C#, a *short* can contain integer values between -32,768 and 32,767. The following code demonstrates arithmetic overflow in Java:

```
short x = 32767;
x++;
System.out.println(x);
```

The output from the above code will be -32768.

Java handles integral arithmetic overflow by truncating the high-order bits, resulting in the cyclical effect just demonstrated. In C#, the *checked* and *unchecked* keywords allow control of the compile-time and run-time handling of integral arithmetic overflow.

Technically, the *checked* and *unchecked* keywords are operators as well as statements. The *checked* and *unchecked* keywords use the same syntax. An example of a *checked* expression and statement is included in the following code fragment:

```
// A checked expression
int b = checked (x * 5);

// A checked statement block
checked {
    int p = x++;
    int q = x * 5;
    int r = p * q;
}
```

A compiler error is reported if the value of the *checked* expression can be resolved at compile time and overflow occurs. If the value of the *checked* expression cannot be determined until run time, overflow causes a *System.OverflowException* to be thrown. The use of the *unchecked* keyword forces truncation, causing any errors or exceptions to be suppressed and resulting in the same cyclic behavior seen with Java.

If neither *checked* nor *unchecked* is specified in the code, the following defaults are used:

■ For constant values, the compiler checks for overflow and an error will be reported, as though the *checked* keyword had been specified.

■ For variable values, the runtime will allow truncated values, as though the *unchecked* keyword had been specified.

The default compile-time overflow checking can be modified by using the */checked* compiler flag. See Chapter 3 for details of compiler flags.

The *using* Statement

The *using* keyword represents both a statement and a directive. The *using* directive is for importing namespaces into an application. See the "Namespaces" section earlier in this chapter for details. The *using* statement is a mechanism for efficiently acquiring, using, and disposing of a class or struct that implements the *System.IDisposable* interface. For example, if *MyClass* and *MyStruct* are types that implement *IDisposable*, the syntax of the *using* command is as follows:

```
using (MyClass x = new MyClass(), MyStruct y = new MyStruct()) {
    // do something with x and y
    x.someMethod();
    y.someOtherMethod();
} // x and y are automatically disposed of
```

The objects specified in the *using* statement are available within the scope of the statement block. At the end of the statement block, the *Dispose* method of the *IDisposable* interface is automatically called on each object. The *using* statement automatically wraps the necessary *try...catch...finally* structure around the statement block. This ensures that the objects are disposed of irrespective of whether an exception causes the program to leave the statement block or the statement exits normally.

The *fixed* Statement

For information on the *fixed* statement, see the "Unsafe Code" section in Chapter 6.

Summary

This chapter has described the fundamentals of the C# language, comparing and contrasting them with the Java language. We have shown that great similarities exist between C# and Java but that there are also occasional, often subtle differences of which the Java programmer must be wary. We have also introduced a number of new features that a Java programmer must become familiar with in order to become proficient with C#.

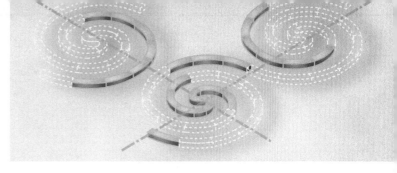

5

Data Types

This chapter discusses the data types provided by C#. Although C# maintains strong parallels with the data types offered by Java, the designers of C# have also drawn heavily on the features of C and C++. For the Java programmer, C# data types include many subtle and confusing differences as well as some new features to learn.

We begin with a broad discussion of the unified type system provided by the Microsoft .NET Framework and the fundamental division of data types into value and reference types. We then cover each of the data types in detail, describing how and when each type can be used and the functionality it provides. Next we detail each of the member types that can be used within interfaces, classes, and structs. Many of these member types will be familiar to the Java developer, but C# also defines new member types that provide clean and powerful language-based implementations of common programming models. Finally we discuss the types of variables in C# and in particular the features for passing variables by reference instead of value.

Types

Java has *primitive* and *reference* types; C# refers to them as *value* and *reference* types. *Value* types include *byte*, *int*, *long*, *float*, and *double*. *Reference* types include *class*, *interface*, and *array*. C# has a third type category, the infamous *pointer*. Java does not provide a *pointer* type, primarily because of the complexity of these types and the dangers they pose to application stability when used incorrectly. Pointers are discussed in the context of unsafe code in Chapter 6, "Advanced Language Features."

Despite the apparent similarities, a closer inspection reveals fundamental differences in the C# type system:

- The common language runtime (CLR) unified type system extends object capabilities to value types.

- A richer set of inbuilt value types provides additional flexibility.

- The introduction of the *struct* data type provides stack-based objects.

- The *delegate* reference type provides a safe, object-oriented approach to method pointers.

- Enumerations provide a mechanism to group and name a related set of constant values.

Apart from the pointer, we'll discuss all C# types in the following sections.

> **More Info**   Attributes are applicable to the declaration of all types. However, we won't discuss attributes in this chapter, saving them instead for a detailed discussion in Chapter 6.

Unified Type System

The Microsoft .NET Framework considers every data type to be ultimately derived from *System.Object*. This gives all value types, including primitives such as *int* and *long*, object capabilities. This has two consequences:

- Methods can be invoked against value types. This is more important for structs, which can implement new function members.

- Value types can be passed as object and interface references.

To understand the significance of the unified type system, it's important to understand the traditional differences between value and reference types. These are summarized in Table 5-1.

Table 5-1   The Difference Between Value and Reference Types

Characteristic	Value Types	Reference Types
Memory allocation	Stack. However, value-type members of heap-based objects are stored inline, meaning that they are allocated memory on the heap within the containing object.	Heap
Contents	Data.	Reference to data
Disposal	Immediately as they leave scope.	Garbage collected

In Java, the benefit of value types stems from their simplicity relative to objects, resulting in performance benefits and memory savings compared with the alternative of implementing everything as objects.

The CLR maintains speed and memory savings by treating value types as objects only when required, minimizing the impact of providing value types with object capabilities. When a value type is used as an *object* or cast to an *interface* type, a process called *boxing* is used to automatically convert the value type to a reference type. Boxing and its counterpart, *unboxing*, provide the run-time bridge between value and reference types. The net effect is similar to that of using the wrapper classes in Java, such as the *Integer* and *Double* classes, but in C#, the CLR takes care of the details automatically.

Boxing

Boxing takes an instance of a value type and converts it to an *object* or *interface* type. For example:

```
// Box an int variable
int myInt = 100;
object myIntObject = myInt;
System.Console.WriteLine("myIntObject = " + myInt.ToString());

// Box a long literal
object myLongObject = 4500L;
```

This example uses simple data types, but the same syntax also works for boxing structs. Structs can also be boxed into instances of interfaces they implement. For example, boxing a struct named *MyStruct* that implements the interface *ISomeInterface* is achieved as follows:

```
MyStruct x = new MyStruct();
ISomeInterface y - x;
```

The runtime implements boxing by instantiating a container object of the appropriate type and copying the data from the value type into it. It's important to understand that the boxed instance contains a copy of the source value. Any changes made to the original value are not reflected in the boxed instance.

Implicit boxing   The C# compiler will implicitly box value types as required—for example, invoking a function member of a struct or passing a value type where an object is expected. Given the overheads associated with boxing, overuse can affect program performance. Where performance is an issue, you should write programs to avoid the unnecessary use of implicit boxing.

Unboxing

Unboxing is the reverse of boxing. It takes an object representing a previously boxed value and re-creates a value type from it. For example:

```
// Box an int variable
int myInt = 100;
object myIntObject = myInt;
System.Console.WriteLine("myIntObject = " + myInt.ToString());

// Unbox
int myOtherInt = (int)myIntObject;
```

As can be seen in this example, the previously boxed object must be explicitly cast to the appropriate type. The runtime checks that the boxed instance is being unboxed as the correct type; otherwise, it throws a *System.InvalidCastException*.

It isn't possible to create a value type representation of any reference type using unboxing; unboxing works only on objects that contain previously boxed values.

Value Types

All value types in C# are of type *struct* or *enum*. Both *struct* and *enum* are types that were not implemented in Java, an omission that is frequently debated by language theorists. A set of inbuilt value types in C#, referred to as simple types, provides the same functionality as primitive types (*int, long, float,* and so forth) in Java, but their implementation is very different. All .NET inbuilt value types are implemented as structs; this is essential to enabling the boxing of inbuilt value types.

Structs

A struct is a data structure that is similar to a class. The most important differences between classes and structs are a consequence of structs being a value type:

- When instantiated, a struct is allocated memory on the stack or inline if it's a member of a heap resident object, such as a class.

- Memory allocated to a struct instance contains the member data, not references to the data.

- Struct instances are disposed of as soon as they lose scope; they are not garbage collected.

Declaration   A *struct* declaration takes the following form:

[attributes] [modifiers] struct identifier : interfaces {body}

Apart from the fact that structs do not support inheritance (discussed in the next section), structs are declared the same way as classes. For example, a *public* struct named *MyStruct* that implements the *IMyInterface* interface is declared as follows:

```
public struct MyStruct : IMyInterface {
    // function and data members
}
```

Inheritance   Structs do not support user-defined inheritance. However, all structs implicitly derive from *System.ValueType*, which is in turn derived from *System.Object*.

Modifiers   The applicability of modifiers to a *struct* declaration depends on the context in which the struct is declared. Structs can be declared as top-level types (that is, direct members of an enclosing namespace) or nested within the definition of another struct or class. Table 5-2 summarizes modifier availability.

Table 5-2   Struct Declaration Modifier Availability

	Struct Declaration Context		
	Member of Namespace	**Member of Class**	**Member of Struct**
Accessibility			
public	✓	✓	✓
protected	N/A	✓	N/A
private	N/A	(default)	(default)
internal	(default)	✓	✓

(continued)

Table 5-2   Struct Declaration Modifier Availability   *(continued)*

	Struct Declaration Context		
	Member of Namespace	**Member of Class**	**Member of Struct**
protected internal	N/A	✓	N/A
Inheritance			
new	N/A	✓	N/A
abstract	N/A	N/A	N/A
sealed	(implicit)	(implicit)	(implicit)
virtual	N/A	N/A	N/A
override	N/A	N/A	N/A
Other			
readonly	N/A	N/A	N/A
volatile	N/A	N/A	N/A
static	N/A	N/A	N/A
extern	N/A	N/A	N/A

Empty constructors and structs   An empty constructor is one that takes no parameters. Although it's valid to define an empty constructor for a class, it's not valid to define one for a struct. The compiler implicitly defines an empty constructor for a struct, the body of which sets all of the struct members to their default values. This means that it's impossible to stop the instantiation of a struct using a *private* empty constructor. If the accessibility of the struct makes it visible, it can always be instantiated.

Instantiation   Unlike classes, struct instances are allocated memory as soon they are declared; the *new* keyword is not required. However, if the *new* keyword is not used, all field members of the struct must be explicitly assigned values prior to use; otherwise, a compiler error occurs. If the *new* keyword is used, the field members of the struct will be initialized to their default values. Struct variables can never be assigned the value *null*.

Members   Structs can contain the following member types: constant, field, method, property, event, indexer, operator, instance constructor, static constructor, and nested type declarations. Structs cannot contain destructors, as stack-based object structs are not subject to the garbage collection process.

> **More Info**   For comprehensive coverage of these member types, see the "Members" section later in this chapter (beginning on page 88).

Assigning and passing structs   If a struct instance is passed as a function member parameter, returned from a function member, or assigned to a variable, a copy of the complete struct will be created. The copy is independent of the original struct; any changes made to the content of the new struct will not be reflected in the original.

Should the need arise to pass a struct reference, use the *ref* or *out* modifier on the parameter. The need to use *ref* may indicate that a class would be a more appropriate alternative. See the "Variables" section later in this chapter for full details of the *ref* and *out* parameter modifiers.

Issues with structs   Thought should be given to how a data structure will be used before deciding whether to implement a class or a struct. The decision can affect the performance of an application. There are no definitive rules; only guidelines can be offered:

- As a general rule, small and simple favors structs. The larger and more complex a data structure is, the more likely it should be implemented as a class.

- When working in a resource-constrained environment where memory needs to be freed quickly, structs will provide a benefit over the non-deterministic garbage collection of classes. Because structs are allocated on the stack, their memory is freed as soon as they go out of scope.

- If speed is of paramount importance, efficiency will be gained from the stack-based nature of structs.

- Frequently passing a struct as a parameter or assigning structs to variables can be expensive; bear in mind that a complete copy of the contents of that struct is created each time and is more costly than copying an object reference.

- Frequent method calls are better served by classes; the overhead of implicit boxing can forfeit benefits gained from the fact that structs are stack-based.

■   When a data structure will be used inside a containing structure, the approach used by the container to manage its contents can dramatically affect overall performance. In a collection, a struct will be repeatedly boxed as the *Equals* or *GetHashCode* method is called. This will cause a significant performance overhead. In an array, a struct can provide higher efficiency than a class, as there is no need to look up references.

Simple Types

C# provides a rich selection of predefined value types that are collectively known as simple types, including types equivalent to the primitive types available in Java. C# also provides unsigned versions of all the integer types, as well as a new type called *decimal*. The *decimal* is a high-precision fixed-point value type designed for use in calculations in which the rounding issues associated with floating-point arithmetic are problematic.

Each of the predefined value types is a struct implemented in the *System* namespace of the .NET class library. For convenience, C# provides keywords to reference these simple types. Either the keyword or the struct name can be used in a program.

Table 5-3 details the predefined simple type keywords, the Java equivalents, the structs that the keywords are aliases for, the range of values supported by each type, and the default values.

Table 5-3   C# Simple Data Types

Java Type	C# Keyword	.NET Struct	Values	Default Value
boolean	*bool*	*System.Boolean*	*true* or *false*	*False*
byte	*sbyte*	*System.SByte*	8-bit signed integer (-128 to 127)	0
N/A	*byte*	*System.Byte*	8-bit unsigned integer (0 to 255)	0
short	*short*	*System.Int16*	16-bit signed integer (-32768 to 32767)	0
N/A	*ushort*	*System.UInt16*	16-bit unsigned integer (0 to 65535)	0
int	*int*	*System.Int32*	32-bit signed integer (-2147483648 to 2147483647)	0
N/A	*uint*	*System.UInt32*	32-bit unsigned integer (0 to 4294967295)	0
long	*long*	*System.Int64*	64-bit signed integer (-9223372036854775808 to 9223372036854775807)	0

Table 5-3   C# Simple Data Types   *(continued)*

Java Type	C# Keyword	.NET Struct	Values	Default Value
N/A	*ulong*	*System.UInt64*	64-bit unsigned integer (0 to 18446744073709551615)	0
float	*float*	*System.Single*	32-bit double-precision floating-point	0
double	*double*	*System.Double*	64-bit double-precision floating-point	0
N/A	*decimal*	*System.Decimal*	128-bit high-precision decimal number with 28 significant digits	\u0000
char	*char*	*System.Char*	2-byte Unicode	0

Enumerations

An enum (short for enumeration) is a data type that declares a set of named integer constants. Enums are data structures that have no direct equivalent in Java; the closest Java alternative is a set of individually defined constant values. However, enums offer advantages over the use of constants:

- Using enum types as parameters in function members restricts the range of valid values that can be passed during calls.

- There is a logical connection between the member values of an enum as opposed to discrete constants.

Declaration   An *enum* declaration has the form

[attributes] [modifiers] enum identifier [:base] {body}

The *base* component of the *enum* declaration specifies the underlying type of the enum and can be any of the simple integer types; the default is *int*. The base type limits the range of values that can be assigned to the enum members.

The *body* of the *enum* declaration contains a list of member names with optional values. Member names must be unique, but multiple members can have the same value. By default, the first member will have the integer value 0 and subsequent members will be assigned values sequentially.

Using explicit numbering, the programmer can assign an integer value to each enum member. The assigned value must be valid for the specified base type. Any members without explicit values are assigned a value sequentially based on the value of the previous member.

The following example declares an enum named *PokerChip* with a *byte* base type:

```
public enum PokerChip : byte {

    Blue = 1,
    Green,              // Automatically assigned the value 2 (Blue + 1)
    Red = 5,            // Explicitly assigned the value 5
    Orange = 10,
    Brown = 25,
    Silver = 50,
    Gold = Silver * 2, // Any determinable constant is acceptable
    Min = Blue,         // Multiple members with the same value are ok
    Max = Gold
}
```

The following example demonstrates the *PokerChip* enum used as a method argument and a switch statement expression:

```
public void PlaceBet(PokerChip chip) {
    switch (chip) {
        case PokerChip.Blue:
            //Do something
            break;
        case PokerChip.Green:
            //Do something else
            break;
        default:
            //Do something else
            break;
    }
}
```

As shown in the *PlaceBet* method, function members can specify *enum* types as arguments. Using an *enum* type argument restricts the range of values that are valid for the argument. However, the integer constant 0 (zero) is implicitly convertible to any *enum* type and can always be passed in place of a valid enum member.

Modifiers   Enums can be declared as top-level structures or contained within a class or struct. The modifiers available depend on the context of the *enum* declaration. Table 5-4 summarizes the available modifiers for each context.

Table 5-4   Enum Declaration Modifier Availability

	Enum Declaration Context		
	Member of Namespace	**Member of Class**	**Member of Struct**
Accessibility			
public	✓	✓	✓
protected	N/A	✓	N/A
private	N/A	(default)	(default)
internal	(default)	✓	✓
protected internal	N/A	✓	N/A
Inheritance			
new	N/A	✓	N/A
abstract	N/A	N/A	N/A
sealed	(implicit)	(implicit)	(implicit)
virtual	N/A	N/A	N/A
override	N/A	N/A	N/A
Other			
readonly	N/A	N/A	N/A
volatile	N/A	N/A	N/A
static	N/A	N/A	N/A
extern	N/A	N/A	N/A

Members and inheritance   The user-defined members of an enum are restricted to the set of public name/value pairs contained within the enum. Enums do not support user-defined inheritance, but all enums implicitly derive from *System.Enum*, which derives from *System.ValueType* and ultimately from *System.Object*. The *System.Enum* class provides a number of static methods for working with enum member names and values, summarized in Table 5-5.

Table 5-5   *System.Enum* Methods

Method	Description
GetName()	Gets the name of the member with the specified value in an enum.
GetNames()	Gets an array of the member names contained within an enum.
GetUnderlyingType()	Gets the underlying base type of the enum.
GetValues()	Gets an array of the member values contained within an enum.
IsDefined()	Determines whether the enum has a member with the specified value.

Reference Types

In C#, reference types include class, interface, array, and delegate. With the exception of delegate, Java developers will be familiar with all of these. We discuss each reference type in detail in the following sections.

Classes

The implementation of classes in C# mirrors that of Java. Both are reference types, supporting single implementation inheritance and multiple interface implementations. The few differences that do exist are predominantly syntax changes or are required to support the modifiers and member types introduced by C#. Only Java *anonymous* and *local* classes have no C# equivalent.

Declaration   A C# class declaration takes the following form:

[attributes] [modifiers] class identifier [:superclass] [interfaces] {body}

The Java keywords *extends* and *implements* are not used. C# uses the colon to separate the class name from its superclasses and interfaces. Commas are used to separate the superclass and each subsequent interface name; the superclass must come first, or a compiler error will occur.

For example, the following is the C# code to declare a public class named *MyClass* that inherits from the superclass *MyBaseClass* and implements two interfaces named *IAnInterface* and *IAnotherInterface*:

```
public MyClass : MyBaseClass, IAnInterface, IAnotherInterface {
    // Implementation code
}
```

Modifiers   The applicability of modifiers to class declarations depends on the context in which the class is declared. Classes can be declared as a top-level type, being direct members of an enclosing namespace, or they can be nested within the definition of a class or struct. Table 5-6 summarizes modifier availability for classes.

Table 5-6   Class Declaration Modifier Availability

	Class Declaration Context		
	Member of Namespace	**Member of Class**	**Member of Struct**
Accessibility			
public	✓	✓	✓
protected	N/A	✓	N/A
private	N/A	(default)	(default)

Table 5-6   Class Declaration Modifier Availability   *(continued)*

	Class Declaration Context		
	Member of Namespace	**Member of Class**	**Member of Struct**
internal	(default)	✓	✓
protected internal	N/A	✓	N/A
Inheritance			
new	N/A	✓	N/A
abstract	✓	✓	✓
sealed	✓	✓	✓
virtual	N/A	N/A	N/A
override	N/A	N/A	N/A
Other			
readonly	N/A	N/A	N/A
volatile	N/A	N/A	N/A
static	N/A	N/A	N/A
extern	N/A	N/A	N/A

Members   Classes can contain the following member types: constant, field, method, property, event, indexer, operator, instance constructor, static constructor, and nested type declarations. For comprehensive coverage of member types, see the "Members" section later in this chapter.

Abstract classes   The implementation of interface members represents an important difference in the default behavior of how abstract classes are handled in Java and C#. In Java, any interface members that are not implemented simply become abstract members that concrete classes must implement. C# abstract classes must provide implementations for all interface members, but the abstract class may declare the member as abstract. For example:

```
public interface MyInterface {
    int MyMethod(int x);
}

public abstract class MyClass : MyInterface {
    // Compile time error if the following declaration is missing
    public abstract int MyMethod(int x);
}
```

Default constructor accessibility   The C# compiler, like the Java compiler, will provide a default constructor if one is not explicitly defined for a class. The accessibility Java assigns to this default constructor is the same as the accessibility of the containing class; C# defines the default constructor as *protected* if the class is abstract, otherwise as *public*.

Preventing class instantiation   Both Java and C# offer the same capabilities for creating concrete classes that cannot be instantiated. Declaring at least one constructor ensures that the compiler does not generate a default constructor. Declaring this constructor *private* renders it inaccessible to other code, so the class cannot be instantiated.

Anonymous and local classes   It's not possible to define anonymous or local classes in C#; all classes must be explicitly defined before use. Java anonymous classes are regularly used for event handling, especially with GUI components. See the "Events" section later in this chapter for details of event handling in C#.

Interfaces

Interfaces serve the same purpose in C# as Java. There are some differences in the declaration syntax, but the primary difference is that constants cannot be declared within the context of a C# interface.

Declaration   A C# interface declaration takes the following form:

[attributes] [modifiers] interface identifier [:superinterfaces] {body}

For example, the C# code to declare a *public* interface named *MyInterface* that extends the superinterfaces *IAnInterface* and *IAnotherInterface* follows:

```
public MyInterface : IAnInterface, IAnotherInterface {
    // member declarations
}
```

C# uses a colon followed by a comma-separated list of superinterfaces to specify inheritance.

Modifiers   The applicability of modifiers to an interface declaration depends on the context in which the interface is declared. Interfaces can be declared as a top-level type, being direct members of an enclosing namespace, or they can be nested within the definition of a class or struct. Table 5-7 summarizes modifier availability.

Table 5-7   Interface Declaration Modifier Availability

	Interface Declaration Context		
	Member of Namespace	**Member of Class**	**Member of Struct**
Accessibility			
public	✓	✓	✓
protected	N/A	✓	N/A
private	N/A	(default)	(default)
internal	(default)	✓	✓
protected internal	N/A	✓	N/A
Inheritance			
new	N/A	✓	N/A
abstract	N/A	N/A	N/A
sealed	✓	✓	✓
virtual	N/A	N/A	N/A
override	N/A	N/A	N/A
Other			
readonly	N/A	N/A	N/A
volatile	N/A	N/A	N/A
static	N/A	N/A	N/A
extern	N/A	N/A	N/A

Members   Interfaces can contain the following member types: method, property, event, and indexer. Aside from support for the member types introduced by C#, the major difference from Java is that constants cannot be declared in interfaces. The alternative provided by C# is to use a peer-level enum; however, this does not keep associated constants together with the interface.

> **More Info**   For comprehensive coverage of the members applicable in the context of an interface declaration, see the "Members" section later in this chapter.

Implementing interfaces   C# classes and structs implement interfaces using the same syntax. The following example shows a struct *MyStruct* and a class *MyClass* both declaring the implementation of two interfaces *IAnInterface* and *IAnotherInterface*:

```
public struct MyStruct :IAnInterface, IAnotherInterface {
    // Implementation code
}

public class MyClass :IAnInterface, IAnotherInterface {
    // Implementation code
}
```

Explicit interface implementation   C# includes a feature called *explicit interface implementation*, which gives greater control over interface member implementations. Explicit interface implementation is most commonly used when implementing multiple interfaces that contain members with conflicting names or signatures. The only mandatory use of explicit interface implementation is when implementing an indexer declared in an interface.

The following is an example of a class implementing two interfaces with conflicting member declarations. Explicit interface implementation is used to differentiate between the implementation of the interface methods.

```
 public interface IMyInterface {
    void SomeMethod();
}

public interface IMyOtherInterface {
    void SomeMethod();
}

public class MyClass : IMyInterface, IMyOtherInterface {
    void IMyInterface.SomeMethod() {
        // Implementation Code
    }
    void IMyOtherInterface.SomeMethod() {
        // Implementation Code
    }
}
```

Each implementation of *SomeMethod* is qualified using the name of the interface from which it's derived.

Explicit interface implementation provides the following benefits:

■   An implementation can differentiate between interface members that have the same signature and return type. In Java, and nonexplicit member implementations in C#, a single implementation is used to satisfy all matching interface members.

■   An implementation can differentiate between interface members that have the same signature and different return types. This is not possible in Java.

■   If an interface that derives from a superinterface has hidden an inherited member, explicit interface implementation is used to differentiate between the implementation of the parent and child members.

The use of explicit interface implementation has some consequences worth mentioning:

■   The members can no longer be accessed through a class instance; they must be accessed through an instance of the interface in which the member is declared.

■   A compile-time error will occur if any access modifiers are applied to the member. The accessibility of an explicitly implemented member is a special case: it is never accessible through the class instance but always accessible through the interface instance.

■   A compile-time error will occur if the *abstract, virtual, override,* or *static* modifier is applied to the explicit implementation.

Arrays

Arrays are reference types in both C# and Java. Because of their importance, both languages implement native language syntax to declare and manipulate arrays.

Declaration and creation   C# provides three syntax variants for declaring arrays, including two variants to deal with arrays of multiple dimensions: single-dimensional, multidimensional (rectangular), and jagged (arrays of arrays). Java makes no distinction between multidimensional and jagged arrays.

The syntax for array declaration and creation in C# is less flexible than in Java; the square brackets must follow the type specification. If anything, however, this avoids confusion, improving code clarity without reducing functionality.

Table 5-8 demonstrates the Java and C# syntax for array declaration and creation. We use arrays of type *int* in these examples, but C#, like Java, will support arrays of any valid type, including delegates, interfaces, and abstract classes.

Table 5-8 A Cross-Language Array Comparison

	Java	C#
Single-dimensional	*int[] x = new int[5]*	*int[] x = new int[5]*
Multidimensional	*int[][] x = new int[5][5]*	*int[,] y = new int[5,5]*
or rectangular	*int[][][] y = new int[5][5][5]*	*int[,,] z = new int[5,5,5]*
Jagged, or	*int[][] x = new int[5][5]*	*int[][] x = new int[5][]*
array of arrays	*int[][][] x = new int [5][5][5]*	*int[][,] y = new int[5][,]*

Initialization   As with Java, it's possible to initialize a declared array without explicitly creating it. An array of the appropriate size will be implicitly created based on the initialization values. For example, the following two statements are equivalent:

```
int[,,] x = {{{2,3,4}, {5,8,2}}, {{4,6,8}, {7,9,0}}};
int[,,] x = new int [2,2,3] {{{2,3,4}, {5,8,2}}, {{4,6,8}, {7,9,0}}};
```

The *foreach* statement   C# provides the *foreach* statement that simplifies the syntax required to iterate over the elements of an array. Full details of the *foreach* statement are included in the "Statements" section in Chapter 4, "Language Syntax and Features."

Arrays as objects and collections   Arrays are considered objects in both Java and C#; however, the objectlike features of arrays in C# are more extensive than those in Java. In Java, arrays are not directly exposed as objects, but the runtime enables an instance of an array to be assigned to a variable of type *java.lang.Object* and for any of the methods of the *Object* class to be executed against it.

In C#, all arrays inherit from the abstract base class *System.Array*, which derives from *System.Object*. The *System.Array* class provides functionality for working with the array, some of which is available in *java.util.Arrays*. Arrays are also considered to be one of the fundamental collection types.

> **More Info**   Both the object and collection characteristics of arrays are covered in detail in Chapter 9, "Collections."

Delegates

Delegates are a type introduced by C# that has no direct analogue in Java. Delegates provide an object-oriented type-safe mechanism for passing method references as parameters without using function pointers. Delegates are primarily used for event handling and asynchronous callbacks.

Instances of delegates contain references to one or more methods; this is known as an *invocation list*. Methods are added to the invocation list through the delegate constructor and subsequent use of simple operators. Through the delegate, the methods on the invocation list can be executed.

Delegates do not provide functionality that is impossible to achieve in Java. The use of appropriate design patterns and interfaces in Java can provide equivalent capabilities; however, delegates are an elegant and powerful feature. Since delegates are used extensively throughout the .NET class libraries, a detailed understanding of how they work is important.

Declaration   A *delegate* declaration takes the following form:

[attributes] [modifiers] delegate type identifier (parameters);

The *type* and *parameters* of the *delegate* declaration define the return type and signature template a method must have so that it can be added to the delegate invocation list. For example:

```
//Declare a new delegate type
public delegate int MyDelegate(int x, string y);

//The following methods are valid delegate references
public int Method1(int a, string b) { /* … */}
public int Method2(int e, string f) {/* … */}
public int Method3(int p, string q) {/* … */}

//The following methods are not valid
public void Method4(int p, string q) {/* … */}
public int Method5(ref int p, string q) {/* … */}
```

In this example, *Method1*, *Method2*, and *Method3* are all valid to be used with *MyDelegate*. *Method4* and *Method5* are not because their return types and signatures do not match those defined in the *MyDelegate* declaration.

Instantiation   Delegates are instantiated using a single parameter: the name of a method that matches the template specified in the delegates declaration. Existing delegate instances can also be assigned to another instance of the same delegate type, in which case a copy of the delegate invocation list will be assigned to the target delegate.

Delegates can be added together using the + and += operators. This results in the target delegate having the combined invocation list of the two operand delegates. Method references are maintained in the order in which they are added. Adding the same method twice results in two references to the same method being maintained on the invocation list.

Removing method references from a delegate instance is achieved using the - or -= operator. Where there are multiple references to the method, only the last instance will be removed. Attempting to remove a method that is not on the invocation list is not an error. Continuing from the foregoing example:

```
//Instantiating and modifying delegates
MyDelegate d1 = new MyDelegate(Method1);
MyDelegate d2 = new MyDelegate(Method2);
MyDelegate d3 = d1 + d2;
d3 += new MyDelegate(Method3);
d3 -= d1;
d3 -= new MyDelegate(Method3);
```

A delegate is concerned only with the signature and return type of a method, not the type that implements the method; any instance or static method that matches the template can be used with a delegate.

Invoking a delegate   Invoking a delegate is achieved using the delegate instance as if it were a method with the return type and parameters specified in the delegate declaration. For example:

```
//Invoking a delegate
int i = d3(6, "Test");
```

This will cause each method on the invocation list to be called in sequence using the parameters provided. If passing an object reference or using a *ref* parameter, subsequent methods will see any changes made to the arguments by previous methods. The return value will be the value returned from the last method in the invocation list.

Modifiers   The applicability of modifiers to a *delegate* declaration depends on the context in which the delegate is declared. Delegates can be declared as a top-level type, being direct members of an enclosing namespace, or they can be nested within the definition of a class or struct. Table 5-9 summarizes modifier availability.

Table 5-9   *Delegate* **Declaration Modifier Availability**

	Delegate **Declaration Context**		
	Member of Namespace	**Member of Class**	**Member of Struct**
Accessibility			
public	✓	✓	✓
protected	N/A	✓	N/A
private	N/A	(default)	(default)
internal	(default)	✓	✓
protected internal	N/A	✓	N/A
Inheritance			
new	N/A	✓	N/A
abstract	N/A	N/A	N/A
sealed	(implicit)	(implicit)	(implicit)
virtual	N/A	N/A	N/A
override	N/A	N/A	N/A
Other			
readonly	N/A	N/A	N/A
volatile	N/A	N/A	N/A
static	N/A	N/A	N/A
extern	N/A	N/A	N/A

Events   In the .NET Framework, delegates are most frequently used in conjunction with event members. For a complete description of events, see the "Events" section later in this chapter.

Conversion

Converting instances of one type or value to another can be implicit or explicit. The compiler handles implicit conversions automatically; the programmer need take no action. Implicit conversions can occur when conversion of one type to another will not cause loss of information.

When no implicit conversion exists between two types, explicit conversion is used. The programmer forces explicit conversion using casts. If a cast is not specified when an explicit cast is required, a compiler error will occur.

The .NET class library includes the *System.Convert* utility class to convert between different types. This includes the conversion between string, Boolean, date, and value types.

Implicit Conversion

Different data types support different implicit conversions. We discuss these in the following sections.

Implicit numeric conversion   For the simple numeric types, the implicit conversions described in Table 5-10 are possible.

Table 5-10 Supported Implicit Numeric Conversions

From Type	To Types
sbyte	*short, int, long, float, double*, or *decimal*
byte	*short, ushort, int, uint, long, ulong, float, double*, or *decimal*
short	*int, long, float, double*, or *decimal*
ushort	*int, uint, long, ulong, float, double*, or *decimal*
int	*long, float, double*, or *decimal*
uint	*long, ulong, float, double*, or *decimal*
long or *ulong*	*float, double*, or *decimal*
char	*ushort, int, uint, long, ulong, float, double*, or *decimal*
float	*double*

Implicit enumeration conversion   The integer literal 0 (zero) implicitly converts to any enumeration type. Function members should accommodate the fact that 0 is valid where an *enum* type is expected.

Implicit reference conversion   Implicit reference conversion allows use of a reference type where an instance of a different reference type is expected.

- Any reference type is implicitly convertible to *System.Object*.

- Any reference type is implicitly convertible to any class it derives from.

- Any reference type is implicitly convertible to any interface it implements.

- Any array type is implicitly convertible to *System.Array*.

- Arrays of the same dimension with underlying types that support implicit conversion are implicitly convertible.

■   Any delegate type is implicitly convertible to *System.Delegate.*

■   The *null* value is implicitly convertible to any reference type.

Implicit boxing conversion   Implicit boxing conversion allows the conversion of any value type to *System.Object* or any interface that the value type implements. The process of boxing is discussed in the "Boxing" and "Unboxing" sections earlier in this chapter.

Explicit Conversion

Explicit conversion requires the use of the cast expression; this is the same as Java, where the type to be cast is preceded by a set of brackets containing the target type. For example:

```
float f = 23897.5473F;
byte b = (byte)f;          // cast float to byte (losing data)
```

Using a cast where an implicit conversion exists incurs no penalty and can improve the readability of code, clarifying the programmer's intentions. We discuss the different types of explicit conversion in the following sections.

Explicit numeric conversion   Explicit numeric conversion allows conversion from any numeric type to another. Depending on the types and values converted, information loss or exceptions can occur. See the section "The *checked* and *unchecked* Keywords" in Chapter 4 for details of how to handle numeric overflow.

Explicit enumeration conversion   Explicit enumeration conversion supports the following conversions:

■   From all simple numeric types to any *enum* type

■   From any *enum* type to any simple numeric type

■   From any *enum* type to any other *enum* type

Explicit reference conversion   Explicit reference conversion permits the conversion of one reference type to another. If an explicit reference conversion fails at runtime, the CLR will throw a *System.InvalidCastException.*

Explicit unboxing conversion   Unboxing conversions allow a previously boxed value type to be unboxed. The process of unboxing is discussed in the "Boxing" and "Unboxing" sections earlier in this chapter.

User-Defined Conversion

C# allows the programmer to define custom mechanisms for the implicit and explicit conversion of user-defined types. We'll discuss the syntax for defining custom conversions in the "Operators" section later in this chapter.

Members

Members are the programming elements and constructs that are contained in namespaces, classes, structs, and interfaces. Members are divided into three categories: functional, data, and type. Functional members are those that contain executable code, data members are constant or variable values, and type members are nested type declarations.

Member Types and Declaration Context

Table 5-11 contrasts the member types available in Java and C#. A Java developer will be familiar with many of the C# member types, but C# also adds some new ones. For the C# member types, we identify their valid declaration contexts.

Table 5-11   A Cross-Language Comparison of Member Types

		C# Member Context			
Java Member	**C# Member**	**Namespace**	**Class**	**Struct**	**Interface**
Functional Members					
Constructor	Instance constructor	N/A	✓	✓	N/A
Instance initializer	N/A	N/A	N/A	N/A	N/A
Static initializer	Static constructor	N/A	✓	✓	N/A
Finalizer	Destructor	N/A	✓	N/A	N/A
Method	Method	N/A	✓	✓	✓
N/A	Property	N/A	✓	✓	✓
N/A	Event	N/A	✓	✓	✓
N/A	Indexer	N/A	✓	✓	✓
N/A	Operator	N/A	✓	✓	N/A
Data Members					
Constant	Constant	N/A	✓	✓	N/A
Field	Field	N/A	✓	✓	N/A

Table 5-11   A Cross-Language Comparison of Member Types   *(continued)*

Java Member Type Members	C# Member	C# Member Context			
		Namespace	**Class**	**Struct**	**Interface**
Class	Class	✓	✓	✓	N/A
Interface	Interface	✓	✓	✓	N/A
N/A	Delegate	✓	✓	✓	N/A
N/A	Struct	✓	✓	✓	N/A
N/A	Enum	✓	✓	✓	N/A

Versioning and Inheritance of Members

In Java, all methods not declared *static* or *final* are implicitly declared *virtual*. A derived class that implements a method with the same signature and return type as an inherited *virtual* method implicitly overrides that method. When a method is invoked on an object, the most overridden version of the method available to the runtime type of the object is used irrespective of the reference type used to refer to the object. This behavior is the basis of polymorphism.

This approach can cause problems in derived classes when releasing new versions of a base class:

■   If a new version of a base class introduces a method with the same signature and return type as a method already declared in a derived class, any attempts to invoke that method will result in the invocation of the overridden method in the derived class. This will almost certainly give results different from those intended by the base class developers. If the method is marked as *final* to avoid this, the derived class will fail to compile.

■   If a new version of the base class introduces a method with the same signature but different return type from a method already declared in a derived class, the derived class will fail to compile.

Although not common, these problems are more probable when deriving from third-party classes, where it's not possible to coordinate versioning. To overcome these problems, C# offers two alternative approaches to member inheritance: overriding and hiding.

Overriding

Overriding is the same as the default behavior of Java; however, this is not the default C# behavior. The *virtual* modifier must be used to explicitly declare a member as virtual. When a derived class declares a new implementation of an inherited virtual member, the *override* modifier must be used to explicitly confirm the programmer's intention to override the inherited member. If the *override* modifier is not used, the new member hides the inherited member, and a compiler warning occurs. If a derived class attempts to override a nonvirtual inherited member, a compiler error will occur.

Hiding

By default, members are not virtual. A derived class that implements a member with the same name and signature as a nonvirtual inherited member must use the *new* modifier to explicitly declare the programmer's intention to hide the inherited member. Although hiding is the default behavior of C#, a compiler warning will occur if the *new* modifier is not used.

Hiding breaks the polymorphic behavior provided by virtual members. When invoking nonvirtual members, the type of variable used to reference an object determines which member gets invoked. No attempt is made to execute a more derived version of the member based on the runtime type of the object.

In Java, hiding is possible only with static methods, and not instance methods. As a Java developer learning C#, it can be frustrating having to remember to make members virtual and overridden, but the support for both overriding and hiding inherited members provided by C# gives a level of flexibility unavailable in Java.

New Virtual Members

It's possible to use the *new* modifier in conjunction with the *virtual* modifier. This results in a new point of specialization in the inheritance hierarchy. Methods derived from the class implementing a new virtual member will inherit the virtual member. Classes further up the inheritance chain will still perceive the member to be nonvirtual.

Sealed Members

A member that is overriding an inherited virtual member can use the *sealed* modifier to ensure that no further derived classes can override the member. This is similar to the use of the *final* modifier in Java. However, the *sealed* modifier is valid only in conjunction with the *override* modifier. This means that the original declaration of a member cannot guarantee that it won't be overridden. Only through marking an entire class as *sealed* can the programmer ensure that a member cannot be overridden.

Base Class Member Access

A derived class can access members in a superclass by using the *base* keyword. This has the same function and syntax as the *super* keyword in Java.

Static Members

C# static members are not accessible through instances of the containing type; accessing a static member is possible only through reference to its containing type.

Member Attributes

Attributes are applicable to the declaration of all member types. We'll save detailed discussion of them until the "Attributes" section in Chapter 6.

Member Modifiers

Each member type can take a subset of the valid modifiers, depending on the context in which it's declared. The valid modifiers for each member type are detailed in the member sections that follow. Details of each modifier type can be found in the "Modifiers" section in Chapter 4.

Constants

C# and Java constants represent a fixed value that is determined at compilation. However, a C# constant is a unique member type, whereas a Java constant is a field modified using the *final* modifier. In declaration and behavior, Java constants are more like C# *readonly* fields, which we'll discuss in the "Fields" section coming up.

Declaration

Constant declarations have the following syntax:

[attributes] [modifiers] const type identifier = value;

More than one constant can be declared on a single line, each having the same type and accessibility but different values. For example:

```
public const int MyConstant = 60;
private const byte A = 5, B = 10, C = 20;
protected const string MyName = "Allen", HisName = null;
internal const MyClass X = null;
protected internal const int MyOtherConstant = MyConstant * 2;
```

Constants can be declared as any of the inbuilt simple types as well as *string*, *enum*, or any reference type. However, the only valid values for reference type constants are string literals and *null*.

A constant must be assigned a value at declaration, or a compile-time error will occur. No default values are assigned by the compiler. This value can depend on other constants as long as no circular reference is created.

Modifiers

The modifiers applicable to constants depend on the context of their declaration. Table 5-12 summarizes the available modifiers for each context.

Table 5-12   *Constant* **Declaration Modifier Availability**

	Constant **Declaration Context**	
	Member of Class	**Member of Struct**
Accessibility		
public	✓	✓
protected	✓	N/A
private	✓	✓
internal	✓	✓
protected internal	✓	N/A
Inheritance		
new	✓	N/A
abstract	N/A	N/A
sealed	N/A	(implicit)
virtual	N/A	N/A
override	N/A	N/A
Other		
readonly	N/A	N/A
volatile	N/A	N/A
static	(implicit)	N/A
extern	N/A	N/A

Fields

Like Java fields, C# fields represent changeable, variable values and are used to hold object state.

Declaration

Field declarations have the following syntax:

[attributes] [modifiers] type identifier = value;

A field can be declared with any reference or value type. As with Java, it's possible to declare more than one field per declaration. Each field will have the same type and accessibility. For example:

```
public int MyField;
public byte X = 5, Y, Z = 10;
```

As before, fields can be initialized at declaration. However, if a field is not initialized, the compiler will assign it a default value based on its type. Details of default values for each type can be found in the "Types" section earlier in this chapter.

Modifiers

The modifiers applicable to fields depend on the context of their declaration. Table 5-13 summarizes the available modifiers for each context.

Table 5-13   Field Declaration Modifier Availability

	Field Declaration Context	
	Member of Class	**Member of Struct**
Accessibility		
public	✓	✓
protected	✓	N/A
private	✓	✓
internal	✓	✓
protected internal	✓	N/A
Inheritance		
new	✓	N/A
abstract	N/A	N/A
sealed	N/A	N/A
virtual	N/A	N/A
override	N/A	N/A
Other		
readonly[*]	✓	✓
volatile[*]	✓	✓
static	✓	✓
extern	N/A	N/A

[*] *readonly* and *volatile* are mutually exclusive.

Fields as Struct Members

A compile-time error occurs if an attempt is made to assign an initial value to a field that is a member of a struct. For example:

```
public struct MyStruct {
    //This will cause a compile time error
    int MyInt = 6;
}
```

As long as the *new* keyword is used to instantiate a struct, all the member fields will be initialized to their default values. If the *new* keyword is not used, each field must be manually assigned a value before an attempt is made to use the fields.

Read-Only Fields

Fields marked with the *readonly* modifier are the C# equivalent of Java constants. Read-only fields can be assigned a value only at declaration or in a constructor appropriate to the type of field: instance or static. Because read-only fields are unchangeable once initialized, a compile-time error occurs if an attempt is made to pass a read-only field as an *out* or *ref* parameter outside the context of a constructor.

The use of both *static* and *readonly* modifiers provides a useful alternative to the C# constant in situations in which a type is needed that is not supported by the constant member type, or in which the value cannot be determined at compile time. In the following example, the *anObject* field cannot be a constant but can be read-only. Although the *anInteger* field could be a constant, we would have to assign it a value at declaration instead of waiting until the *SomeOtherClass* was instantiated.

```
public class SomeClass {
    // SomeClass implementation
}

public class SomeOtherClass {
    readonly SomeClass anObject;
    readonly int anInteger;

    public SomeOtherClass () {
        anObject = new SomeClass();
        anInteger = 5;
    }
}
```

Static and Instance Constructors

Constructors serve the same purpose in C# as they do in Java, although C# uses different syntax for calling superclass and overloaded constructors. C# also extends the use of constructors to the initialization of structs. More significantly, C# does not support instance initialization blocks, requiring that any instance initialization be carried out within the context of a constructor. With static initialization blocks, C# applies a more constructorlike syntax; this is discussed later in this section.

Declaration

Constructor declarations have the following form:

[attributes] [modifiers] identifier ([parameters])[:initializer([parameters])] {body}

The following Java code demonstrates a class named *MyClass* with a public constructor that passes control to a constructor of its superclass:

```
class MyClass extends MySuperClass{

    public MyClass(int x, String y) {
        super(x, y);
        //other constructor code
    }
}
```

Java constructors use the *super* keyword to pass control to a superclass constructor, which must be the first statement in the constructor. C# adopts a different syntax, using the *base* keyword to identify the superclass constructor to call, as highlighted in the following example:

```
class MyClass : MySuperClass {

    public MyClass(int x, string y): base(x, y) {
        //other constructor code
    }
}
```

The *this* keyword is used instead of *base* to call an overloaded constructor in the same class, as highlighted in the following example:

```
class MyClass : MySuperClass {

    public MyClass(string y): this(5, y) {
        //any other constructor code will be executed
        //after the call to the overloaded constructor
    }
```

(continued)

```
public MyClass(int x, string y): base(x, y) {
    //other constructor code will be executed after
    //the call to the superclass constructor
}
}
```

Modifiers

The modifiers applicable to constructors depend on the context of their declaration. Table 5-14 summarizes the available modifiers for each context.

Table 5-14   Constructor Declaration Modifier Availability

	Constructor Declaration Context	
	Member of Class	**Member of Struct**
Accessibility		
public	✓	✓
protected	✓	N/A
private	✓	✓
internal	✓	✓
protected internal	✓	N/A
Inheritance		
new	N/A	N/A
abstract	N/A	N/A
sealed	N/A	N/A
virtual	N/A	N/A
override	N/A	N/A
Other		
readonly	N/A	N/A
volatile	N/A	N/A
static	✓	✓
extern	✓	✓

Static Constructors

C# *static constructors* are the equivalent of Java *static initialization* blocks. The syntax of a C# static constructor is similar to that of an instance constructor, supporting attributes and the *extern* modifier. No other modifiers are supported, including access modifiers. For example:

```
public class MyClass {
    // This is a static constructor
    static MyClass() {
        // Static Constructor code goes here
    }
}
```

Only one static constructor can be defined per class; Java supports multiple static initialization blocks.

Destructors

Destructors are the C# equivalent of Java finalizers. To implement a finalizer in Java, a class overrides the *java.lang.Object.Finalize* method. In C#, a destructor is a method with a name equal to the class name, preceded by a tilde (~). Destructors are used by the garbage collector to allow the CLR to reclaim resources. The following example demonstrates the declaration of a destructor:

```
public class MyClass {
    // The following method is the destructor for MyClass
    ~MyClass() {
        // Destructor Code
    }
}
```

Although destructors are methods, the following limitations apply:

■ Classes can define only one destructor.

■ Structs cannot define destructors. Structs are allocated memory on the stack, not the managed heap. Stack memory is freed as soon as a struct goes out of scope; hence, the garbage collector is not involved.

■ A destructor never takes parameters or returns a value.

■ The only modifier applicable to a destructor is *extern*.

■ Destructors are not inherited by derived classes.

■ Destructors cannot be explicitly called; they can be invoked only by the garbage collector.

■ Destructors implicitly call the *Finalize* method on the object base class.

> **Warning** As in Java, destructors must be used with care and planning. The incorrect use of destructors can introduce unexpected behavior into an application. Destructors are covered in more detail in Appendix D, "Garbage Collection."

IDisposable

As an alternative to destructors, C# provides the *System.IDisposable* interface for clearing up object resources without waiting for the automated garbage collection process to call a destructor. A class that implements *IDisposable* should correctly release any resources it holds when its *Dispose* method is called.

C# provides the *using* statement, which is shorthand syntax for acquiring and disposing of objects that implement the *IDisposable* interface. See the "Statements" section in Chapter 4 for complete details of the *using* statement.

Methods

The only difference between C# and Java is the additional types of parameters available.

Declaration

Method declarations have the following syntax:

[attributes] [modifiers] return-type identifier (parameter-list) {body}

For example, a *protected static* method named *MyMethod* that returns an integer and takes a *string* and a *bool* as parameters is declared as follows:

```
protected static int MyMethod (string s, bool b) {
    // implementation code
}
```

Modifiers

The modifiers applicable to methods depend on the context of their declaration. Table 5-15 summarizes the available modifiers for each context.

Table 5-15   Method Declaration Modifier Availability

	Method Declaration Context		
	Member of Class	**Member of Struct**	**Member of Interface**
Accessibility			
public	✓	✓	(implicit)
protected	✓	N/A	N/A
private	✓	✓	N/A
internal	✓	✓	N/A
protected internal	✓	N/A	N/A
Inheritance			
new	✓	N/A	✓
abstract	✓	N/A	(implicit)
sealed	✓	N/A	✓
virtual	✓	N/A	N/A
override	✓	N/A	N/A
Other			
readonly	N/A	N/A	N/A
volatile	N/A	N/A	N/A
static	✓	✓	N/A
extern	✓	✓	N/A

When applying modifiers to method declarations, the following restrictions apply:

- The *static*, *virtual*, and *override* modifiers are mutually exclusive.

- The *new* and *override* modifiers are mutually exclusive.

- If the method is *abstract*, it cannot be *static*, *virtual*, or *extern*.

- If the method is *private*, it cannot be *virtual*, *override*, or *abstract*.

- The *sealed* modifier must be accompanied by *override*.

Parameters

All parameters are passed by value in Java. In addition to pass-by-value parameters, C# supports two new parameter types: reference and output parameters. C# also provides a mechanism called *parameter arrays*, which is used to pass a variable number of arguments to a method. We discuss parameter arrays in the following section. See the "Variables" section later in this chapter for a complete coverage of value, reference, and output parameters.

Parameter arrays   Parameter arrays are a feature with no direct parallel in Java. The use of a parameter array allows the caller of a method to provide a variable number of arguments when invoking a method; these are passed into the method in the form of an array.

A method is declared to use a parameter array using the *params* keyword as follows:

```
public void MyMethod(string someParam, params byte[] args) {
    // implementation code
}
```

As illustrated here, if a method takes multiple parameters, the parameter array must be the rightmost parameter declared. The *params* declaration must indicate the type of array that the method expects to receive; the array can be composed of simple or reference types. Within the body of the method, the *params* argument is processed as a normal array. The method just shown can be invoked in the following ways:

```
byte[] b = {5, 2, 6, 8} ;
string test = "hello" ;

MyMethod(test);            // call with no parameters
MyMethod(test, 3);         // call with a single parameter
MyMethod(test, 2,7,1);     // call with more than one parameter
MyMethod(test, b);         // call using an actual array
```

Events

Events are a formalization of the observer pattern, providing a generic mechanism through which a collection of registered listeners is notified when events occur. For example, program elements might need to know when a user clicks a button or closes a window. Events leverage delegates as the mechanism for event distribution. Objects interested in receiving event notifications register a delegate instance with the event. When triggered, the event invokes all registered delegates. We discussed delegates in the "Types" section earlier in this chapter.

Like delegates, events do not provide functionality that cannot be implemented in Java using the appropriate patterns and interfaces; the observer pattern is used extensively throughout the Java class library. However, events do provide a clean syntax, freeing the programmer from implementing listener management and event distribution mechanisms.

Declaration

An *event* declaration takes the following form:

[attributes] [modifiers] event type identifier [{access-declarations}];

The *event* type must be an already defined and accessible *delegate* type. The optional *access-declarations* element provides the functionality for adding and removing event listeners. If this element is omitted, the compiler provides a default implementation suitable for most purposes. We'll discuss custom access-declarations later in this section.

Event invocation and usage   An event can be triggered only from within the type that declared it, irrespective of the accessibility modifiers applied to the event. An event is triggered as if invoking a delegate of the type used to declare the event. Triggering an event causes all delegate instances registered with the event to be invoked with the specified argument values. It makes no sense to trigger an event that has no registered listeners. An *event* will evaluate to *null* if it has no registered listeners. An *if* statement can be used to determine whether it's necessary to trigger an event. To remove all registered listeners from an event, set the value of the event to *null*.

The following code demonstrates the use of events. The example defines a *TempSource* class that has a read-only property *Temp* for setting the current temperature. *TempSource* notifies all registered listeners when the temperature is set. We define a *TempListener* class to listen to temperature change events and output a message to the console in response.

```
using System;

// Declare a delegate for event notifications
public delegate void
    TemperatureEventHandler (string source, int temp);

// Declare the event source object
public class TempSource {
    private string Name;
    private int temp = 0;
    public event TemperatureEventHandler TemperatureChange;

    //Constructor takes a name for the Temperature Source
    public TempSource (string name) {
        Name = name;
    }

    // Declare a property to set the current temperature
    public int Temp {
        set {
```

(continued)

```csharp
            temp = value; // set the temperature

            // Raise the event if there are any listeners
            if (TemperatureChange != null) {
          TemperatureChange(Name, temp);
            }
        }
    }

    // Declare a method to remove all registered listeners
    public void Reset() {
        TemperatureChange = null;
    }
}

// Declare the event listener
public class TempListener {
    private string Name;

    // Constructor that takes Listener name and an array of source
    public TempListener(string name, params TempSource[] sources) {

        Name = name;

        // Register with each of the temperature sources
        foreach (TempSource t in sources) {
            t.TemperatureChange +=
                new TemperatureEventHandler(this.TempChanged);
        }
    }

    public void TempChanged(string src, int temp) {
        Console.WriteLine(Name + " : Temp is " + temp
            + " F in the " + src);
    }

    public static void Main() {
        TempSource g = new TempSource("garden");
        TempSource r = new TempSource("refrigerator");

        new TempListener("Listener1", new TempSource[] {g, r});
        new TempListener("Listener2", new TempSource[] {g, r});

        g.Temp = 34;
        r.Temp = 16;
    }
}
```

This example demonstrates multiple listeners registering with a single source as well as a listener receiving events from multiple sources. When run, the example produces the following output:

```
Listener1 : Temp is 34 F in the garden.
Listener2 : Temp is 34 F in the garden.
Listener1 : Temp is 16 F in the refrigerator.
Listener2 : Temp is 16 F in the refrigerator.
```

.NET implementation guidelines   The .NET class libraries use events extensively, especially with GUI components. Events can utilize any delegate, but .NET standardizes the delegate signature used with events and provides a concrete implementation in the *System.EventHandler* delegate with the following signature:

```
public delegate void EventHandler(object sender, EventArgs e);
```

The *sender* is a reference to the object that contains and raises the event; *e* is an object that derives from *System.EventArgs*. *System.EventArgs* contains no specialized functionality. An event that needs to distribute event data should derive an event-specific class from *EventArgs* with the additional functionality it requires.

Events and inheritance   Because events can be called only from within the context of the containing type, derived classes cannot trigger events in superclasses; *protected* methods must be declared to indirectly trigger the event where required.

Modifiers   The modifiers applicable to event declarations are dependent upon the context in which the delegate is declared, as summarized in Table 5-16.

Table 5-16 Event Declaration Modifier Availability

	Event Declaration Context		
	Member of Class	**Member of Struct**	**Member of Interface**
Accessibility			
public	✓	✓	(implicit)
protected	✓	N/A	N/A
private	(default)	(default)	N/A
internal	✓	✓	N/A
protected internal	✓	N/A	N/A

(continued)

Table 5-16 **Event Declaration Modifier Availability** *(continued)*

	Event Declaration Context		
	Member of Class	**Member of Struct**	**Member of Interface**
Inheritance			
new	✓	N/A	✓
abstract	✓	N/A	(implicit)
sealed	✓	N/A	✓
virtual	✓	N/A	N/A
override	✓	N/A	N/A
Other			
readonly	N/A	N/A	N/A
volatile	N/A	N/A	N/A
static	✓	✓	N/A
extern	✓	✓	N/A

Accessors   Event accessors provide the functionality called when the += or -= operator is used to add and remove event listeners. In most cases, the default implementations provided by the compiler are sufficient. If custom behavior is required, syntax similar to that used in a property is employed. However, the two methods are named add and remove. The following code fragment shows the syntax used:

```
public event SomeEventHandler SomeEvent {
    add {
        // Functionality to add event listener
    }
    remove {
        // Functionality to remove an event listener
    }
}
```

Both *add* and *remove* blocks can take attributes but do not take any modifiers or parameters. The only parameter available in *add* and *remove* is an implicit parameter named *value* that contains a reference to the delegate instance being added or removed.

Use of custom accessors means the programmer is responsible for implementing the necessary functionality to track registered listeners and also for using the registered delegates to raise events. It's no longer possible to clear the event listeners by nulling the event, nor can the event be compared with *null* to determine whether there are any registered listeners.

Properties

Properties are a feature of C# that allows seemingly direct access to the state of a class or struct while still giving the control associated with providing access through methods. Properties provide a formalization of the getter/setter pattern. This pattern is a convention used extensively throughout Java class libraries and packages, although the Java language lacks a formal syntax to support or enforce the pattern.

To demonstrate the benefit of properties, consider an instance of a class *Person* that contains a member field to hold a person's age. To avoid exposing a public *age* field, a common approach is to implement *getAge* and *setAge* methods to allow controlled manipulation of the field. These would be used as follows:

```
aPerson.setAge(34);
int age = aPerson.getAge();
```

C# properties allow this manipulation to take the following form:

```
aPerson.Age = 34;
int age = aPerson.Age;
```

The benefits become more apparent when using the property in conjunction with operators, for example:

```
aPerson.Age += 5;
aPerson.Age++;
```

To the code consumer, it's as though there is a directly accessible member field named *Age*. In reality, there is no field named *Age*: the code is calling special accessor methods to interact with the object state.

The use of properties provides clean and intuitive code, but for a Java developer this can be confusing. It's often hard to determine the difference between working with a public field and working with a property.

Declaration

Properties provide a means to manipulate object state but are not stateful mechanisms themselves; something else, often a field member, is the target of the manipulation. The property declaration imposes no requirements on the containing type as to what the stateful item is, or is called.

Property declarations have the following syntax:

[attributes] [modifiers] type identifier {accessor-declaration}

The property type can be any value or reference type and specifies both the data type that can be assigned to the property and the type returned when the property itself is assigned to something else.

Here's a Java implementation of the getter/setter pattern for the *Person* class discussed previously:

```java
public class Person {

    private int thePersonsAge;

    public void setAge(int p_age) {
        // Do some validation
        thePersonsAge = p_age;
    }

    public int getAge() {
        return thePersonsAge;
    }
}
```

The equivalent C# implementation using properties is

```csharp
public class Person {
    private int thePersonsAge;

    public int Age {
        get {
            return thePersonsAge;
        }
        set {
            thePersonsAge = value;
        }
    }
}
```

The *get* and *set* accessors in this example are simplistic and provide no additional benefit compared with making the *thePersonsAge* field public; however, as function members, properties can contain any executable code.

The undeclared variable *value* used in the *set* accessor is implicitly provided by the compiler, containing the value the caller has assigned to the property. The type is the same as that of the property declaration, in this example an *int*.

It's possible to implement only the *get* or the *set* accessor, thus providing a read-only or write-only property. However, if the intention is to use the prefix or postfix increment (++) or decrement (--) operator, or any of the compound assignment operators (+=, −=, and so on), both the *get* and *set* accessors must be declared. Attempting any action on a property that requires an accessor that has not been implemented will result in a compiler error being raised.

Modifiers

The modifiers applicable to properties depend on the context of their declaration. Table 5-17 summarizes the available modifiers for each context.

Table 5-17   Property Declaration Modifier Availability

	Property Declaration Context		
	Member of Class	**Member of Struct**	**Member of Interface**
Accessibility			
public	✓	✓	(implicit)
protected	✓	N/A	N/A
private	✓	✓	N/A
internal	✓	✓	N/A
protected internal	✓	N/A	N/A
Inheritance			
new	✓	N/A	✓
abstract	✓	N/A	N/A
sealed	✓	N/A	N/A
virtual	✓	N/A	N/A
override	✓	N/A	N/A
Other			
readonly	N/A	N/A	N/A
volatile	N/A	N/A	N/A
static	✓	✓	N/A
extern[*]	✓	✓	N/A

[*]   When the *extern* modifier is used, the *get* and *set* accessor bodies should be empty statements.

Properties as Members of Interfaces

A property can be a member of an interface. The structure of the property declaration is the same as discussed earlier in this section; however, the body of the *get* and *set* accessors is an empty statement. If only one of the accessors is required, specify this in the interface. For example:

```
public interface IPerson {
    int Age {get; set;}
    string PayrollNumber {get;}    // No set accessor required.
}
```

Indexers

Sometimes it makes sense to access a class or struct by using index syntax, similar to that used with arrays. This is particularly appropriate if the class contains some collection of related information. C# provides the *indexer* member type for achieving this functionality.

Instead of making field members directly accessible or defining a series of methods for manipulating the underlying data, indexers provide indirect access to state using the familiar array-style index. Like properties, the indexer provides indirect access to the data via definable *get* or *set* methods. The index can be any value or reference type.

The .NET class libraries make extensive use of indexers to provide access to collections. See Chapter 9 for complete details.

Declaration

Indexers are similar to properties in that they provide a means to manipulate object state but are not stateful mechanisms themselves. As with properties, the containing class or struct must implement some other program element as the target of the manipulation. The indexer imposes no requirements as to how this is done.

Index declarations have the following syntax:

[attributes] [modifiers] type this [parameters] {accessor-declarations}

Use of an indexer is never performed explicitly through a member name, so indexers do not have identifiers. As a consequence of an unfortunate syntax choice, indexers are declared using the keyword *this*.

The indexer type can be any value or reference type and specifies both the data type that can be assigned to an indexer element and the type of the indexer element returned when assigned to something else. At least one parameter must be specified in the indexer declaration. Multiple parameters result in a multidimensional index, as in the case of a multidimensional array. For example:

```
public string this [int index1, byte index2, string index3] {…}
```

Parameters can be of any value or reference type, but it is not valid to use the *ref* or *out* modifier.

Multiple indexers can be defined for a single class. Given that all indexers are declared using the *this* keyword, additional indexers must be differentiated with different parameter types.

The following example demonstrates the declaration of an indexer:

```
public class TopTenArtists {

    private string[] artists = new string[10];

    public string this [int index] {
        get {
            if (index > 0 && index < 11) {
                return artists[index-1];
            } else {
                return null;
            }
        }
        set {
            if (index > 0 && index < 11) {
                artists[index-1] = value;
            }
        }
    }
}
```

The undeclared variable *value* used in the *set* accessor is implicitly provided by the compiler. It contains the value the caller is assigning to the property. Its type is the same as that of the property declaration—in this instance, an *int*.

The following code demonstrates how the indexer of the *TopTenArtists* class can be used:

```
public static void Main() {

    TopTenArtists artists = new TopTenArtists();

    artists[1] = "Rubens";
    artists[2] = "Gainsborough";
    artists[3] = "Yevseeva";


    for (int x = 1; x < 11; x++) {
        System.Console.WriteLine("Artist {0} is {1}", x, artists[x]);
    }
}
```

This example produces the following output:

```
Artist 1 is Rubens
Artist 2 is Gainsborough
Artist 3 is Yevseeva
Artist 4 is
Artist 5 is
Artist 6 is
```

(continued)

```
Artist 7 is
Artist 8 is
Artist 9 is
Artist 10 is
```

As was the case with properties, indexers can implement only the *get* or *set* accessor; this provides a read-only or write-only member. As with properties, if the intention is to use the prefix or postfix increment or decrement operators, or any of the compound assignment operators, both the *get* and *set* accessors must be declared.

Modifiers

The modifiers applicable to indexers depend on the context of their declaration. Table 5-18 summarizes the available modifiers for each context.

Table 5-18   Indexer Declaration Modifier Availability

	Indexer Declaration Context		
	Member of Class	**Member of Struct**	**Member of Interface**
Accessibility			
public	✓	✓	(implicit)
protected	✓	N/A	N/A
private	✓	✓	N/A
internal	✓	✓	N/A
protected internal	✓	N/A	N/A
Inheritance			
new	✓	N/A	✓
abstract	✓	N/A	N/A
sealed	✓	N/A	N/A
virtual	✓	N/A	N/A
override	✓	N/A	N/A
Other			
readonly	N/A	N/A	N/A
volatile	N/A	N/A	N/A
static[*]	N/A	N/A	N/A
extern[†]	✓	✓	N/A

[*] Static indexers are not permitted.

[†] When the *extern* modifier is used, the *get* and *set* accessor bodies should be empty statements.

Indexers as Members of Interfaces

Indexers can be declared in interfaces. As with properties, the *get* and *set* accessors must be specified as an empty statement. To implement a read-only or write-only indexer, simply omit the accessor that is not required. When implementing the interface, explicit interface implementation must be used to identify the indexer implementation. For example:

```
public interface IMyInterface {
    string this [int index] {get; set;}
}

public class MyClass : IMyInterface {
    string IMyInterface.this [int index] {
        get {
            // implementation
        }
        set {
            // implementation
        }
    }
}
```

The problem with this approach is that the indexer cannot be accessed through an instance of the class, only through an instance of the interface. For example:

```
// This is a compile-time error
MyClass a = new MyClass();
string b = a[1];

// The following statements are valid
MyClass p = new MyClass();
string q = ((IMyInterface)p)[1];    // Cast to an interface instance

IMyInterface x = new MyClass();
string y = x[1];
```

Operators

In this section, we'll consistently refer to this member type as an *operator member* to avoid confusion with regular operators such as + and !=. The operator member enables a programmer to specify the behavior when an instance of a class or struct is used in either of the following ways:

- Is used in conjunction with an operator such as + or !=. This is called *operator overloading*.

- Is implicitly or explicitly converted to another type, known as *custom conversion*.

Operator members provide syntactic convenience resulting in clean and logical code when used correctly; however, when used inappropriately or in idiosyncratic ways, operator members result in code that is difficult to understand and types that are difficult to use. For example, it makes sense for a class *CalendarDay* that represents a calendar day to support the ++ operator to increment the day being represented, but use of the + operator to add two *CalendarDay* instances together is not logical and constitutes confusing behavior.

Declaration

The declaration of an operator member takes the following general form:

[attributes] [modifiers] operator operator-token (parameters) {body}

The type of operator member determines the specific declaration syntax required, but there are a number of restrictions common to all operator members:

- Operator members are always associated with types and must be *public* and *static*.

- The only optional modifier is *extern*, in which case the body of the operator member must be an empty statement.

- Arguments to operator members cannot be *ref* or *out* parameters.

- Derived classes inherit operator members but cannot override or hide them.

- Operator members cannot return *void*.

There are three categories of operator members: unary, binary, and conversion. We discuss each of these in the following sections.

Unary operators   Unary operator members allow the following operators to be overloaded: +, -, !, ~, ++, --, *true*, and *false*. The *true* and *false* operators must be implemented as a pair, or a compiler error will occur. Unary operator members take a single argument of the type the operator member is declared in. The return type depends on the overloaded operator. Table 5-19 summarizes the return type for each operator.

Table 5-19   Unary Operator Return Types

Operator	Return Type
+, -, !, ~	Any
++, --	The type containing the operator member
true, false	*bool*

The following example demonstrates the syntax used to declare a variety of unary operators as members of a class named *SomeClass*. We have highlighted the operator keywords and tokens for clarity.

```
public class SomeClass {

    // +, -, !, and ~ operators can return any type
    public static int operator +(SomeClass x) {/*...*/}
    public static SomeOtherClass operator ~(SomeClass x) {/*...*/}

    // ++ and -- operators must return an instance of SomeClass
    public static SomeClass operator ++(SomeClass x) {/*...*/}

    // true and false operators must be declared as a pair
    // and return bool
    public static bool operator true(SomeClass x) {/*...*/}
    public static bool operator false(SomeClass x) {/*...*/}
}
```

Given the declaration of *SomeClass*, the following statements are valid:

```
SomeClass x = new SomeClass();    // Instantiate a new SomeClass
SomeClass y = +x;                 // Unary + operator
SomeOtherClass z = ~x;            // Bitwise compliment operator

while (x) {                       // true operator
    x++;                          // postfix increment operator
}
```

Binary operators   Binary operator members allow the following operators to be overloaded: +, -, *, /, %, &, |, ^, <<, >>, ==, !=, >, <, >=, and <=.

The following binary operators must be overloaded in pairs:

- == and !=

- > and <

- >= and <=

Binary operator declarations must specify two arguments, one of which must be the type that the operator member is declared in. The order of the arguments must match the order of operands when the overloaded operator is used. The return value can be of any type. Paired operator declarations must have the same argument types and order.

When a binary operator is overloaded, the corresponding compound assignment operator (if any) is implicitly overloaded. For example, overloading the * operator implicitly overloads the *= operator. If a type overloads the == or != operator, a compiler warning is generated if the type does not override the inherited *Object.Equals* and *Object.GetHashCode* methods. Although the && and || operators cannot be directly overloaded, they are supported through the implementation of the & and | operators. Using the && operator as an example, the & operator must be overloaded, taking two arguments of the type in which the operator member is declared and returning the same type.

The following example demonstrates a number of binary operator member declarations as members of a struct named *SomeStruct*. We have highlighted the operator keywords and tokens for clarity.

```
public struct SomeStruct {

    // The == and != operators must be declared in pairs
    // The same arguments types and order must be used
    public static bool operator == (SomeStruct x, int y) {/*…*/}
    public static bool operator != (SomeStruct x, int y) {/*…*/}

    // Binary + operator causes += to be implicitly overloaded
    public static SomeStruct operator + (SomeStruct x, long y) {/*…*/}

    // Binary & operator declared to support usage with "&&" statements
    public static SomeStruct operator & (
        SomeStruct x, SomeStruct y) {/*…*/}

}
```

Given the declaration of *SomeStruct*, the following code fragments are valid:

```
SomeStruct x = new SomeStruct();    // Instantiate a new SomeStruct
SomeStruct y = new SomeStruct();    // Instantiate a new SomeStruct

if (x && y) {    // correctly implemented "&" operator supports this
    x += 45 ;    // implicitly provided by overloading "+" operator
}
```

Conversion operators   Conversion operator members allow the programmer to define the logic used to convert an instance of one type (the source) to an instance of another (the target). The compiler will use available conversion operators to perform implicit and explicit data type conversions. See the "Types" section earlier in this chapter for details of implicit and explicit conversions.

Conversion operator declarations include the keyword *implicit* or *explicit*. This determines where the compiler will use the conversion operator. Conversion operator members take a single parameter and return a value of any type. The parameter is the source type and the return value is the target type of the conversion. For example, the declaration of an implicit conversion operator to convert a *string* to an instance of *SomeClass* is as follows:

```
public static implicit operator SomeClass(String x) {/*…*/}
```

The declaration of an explicit conversion operator to convert an instance of *SomeStruct* to an *int* is as follows:

```
public static explicit operator int (SomeStruct x) {/*…*/}
```

The following restrictions apply to conversion operators:

■ Either the return type or the argument must be the type in which the conversion operator is declared.

■ It is not possible to declare a conversion operator to redefine an already existing conversion, meaning that it is not possible to define both an *explicit* and an *implicit* conversion operator for the same types.

■ A conversion operator must convert between different types.

■ Conversion to or from interface types is not possible.

■ No inheritance relationship can exist between the target and source types.

Cross-Language Considerations

Many languages do not support operator overloading, and it is not part of the Common Language Specification (CLS). To provide cross-language support, it's necessary to provide method alternatives to any overloaded operators. The CLS provides recommendations on appropriate names for each operator type.

Nested Types

As with Java, C# supports nested type declarations. Full details can be found in the "Types" section earlier in this chapter.

Variables

Both Java and C# are strongly typed languages, meaning variables must be declared with a specific type before they are used and can hold only values compatible with that declared type. Both Java and C# define seven types of variables. Despite this coincidence, significant differences exist in how each language categorizes its variable types, as described in Table 5-20.

Table 5-20   A Comparison of Variable Types in Java and C#

Java	C#	Includes
class variable	static variable	Fields declared using the *static* modifier. In Java, this also includes any fields declared in interfaces. Refer to the "Members" section earlier in this chapter for full details.
instance variable	instance variable	Fields declared as members of a class (or struct in C#) that are not declared with the *static* modifier. Refer to the "Members" section earlier in this chapter for full details.
array component	array element	The elements contained within an array. Refer to the "Types" section earlier in this chapter for full details.
local variable	local variable	Variables declared within the scope of a function member, statement block, *for* statement, or *switch* statement. Also, in C#, a *using* statement, a *foreach* statement, or a *catch* clause.
		The C# compiler will raise a warning if any declared local variables are not used.
method parameter	value parameter	Refer to the "Value Parameters" section later in this chapter for full details.
N/A	reference parameter	Refer to the "Reference Parameters" section later in this chapter for full details.
N/A	output parameter	Refer to the "Output Parameters" section later in this chapter for full details.

Table 5-20   A Comparison of Variable Types in Java and C#   *(continued)*

Java	C#	Includes
constructor parameter	N/A	Java differentiates between parameters used in normal methods and those used in constructors. C# considers these to be the same as value parameters.
exception-handler parameter	N/A	A variable created to hold the exception instance that has been caught in a *try...catch* statement. C# considers these to be local variables.

Value Parameters

All parameters specified in function member declarations are considered to be value parameters unless they are preceded by the *ref* or *out* keyword. We'll discuss these two keywords shortly.

When a function member is invoked, variables are created for each parameter specified in the member declaration and are automatically initialized to the default value of the arguments provided in the member invocation. These variables are accessible within the scope of the member using the names assigned to the parameter in the member declaration.

This leads to reference type parameters pointing to the object instances provided as arguments and value type parameters containing a copy of the argument value provided by the caller, meaning that although the contents of any referenced objects can be affected, the actual values of any variables used by the caller to invoke the member remain unchanged. For example:

```
public class SomeObject {
    // implementation details
}

public class MyClass {

    public static void ValParamTest(SomeObject x, int y) {
        x = new SomeObject();
        y = y * 2;
    }

    public static void Main() {
        SomeObject p = null;
        int q = 3;
        MyClass.ValParamTest(p, q);
    }
}
```

After running this example, *p* is still *null* and *q* is still equal to 3. This is the default behavior in C# and the only behavior available in Java.

Reference Parameters

Use of the *ref* keyword creates a reference parameter. When a function member is invoked using a *ref* parameter, the function member parameter variable represents the same variable used by the caller instead of a new variable being created and assigned the value of the calling argument.

The importance of this is that any changes made within the function member to the variables will be visible to the caller. For example:

```
public class SomeObject {
    // implementation details
}

public class MyClass {

    public static void RefParamTest(ref SomeObject x, ref int y) {
        x = new SomeObject();
        y = y * 2;
    }

    public static void Main() {
        SomeObject p = null;
        int q = 3;
        MyClass.RefParamTest(ref p, ref q);
    }
}
```

Note the use of the *ref* keyword in both the method declaration and the method invocation. After the execution of this code, *p* will reference an instance of *SomeClass* and *q* will equal 6. This is distinctly different from the behavior of value parameters, discussed earlier.

The use of reference parameters is a simple way to overcome the limitation that function members can return only a single value. In Java, a container class would be created to hold the values to pass into the method. C# reference parameters provide a simple solution to this problem in situations that do not warrant the use of a more structured approach.

Output Parameters

The *out* keyword is used the same and has the same effect as *ref,* but variables modified with the *out* keyword don't have to be initialized before they're passed into a function member. In the following example, without the use of the *out* keyword in the declaration and invocation of the *OutParamTest* method, a compiler error would be raised because the variable *x* is not initialized before it's used:

```
public class MyClass {

    public static void OutParamTest(out int x) {
        x = 5;
    }

    public static void Main() {
        int x;
        MyClass.OutParamTest(out x);
        System.Console.WriteLine("x = " + x);
    }
}
```

Within the called function member (*OutParamTest*), any *out* parameters are initially unassigned, as the compiler does not assign them default values. Hence they must be manually initialized before they can be used; otherwise, a compile-time error will occur. A compile-time error will also occur if the *out* parameter is not assigned a value before the member returns.

Summary

Java provides a set of data types suitable for the resolution of most contemporary business computing problems. However, the unified type system provided by the .NET Framework, as well as the extended selection of C# data and member types, offers greater flexibility and more control to the programmer.

6

Advanced Language Features

This chapter explores some advanced features of the C# language, including exception handling, attributes, preprocessor directives, and unsafe code. Although the Java programmer will be familiar with exception handling, many of these features have no analog in Java and demonstrate the strong C/C++ heritage of C#.

Threading and Synchronization

C# and Microsoft .NET provide a richer set of threading and synchronization capabilities than Java. As with Java, most of these capabilities are exposed through the class libraries, not the language syntax. The *lock* keyword is the only C# statement related to threading and synchronization. See the "Statements" section in Chapter 4, "Language Syntax and Features," for a complete description of the lock statement.

> **More Info** For complete coverage of threading and synchronization, see Chapter 13, "Threading and Synchronization."

Exceptions and Exception Handling

The exception-handling features of C# will be familiar to the Java programmer; the exception-handling syntax is predominantly the same, although the languages differ significantly in their exception declaration requirements.

Declaring Exceptions

There is no requirement, and no ability, in C# for a function member to programmatically declare the exceptions it might throw. The only way to do so is in the API documentation. This has two consequences:

- Java developers are accustomed to methods explicitly declaring the checked exceptions they might throw. The absence of a *throws* declaration means that the programmer is more reliant on API documentation than on the compiler.

- Interface members cannot specify which exceptions the member implementations are expected to throw. A full and accurate implementation of an interface member can be achieved only by a disciplined developer referring to and accurately interpreting the interface documentation.

Catching Exceptions

The following example demonstrates the familiar *try...catch...finally* exception-handling syntax, along with new *catch* syntax introduced by C#:

```
try {
    // code that might throw an exception

} catch (ExceptionClass1 ex1) {        // catch clause 1
    // code to handle exceptions of class ExceptionClass1
    // with access to the thrown exception named ex1

} catch (ExceptionClass2) {        // catch clause 2
    // code to handle exceptions of class ExceptionClass2
    // but without access to the Exception instance

} catch {     // catch clause 3
    // code to handle any Exception, but without access
    // to the Exception instance
```

```
} finally {
    // code that executes no matter whether
    // the try block succeeds or fails
}
```

The example shows that

- Catch clause 1 is exactly the same as the Java syntax.

- Catch clause 2 allows the programmer to catch an exception without declaring a local variable; there is no access to the exception caught.

- Catch clause 3, known as a general catch clause, is used to capture any previously unhandled exception regardless of type. Because all run-time exceptions inherit from *System.Exception*, it is simply a shorthand form of writing the following:

```
try {
    // Some code
} catch (System.Exception) {
    // Some exception-handling code
}
```

Throwing Exceptions

Throwing exceptions is the same in C# as in Java. For example:

```
throw new ExceptionClass();
```

C# introduces a shorthand syntax for rethrowing caught exceptions: the *throw* statement with no parameters. This is required when using the new *catch* syntax described in the preceding section. For example:

```
try {
    // Some code
} catch {
    // Some exception handling code
    // Rethrow the caught exception
    throw;
}
```

> **Tip** The same performance issues with exceptions exist in C# as in Java. Throwing exceptions can be expensive and should not be used as a general flow control mechanism.

The Exception Hierarchy

The *java.lang.Throwable* class is the root of the Java exception class hierarchy. Two classes derive directly from *Throwable*: *java.lang.Exception* and *java.lang.Error*. Derived from *Exception* is a class named *java.lang.RuntimeException*. The *Exception*, *Error*, and *RuntimeException* subclasses of *Throwable* are central to the Java classification of exceptions into the *checked* and *unchecked* categories.

Unchecked exceptions are those derived from either the *Error* or *RuntimeException* class. The compiler makes no attempt to ensure that these exceptions are handled by the developer since they generally occur because of a run-time or program error that should be fixed.

Checked exceptions are those that the compiler ensures are caught and handled within the code or are declared in the *throws* clause of the method declaration. Checked exceptions include all exceptions derived from *java.lang.Exception*, excluding *RuntimeException* and its subclasses.

Because C# function members cannot declare exceptions, the compiler makes no attempt to ensure that exceptions are caught and handled correctly. All .NET exceptions can be considered to be unchecked exceptions in Java terminology.

.NET takes a simpler approach to classifying exceptions based on whether it is a system or an application-related exception. This is merely a convention and is not enforced by the compiler or the runtime.

The root of the exception hierarchy in .NET is *System.Exception*. System exceptions are represented by *System.SystemException* and application exceptions by *System.ApplicationException*, both of which are derived from *System.Exception*.

The *System.Exception* Class

Table 6-1 compares the functionality of .NET's *System.Exception* class with that of the Java *java.lang.Throwable* class. Although not a part of either language specification, the use of exceptions is tightly integrated with both Java and C# and is appropriate to this chapter. Java and .NET both rely on the exception inheritance hierarchy as a classification mechanism to support the use of the *catch* clause.

Exception Chaining

Both .NET and Java version 1.4 support a standardized approach to exception chaining. This allows exceptions to be created and store a reference to another exception internally. The inner exception would usually be a reference to an exception that prompted the outer exception to be raised.

Table 6-1   Comparison of Java and C# Exception Members

Java	C#	Comments
Constructors		
Throwable()	*Exception()*	Constructs a new exception instance.
Throwable(String)	*Exception(string)*	Constructs an exception with the specified message.
Throwable(String, Throwable)	*Exception(string, Exception)*	Constructs an exception with the specified message and chained exception.
Throwable(Throwable)	N/A	Not supported in .NET; use the previous constructor.
N/A	*Exception(SerializationInfo, StreamingContext)*	Constructs an exception from a previously serialized exception. See *GetObjectData* near the end of this table.
Member		
fillInStackTrace()	N/A	Not supported. (Although *Environment.StackTrace* can be used if only a stack trace is needed.)
getCause()	*InnerException*	Gets the chained exception, or *null* if one has not been specified.
getLocalizedMessage()	N/A	.NET recommends that the message available through the *Message* property be localized. Java provides this second method, which should be overridden by deriving classes to return a localized version of the message.
getMessage()	*Message*	Gets a message that describes the exception.
getStackTrace()	*StackTrace*	Gets the stack trace from the exception as a string.
initCause()	N/A	Sets the chained exception reference. .NET allows this reference to be set only during construction.
printStackTrace()	N/A	Not supported. Use the *ToString* method followed by the appropriate *Stream* or *Console* method.
setStackTrace()	N/A	Not supported.

(continued)

Table 6-1   Comparison of Java and C# Exception Members   *(Continued)*

Java	C#	Comments
N/A	*HelpLink*	Gets or sets a link to related help information. Should be in the form of a URN or URL.
N/A	*Source*	Gets or sets the name of the application or object that caused the exception. By default, this will be the assembly name.
N/A	*TargetSite*	Gets a *MethodBase* class representing the method that threw the exception.
N/A	*GetBaseException()*	Returns the original exception at the root of the exception chain.
N/A	*GetObjectData()*	Serializes an exception.
N/A	*HResult*	Gets or sets a coded number that uniquely identifies an exception. Predominantly for legacy integration.

Attributes

Attributes are a .NET feature with no direct Java equivalent. For a Java developer new to C#, attributes may well be one of the hardest language features to appreciate. However, knowledge of attributes is essential to use the .NET Framework for anything but the most trivial programs.

Attributes are a generic mechanism for associating declarative information (metadata) with program elements. This metadata is contained in the compiled assembly, allowing programs to retrieve it through reflection at run time. Other programs, particularly the common language runtime (CLR), use this information to determine how they should interact with and manage program elements.

There are many predefined attributes in the .NET class libraries, but the power and flexibility of attributes stem from the fact that they are classes. Custom attributes can be created by deriving a class from the abstract base class *System.Attribute*. This provides a metadata mechanism that is extensible beyond the scope of the default .NET class libraries.

This section looks first at how to assign existing attributes to elements of code and then at how to define custom attributes. We don't discuss all the attributes included in the .NET class libraries; these will be discussed throughout the rest of the book in sections relevant to their purpose.

> **More Info**   The mechanisms used to access attribute metadata at run time are covered in Chapter 12, "Reflection."

Attribute Names

The names of all attribute classes defined in the .NET class libraries end with the word *Attribute*. However, attribute classes are normally referenced using short names without the word *Attribute* appended. When using attributes, the programmer has the choice of using either form; use of the short name improves readability, and the C# compiler will automatically generate the appropriate full name. For example, the *Serializable* and *SerializableAttribute* attribute names represent the same attribute within a C# program and can be used interchangeably.

Attribute Specification

Applying previously defined attributes to program elements is called *attribute specification*. Attributes can be specified on the following target elements: assembly, class, constructor, delegate, enum, event, field, interface, method, module, parameter, property, return value, and struct. There is also a meta-attribute specifically applicable to attribute declarations. Valid target elements are defined as part of an attribute declaration.

Attribute specification involves placing the attribute name and any necessary parameters in square brackets immediately preceding the target element. If you apply more than one attribute to a target, place each attribute in its own set of square brackets. Alternatively, use a comma-separated list of attributes in a single set of square brackets. The ordering of attributes is not important. The following code fragment demonstrates the syntax of attribute specification:

```
// Single attribute specified on a class definition
[Serializable] public class MyClass {

// Two attributes specified separately on a method
    [CLSCompliant(true)]
    [WebMethod(false, Description="My Web Method")]
    public int MyMethod(int someParam) {
    // implementation
    }

    // Two attributes specified in a single line on a method
    [WebMethod(true, Description="My Other Web Method"),
```

(continued)

```
        CLSCompliant(true)]
    public int MyOtherMethod(string someParam) {
    // implementation
    }
}
```

In this example, we've used three different attributes. The *Serializable* attribute was placed on the same line as the target class declaration. The *CLSCompliant* and *WebMethod* attributes are both specified on two method declarations. For the first method, each attribute is on a separate line; for the second method, they are placed together in a single set of square brackets on a single line. Both approaches have the same effect.

Attribute Parameters

The foregoing examples also demonstrate how parameters are passed to attributes. The *Serializable* attribute takes no parameters. The *CLSCompliant* attribute takes one positional parameter, and the *WebMethod* attribute takes one positional and one named parameter. The way the compiler handles attribute parameters is one of the key behaviors that differentiate attributes from other classes.

Positional parameters   Positional parameters are the same as parameters in any normal instance constructor. They are expected in a predefined order, must be of the correct type, and must appear before any named parameters.

Named parameters   Named parameters are specified by providing a comma-separated list of name/value pairs. Named parameters must be placed after all positional parameters; their order is not important. Providing named parameters that are not supported by an attribute or values that cannot be implicitly converted to the expected type will cause a compile-time error.

Attribute Target Specification and Global Attributes

The target of an attribute is normally apparent by its position preceding the target element. However, there are circumstances in which the target is a module or an assembly, or in which the target is ambiguous. Ambiguity occurs most frequently when specifying an attribute on a member that returns a value; both the method and the return value are valid attribute targets.

In these situations, the programmer must clarify the target by prefixing the attribute name with the appropriate *attribute target specifier* from the following list: assembly, field, event, method, module, param, property, return, or type. The most common use of the attribute target specifier is to identify an assembly or module as the target of an attribute; these are called *global attributes*. For example:

```
[assembly:CLSCompliant(true)]
[module:DynamicLoad]
```

For global attributes, these statements must occur after any top level *using* statements but before any namespace or type declarations.

> **Tip**   It's common to put assembly attributes in a separate file. The wizard-generated projects in Microsoft Visual Studio .NET take this approach, using a file named AssemblyInfo.cs.

Custom Attributes

An attribute is a class that derives from *System.Attribute*. The following is an example of a simple attribute used to identify the developer who created a class or assembly:

```
using System ; // Needed for Attributes

[AttributeUsage(AttributeTargets.Class | AttributeTargets.Assembly,
    AllowMultiple=true, Inherited = false)]
public class CreatorAttribute: System.Attribute {

    private String name;    // creator's name
    private String email;   // creator's email

    // Declare public constructor
    public CreatorAttribute (String creator) {
        name = creator;
        email = "";
    }

    // Declare a property to get/set the creator's email address
    public string Email {
        get {
            return email;
        }
        set {
            email = value;
        }
    }
}
```

(continued)

```
// Declare a property to get the creator's name
public string Name {
    get { return name;}
}
}
```

The following examples demonstrate the use of this attribute:

```
[assembly:Creator("Bob")]
[assembly:Creator("Jim" , Email = "Jim@somecompany.com")]

[Creator ("Judy", Email = "Judy@someothercompany.com")]
public class MyClass {
    // class implementation
}
```

The *System.AttributeUsage* Attribute

The *AttributeUsage* attribute defines how a new attribute can be used. *Attribute-Usage* takes one positional and two named parameters, which are described in Table 6-2. The table also specifies the default value applied to an attribute declaration if the *AttributeUsage* attribute is omitted or a parameter isn't specified.

A compiler error occurs if an attempt is made to use the *AttributeUsage* attribute on a class that is not derived from *System.Attribute*.

Table 6-2   *AttributeUsage* Parameter Description

Parameter	Type	Description	Default
validOn	positional	Identifies which program elements the attribute is valid against. Valid values are any member of the *System.AttributeTargets* enumeration.	*AttributeTargets.All*
AllowMultiple	named	Whether the attribute can be specified more than once for a single element.	*false*
Inherited	named	Whether the attribute is inherited by derived classes or overridden members.	*true*

Attribute Declaration

The remainder of the attribute declaration is the same as for any other class; however, all attribute classes must be declared *public*.

> **Important**   The documentation for the first release of .NET states that all user-defined attributes will implicitly have the *Attribute* string appended to their class name if not done so manually. However, our experience shows that this is not the case. Custom attributes should always be given a name ending in the word *Attribute* to maintain consistency, enabling the C# compiler to support the dual-name behavior described earlier.

Attribute Constructors

A custom attribute must have at least one public constructor. The constructor parameters become the attribute's positional parameters. As with any other class, more than one constructor can be specified; providing overloaded constructors gives the users of the attribute the option of using different sets of positional parameters when specifying the attribute.

Named Parameters

Any public read/write fields and properties contained in an attribute are automatically exposed as named parameters. In the foregoing example, the *Email* property is exposed as a named parameter, but the *Name* property is read-only, meaning that it cannot be used as a named parameter.

Compile-Time Attributes

While the majority of attributes are used for specifying run-time-accessible metadata, a number of them are evaluated at compile time. The *Attribute-Usage* attribute discussed earlier is evaluated at compile time. Two other important compile-time attributes are discussed in the following sections.

System.Diagnostics.ConditionalAttribute

The *Conditional* attribute marks a method whose execution depends on the definition of a preprocessor symbol. (See the "*#define* and *#undef*" section within the "Preprocessor Directives" section later in this chapter.) If a method is marked with the *Conditional* attribute, any attempts to execute the method will be removed by the compiler if the specified preprocessor symbol is not defined at the calling point.

The *Conditional* attribute is a more elegant but less flexible alternative to using *#ifdef* preprocessor directives. It centralizes the conditional logic rather than having many *#ifdef* statements throughout the code. To be a valid target of the *Conditional* attribute, a method must return *void*; otherwise, it won't be possible to remove references without breaking the calling code.

For example, to define a method whose execution is conditional on the declaration of the symbol *DEBUG*, use the following syntax:

```
//The following method will execute if the DEBUG symbol is defined
[Conditional("DEBUG")]
public void SomeMethod() { // implementation here}
```

Multiple instances of the *Conditional* attribute can be specified for a method producing a logical OR behavior. For example:

```
// The following method will execute if WIN95 OR WIN2000
// symbols are defined
[Conditional("WIN95"), Conditional("WIN2000")]
public void SomeMethod() { // implementation here}
```

Achieving logical AND behavior is messy, involving the unpleasant use of intermediate *Conditional* methods. For example:

```
// The following method will execute if the DEBUG symbol is defined
[Conditional("DEBUG")]
public void SomeMethod() {
SomeOtherMethod()
}
```

```
// The following method will only execute if the WIN95 symbol is defined.
// When called from SomeMethod above, this has the effect of only executing
// SomeOtherMethod if both the DEBUG AND WIN95 symbols are defined
[Conditional("WIN95")]
private void SomeOtherMethod() { // implementation here}
```

System.ObsoleteAttribute

The *Obsolete* attribute marks a program element as obsolete and forces the compiler to raise a warning or an error when other code attempts to use the element. This is similar to marking an element as *deprecated* in Java but places more control in the hands of the code's author.

The two positional parameters of the *Obsolete* attribute specify the message to be displayed by the compiler and whether the compiler raises a warning or an error. For example:

```
// Specifying true as the second argument means that code referencing
// the following method will generate a compiler error about the
// method being deprecated.
[Obsolete("This method has been deprecated.", true)]
public string MyMethod() { // implementation here}

// Specifying false as the second argument means that code referencing
// the following method will generate a compiler warning that the
// method is in the process of being phased out.
[Obsolete("This method is being phased out, use SomeMethod().", false)]
public string MyOtherMethod() { // implementation here}
```

The *Obsolete* attribute is not limited to specification on methods. Valid targets are class, struct, enum, constructor, method, property, field, event, interface, and delegate.

Assertions

Assertions are new to Java version 1.4 and have no direct equivalent in C#. However, the .NET class libraries include a superset of the Java assert functionality through the static methods contained in both the *System.Diagnostics.Debug* and *System.Diagnostics.Trace* classes. A discussion of the *Debug* and *Trace* classes is beyond the scope of this book. Consult the Microsoft .NET documentation for more information.

Preprocessor Directives

Preprocessor directives are instructions to the C# compiler to perform some action during compilation. There is no equivalent functionality in Java. The term *preprocessor directive* is misleading because the compilation process does not include a preprocessing step, but the term is a legacy of C/C++ and has remained to avoid confusion.

Preprocessor directives are used to

■   Conditionally include and exclude sections of code during compilation.

■   Force the compiler to issue warnings and errors.

- Group related sections of source code.

- Alter the line number and file-name references displayed by the compiler for errors and warnings.

Preprocessor directives are preceded by the # symbol and must be the only command on a line. They are not terminated with semicolons.

#define and *#undef*

The *#define* and *#undef* directives are used to define and undefine conditional compilation symbols. The *#if* directive, described in the next section, uses these symbols to control conditional compilation. The following example demonstrates the use of the *#define* and *#undef* directives:

```
#define release
#define win2000
#undef release
```

This example defines the symbols *release* and *win2000*. It then undefines *release*. Only the *win2000* symbol is defined at the end of the code fragment. Unless explicitly defined, a symbol is undefined. Once a symbol is defined, it remains defined until it is explicitly undefined or the end of the file is reached. Any preprocessor definition, either a *#define* or an *#undef*, must be placed before any code, including a *using* directive, or else a compiler error will occur. Symbols can also be defined using the */d* switch during compilation. Compiler options are discussed in Chapter 3, "Creating Assemblies."

#if, #elif, #else, and *#endif*

The *#if, #elif, #else,* and, *#endif* directives provide conditional compilation based on the definition of symbols as described in the preceding section. The structure and behavior of the *#if* directive are the same as those of a normal *if* conditional statement in C# and Java except that the *#if* directive is terminated with an *#endif* directive. The compiler evaluates each *#if* and *#elif* clause until it finds one that evaluates to true. It then evaluates the enclosed code for possible inclusion in compilation.

If no *#if* or *#elif* clause evaluates as true and there is an *#else* clause, the enclosed code will be evaluated. The following example determines the content of the string *welcomeString* during compilation based on which preprocessor symbol is defined:

```
string welcomeString = null;

#if win2000    //compiling for Windows 2000 platform
    welcomeString = "Welcome to Windows 2000";
#elif win98    //compiling for Windows 98 platform
    welcomeString = "Welcome to Windows 98";
#elif win95    //compiling for Windows 95 platform
    welcomeString = "Welcome to Windows 95";
#else          //compiling for all other platforms
    welcomeString = "Welcome to Windows";
#endif
```

The test condition supports logical operators and brackets to enable complex conditions to be represented. The supported logical operators available are described in Table 6-3.

Table 6-3   Supported Logical Operators for *#if* Clause Conditionals

Operator	Example	Comment
==	*#if win2000 == true*	Equality. Expression will evaluate to *true* if the *win2000* symbol has been defined.
!=	*#if win2000 != true*	Inequality. Expression will evaluate to *true* if the *win2000* symbol has not been defined.
&&	*#if win2000 && release*	Logical AND. Expression will evaluate to *true* only if both the *win2000* AND *release* symbols have been defined.
||	*#if win2000 || release*	Logical OR. Expression will evaluate to *true* if either the *win2000* OR *release* symbol has been defined.
( )	*#if (win2000 && release) || win95*	Parentheses. Used to group expressions. Expression will evaluate to *true* if either the *win2000* AND *release* symbols are defined OR the *win95* symbol is defined.

It's possible to nest *#if* directives, but the overly complex use of conditional compilation directives will make code difficult to understand and debug.

> **More Info**   An alternative approach for conditional compilation is the use of the *Conditional* attribute, which is discussed in the "*System.Diagnostics.ConditionalAttribute*" section earlier in this chapter.

#region and #endregion

The *#region* and *#endregion* directives mark a block of code. These directives have no meaning in the context of C# but are implemented for the benefit of developers and tools. For example:

```
#region SomeClass related code
public class SomeClass{
    #region SomeClass data members
    // Declare fields and constants
    #endregion

    #region SomeClass function members
    // Declare methods, properties and operators
    #endregion
}
#endregion
```

The Visual Studio .NET development environment uses these directives to allow a developer to collapse and expand blocks of code to improve readability during development.

Note the following:

■   A compiler error will occur if there are not enough matching *#region* and *#endregion* directive pairs to close all regions correctly.

■   Overlapping regions cannot be created. There is no way to map an *#endregion* to a specific *#region* directive.

■   The comments on the *#region* and matching *#endregion* directives are not related and can be different.

#warning and #error

The *#warning* and *#error* directives explicitly generate warnings and errors during code compilation. The message the compiler should display follows the directive. There is no need to place the message in quotation marks. This directive can be used in conjunction with the conditional compilation directives already discussed. For example:

```
#warning TODO: Need to rework method to be more efficient

#if (debug && release)
    #error Multiple build version symbols specified
#endif
```

This code will always generate the *TODO...* warning when compiled but will generate the *Multiple build...* error only if both the *debug* and *release* symbols have been defined using *#define* or the */d* compiler flag.

#line

The purpose of the *#line* directive is to modify the line numbers and source file names reported in warnings and errors generated by the compiler. This directive is aimed at tools that generate C# code and will not be useful to most developers. In the following example:

```
#line 100 "MyFileName"
```

The compiler will consider the line immediately following this directive to be line 100 and the file name to be *MyFileName*. These settings will remain in force until the end of the file or until a new *#line* directive is encountered. Subsequent instances of the *#line* directive override previous *#line* directives.

To undo the effects of any existing *#line* directives, use the following directive:

```
#line default
```

Unsafe Code

C#'s support for unsafe code is the language's most significant divergence from Java. Unsafe code provides access to pointer data types and allows the programmer to work directly with the contents of memory. Unsafe features can be dangerous, are rarely needed, and should be avoided if possible. However, unsafe code is required when calling pre-.NET dynamic-link libraries (DLLs) that take pointers as arguments.

The *unsafe* Modifier

The unsafe features described in this section are available only within an unsafe context, declared using the *unsafe* modifier. The *unsafe* modifier is applicable to the declaration of classes, structs, interfaces, delegates, fields, methods, properties, events, indexers, operators, constructors, destructors, and statement blocks. The presence of the *unsafe* modifier in the declaration of these program elements signals to the compiler that the element contains unsafe code. The *unsafe* modifier is not applicable to local variables; they must be used within the unsafe context of one of the program elements previously mentioned.

The following code demonstrates an unsafe context applied to a statement block, a method declaration, and a member field; we'll discuss the pointer syntax later in this section.

```
// Unsafe statement block containing pointer-type local variable
unsafe {
    float* f;
}

// Unsafe method declaration with pointer arguments
protected unsafe int SomeMethod (int* p1, byte* p2, short* p3) { /*...*/}

// Unsafe member field
class SomeClass {
    private unsafe char* SomeField;
}
```

With functional members, the unsafe context includes the function parameters allowing *pointers* as arguments.

The */unsafe* Compiler Flag

The */unsafe* flag must be used when compiling an application that contains unsafe code, or a compiler error will occur. Compiler options are discussed in Chapter 3.

Managed and Unmanaged Types

The CLR distinguishes between managed and unmanaged data types. A compiler error will occur if pointers or unsafe operators are used to reference managed types. Managed types include all reference types and any struct that contains or inherits a reference-type field. Unmanaged types include the following:

- All of the inbuilt simple types (*sbyte*, *ushort*, *float*, *decimal*, and so on)

- Any *enum* type

- Any *pointer* type

- Any user-defined struct that contains only fields of unmanaged types

The *sizeof* Operator

The *sizeof* operator returns the memory size (in bytes) occupied by a variable of a specified unmanaged type. The size of the inbuilt simple types is fixed, so *sizeof* provides negligible value. However, *sizeof* also returns the size of user-defined structs, which may be useful when working with unsafe code. The following example demonstrates use of the *sizeof* operator to get the size of the struct *SomeStruct*:

```
public struct SomeStruct {
    int x;          // 4 bytes
    byte y;         // 1 byte
    float z;        // 4 bytes

    unsafe public static void Main() {
        System.Console.WriteLine("Size = " + sizeof(SomeStruct));
    }
}
```

The output of the above example is

```
Size = 12
```

As can be seen from the output, the size of a struct is not necessarily the sum of the size of the individual member types. The compiler determines how to allocate space within a struct and may pad the member values to align the data correctly for the underlying hardware platform.

Pointers

A pointer variable holds a memory address that references another data item. Pointers are similar to Java and C# reference types except that pointers give the developer access to both the memory address referenced by the pointer and the data at that address. Pointers are unique in that they do not derive from *System.Object*.

Declaration

A pointer declaration takes the following form:

referent-type * *identifier;*

The *referent-type* specifies the type of value the pointer is referencing and can be any unmanaged type. The *referent-type* can be *void*, declaring a pointer to an unknown type. The *token identifies this as a pointer-type declaration. The following example demonstrates four pointer declarations:

```
int* a, b, c;      // Declare 3 integer pointers
char** d;          // Declare a pointer to a character pointer
byte*[] e;         // An single dimension array of pointers to bytes
void* f;           // A pointer to an unknown type
```

Address-Of Operator and Pointer Indirection

The address-of operator (&) gets the address of an existing unmanaged variable for assignment to a pointer. Pointer indirection (*) enables the programmer to get or set the data value that the pointer references. The following code demonstrates the address-of and pointer indirection operators:

```
unsafe {
    // Declare and initialize an int variable
    int SomeInt = 500;

    // Declare a pointer to an int
    int* SomePtr;

    // Use address-of (&) operator to get the address of SomeInt
    // and assign to SomePtr
    SomePtr = &SomeInt;

    // Use indirection (*) to get value of the int referenced by SomePtr
    System.Console.WriteLine("Value of a = " + *SomePtr);

    // Use indirection (*) to set value of int pointed to by SomePtr
    *SomePtr = 300;
}
```

The output of the above example is

```
Value of a = 500
```

Pointer Member Access

When a pointer references a struct, the -> token is used to access members of the struct. For example:

```
public struct SomeStruct {
    public int SomeField;
    public byte SomeOtherField;
}
public class SomeClass {
    public unsafe static void Main() {
        SomeStruct s = new SomeStruct();
```

```
        SomeStruct* p = &s;
        p->SomeField = 234;
        int x = p->SomeField;
        p->SomeOtherField = 5;
    }
}
```

Pointer Element Access

Pointer element access enables the developer to access the data referenced by a pointer as if it were an array of values. For example:

```
public unsafe char* CharCopy (char* chars, int size) {
    char* r = stackalloc char[size];
    for (int x = 0 ; x < size ; x++ ) {
        r[x] = chars[x];
    }
    return r;
}
```

Pointer Arithmetic

Pointer types support the increment (++) and decrement (--) operators as well as the addition (+) and subtraction (-) operators. These operators affect the memory address contained in the pointer, not the value referenced. However, the value being added to or subtracted from the pointer is implicitly multiplied by the size (in bytes) of the underlying type the pointer references. For example:

```
unsafe {
    byte a = 5;
    long b = 1000;

    byte* x = &a;   // Declare a pointer to a byte
    x++;            // Increments by 1, the size of a byte = 1
    x += 4;         // Adds 4 x 1 = 4,  because the size of a byte = 1

    long* y = &b;   // Declare a pointer to a long
    y++;            // Increments by 8, the size of a long = 8
    y += 4;         // Adds 4 * 8 = 32, because the size of a long = 8
}
```

Pointer Comparison

Pointers can be compared using the following operators: ==, !=, >, <, <=, and >=. These operators compare the address contained in the pointer operands.

Pointer Conversion

Pointers of one type can be explicitly converted to pointers of any other type. Pointers can also be explicitly converted to and from any integer value type. Conversion of a pointer to an integer type results in unpredictable behavior if the integer type isn't large enough to hold the full memory address referenced by the pointer. Overflow checking isn't performed on pointer conversions, and the *checked* keyword isn't applicable. See the section "The *checked* and *unchecked* Keywords" in Chapter 4 for details of the *checked* keyword.

A common use of pointer conversion to integer types is to display the referenced memory address. The *String* class doesn't support concatenation with pointer types, and the *Console.Write* and *WriteLine* methods don't have overloads that take pointer arguments. The following code demonstrates pointer conversion:

```
unsafe {
    int a = 30;          //Declare an int
    int* x  = &a;        //Pointer to int
    byte* y = (byte*)x;  //Cast int* to byte*

    // Display the referenced address by casting to uint
    System.Console.WriteLine("Address of a = " + (uint)y);
}
```

All pointers are implicitly convertible to the *void* pointer type (*void**).

The *fixed* Statement

Although unsafe code cannot be used with managed data types, it can be used with accessible unmanaged fields contained in managed types. However, the garbage collector doesn't track pointer references and can feasibly move or collect an object containing a field referenced by a pointer.

The *fixed* statement forces the CLR to pin an object in memory so that the garbage collector won't move the referenced field. The *fixed* statement both declares and initializes a pointer. It has the following form:

fixed (type* identifier = expression) statement

The expression used to initialize the pointer must be implicitly convertible to a pointer of the type specified. If multiple pointers of the same type are required within the statement, use a comma-separated list of declarations in a single *fixed* statement. Alternatively, use multiple *fixed* statements.

The following code demonstrates the use of multiple *fixed* statements to access the members of a *SomeClass* instance using pointers:

```
using System;

public class SomeClass {
    public int FirstField = 4;
    public int SecondField = 5;
```

```
public byte ThirdField = 22;

public unsafe static void Main() {

    //Instantiate SomeClass
    SomeClass x = new SomeClass();

    //Fix the fields and use them
    fixed (int* a = &x.FirstField, b = &x.SecondField)
    fixed (byte* c = &x.ThirdField) {
        Console.WriteLine("First + Second Field = " + (*a + *b));
        Console.WriteLine("Third Field = " + *c);
    }
  }
}
```

The pointer variables are read-only and exist only for the scope of the *fixed* statement block. As soon as execution leaves the *fixed* statement block, all objects become unfixed and are subject to normal garbage collection.

The *stackalloc* Command

The *stackalloc* command allocates memory from the stack and returns the address of the allocated memory. The returned address must be assigned to a local pointer variable as part of the variable's declaration.

The *stackalloc* command takes an unmanaged data type and a quantity as arguments, calculates the size of the memory block to accommodate the specified number of instances, allocates memory from the stack, and returns a pointer to the newly allocated memory block. The initial content of the memory is undefined.

The following code demonstrates a number of *stackalloc* operations:

```
unsafe {
    //Allocate stack memory for 50 int values
    int* a = stackalloc int [50];

    //Allocate stack memory for 30 char values
    char* b = stackalloc char [30];
}
```

No mechanism exists to explicitly free memory allocated using the *stackalloc* command. Stack-allocated memory is freed when the function member returns.

Summary

This chapter has detailed advanced features of C#. Some of these features will be familiar to the Java developer, while many will be completely new unless the developer also has C/C++ experience. Although perhaps initially frustrated, the Java programmer should have little trouble adapting to the differences between Java and C# exception handling. It's possible that many programmers will never need to use preprocessor directives or unsafe code; however, an understanding of attributes is essential for developing applications for Microsoft .NET by using C#.

III

Programming .NET with C#

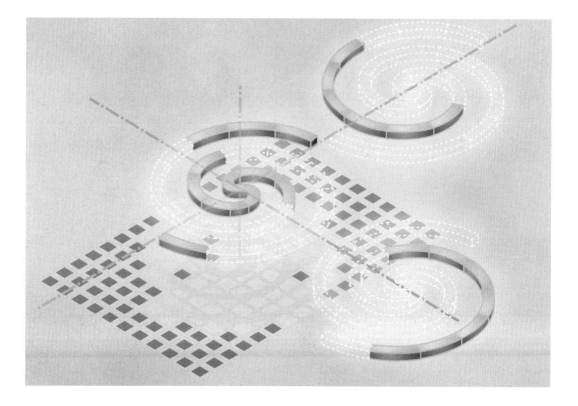

7

Strings and Regular Expressions

Java and C# both recognize that string handling and manipulation are key functions required by almost every application, and they provide language-level support to make working with strings simple and a rich API to support advanced string manipulation. The basic capabilities of strings and the C# syntax used to manipulate them are covered in Chapter 4, "Language Syntax and Features." This chapter focuses on the Microsoft .NET *System.String* class and the functionality available in the Microsoft .NET class library for working with strings.

Java developers will find support in .NET for all the string-handling mechanisms they are accustomed to in Java. This includes the more advanced features such as byte encoding, text formatting, and regular expressions. While there are many implementation differences, a Java developer will have little trouble adapting to the .NET methodology.

Strings

The .NET *System.String* class is equivalent to the *java.lang.String* class. Both classes offer predominantly the same functionality, although the implementation specifics present significant differences in how common tasks are accomplished. This section discusses and contrasts the functionality of both *String* classes in the context of describing everyday string manipulations.

As pointed out in Chapter 4, the C# keyword *string* is an alias for the .NET *System.String* class; we'll use both conventions in the examples throughout this chapter.

Creating Strings

Both Java and C# support the use of assignment operators to create new instances of string objects from literals and other string instances, as illustrated in this fragment of C# code:

```
String someString = "This is a string.";
String someOtherString = someString;
```

Notice that the .NET *String* class doesn't provide constructor equivalents of these assignment statements.

The only other difference of note is the support .NET provides for creating a string given a pointer to a *char* or *byte* array. Because they use pointers, these constructors are unsafe. See the "Unsafe Code" section in Chapter 6, "Advanced Language Features," for details on unsafe code.

Table 7-1 summarizes the Java and .NET string constructors.

Table 7-1   Creating Strings in Java and .NET

Java	.NET	Comments
new String()	*String.Copy("")*	The .NET *String* class doesn't provide empty constructor support. The static *String.Copy* method can be used, although it's easier to use direct assignment of an empty string.
new String(String)	*String.Copy(String)*	The .NET *String* class doesn't provide a constructor that takes a *String* as an argument. The static *String.Copy* method can be used, although it's easier to use direct assignment.
new String(byte[]) *new String(byte[],int,int)*	*new String(sbyte*)* *new String(sbyte*,int,int)*	Takes a pointer to a *byte* array. These constructors are unsafe because they use pointers.
new String(byte[], charset) *new String(byte[],int,int,charset)*	*new String(sbyte*,int,int,Encoding)*	Reads from *byte* array using the specified encoding scheme. This constructor is unsafe because it uses pointers.

Table 7-1   Creating Strings in Java and .NET   *(continued)*

Java	.NET	Comments
new String(char[]) *new String(char[],int,int)*	*new String(char[])* *new String(char[],int,int)* *new String(char*)* *String(char*,int,int)*	Supports both a *char* array and a pointer to a *char* array. The two constructors that take pointers to *char* arrays are unsafe.
String(StringBuffer)	*StringBuilder.ToString()*	
N/A	*String(char, int)*	Creates a string that contains a *char* repeated *int* times.

Comparing Strings

Java does not provide support for comparing strings using operators. The == or != operator in Java will compare object references and not the contents of the string. In C# support for operator overloading, the == and != operators have been implemented to support the comparison of string content. Both operators are backed by the *String.Equals* method. The following C# statements demonstrate the use of the overloaded == operator to compare a string variable with a string literal:

```
if (someString == "This is a string.") {
    // some statements
}
```

Java and .NET both provide methods for comparing whole or partial strings. These are summarized in Table 7-2.

Table 7-2   String Comparison in Java and .NET

Java	.NET	Comments
N/A	==	String equality operator.
N/A	!=	String inequality operator.
equals()	*Equals()*	.NET also provides an overloaded static *Equals* method for comparing two strings.
equalsIgnoreCase()	*Compare()*	The .NET *String* class provides static, overloaded *Compare* methods for the case-insensitive comparison of strings and substrings.

(continued)

Table 7-2   String Comparison in Java and .NET   *(continued)*

Java	.NET	Comments
N/A	*CompareOrdinal()*	The .NET *String* class provides static, over-loaded *CompareOrdinal* methods for the case-insensitive comparison of strings and sub-strings, ignoring localization.
compareTo()	*CompareTo()*	
compareToIgnoreCase()	*Compare()*	
contentEquals()	N/A	
endsWith()	*EndsWith()*	
regionMatches()	*Compare()*	
startsWith()	*StartsWith()*	

Copying Strings

Java and C# both provide operator support for copying strings. The = operator is used to assign a string literal or variable to another string variable; .NET also provides the static *String.Copy* method, which can be used to copy strings. For example, the following two C# statements have the same effect:

```
string SomeString = "Some string value.";
string SomeOtherString = string.Copy("Some string value.");
```

String Length

The length of a Java *String* is obtained by calling the *String.length* method; .NET provides the read-only property *String.Length*.

String Concatenation

Like Java, C# provides both operator and method support for concatenating strings. The support in C# is the same as in Java and allows the use of both the + and += operators. Method-based concatenation support in .NET is more extensive than that provided in Java. Java provides the *String.concat* method, which is equivalent to the operator syntax described earlier. .NET provides a set of static, overloaded *String.Concat* methods that concatenate a variable number of strings and string representations of objects into a single string.

The static *String.Join* methods provide a mechanism to concatenate an array of strings into a single string separating each component with a config-urable string token. This is useful for creating strings that represent hierarchical information such as IP addresses, URLs, or file names. For example:

```
string[] names = {"www", "microsoft", "com"};
string nameString = System.String.Join(".", names);
```

The value of *nameString* will be *www.microsoft.com.*

Changing Case

Both Java and .NET provide capabilities to convert the case of a string. The equivalent methods are shown in Table 7-3.

Table 7-3 String Case Conversion in Java and .NET

java.lang.String	*System.String*
toUpperCase()	*ToUpper()*
toLowerCase()	*ToLower()*

Working with Characters

Both Java and .NET provide mechanisms to retrieve, remove, and replace the individual characters contained within a string. .NET provides a superset of the Java functionality and provides two particularly useful features:

- Implementation of an *indexer* to provide read access to the characters that constitute the string.

- The *String.GetEnumerator* method returns an *IEnumerator* that can be used in a *foreach* statement to iterate through the characters in a string. This is similar to the *java.text.StringCharacterIterator* class.

Because strings are immutable, these methods do not modify the string instance, instead returning a new string containing any modifications. If performing many edit operations, it's more efficient to use the *StringBuilder* class, discussed later in this chapter. When performing complex or repeated matching operations, regular expressions (discussed later in this chapter) provide a more flexible solution. The methods for character access are summarized in Table 7-4.

Table 7-4 String Character Manipulation in Java and .NET

Java	.NET	Description
charAt()	*<string>[key]*	Indexer that returns the character at a specific index within the string.
N/A	*GetEnumerator()*	Returns an *IEnumerator* that supports iteration across the characters of a string.

(continued)

Table 7-4   String Character Manipulation in Java and .NET   *(continued)*

Java	.NET	Description
getChars()	*CopyTo()*	Extracts a specified number of characters from a string and places them in a character array.
toCharArray()	*ToCharArray()*	Copies the characters making up the string to a character array.
indexOf()	*IndexOf()*	Returns the index of the first occurrence of a specified character.
N/A	*IndexOfAny()*	Returns the index of the first occurrence of any of the characters contained in a character array.
lastIndexOf()	*LastIndexOf()*	Returns the index of the last occurrence of a specified character.
N/A	*LastIndexOfAny()*	Returns the index of the last occurrence of any of the characters contained in a character array.
replace()	*Replace()*	Replaces all instances of a specified character with another character.
N/A	*Remove()*	Removes a specified range of characters from a string.
trim()	*Trim()*	Removes white space or specified characters from the beginning and end of a string.
N/A	*TrimEnd()*	Removes white space or specified characters from the end of a string.
N/A	*TrimStart()*	Removes white space or specified characters from the beginning of a string.
N/A	*PadLeft()*	Right-justifies a string and pads the left side with white space or a specified character to make it the required length.
N/A	*PadRight()*	Left-justifies a string and pads the right side with white space or a specified character to make it the required length.

Working with Substrings

Java and .NET both provide mechanisms for locating and modifying substrings within an existing string. As with the character access just discussed, the use of *StringBuilder* or regular expressions can provide a more efficient alternative. The substring manipulation methods are summarized in Table 7-5.

Table 7-5   **Substring Manipulation in Java and .NET**

Java	.NET	Description
replaceAll() *replaceFirst()*	*Replace()*	Replaces all instances of a specified substring with another string. Java methods are actually exposing regular expression functionality. See later in this chapter for details.
N/A	*Insert()*	Inserts a substring into the string at the specified index.
indexOf()	*IndexOf()*	Returns the index of the first occurrence of a specified substring within the string.
lastIndexOf()	*LastIndexOf()*	Returns the index of the last occurrence of a specified substring within the string.
substring()	*Substring()*	Returns a substring from between the specified index range in the string.

Splitting Strings

Both the Java and .NET *String* classes provide methods to split a string based on the occurrence of tokens within a string. The Java *String.split* method exposes regular expression functionality, discussed later in this chapter. Java also provides the *java.util.StringTokenizer* as a flexible mechanism to split strings without using regular expressions; .NET has no direct equivalent.

The .NET *String.Split* method splits a string into component parts based on the location of a definable set of characters, returning an array of components from the source string.

Strings as Keys

It's common to use strings as keys in collections such as dictionaries. The *GetHashCode* and *Equals* methods inherited from *System.Object* are the basis for key comparison. The *String* class has overridden these two methods to provide appropriate behavior for key comparison. The *GetHashCode* method returns a hash code based on the entire contents of the string, not the object reference. The *Equals* method is discussed earlier in this chapter.

Parsing Strings

Parsing is the process used to create date and numeric data types from strings, for example, creating an *int* from the string *600*. The .NET Framework provides a parsing mechanism that is similar to the Java static *parseXXX* methods in the primitive wrapper classes. Because all .NET value types are objects, there is no need for wrapper classes. In .NET, all of the simple data types (*Byte*, *Int32*, *Double*, and so forth) have static methods named *Parse* that take a *String* and return an instance of the appropriate value type. An exception will be thrown if

■   The string to be parsed is *null*.

■   The string contents cannot be parsed into the target type.

■   The parsed string would exceed the minimum or maximum value of the data type.

System.DateTime, *System.TimeSpace*, and *System.Enumeration* classes also implement *Parse* methods for parsing strings.

.NET also defines the *System.Convert* class, which provides an impressive selection of static methods for converting between data types; however, all the methods that convert strings simply call the *Parse* method of the target type.

Formatting Strings

.NET provides functionality for creating strings that contain formatted representations of other data types. This includes the use of formatting conventions for different regions, cultures, and languages. Java provides similar capabilities through the *java.text.MessageFormat* class, among others; however, the implementations are sufficiently different that it is easier, and more instructive, just to discuss the .NET implementation on its own.

Formatting functionality is exposed through overloaded methods in a number of classes in which string output is generated. The most commonly used methods are

■   *System.String.Format*

■   *System.Text.StringBuilder.AppendFormat*

■   *System.Console.WriteLine* and *System.Console.Write*

■   *System.IO.TextWriter.WriteLine* and *System.IO.TextWriter.Write*

> **More Info**   Details of the *System.Console* and *System.IO.TextWriter* classes are provided in Chapter 10, "Streams, Files, and I/O."

Most of these classes provide overloaded methods that take different numbers of parameters. For our discussion, we'll consider the most general case of the *System.Console.WriteLine* method, which takes a variable number of arguments through the use of a *params* parameter. The signature is as follows:

```
public static void WriteLine(string format, params object[] args);
```

The *format* parameter is a string that contains both the standard text to output and embedded format specifiers at locations where formatted data will be inserted.

The *args* array contains the objects to be formatted and inserted into the resulting string. The method will accept a variable number of arguments through the use of the *params* keyword. The order of these arguments determines the index they occupy in the object array. The array index of each object is used in the *format* string to identify where each formatted object should be inserted. The best way to convey how this works is by example. This code

```
double a = 345678.5678;
uint b = 12000;
byte c = 254;
Console.WriteLine("a = {0}, b = {1}, and c = {2}", a, b, c);
Console.WriteLine("a = {0:c0}, b = {1:n4}, and c = {2,10:x5}",
    a, b, c);
```

will result in the following output:

```
a = 345678.5678, b = 12000, and c = 254
a = £345,679, b = 12,000.0000, and c =      000fe
```

The codes in the braces, highlighted in the example, are called *format specifications*. Changing the contents of the format specification changes the format of the output. The current cultural and regional settings can affect the formatted output. As in the example, the currency symbol, thousands separator, and decimal separator are all affected by localization settings.

Format specifications have the general form

```
{N,[M][:F]}
```

where:

- *N* is the zero-based index, which indicates the formatted argument to insert.

- *M* is an optional integer that specifies the minimum width of the inserted element. If *M* is positive, the formatted value is right-justified, and left-justified if *M* is negative. The value will be padded with white space to ensure that it fills the minimum specified width.

■ *F* is an optional set of formatting codes called a *format string*. Format strings determine how the data item is to be formatted when rendered to a string value. Different data types support different format strings.

Any object can be passed as a parameter for formatting, although only types that implement the *IFormattable* interface support format strings. Any type that doesn't implement *IFormattable* will always be rendered to a string using the inherited *Object.ToString* method, irrespective of any format strings provided. Attempts to use invalid format strings on *IFormattable* objects will cause a *FormatException* exception to be thrown.

All of the simple types, as well as *System.DateTime*, *System.TimeSpan*, and *System.Enum*, implement *IFormattable*. We'll discuss some of the more common format strings in Chapter 8, "Numbers and Dates," but the .NET documentation provides complete coverage.

The *IFormattable* Interface

Any class or struct that needs to support formatting must implement the *IFormattable* interface. This interface contains a single member with the following signature:

```
string ToString(string format, IFormatProvider formatProvider);
```

The *format* argument is a string containing the format string. This is the portion of the format specifier that follows the colon and contains instructions on how the object should create a string representation of itself; this will be *null* if no format string was specified.

The *formatProvider* argument provides a reference to an *IFormatProvider* instance. An *IFormatProvider* contains information about the current system settings, culture, region, and preferences. The *IFormattable* object being formatted can refer to the *IFormatProvider* to decide how best to render itself to a string given the current environment. The decision can take into consideration such elements as the appropriate currency symbol to use and how many decimal places are required by a given locale.

By default, *formatProvider* will be *null*, which means that the default settings of the current system are to be used. However, it is possible to specify a different value in some of the overloaded string formatting methods.

The following example demonstrates a class named *MyNumber* that implements the *IFormattable* interface. The class holds an integer. If used in a formatted string, *MyNumber* can render itself either to digits or to words depending on the format specifier used. Either *w* or *W* signals that words should be output.

```
using System;
using System.Text;

public class MyNumber : IFormattable {
    private int val;

    public MyNumber(int v) { val = v; }

    public string ToString(string format, IFormatProvider provider) {
        if (format != null && format.ToLower() == "w") {
            switch (val) {
                case 1 : return "one";
                case 2 : return "two";
                case 3 : return "three";
                default: return "unknown";
            }
        } else {
            return val.ToString();
        }
    }

    public static void Main() {

        MyNumber numberOne = new MyNumber(3);
        MyNumber numberTwo = new MyNumber(1);

        Console.WriteLine("The first number is {0} and the second is {1}",
            numberOne, numberTwo);
        Console.WriteLine("The first number is {0:w} and the second is " +
            "{1:w}", numberOne, numberTwo);
    }
}
```

When this example is executed, the following output is produced:

```
The first number is 3 and the second is 1
The first number is three and the second is one
```

Encoding Strings

Java and .NET both support Unicode and encode characters internally using the UTF-16 scheme. However, Unicode is not the only character-encoding scheme, nor is UTF-16 the only scheme for encoding Unicode. Support for different character encodings is essential for providing cross-platform support and integration with legacy systems.

Java has provided support for character encoding since version 1.1; however, these capabilities were accessible only through other classes such as *java.lang.String* and *java.io.InputStreamReader*. The model introduced in Java version 1.4 offers greater flexibility, providing direct access to the underlying encoding mechanisms. The character encoding functionality in Java version 1.4 and .NET is predominantly the same. The most significant difference is how encoding classes are instantiated.

The *java.nio.charset.Charset* class represents a mapping between 16-bit Unicode characters and encoded bytes. The static factory method *Charset.forName(String charsetName)* returns a *Charset* instance for a specific encoding scheme based on a name. The following example demonstrates instantiation of a *Charset* for performing UTF-8 encoding:

```
Charset x = Charset.forName("UTF-8");
```

The .NET equivalent of the *Charset* class is the abstract class *System.Text.Encoding*. The *Encoding* class provides base functionality and factory methods for a number of encoding-specific classes contained in the *System.Text* namespace. Concrete implementations are provided for UTF-7, UTF-8, Big-Endian and Little-Endian UTF-16, and ASCII. The .NET Framework relies on the underlying operating system to provide support for other encoding schemes, adopting the Java model of returning an *Encoding* instance based on a scheme name to expose this functionality.

Table 7-6 maps commonly used Java scheme names against their .NET equivalents. The table also shows how to instantiate an *Encoding* object using the static methods and properties of *Encoding*. The concrete *Encoding* subclasses also offer instantiation via constructors.

Table 7-6   Java and .NET Character Encoders

Java Encoding Name	.NET Class	Obtain By
US-ASCII	*ASCIIEncoding*	*Encoding.ASCII*
Cp1252	*Encoding*	*Encoding.GetEncoding(1252)*
UTF-8	*UTF8Encoding*	*Encoding.UTF8*
UTF-16BE	*UnicodeEncoding*	*Encoding.BigEndianUnicode*
UTF-16LE	*UnicodeEncoding*	*Encoding.Unicode*

ASCIIEncoding, UTF8Encoding, and *UnicodeEncoding* derive from *Encoding* but do not introduce any new functionality. Table 7-7 provides a summary of the *Encoding* functionality.

Table 7-7   **Member Summary for *System.Text.Encoding***

Encoder	Description
Properties	
ASCII	Static read-only property used to get an *ASCIIEncoding* instance.
BigEndianUnicode	Static read-only property used to get a *UnicodeEncoding* instance configured for big-endian byte ordering.
BodyName	Gets the name for the encoding that can be used in mail agent body tags.
CodePage	Gets the code page identifier for the encoding.
Default	Static read-only property used to get an encoding for the system's current ANSI code page.
EncodingName	Gets a human-readable name for the encoding.
HeaderName	Gets the name for the encoding for use in mail agent header tags.
IsBrowserDisplay	Gets an indication of whether the encoding can be used for display in browser clients.
IsBrowserSave	Gets an indication of whether the encoding can be used for saving by browser clients.
IsMailNewsDisplay	Gets an indication of whether the encoding can be used for display in mail and news clients.
IsMailNewsSave	Gets an indication of whether the encoding can be used for saving by mail and news clients.
Unicode	Static read-only property used to get a *UnicodeEncoding* instance configured for little-endian byte ordering.
UTF7	Static read-only property used to get a *UTF7Encoding* instance.
UTF8	Static read-only property used to get a *UTF8Encoding* instance.
WebName	Gets the IANA registered name for the encoding.
WindowsCodePage	Gets the Windows code page that most closely corresponds to the encoding.
Methods	
Convert()	A static method that converts a byte array between two encoding schemes.
GetByteCount()	Calculates the exact number of bytes required to encode a specified *char[]* or *string*.
GetBytes()	Encodes a *string* or *char[]* and returns a *byte[]*.
GetCharCount()	Calculates the exact number of characters produced from decoding a specified *byte[]*.
GetChars()	Decodes a *byte[]* into a *char[]*.

(continued)

Table 7-7   Member Summary for *System.Text.Encoding*   *(continued)*

Encoder	Description
GetDecoder()	Returns a *System.Text.Decoder* instance for the encoding. See Table 7-10 for details of the methods provided by the *Decoder* class.
GetEncoder()	Returns a *System.Text.Encoder* instance for the encoding. See Table 7-9 for details of the methods provided by the *Encoder* class.
GetEncoding()	Static factory method that returns an encoding instance for a named encoding scheme.
GetMaxByteCount()	Calculates the maximum number of bytes that will be required to encode a specified number of characters.
GetMaxCharCount()	Calculates the maximum number of characters that will be produced by decoding a specified number of bytes.

Both the *Charset* and *Encoding* classes provide convenience methods for performing single-call transformations and provide factory methods to create stateful encoding and decoding objects for processing longer *char* and *byte* arrays. These methods are contrasted in Table 7-8.

Table 7-8   *Charset* and *Encoding* Mechanisms for Encoding/Decoding

Java *Charset*	.NET *Encoding*	Description
encode()	*GetBytes()*	Encodes a string or a sequence of characters into a *byte* array.
decode()	*GetChars()*	Decodes a *byte* array into a sequence of characters.
newEncoder()	*GetEncoder()*	Java returns a *java.nio.charset.CharsetEncoder* instance; .NET returns *System.Text.Encoder*.
newDecoder()	*GetDecoder()*	Java returns a *java.nio.charset.CharsetDecoder* instance; .NET returns *System.Text.Decoder*.

The .NET *Encoder* and *Decoder* classes are simpler than their Java counterparts and are summarized in Tables 7-9 and 7-10.

Table 7-9   Members of *System.Text.Encoder*

Member	Description
GetByteCount()	Calculates the number of bytes *GetBytes* would return if passed a specified *char* array.
GetBytes()	Takes an array of Unicode characters as an argument and encodes the characters as bytes. Any partial-character sequences at the end of the *char* array are stored and prepended to the *char* array provided in the next call to the *GetBytes* method.

Table 7-10   Members of *System.Text.Decoder*

Member	Description
GetCharCount()	Calculates the number of characters *GetChars* would return if passed a specified *byte* array.
GetChars()	Takes an array of bytes as an argument and decodes the bytes as Unicode characters. Any partial-byte sequences at the end of the *byte* array are stored and prepended to the *byte* array provided in the next call to the *GetChars* method.

The following code demonstrates the use of the encoding and decoding functionality we've discussed in this section:

```
// Instantiating an Encoding that supports UTF-8
Encoding myEncoding = Encoding.UTF8;

//Instantiating a UTF-8 Encoder
Encoder myEncoder = myEncoding.GetEncoder();

//Determine the byte array size required to encode a String
char[] myChars = "Hello world !".ToCharArray();
int size = myEncoder.GetByteCount(myChars, 0, 13, true);

//Convert the character array to a UTF-8 byte array
byte[] myBytes = new byte[size];
myEncoder.GetBytes(myChars, 0, 13, myBytes, 0, true);

// Encode the byte stream as UTF-7 using Encoding.Convert()
myBytes = Encoding.Convert(Encoding.UTF8, Encoding.UTF7, myBytes);

// Convert the bytes back to Unicode from UTF-7
String myString = new String(Encoding.UTF7.GetChars(myBytes));

//Display result string
System.Console.WriteLine(myString);
```

Like Java, .NET also provides access to encoding mechanisms through other relevant classes. The *String* class provides a constructor that takes an *Encoding* to create a Unicode string from an encoded *byte* array. Also, the *StreamReader* and *StreamWriter* classes in the *System.IO* namespace provide constructors that allow an *Encoding* to be specified, forcing all strings written and read through the stream to be encoded and decoded using the specified scheme.

> **More Info** The *StreamReader* and *StreamWriter* classes, as well as examples of using string encoding in the context of stream and file operations, can be found in Chapter 10.

Dynamically Building Strings

The immutability of strings means that manipulation and concatenation result in new string instances being created instead of the contents of existing strings being modified. The overhead of creating many new string instances can dramatically affect the performance of an application. Java and .NET both provide similar solutions to this problem. Java provides the *java.lang.StringBuffer* class, and .NET provides the *System.Text.StringBuilder* class. Both classes represent a sequence of Unicode characters that can be modified in situ, extended if necessary, and rendered to a string as required.

The .NET *StringBuilder* class provides better functionality for formatting and manipulating contents of the character data but lacks some of the *StringBuffer* capability of inspecting the contents of, and extracting substrings from, the underlying character sequence. Table 7-11 compares the functionality of the *StringBuffer* and *StringBuilder* classes.

Table 7-11 Comparison of *java.lang.StringBuffer* and *System.Text.StringBuilder*

Java	.NET	Comments
append()	*Append()*	Numerous overloaded methods that append the string representation of different values to the end of a *StringBuilder*.
N/A	*AppendFormat()*	.NET includes numerous overloaded methods that append formatted strings to the end of a *StringBuilder*.

**Table 7-11 Comparison of *java.lang.StringBuffer* and
*System.Text.StringBuilder*** *(continued)*

Java	.NET	Comments
capacity()	*Capacity*	In a difference from Java, *Capacity* is a property and supports both the getting and setting of the *StringBuilder* capacity. However, an *ArgumentOutOfRangeException* will be thrown if an attempt is made to set the capacity lower than the length of the current contents.
N/A	*MaxCapacity*	A read-only property used to get the maximum capacity for a *StringBuilder* class. This is platform dependent.
charAt() *setCharAt()*	*<StringBuilder>[key]*	An indexer that provides a zero-based integer index into the characters of a *StringBuilder*
delete() *deleteCharAt()*	*Remove()*	Deletes a range of characters from a *StringBuilder*.
ensureCapacity()	*EnsureCapacity()*	Ensures that the capacity of a *StringBuilder* is at least the specified value.
getChars()	N/A	
indexOf()	N/A	
insert()	*Insert()*	Numerous overloaded methods insert the string representation of different values at a specified location within a *StringBuilder*.
lastIndexOf()	N/A	Unsupported.
length() *setLength()*	*Length*	A property used to get and set the current length of the *StringBuilder* contents. As with Java, if the new length is shorter than the current contents, the contents will be truncated. If the new length is greater, the end of the string will be padded with spaces.
replace()	*Replace()*	The Java *StringBuffer* method replaces characters at the specified location range. Overloaded versions of the *StringBuilder* method replace matching characters or substrings.
reverse()	N/A	
subSequence()	N/A	
substring()	N/A	
toString()	*ToString()*	Returns the current contents of a *StringBuilder* as a *string*.

Regular Expressions

The comparison and manipulation features provided by the *String* and *String-Builder* classes are adequate for simple operations. However, when complex string manipulations are required or large amounts of text need to be processed, regular expressions can provide a more efficient solution. Although regular expressions are new to Java version 1.4, many third-party Java regular expression libraries have been available for some time. .NET includes regular expression functionality as part of the standard class libraries in the *System.Text.RegularExpressions* namespace.

The .NET regular expression implementation is refreshingly straightforward and contains some functionality not available in the Java implementation. In the following sections, we'll cover the use of the .NET regular expression classes; where appropriate, we'll contrast them with those provided in Java version 1.4.

Compiling Regular Expressions

The *java.util.regex.Pattern* class represents a compiled regular expression; the .NET equivalent is *System.Text.RegularExpressions.Regex*. Whereas Java provides a static factory method for creating *Pattern* instances, *Regex* uses a constructor; we contrast these approaches in Table 7-12. Both implementations offer two overload versions with similar signatures and return an immutable representation of a compiled regular expression. The first version takes a *string* containing a regular expression. The second takes both a regular expression and a bit mask containing compilation flags; we discuss these flags later in this section.

Table 7-12 Regular Expression Creation in Java and .NET

java.util.regex.Pattern	*System.Text.RegularExpressions.Regex*
Pattern.compile(String)	*Regex(string)*
Pattern.compile(String, flags)	*Regex(string, RegexOptions)*

The following example shows the Java and C# statements required to compile a regular expression that matches name/value pairs of the form *author = Adam Freeman*:

```
// Java
Pattern p = Pattern.compile("\\b\\w+\\s*=\\s*.*");

// C#
Regex r = new Regex(@"\b\w+\s*=\s*.*");
```

Note the following:

- The C# example uses the @ symbol to indicate a verbatim string. This permits the inclusion of \ characters without the need to escape them as seen in the Java equivalent.

- The regular expression $"\b\w+\s*=\s*.*"$ used in the preceding example can be broken down as follows:

  - ❑ \b matches a word boundary.

  - ❑ \w+ matches one or more word characters.

  - ❑ \s* matches zero or more white-space characters.

  - ❑ = matches the equal sign.

  - ❑ .* matches any character except the newline character \n.

More Info   For a complete description of the syntax supported by .NET regular expressions, refer to the .NET documentation.

Regular Expression Compilation Flags

When a regular expression is constructed, compilation flags can be provided to modify its behavior. In .NET, these flags are specified as a bit mask using members of the *System.Text.RegularExpressions.RegexOptions* enumeration. Table 7-13 summarizes the more useful flags alongside their Java equivalents.

Table 7-13   Regular Expression Compilation Flags in Java and .NET

Java	.NET	Description
COMMENTS	*IgnorePatternWhitespace*	Ignores any white space and comments without the need to escape them.
N/A	*Compiled*	Compiles the regular expression to MSIL code. See the next section for more details.
N/A	*ExplicitCapture*	Only explicitly named or numbered groups are valid captures.
CASE_INSENSITIVE *UNICODE_CASE*	*IgnoreCase*	The Java *CASE_INSENSITIVE* flag works only for ASCII characters. It must be used in conjunction with *UNICODE_CASE* to support case-insensitive Unicode.
MULTILINE	*Multiline*	Specifies multiline mode.

(continued)

Table 7-13 Regular Expression Compilation Flags in Java and .NET *(continued)*

Java	.NET	Description
N/A	*RightToLeft*	Specifies that searches should go from right to left.
DOTALL	*Singleline*	Specifies single-line mode.
N/A	*ECMAScript*	Enables ECMAScript-compliant behavior.

The *RegexOptions.Compiled* Flag

Given that all regular expressions must be compiled, the name of this flag is a little confusing. However, a regular expression is normally compiled to an intermediate form that is interpreted by the regular expressions engine at run time. The *RegexOptions.Compiled* flag forces compilation of the regular expression down to MSIL code. This results in faster execution but slower loading.

Use the *Compiled* flag sparingly. The common language runtime (CLR) cannot unload generated MSIL code without unloading the entire application domain. Using the *Compiled* flag frequently will result in compiled regular expressions consuming system resources.

Manipulating Text

Once a compiled regular expression instance has been created, it can be used against input text to

- Locate matching substrings.

- Perform substring replacement.

- Split the input text into component parts.

In .NET, these actions are all initiated through methods of the *Regex* instance. In Java, splitting the input text is initiated from the *Pattern* instance, but matching and replacing requires the instantiation of a *java.util.regex.Matcher* object using the *Pattern.matcher* factory method. This is where the .NET and Java models diverge significantly.

We'll cover matching, replacing, and splitting of input text in the following sections.

Matching Regular Expressions

If we are concerned only with determining whether an input text contains an occurrence of the regular expression, we use the *Regex.IsMatch* method. This returns a *bool* indicating whether a match was found but does not give access to any further match details. For example:

```
// Create an input text string
string input = "author = Allen Jones, author = Adam Freeman";

// Compile regular expression to find "name = value" pairs
Regex r = new Regex(@"\b\w+\s*=\s*.*");

// Test for a match
bool b = r.IsMatch(input);          // b = true;
```

If we need access to the number and location of matches found, two approaches are available. First, the *Regex.Match* method returns an instance of *Match*, which represents the result of a single match operation. The *Match.Success* property signals whether the match was successful. *Match.NextMatch* returns a new *Match* instance representing the next match in the input text. The use of *Regex.Match, Match.Success,* and *Match.NextMatch* enables the programmer to sequentially step through the matches in an input text. This is similar to the Java model of using repeated calls to *Matcher.find*.

Alternatively, the *Regex.Matches* method returns an instance of *MatchCollection* containing an enumerable set of *Match* instances representing all matches in the input text. Either the *MatchCollection* indexer or *MatchCollection.GetEnumerator* can be used to iterate across the set of *Match* instances. We demonstrate both the use of *Match.NextMatch* and *MatchCollection.GetEnumerator* in the following example:

```
// Create an input text string
string input = "author = Allen Jones \n author = Adam Freeman";

// Compile regular expression to find "name = value" pairs
Regex r = new Regex(@"\b\w+\s*=\s*.*");

// Using Match.NextMatch() to process all matches
Match m = r.Match(input);
while (m.Success) {
    System.Console.WriteLine(m.Value);
    m = m.NextMatch();
}

// Using MatchCollection to process all matches
MatchCollection mc = r.Matches(input);
foreach (Match x in mc) {
    System.Console.WriteLine(x.Value);
}
```

Both loops in this example produce the same output, resulting in the following display:

```
author = Allen Jones
author = Adam Freeman
author = Allen Jones
author = Adam Freeman
```

The *Match* instance provides access to details of the match, including the results of each capture group and subexpression capture. The members of the *Match* and *MatchCollection* classes are summarized in Tables 7-14 and 7-15.

Table 7-14   *System.Text.RegularExpressions.Match* Member Summary

Member	Description
Properties	
Captures	Returns a *CaptureCollection* containing a set of all subexpression captures represented by *Capture* objects.
Groups	Returns a *GroupCollection* containing a set of *Group* objects representing the groups matched by the regular expression.
Index	The position in the input string where the first character of the match was located.
Length	The length of the captured substring.
Success	Indicates whether the match was a success.
Value	The captured substring.
Methods	
NextMatch()	Returns a *Match* instance that represents the next match in the input text.
Result()	Returns the expansion of a specified replacement pattern.
Synchronized ()	Returns a thread-safe instance of the *Match* object.

Table 7-15   *System.Text.RegularExpressions.MatchCollection* Member Summary

Member	Description
Indexers	
<MatchCollection>[key]	Gets the *Match* object at the specified index.
Properties	
Count	Gets the number of *Match* instances contained.
Methods	
GetEnumerator()	Gets an *IEnumerator* that is used to iterate over the collection of *Match* objects.

The *Match* class is derived from *Group*, which in turn is derived from *Capture*. The *Capture* and *Group* instances retrievable through the *Match* class represent the specific group and subexpression matches that constitute a successful match. The *CaptureCollection* and *GroupCollection* classes provide the same functionality for the *Group* and *Capture* objects that the *MatchCollection* provides for the *Match* object. The members of *Capture, Group, CaptureCollection,* and *GroupCollection* are similar to those of *Match* and *MatchCollection*, discussed previously, and will not be covered in detail. Refer to the .NET documentation for complete details.

Replacing Substrings

There are two approaches to substring replacement. First, the *Regex.Replace* method replaces any matches in an input text with a specified substitution string. Overloaded versions of *Replace* allow the specification of a maximum number of replacements to make and a search starting position in the input text.

Alternatively, an overloaded version of the *Replace* method takes a *MatchEvaluator* delegate as an argument. For each match that occurs, the delegate is invoked. The delegate is passed a *Match* instance that represents the current match. The delegate implements any decision-making logic required and returns a string that will be used as the substitution string.

The *MatchEvaluator* delegate has the following signature:

```
public delegate string MatchEvaluator(Match match);
```

The following example demonstrates both of these approaches:

```
using System;
using System.Text.RegularExpressions;

public class REReplace {

    // Declare MatchEvaluator delegate target method
    public static string MyEval(Match match) {
        switch (match.Value) {
            case "fox" : return "cow";
            case "dog" : return "pig";
            default : return match.Value;
        }
    }

    public static void Main() {

        // Create an input text
        string text =
            "the quick red fox jumped over the lazy brown dog.";
```

(continued)

```
// Perform a complete replacement of "the" with "a"
Regex r = new Regex("the");
System.Console.WriteLine(r.Replace(text, "a"));

// Perform evaluated replacement of any word that
// has the lower case letter "o" in, but not at
// the beginning or end.
r = new Regex(@"\w+o\w+");
System.Console.WriteLine(r.Replace(text,
    new MatchEvaluator(REReplace.MyEval)));
    }
}
```

The output from the example with the replacements highlighted is

```
a quick red fox jumped over a lazy brown dog
the quick red cow jumped over the lazy brown pig
```

Note that in the second line of output, although *brown* matches our regular expression, it is not replaced based on the logic in the *MyEval* delegate.

Splitting Strings

The splitting of an input text around a regular expression is handled using the *Regex.Split* method. *Split* takes an input string and an optional integer that sets the maximum number of splits to perform and returns a string array containing the extracted substrings. This is demonstrated in the following code fragment:

```
// Split the String at the first two occurrences of the regex "and"
string input = "bill and bob and betty and dave";
Regex r = new Regex(" and ");
string[] result = r.Split(input, 3);
foreach (string s in result) {
    System.Console.WriteLine(s);
}
```

The code produces the following output:

```
bill
bob
betty and dave
```

Note that we specified a maximum of three splits in *Regex.Split*, so *betty and dave* remains unsplit.

Ad Hoc Regular Expressions

Both Java and .NET provide support for ad hoc regular expression usage without the need to explicitly instantiate any regular expression objects. Java exposes these capabilities predominantly through the *String* class, whereas .NET provides static methods in the *Regex* class. If access to the match data isn't required, both platforms offer the same capabilities. However, the .NET static methods provide a better solution if access to the match results is required. Both approaches are equivalent to compiling a regular expression, using it, and discarding it, so if the regular expression is to be used more than once, explicit instantiation and reuse is more efficient. These methods are contrasted in Table 7-16.

Table 7-16   Ad Hoc Regular Expression Functionality in Java and .NET

Java	.NET	Description
Pattern.matches() *String.matches()*	*Regex.IsMatch()*	Searches an input string for an occurrence of a regular expression and returns a *bool* value indicating whether a match was found. Access to the match results is not possible.
N/A	*Regex.Match()*	Returns the first regular expression match in an input string.
N/A	*Regex.Matches()*	Returns a *MatchCollection* of all regular expression matches in an input string.
String.replaceAll()	*Regex.Replace()*	Replaces all occurrences of a matched expression with a provided string. An overloaded version also supports the use of a delegate as a callback mechanism to provide per-match decision making capabilities.
String.replaceFirst()	N/A	Not directly supported but can be achieved using the correct regular expression syntax.
String.split()	*Regex.Split()*	Splits an input string into a string array around matches.

Summary

This chapter has demonstrated the features of the *String* class and the functionality provided by the .NET class libraries to support string manipulation. We have shown that the support in both Java and .NET is broadly the same with respect to simple string manipulation, dynamic string building, and string encoding.

The string formatting features of .NET, however, offer better integration with the rest of the class library than the equivalent functionality in Java, and the C# *params* support results in cleaner syntax. The use of the *IFormattable* interface and the encapsulation of rendering logic within the target class provide a flexible architecture.

The regular expression implementation provided in .NET is strong and offers a superset of the functionality provided in Java version 1.4. The stateless, collection-oriented match capabilities are useful, and the ability to search text right to left provides support for localized searching.

8

Numbers and Dates

This chapter compares the support for numbers, dates, and times provided in the Java class library with those in Microsoft .NET. Java and C# both provide language-level support for straightforward numeric operations; more complex features are implemented in the class libraries. Conversely, neither Java nor C# provides language-level support for working with dates and times; classes offer a better solution to the complexities of localization.

Numbers

The .NET numeric types and the C# language syntax used to manipulate them are discussed in Chapter 5, "Data Types." As described in Chapter 5, .NET value types are implemented as structs and have object capabilities. This section discusses the object features of the numeric types, particularly those that support comparison, conversion, and formatting. In Java, the primitive wrapper classes such as *java.lang.Integer* and *java.lang.Double* predominantly provide these features. This section also covers the facilities provided by .NET to perform mathematical operations and generate pseudorandom numbers; both provide direct equivalents of the facilities offered by Java.

Numbers as Objects

.NET implements all inbuilt numeric data types as structs in the *System* namespace. C# defines convenient keyword aliases for the fully qualified struct names, so the full names are rarely used. We discussed the C# keywords and their equivalent fully qualified struct names in Chapter 4, "Language Syntax and Features."

All of the numeric structs derive from the *System.ValueType* class, which derives from *System.Object*. The *Equals*, *GetHashCode*, and *ToString* methods inherited from *Object* are overridden to provide behavior more appropriate to numeric types. *GetType* still returns a *Type* object for the struct instance. We'll discuss these methods in the "Members" section later in this chapter. Additionally, all numeric structs implement a standard set of interfaces, provide type-specific members, and are serializable.

> **More Info**   For a complete discussion of serialization, see Chapter 10," "Streams, Files, and I/O."

Interfaces

All of the inbuilt numeric types implement the *IComparable*, *IFormattable*, and *IConvertible* interfaces from the *System* namespace.

IComparable   The *IComparable* interface specifies the implementation of the following method:

```
int CompareTo(object obj);
```

The *CompareTo* method enables instances of numeric types to be compared with other numbers, with the return value indicating their relative ranking. This is the same as the Java *java.lang.Comparable* interface, and the return values are

- < 0 if the instance value is less than the value of *obj*.

- 0 if the instance value is equal to the value of *obj*.

- > 0 if the instance value is greater than the value of *obj*.

Unfortunately, although the *CompareTo* method accepts any *Object* reference as an argument, the numeric types throw a *System.ArgumentException* if the object and the argument are different types. No implicit conversion is performed; the types must match or have been explicitly cast to the same type. The value *null* is a valid value and is always considered less than any other value.

Implementation of the *IComparable* interface is useful when numeric types are used in collections, but for general purposes the >, ==, and < operators offer a simpler solution.

> **More Info**   See Chapter 9," "Collections," for information on the use of *IComparable* in collections.

IFormattable   *IFormattable* specifies the implementation of an overloaded *ToString* method that supports the rendering of numeric types to strings. Format specifiers and localization settings provide extensive control over the format of the string representation. See the "Formatting Numbers" section later in this chapter for more information.

> **More Info**   The *IFormattable* interface is discussed in detail in Chapter 7, "Strings and Regular Expressions."

IConvertible   The *IConvertible* interface specifies methods for converting the implementing class to a set of target representations. The methods are *ToBoolean, ToByte, ToChar, ToDataTime, ToDecimal, ToDouble, ToInt16, ToInt32, ToInt64, ToSByte, ToSingle, ToString, ToType, ToUInt32,* and *ToUInt64*. All methods take an instance of *IFormatProvider* as an argument. The implementing class refers to the *IFormatProvider* instance to obtain localization settings for use in the conversion process. If *null* is provided, the current default system settings will be used. If no meaningful conversion exists between two types, a *System.InvalidCastException* is thrown.

The *IConvertible* interface also includes the *GetTypeCode* member. *GetTypeCode* returns a member of the *System.TypeCode* enumeration that uniquely identifies the implementing type.

Although the inbuilt numeric types implement *IConvertible*, explicit interface implementation means it is not possible to invoke *IConvertible* members through an instance of the numeric type. The .NET documentation recommends conversion of numeric types be carried out using the static members of the *System.Convert* utility class as opposed to invoking *IConvertible* members directly. Alternatively, the implicit and explicit conversion support in C# is sufficient for most purposes. We'll discuss the *System.Convert* class later, in the "Converting Numbers" section.

Members

Aside from the methods required by the interface implementations described earlier, all numeric types implement the members described in Table 8-1.

Table 8-1   Numeric Type Members

Member	Description
Public Fields	
MaxValue	Constant containing the maximum value representable by the numeric type.
MinValue	Constant containing the minimum value representable by the numeric type.
Methods	
Equals()	Overridden method inherited from *System.Object*. Returns *true* if the argument provided is of the same type and value as the instance; otherwise, returns *false*. Implicit conversion is not used; however, explicitly casting types with the same value will return *true*.
ToString()	The *ToString* method inherited from *System.Object* is overridden and calls the overloaded *IFormattable.ToString* method, passing it default formatting arguments.
GetHashCode()	Overridden. Returns a hash code appropriate to the numeric type.
GetType()	Inherited from *System.Object*. Returns a *Type* object for the numeric type.
Parse()	Converts a string representation of a number to an instance of the numeric type.

Floating-point members   *System.Single* and *System.Double* contain additional members, described in Table 8-2, to support floating-point operations.

Table 8-2   Additional *System.Single* and *System.Double* Members

Member	Description
Public Fields	
Epsilon	Constant containing the smallest positive value greater than 0 representable by the floating-point type.
NaN	Constant representing "Not a Number."
NegativeInfinity	Constant representing negative infinity.
PositiveInfinity	Constant representing positive infinity.
Methods	
IsInfinity	Static method returns *true* if the specified number evaluates to negative or positive infinity.

Table 8-2 Additional *System.Single* and *System.Double* Members   *(continued)*

Member	Description
IsNaN	Static method returns *true* if the specified number evaluates to a value that is not a number.
IsNegativeInfinity	Static method returns *true* if the specified number evaluates to negative infinity.
IsPositiveInfinity	Static method returns *true* if the specified number evaluates to positive infinity.
TryParse()	Converts a string representation of a floating-point number to an instance of the numeric type. Returns *true* if the string is parsed successfully; does not throw an exception.

***Decimal* members**   The *System.Decimal* type directly exposes methods to perform basic mathematical operations on *Decimal* instances. While these may be useful for programmers of languages other than C#, they provide no benefit over using the inbuilt C# syntax and will not be covered here.

Converting Numbers

C# language syntax supports implicit and explicit conversion from one numeric type to another. The .NET class library also includes a utility class named *System.Convert* that contains static methods for converting from one numeric type to another, including support for conversions between numbers and *bool, string*, and *DateTime* values.

The *Convert* class implements the following static methods: *ToBoolean, ToByte, ToChar, ToDateTime, ToDecimal, ToDouble, ToInt16, ToInt32, ToInt64, ToSByte, ToSingle, ToString, ToUInt16, ToUInt32,* and *ToUInt64*. Each of these methods provides overloads that take each of the numeric types and return the appropriately converted value. If no meaningful conversion exists between two types, a *System.InvalidCastException* is thrown.

Formatting Numbers

All numeric types implement the *IFormattable* interface. *IFormattable* specifies the implementation of a *ToString* method with the following signature:

```
string ToString(string format, IFormatProvider formatProvider);
```

The *format* argument takes what's called a *numeric format string*, which determines how the number is formatted. The *formatProvider* argument provides information on localization setting to assist in the formatting process. If *format-Provider* is *null*, default localization settings are used.

In the following example, we use the numeric format string *E2*, which indicates scientific notation to two decimal places, and we specify *null* as the *IFormatProvider* so that the default localization settings are used.

```
int SomeInt = 1234567;

System.Console.WriteLine(SomeInt.ToString("E2", null));
```

The code produces the following output:

```
1.23E+006
```

As shown in this example, the *ToString* method of a numeric type can be called directly; more commonly, a number is formatted indirectly through one of the string formatting methods such as those provided by *Console.WriteLine*. When you're using the string formatting methods, it's important to understand that only the portion of the format specifier after the semicolon is passed to the *ToString* method of the number being formatted. For example, in the following statement:

```
Console.WriteLine("The amount is : {0,15:C2}", 1000000);
```

which, depending on localization settings, produces the following output:

```
The amount is :      $1,000,000.00
```

only the *C2* (in boldface) is used to format the literal *1000000*, equivalent to the following direct *ToString* call:

```
1000000.ToString("C2", null);
```

> **More Info**   String formatting methods are discussed fully in Chapter 7.

Standard Numeric Format Strings

A standard numeric format string is a single letter followed by an optional pair of digits called the *precision specifier*. The purpose of the precision specifier depends on the format string used, and if not provided will default to a setting appropriate for the current system settings. The standard format strings are summarized in Table 8-3. The examples use an overloaded *ToString* method that takes a format string argument but that does not require an *IFormatProvider* instance.

Table 8-3 Numeric Format Strings

Format String	Description and Examples

C or *c*	Formats the number as a currency amount. The currency symbol, thousands separator, and decimal separator are determined by localization settings. The precision specifier controls the number of decimal places displayed. For example:
	
	`1234.ToString("C") = $1,234.00`
	`1234.5678.ToString("c2") = $1,234.57`
	`1234.5678.ToString("C6") = $1,234.567800`

D or *d*	The decimal format string is applicable only to integral types and displays the number as a string of decimal digits. The precision specifier controls the minimum number of digits that appear in the output string; output is left padded with 0s if needed. For example:
	
	`1234.ToString("D7") = 0001234`
	`0xABC.ToString("d") = 2748`

E or *e*	Formats the number in scientific notation with the case of the exponent prefix matching the case of the format string. The precision specifier controls the number of digits displayed after the decimal point. For example:
	
	`1234.ToString("e7") = 1.2340000e+003`
	`12.345678.ToString("E3") = 1.235E+001`

F or *f*	Formats the number to a fixed-point decimal representation. The precision specifier controls the number of digits after the decimal point. For example:
	
	`1234.ToString("F4") = 1234.0000`
	`12.345678.ToString("F3") = 12.346`

G or *g*	Formats the number in the most compact decimal form using fixed or scientific notation. The precision specifier controls the number of significant digits displayed.

N or *n*	Formats the number using the current thousands separator and decimal separator. The precision specifier controls the minimum number of decimal digits displayed. For example:
	
	`1234.56789.ToString("N") = 1,234.57`
	`1234567.89.ToString("N3") = 1,234,567.890`

P or *p*	Multiplies the number by 100 and formats it as a percentage. The percent symbol and its location are determined by localization settings. The precision specifier controls the number of decimal places displayed. For example:
	
	`1.23.ToString("P4") = 123.0000  %`
	`1.234567.ToString("p2") = 123.46  %`

(continued)

Table 8-3 Numeric Format Strings *(continued)*

Format String	Description and Examples
R or *r*	Round-trip formatting is applicable only to floating-point types and guarantees that a floating-point string resulting from formatting will be parsed back into the same numeric value. The precision specifier is not used and is ignored if provided.

X or *x*	The hexadecimal format string is applicable to integral types only and converts the number to a hexadecimal digit representation. The case of the format string controls the case of the hexadecimal digits in the output. The precision specifier controls the minimum number of hexadecimal digits; the output is left padded with 0s if necessary. For example:
	
	`2748.ToString("X") = ABC`
	`2748.ToString("x5") = 00abc`

.NET interprets any format string that is a single character followed by optional digits as a standard numeric format string. If the character doesn't match one of those in Table 8-3, *ToString* throws a *FormatException*. A format string containing more than one character is a custom format string.

Custom Numeric Format Strings

Custom format strings map closely to the formatting functionality provided by the *java.text.DecimalFormat* class; custom format strings offer greater flexibility over how a number will be formatted. Custom format strings use a small selection of symbols to define the desired format of a numeric type. Table 8-4 provides a summary of the available symbols.

Table 8-4 Custom Numeric Format Strings

Format Character	Comments
0	The zero placeholder causes a digit or 0 to appear in the output string. For example: `123.ToString("00000") = 00123`
#	The digit placeholder causes a digit or nothing to appear in the output string. For example: `123.45.ToString("#####") = 123`
.	The decimal point identifies the position of the first decimal place. For example: `123.45.ToString("#####.000") = 123.450`
,	The comma indicates that thousands separators should be used. For example: `12345678.ToString("#,#") = 12,345,678`

Table 8-4 Custom Numeric Format Strings *(continued)*

Format Character	Comments
%	The percent symbol causes the number to be multiplied by 100 and displayed as a percentage. For example: `0.1234.ToString("%#.00") = %12.34`

E0, E+0, E-0,
 	
e0, e+0,e-0
	Use scientific notation. For example:
	
	`1234.ToString("0.##E+000") = 1.23E+003`
	`1234.ToString("0.##e+000") = 1.23e+003`
	`1234.ToString("0.##e0") = 1.23e3`

\	The backslash escapes the next character. For example: `1234.ToString("##\t##") = 12    34`

;	Different formats can be specified for use with positive and negative numbers and 0. The semicolon is used to separate these format elements. For example:
	
	`1234.ToString("##;(##);zero") = 1234`
	`(1234).ToString("##;(##);zero") = (1234)`
	`0.ToString("##;(##);zero") = zero`

Other	Other characters are copied to the output string without affecting numeric formatting. For example: `12345.ToString("A[##][00]") = A[123][45]`

Mathematical Functions

The *java.lang.Math* class is equivalent to the .NET *System.Math* class. Both classes provide a set of constants and static methods for performing mathematical operations. The methods common to both *System.Math* and *java.lang.Math* are, using the .NET names, as follows: *Acos, Asin, Atan, Atan2, Ceiling, Cos, Exp, Floor, IEEERemainder, Max, Min, Pow, Sin, Sqrt,* and *Tan*. Table 8-5 highlights the differences between the *java.lang.Math* and *System.Math* classes.

Table 8-5 Differences in Static Members of *java.lang.Math* and *System.Math*

Java	.NET	Comments
abs()	*Abs()*	.NET provides overloads that take a larger range of parameter types.
N/A	*Cosh()*	Returns the hyperbolic cosine of the specified angle.
log()	*Log()*	.NET provides an overloaded *Log* method that allows the base of the logarithm to be specified.

(continued)

Table 8-5   Differences in Static Members of *java.lang.Math* and *System.Math* *(continued)*

Java	.NET	Comments
N/A	*Log10()*	A convenience method for getting the base 10 logarithm of a number.
random()	N/A	See the next section, "Random Numbers."
rint()	*Round()*	The .NET *Round* method is more like Java *rint* than *round*. It returns a floating-point representation of the rounded number as opposed to an integer value.
round()		
		.NET provides an overloaded *Round* method that supports rounding to a specified precision.
N/A	*Sign()*	Returns a value indicating the sign of the specified number.
N/A	*Sinh()*	Returns the hyperbolic sine of the specified angle.
N/A	*Tanh()*	Returns the hyperbolic tangent of the specified angle.
toDegrees()	N/A	
toRadians()	N/A	

Random Numbers

The Java class *java.util.Random* and the .NET equivalent *System.Random* are simple classes for generating pseudorandom numbers. These classes are not suitable for high-security or cryptography applications.

> **Note**   The .NET *System.Security.Cryptography* namespace includes mechanisms for the generation of secure random numbers (SRNs).

Both *Random* classes act as number generators, providing a stream of random numbers in response to method calls. Instantiation of both classes is the same except when specifying a seed; *java.util.Random* takes a *long*, whereas *System.Random* takes an *int*. Once created, the .NET *System.Random* class cannot have its seed changed, whereas the Java class provides the *setSeed* method.

Java offers greater flexibility in the type of result returned from *Random*, including support for Boolean values and a wider selection of numeric types.

Table 8-6 summarizes the methods of the Java and .NET *Random* classes.

Table 8-6   A Comparison between Java and .NET *Random* Classes

Java	.NET	Comments
Constructors		
Random()	*Random()*	
Random(long)	*Random(int)*	Uses the specified value as the seed for the random number generation algorithm.
Methods		
nextBoolean()	N/A	
nextBytes()	*NextBytes()*	
nextDouble()	*NextDouble()*	
nextFloat()	N/A	
nextGaussian()	N/A	
nextInt()	*Next()*	
nextInt(int)	*Next(int)*	
N/A	*Next(int, int)*	Returns a positive random integer between the specified values.
nextLong()	N/A	
setSeed()	N/A	.NET *Random* seed is set only during construction.

Dates and Times

The primary class for representing an instance of time in Java is *java.util.Date*. Many of the methods in *Date* are deprecated and replaced by functionality contained in the *java.util.Calendar* and *java.text.DateFormat* classes. The .NET mechanism for representing an instant of time is the *System.DateTime* struct. Instances of *DateTime* are always associated with an instance of *System.Calendar*. This relationship allows *DateTime* to provide functionality equivalent to a combination of the Java *Date* and *Calendar* classes. Through implementation of the *IFormattable* interface, described in Chapter 7, and methods to parse string values, the .NET *DateTime* class includes functionality comparable to the Java *DateFormat* class.

A number of fundamental differences exist between how Java and .NET represent dates and times through the *System.DateTime* and *java.util.Date* classes:

■   Java *Date* represents an *int* offset from January 1, 1970, 00:00:00 GMT; .NET *DateTime* represents a *long* offset from January 1, 0001 CE, 12:00:00. CE stands for Common Era and is equivalent to AD in the Gregorian calendar.

- Java *Date* measures the offset in milliseconds. .NET defines the tick that all *DateTime* offsets are measured in. One tick equals 100 nanoseconds; 1 millisecond equals 10,000 ticks.

- .NET *DateTime* is a struct and hence a value type; any calls to methods on a *DateTime* instance will implicitly box the instance.

- .NET *DateTime* is immutable, whereas Java *Date* can be reused through the *setTime* method.

- .NET *DateTime* instances can be compared using standard arithmetic operators such as ==, !=, <, >, >=, and <=.

System.TimeSpan

The *System.TimeSpan* struct is a useful addition to time and date handling with no Java equivalent. The *TimeSpan* struct represents a time interval independent of calendar settings. A *TimeSpan* can be created through constructors or static methods contained in the *TimeSpan* class. The interval represented by the *TimeSpan* is specified in ticks or by specifying the number of days, hours, minutes, seconds, and milliseconds. Because a *TimeSpan* is independent of calendars, the largest unit of time it understands is the day. *TimeSpan* instances can have negative values. Operator overloading allows *TimeSpan* instances to be added, subtracted, negated, and compared using standard operators.

Creating Dates

DateTime instances are created via the *DateTime* constructors or by using the static fields and properties of *DateTime*. Once created, instances of *DateTime* are immutable. Table 8-7 summarizes the most common ways to create *DateTime* instances.

Table 8-7 *DateTime* **Creation Methods**

Creator	Description
Constructors	
DateTime(long)	Creates a *DateTime* instance using the *long* specified as the tick offset.
DateTime(various)	Overloaded constructors support the creation of *DateTime* instances from specified year, month, day, hour, minute, second, and millisecond values.
	It's also possible to specify the *Calendar* instance that will be used by the *DateTime* instance.

Table 8-7 *DateTime* **Creation Methods**   *(continued)*

Creator	Description
Public Fields	
DateTime.MaxValue	Constant representing the largest possible *DateTime* value.
DateTime.MinValue	Constant representing the smallest possible *DateTime* value.
Properties	
DateTime.Now	Static property used to get a *DateTime* that represents the current local date and time.
DateTime.Today	Static property used to get a *DateTime* that represents the current date; the time component will be 00:00:00.
Methods	
DateTime.FromFileTime()	Static method that returns a *DateTime* instance from a file system timestamp.

Manipulating Dates

Java has deprecated the date and time manipulation functions of the *Date* class. The abstract *Calendar* class and the concrete subclasses such as *GregorianCalendar* provide the bridge between *Date* instances and human-readable time and date information.

The relationship between the .NET *DateTime* and *Calendar* classes means that both the *DateTime* and the *Calendar* classes have comparable sets of members for manipulating dates. The *DateTime* members work on the current *DateTime* instance, whereas the *Calendar* members take *DateTime* instances as arguments.

The members of *DateTime* and *Calendar* provide functionality to

- Retrieve any component of a *DateTime*, including ticks, era, year, month, day, and so on.

- Add time intervals to a *DateTime* instance, specified in ticks, hours, days, and so on. It's possible to add a *TimeSpan* instance to a *DateTime* through the methods of *DateTime* or by using the + or - operator overloaded by *DateTime*.

- Convert a *DateTime* instance to and from UTC time.

Formatting Dates

The *DateTime* class implements the *IFormattable* interface. *IFormattable* is discussed in the *"System.IFormattable"* section earlier in this chapter and in Chapter 7. As with numbers, .NET provides a selection of standard and custom format strings for expressing the required format of the returned string representation. Refer to the .NET documentation for a description.

The *DateTime* class implements a number of convenience methods that automatically apply common formatting to *DateTime* instances. These include the following: *ToLongDateString*, *ToLongTimeString*, *ToShortDateString*, and *ToShortTimeString*.

Parsing Strings

The static *Parse* and *ParseExact* methods of the *DateTime* class allow strings to be turned into *DateTime* instances. The *Parse* method makes a best effort to create a *DateTime* based on formatting specified in the current localization settings. Any missing information is filled in using the current date and time; if only a date is specified, the time will default to midnight.

The *ParseExact* method takes a format string—using the same syntax as *IFormattable*—and parses the string. The input string must match the format string exactly, or *System.FormatException* is thrown.

Summary

This chapter has described the support for numbers, dates, and times provided by the .NET class library. Both Java and .NET provide comparable functionality despite implementation differences. The object capabilities provided by the .NET numeric types avoid the need for the separate wrapper and formatting used in Java, although .NET still consolidates conversions into a separate utility class.

.NET provides more unified time and date support. The implementation of the *DateTime* class avoids functionality being spread across multiple related classes, and the use of operators on *DateTime* instances makes for cleaner, more readable code.

9

Collections

Collections are one of the cornerstones of a modern programming language. Java has not always had good collection support, and only since Java 1.2 has the platform benefited from a strong collection class library. The collections provided in Microsoft .NET are less flexible than those in Java but include some interesting features that help to address the differences.

The first part of this chapter covers indexers, which are a useful language construct employed by all of the collection classes. We move on to explain the interfaces that define the basic collection contracts; then we discuss the collections themselves. Much of the chapter is given over to the individual collection classes. The most commonly used collections from Java are available and remain largely unchanged. Some new collections aren't available in Java, and we explain their purpose and use. However, the .NET collection framework also has significant omissions, which Java developers will miss. We finish this chapter with a section on thread-safe collections and the classes that are available to build strongly typed custom collection types.

Indexers

Indexers are a new C# feature that allows classes to be indexed in a similar way to arrays. Indexers are particularly applicable for use in conjunction with collection data members. Using the array-style syntax provides a logical mechanism through which safe access can be provided to the underlying collection data. The .NET standard collection classes use indexers extensively, as we will see later in this chapter.

> **More Info** A comprehensive discussion of the declaration and usage of indexers can be found in Chapter 5, "Data Types."

Of particular use is the ability to overload an indexer, providing access based on different key types. The following example demonstrates the implementation of an indexer to provide access to a collection using both *string* and *int* as keys. This example uses an array as the underlying collection, but the same approach is equally applicable to any collection. The example we use is a set of paintbrushes. A brush can be selected by its position or its color. For the purpose of the example, only three brushes are manually defined.

```csharp
public struct Brush {
    public readonly string Name;
    public readonly byte RedVal, BlueVal, GreenVal;

    public Brush(string name, byte red, byte green, byte blue) {
        Name = name;
        RedVal = red;
        BlueVal = blue;
        GreenVal = green;
    }
}

public class BrushPot {
    private Brush[] Brushes;

    public BrushPot() {
        Brushes = new Brush[3];
        Brushes[0] = new Brush("black",0,0,0);
        Brushes[1] = new Brush("red",255,0,0);
        Brushes[2] = new Brush("blue",0,0,255);
    }

    public Brush this[int key] {
        get {
            return Brushes[key];
        }
        set {
            Brushes[key] = value;
        }
    }
    public Brush this[string key] {
        get{
```

```
        switch (key) {
            case "black":
                return Brushes[0];
            case "red":
                return Brushes[1];
            case "blue":
                return Brushes[2];
        }
        return Brushes[0];
    }
    set {
        switch (key) {
            case "black":
                Brushes[0] = value;
                break;
            case "red":
                Brushes[1] = value;
                break;
            case "blue":
                Brushes[2] = value;
                break;
        }
    }
  }
}
```

The indexers (indicated by boldface) allow a *Brush* to be retrieved using either its position in the array or its color. In the case of the color, we use a *switch* statement because we know the set of brush names. We could have used a *foreach* loop to look through the array and select the brush with the correct name if the number of brushes had been greater.

Collection Interfaces

Like Java, the .NET Framework declares interfaces that define the core collection functionality; these interfaces provide common functionality that can be extended to achieve specialized behavior.

A class that implements one of the collection interfaces is known as a collection class. Note that a collection class is not required to implement every interface member and may throw a *NotSupportedException* when unimplemented members are invoked.

All of the interfaces covered in this section are found in the *System.Collections* namespace.

ICollection

This is the foundation of the collections namespace and is implemented by all the collection classes. It defines only the most basic collection functionality, as shown in Table 9-1.

Table 9-1   The *ICollection* Interface

Member	Description
Properties	
Count	Returns the number of items in the collection.
IsSynchronized	Returns *true* if this instance is thread-safe.
SyncRoot	Returns an object that can be used to provide synchronized access to the collection.
Methods	
CopyTo()	Copies all of the elements in the collection into an array. Throws an exception if more elements are in the collection than can be held in the array or if the elements cannot be implicitly cast to the array type.

The equivalent Java interface is *java.util.Collection*, containing 15 methods that provide commonality across all collection classes. .NET takes the approach of pushing method definitions down into specialized interfaces for lists and dictionaries.

IEnumerable, IEnumerator, and the foreach Keyword

The *IEnumerable* interface is very simple but useful. It contains only one method:

```
IEnumerator.GetEnumerator();
```

Classes that implement this method must return a class that implements the *IEnumerator* interface. The *IEnumerator* interface defines the notion of a cursor that moves over the elements of a collection. It has three members, as described in Table 9-2, for moving the cursor and retrieving elements from the collection.

Table 9-2   The *IEnumerator* Interface

Member	Comments
Properties	
Current	The *Current* property returns the element at the position of the cursor. The type that is returned is determined by the implementation, but the return type is defined as *object*.
Methods	
MoveNext()	By default, the cursor is positioned before the first element in the enumeration. The *MoveNext* method advances the cursor returning *true* if the cursor was successfully advanced to the next element and *false* if the cursor has moved past the last element. The first call to *MoveNext* should position the cursor at the first collection element.

In common with Java, .NET enumerators are not thread safe, and when implementing *IEnumerator*, take care to provide a copy of the elements or to ensure that modifications cannot be made to the underlying data while the enumerator is in use.

The following example demonstrates use of *IEnumerator* and *IEnumerable*:

```
using System ;
using System.Collections ;
class EnumExample : IEnumerator {
    private object[] o_arr;
    private int o_cursor;

    public EnumExample(object[] p_arr) {
        o_arr = p_arr;
        o_cursor = -1;
    }

    public object Current {
        get {
            if (o_cursor > -1 && o_cursor < o_arr.Length) {
                return o_arr[o_cursor];
            } else {
                throw new InvalidOperationException();
            }
        }
    }

    public bool MoveNext() {
        o_cursor++;
        return o_cursor < o_arr.Length;
```

(continued)

```
    }

    public void Reset() {
        o_cursor = -1;
    }
}
```

Here's a fragment that demonstrates using the *EnumExample* class, iterating over a string array:

```
EnumExample x_example = new EnumExample(
    new string[] {"allen", "jones", "adam", "freeman"});

    while (x_example.MoveNext()) {
        Console.WriteLine("Element: " +
            x_example.Current.ToString());
    }
}
```

And here's the output:

```
Element: allen
Element: jones
Element: adam
Element: freeman
```

We can use the *IEnumerator* implementation to provide support for an *IEnumerable* implementation. In this example, we pass the underlying array into the enumerator.

```
class Enumerator : IEnumerable {
    private object[] o_array;

    public Enumerator(object[] p_arr) {
        o_array = p_arr;
    }

    public IEnumerator GetEnumerator() {
        return new EnumExample(o_array);
    }
}
```

To get hold of the enumerator, a call is made to the *GetEnumerator* method.

Any class that implements the *IEnumerable* interface can be iterated over using the *foreach* statement, which provides a clean syntax when iterating over collections. Unfortunately, the *foreach* statement provides no mechanism to access the index of the element being worked with. If index access is a requirement, we suggest using a *for* loop.

> **More Info**   You can find a full discussion of both the *foreach* and *for* statements in Chapter 4, "Language Syntax and Features."

IComparer and *IComparable*

Like Java, .NET defines two interfaces used to sort collections. One is for classes that will make comparisons and the other for classes that will be compared; these are similar to the Java interfaces for sorting. .NET defines the interface *System.IComparable*, which is a direct equivalent of *java.lang.Comparable*. Both the Java and .NET interfaces define a single method that takes an object argument. The return value is an *int* stating the relative rank of the *IComparable* to the object argument. The second interface is *System.Collections.IComparer*, implemented by classes that are able to sort the elements of a collection. The only method in this interface is *Compare*, which takes two object arguments and returns their rankings.

Most of the fundamental classes implement *IComparable*, including the struct implementations of all simple value types, making sorting with simple types straightforward. .NET provides two utility classes that can be used to assist with simple sorting. These are *System.Collection.Comparer* and *System.Collection.CaseInsensitiveComparer*. These classes are used in conjunction with sorting routines such as those implemented by *System.Array*. Here's an example:

```
string[] x_arr = new string[] {"Allen", "Jones",
                 "Adam", "Freeman"};
Array.Sort(x_arr, Comparer.Default);

foreach (string x_str in x_arr) {
    Console.WriteLine("STR: " + x_str);
}
```

The output follows:

```
STR: Adam
STR: Allen
STR: Freeman
STR: Jones
```

Instances of both comparers are obtained using their static *Default* field and are not constructed directly. The single instance can be shared between sorting operations in different threads and classes.

Other Collection Interfaces

Two other collection interfaces are worth noting: *IList* and *IDictionary*. These provide the foundation for indexed array collections (such as *ArrayList*) and key/value collections (such as *Hashtable*). We'll discuss the classes that implement these interfaces in the next section.

Basic Collections

The .NET Framework includes classes that compare to some of the core collections found in Java, but the overall support and flexibility fall short. This section covers the basic .NET collections, which are similar to their Java equivalents. We begin with coverage of arrays; .NET introduces some clever changes that allow arrays to be treated like collections.

Arrays

The most fundamental type of collection is the array. The use of arrays in .NET is similar to that in Java, with one significant enhancement: all arrays derive from the *System.Array* class. By deriving all arrays from the *System.Array* class, .NET provides useful functionality for array creation and manipulation. Although Java arrays are technically classed as objects, the language exposes methods only from the *java.lang.Object* class.

Predominantly, arrays are created, assigned, and accessed using the integral language support provided by C#. For example:

```
int[] x_arr = new int[10];
int[][] x_jagged = new int[2][];
int[,] x_multi = new int[2, 3];
int[] x_defined = new int[] {10, 20, 30};
```

> **More Info**   Comprehensive coverage of the language support provided by C# for array creation and manipulation is in Chapter 5.

The remainder of this section focuses on the object properties of arrays and their use as a collection.

Arrays as Objects

All the array actions that are normally handled using language syntax are possible through the members of *System.Array*. For example, the following code fragments are functionally equivalent:

```
// Using language syntax
int[] x_arr = new int[2];
x_arr[0] = 10;
x_arr[1] = 20;
for (int i = 0; i < x_arr.Length; i++) {
    Console.WriteLine("Index {0}, Value {1}", i, x_arr[i]);
}


// Using System.Array members
Array x_arr = Array.CreateInstance(typeof(int), 2);
x_arr.SetValue(10, 0);
x_arr.SetValue(20, 1);
for (int i = 0; i < x_arr.Length; i++) {
    Console.WriteLine("Index {0}, Value {1}", i, x_arr.GetValue(i));
}
```

These examples demonstrate the object capabilities of .NET arrays. Bear in mind that while it is possible to use the *System.Array* class to handle all array features, there is no need to do so and the native support is recommended for most array operations.

The primary advantage of the *System.Array* class is that it implements *ICollection*, *IList*, and *IEnumerable*, which allow arrays to be treated as collections. In addition, there are some useful static methods in *Array* that support sorting and searching. This feature will not revolutionize programming, but it is clever, and we admire the forethought of the designers.

Table 9-3 summarizes the methods and properties available in the .NET *System.Array* class and identifies their Java equivalents. Because Java doesn't include a class comparable to *System.Array*, the alternatives are all static methods from the *java.util.Arrays* and *java.lang.System* utility classes.

Table 9-3 Comparison Between Java and C# Array Methods

Java	*Member*	Description
N/A	*Array.Rank*	Returns the number of dimensions in the array.
<array>.length	*Array.Length*	Returns the number of elements in the array.

(continued)

Table 9-3   Comparison Between Java and C# Array Methods   *(continued)*

Java	Member	Description
<array>[index].length	*Array.GetLength()*	Gets the number of elements in a specified array dimension.
N/A	*Array.Clear()*	Sets the elements of the array to the default value (which can be *0, false,* or *null,* depending on the array type).
Arrays.binarySearch()	*Array.BinarySearch()*	Searches an array for a key value. Applied to one-dimensional arrays only.
System.arraycopy()	*Array.Copy()*	Copies a region of the array into another array. The .NET implementation will ensure that values are correctly boxed and typed.
System.arraycopy()	*Array.CopyTo()*	Copies all of the elements in a one-dimensional array to another one-dimensional array.
N/A	*Array.CreateInstance()*	Creates a new array. (See foregoing examples.)
N/A	*Array.GetValue()* *Array.SetValue()*	Gets or sets the value of an array element. Equivalent of *<array>[index] = value.*
N/A	*Array.IndexOf()* *Array.LastIndexOf()*	Finds the first (or last) index of a value in a one-dimensional array.
N/A	*Array.Reverse()*	Reverses the order of the elements in a one-dimensional array.
Arrays.Sort()	*Array.Sort()*	Sorts the elements in a one-dimensional array.
N/A	*Array.GetEnumerator()*	Returns an enumerator that can be used to step over the elements.

Hashtable

The *System.Collections.Hashtable* class is similar to the Java *java.util.HashMap* class. The only important difference is that key/value pairs are stored and accessed via an indexer. Here's an example of how to set and get a *Hashtable* element:

```
Hashtable x_hash = new Hashtable();
x_hash["key"] = "value";
object x_value = x_hash["key"];
```

The .NET *Hashtable* also provides the *Add* method, which adds a new key/value pair to the element set only if the key does not already exist. If the key does exist, an exception will be thrown.

Table 9-4 contrasts the principal methods of the *System.Collections.Hashtable* and *java.lang.HashMap* classes.

Table 9-4   Comparison Between C#'s *Hashtable* and Java's *HashMap* Classes

Java *HashMap*	.NET *Hashtable*	Comments
clear()	Clear()	
containsKey()	ContainsKey() Contains()	*Contains* and *ContainsKey* are equivalent.
containsValue()	ContainsValue()	
get()	<hashtable>[key]	Implemented via an indexer.
put()	<hashtable>[key] = value	Implemented via an indexer. Does not accept *null* as a key.
N/A	Add()	Adds a key/value pair, but only if the key does not already exist in the *Hashtable*.
putAll()	N/A	
keySet()	Keys	Returns an *ICollection* of the keys.
values()	Values	Returns an *ICollection* of the values.
isEmpty()	Count == 0	
size()	Count	
remove()	Remove()	
entrySet()	GetEnumerator()	Returns an *IEnumerator* that will return instances of *Dictionary.Entry*, broadly similar to *Map.Entry*.
N/A	IsFixedSize	Determines whether the *Hashtable* has a fixed number of elements.
N/A	IsReadOnly	Determines whether modification can be made to the collection.
N/A	IsSynchronized	Determines whether the *Hashtable* is synchronized.
N/A	Synchronized()	Returns the *Hashtable* in a thread-safe wrapper.

ArrayList

The .NET *System.Collections.ArrayList* is equivalent to *java.util.ArrayList*. Like *Hashtable*, *ArrayList* implements an *indexer* used to get and set the value at a specific index. The *ArrayList* class implements the *IList* interface and provides the unusual static method *Adapter*, which makes the methods for binary searches and sorting available on any *IList* by wrapping the collection in an *ArrayList* instance. This is not as useful as it sounds because the operations aren't optimized for the underlying structure of the list. Apart from the indexer and the adapter support, the Java and .NET classes are much the same. Table 9-5 compares the Java and C# *ArrayList* implementations.

Table 9-5   Comparison of the Java and C# *ArrayList* Implementations

Java *ArrayList*	.NET *ArrayList*	Comments
add()	Add()	
add(int, Object)	Insert()	
addAll()	AddRange()	Adds all of the elements of an *ICollection* (which includes arrays) to the end of the *ArrayList*.
addAll(int, Collection)	InsertRange()	
clear()	Clear()	
contains()	Contains()	
ensureCapacity()	Capacity	.NET property, used to set or get the capacity of the *ArrayList*.
get()	<arraylist>[index]	
indexOf()	IndexOf()	
lastIndexOf()	LastIndexOf()	
isEmpty()	Count == 0	
remove()	RemoveAt()	
removeRange()	RemoveRange()	
set()	<arraylist>[index] = value	
size()	Count	
toArray()	CopyTo()	Copies the contents of the *ArrayList* (or a range) to a one-dimensional array.
trimToSize()	TrimToSize	
N/A	IsFixedSize	Determines whether this is a fixed size *ArrayList*.

Table 9-5   Comparison of the Java and C# *ArrayList* Implementations   *(continued)*

Java *ArrayList*	.NET *ArrayList*	Comments
N/A	*FixedSize()*	Returns a wrapped *ArrayList* that allows elements to be modified but not to be added
N/A	*IsReadOnly*	Determines whether the collection allows changes to the *ArrayList* elements.
Collections. UnmodifiableList()	*ReadOnly()*	Returns an *ArrayList* that does not allow elements to be modified.
Collections.BinarySearch()	*BinarySearch()*	
subList()	*GetRange()*	
iterator()	*GetEnumerator()*	
N/A	*SetRange()*	Sets a range of the *ArrayList* to the values contained in an *ICollection*.
Collections.sort()	*Sort()*	

Queue

A queue is a first in, first out (FIFO) collection, in which objects are retrieved in the order they were added. This is useful for processing messages or events. Although Java doesn't provide a class that enforces the FIFO constraint, we've seen examples of the *LinkedList* class being used to represent a queue. The problem with this approach is that *LinkedList* elements can be manipulated in ways contradictory to the queue model. Happily, .NET provides the *System.Collections.Queue* class, a concrete implementation of a queue that enforces the FIFO rule.

The queue implementation is based on a circular array, and objects are inserted at one end and removed from the other. As with the *ArrayList* class, if the number of elements exceeds the capacity of the queue, the underlying array is resized to provide more space.

Here's a simple example demonstrating how to use the *Queue* class:

```
Queue x_queue = new Queue();
x_queue.Enqueue("first element");
x_queue.Enqueue("second element");
x_queue.Enqueue("third element");

object x_obj = x_queue.Dequeue();
Console.WriteLine("Dequeued: " + x_obj.ToString());
```

(continued)

```
IEnumerator x_num = x_queue.GetEnumerator();
while (x_num.MoveNext()) {
    Console.WriteLine("Element: "
        + x_num.Current.ToString());
}
```

The results of this example follow:

```
Dequeued: first element
Element: second element
Element: third element
```

Elements are added to the *Queue* using the *Enqueue* method and are removed using *Dequeue*. The *Queue* class implements the *IEnumerable* interface and can be used in a *foreach* loop. In contrast with an *ArrayList*, it's not possible to get an element by index. However, it's possible to see what value is at the head of the queue by calling *Peek*. It can be determined that a value is contained in the *Queue* by calling the *Contains* method. The number of elements in the queue is available using the *Count* property.

Stack

Unlike a queue, a stack is a last in, first out (LIFO) collection, in which the most recently added element is the one that will be returned first. Java and .NET both provide stack implementations. The .NET stack class is *System.Collections.Stack*. Here's an example using *Stack*:

```
Stack x_stack = new Stack();
x_stack.Push("first element");
x_stack.Push("second element");
x_stack.Push("third element");

object x_obj = x_stack.Pop();
Console.WriteLine("POPPED: " + x_obj.ToString());

IEnumerator x_num = x_stack.GetEnumerator();
while (x_num.MoveNext()) {
    Console.WriteLine("ELEMENT: " + x_num.Current.ToString());
}
```

The result of this example follows:

```
POPPED: third element
ELEMENT: second element
ELEMENT: first element
```

The Java *java.net.Stack* class has been around since Java 1.0 and is derived from the *Vector* class. This presents a potential misuse problem whereby a reference to a *Stack* can be cast to a *Vector*, allowing the underlying elements to be manipulated as a list. The .NET implementation isn't derived from any other collection and can't be misused in this manner.

Table 9-6 shows the mapping between the Java and .NET stack classes.

Table 9-6 Comparison Between the Java and C# Stack Implementations

Java Stack	.NET Stack
empty()	*Count == 0*
peek()	*Peek()*
pop()	*Pop()*
push()	*Push()*
search()	N/A
clear()	*Clear()*
contains()	*Contains()*
iterator()	*GetEnumerator()*

SortedList

The *System.Collections.SortedList* class is a cross between a *Hashtable* and an *ArrayList*. Two arrays are maintained, one for keys and one for values. The value array is used when a value is requested by index, like an *ArrayList*. When a value is requested by key, the index is obtained by searching the key array and then the matching value is obtained from the value array, which behaves like a *Hashtable* but requires more operations.

When a new item is added, the key array is re-sorted, and the value array is adjusted to reflect the changes. This is an unusual approach, and it can be seen that special support was added to the *System.Array* class to assist in the sort operations. (For example, look at the *Sort(Array, Array)* method as an example of this special support.) The closest analog in Java is the *java.util.SortedSet* interface and related concrete implementations.

In general, requesting values by key is slower with a *SortedList* than a *Hashtable*. However, the advantage of being able to request a value by index makes this class valuable for some problems. Here's a simple example for this class:

```
SortedList x_list = new SortedList();
x_list["allen"] = "jones";
x_list["adam"] = "freeman";
```
(continued)

```
// get the first element
Console.WriteLine("First element: " + x_list.GetByIndex(0));
// get the index of the key "allen"
Console.WriteLine("Index of \"allen\": " +
    x_list.IndexOfKey("allen"));
// get the index of the value "freeman"
Console.WriteLine("Index of value \"freeman\": " +
    x_list.IndexOfValue("freeman"));
```

The output from this fragment is

```
First element: freeman
Index of "allen": 1
Index of value "freeman": 0
```

The sorting operations can be handled by using the *CompareTo* method of classes that implement *IComparable* or by an instance of *IComparator*.

Specialized Collections

The *System.Collections.Specialized* namespace contains a series of collections that either are strongly typed or offer functionality that is not widely required.

Strongly Typed Collections

The strongly typed collections all deal exclusively with strings.

NameObjectCollectionBase and NameValueCollection

The *NameObjectCollectionBase* class is an abstract class that is based on a *Hashtable* but that accepts only strings as key types. The only concrete implementation of this class in the collections namespace is *NameValueCollection*. The *NameValueCollection* class is derived from *NameObjectCollectionBase* but can be used to store multiple values for each key. However, both the key and the values must be strings. The most obvious use of this class is processing HTTP headers. Here's an example:

```
NameValueCollection x_collection = new NameValueCollection();

x_collection.Add("key", "value1");
x_collection.Add("key", "value2");

string[] x_arr = x_collection.GetValues("key");
foreach (string x_str in x_arr) {
    Console.WriteLine("VALUE: " + x_str);
}
```

The result of this fragment follows:

```
VALUE: value1
VALUE: value2
```

StringCollection

The *StringCollection* class represents an implementation of the *IList* interface such that the interface handles only strings.

StringDictionary

The *StringDictionary* class is the dictionary equivalent of the *StringCollection* class. In essence, it's an implementation of a *Hashtable* that accepts only strings as keys.

Unusual Collections

The following two collections have characteristics that make them useful in specific circumstances but not as everyday collections.

ListDictionary

The *ListDictionary* class implements the *IDictionary* interface using a single-linked array. It behaves like a *Hashtable*, which implements the same interface, but is faster when dealing with up to ten items. This is based on the premise that iterating over a small array is faster than computing hash codes. For more than ten items, the iteration takes longer than hashing and the benefits of this class are negated; a *Hashtable* will offer better performance

HybridDictionary

The *HybridDictionary* class provides the best of both a *ListDictionary* and a *Hashtable*. If the number of elements in the collection is small, they are maintained in a *ListDictionary*. Once the number goes above what's optimal for a *ListDictionary*, they are automatically transferred to a *Hashtable* for better performance. This results in a one-off performance hit. If the number of elements falls below the *ListDictionary* threshold, they remain in the *Hashtable*.

The *CollectionsUtil* Class

The *System.Collections.Specialized* namespace also contains the *CollectionUtil* class, which we think would be better located in the main *System.Collections* namespace. Static methods of this factory class create case-insensitive instances of the *ArrayList* and *Hashtable* classes discussed earlier. This is achieved by using case-insensitive implementations of the underlying hash code provider and comparer.

Synchronization

Java has the legacy of the *classic* collections (*Hashtable, Vector,* and so forth) and the *new* collections that were introduced in Java 1.2 (*HashMap, ArrayList,* and so forth). Although some implementation differences exist, the main change was that none of the methods in the new collections are synchronized, but the classic collections are all thread-safe.

.NET has a different approach to thread-safe collections. All of the concrete classes contained in the *System.Collections* namespace are concurrently safe for multiple readers and a single writer. Multiple concurrent writers will cause problems.

A synchronized (thread-safe) implementation of a concrete collection can be obtained by calling the *Synchronized* method, which returns a wrapped version of the collection, just like calling *java.util.Collections.synchronizedCollection.* This wrapped version is thread safe and can be used by concurrent writers.

In addition, the *ICollection* interface provides a method to determine whether a collection is synchronized, and it provides an object that can be used for locking when writing thread-safe wrappers or using monitors.

> **More Info**   See Chapter 13, "Threading and Synchronization," for more information about synchronization in .NET.

Here's an example:

```
Hashtable x_unsafe = new Hashtable();
Console.WriteLine("Sync state: " + x_unsafe.IsSynchronized);
Hashtable x_safe = Hashtable.Synchronized(x_unsafe);
Console.WriteLine("Sync state: " + x_safe.IsSynchronized);
```

The result of these statements is shown below:

```
Sync state: False
Sync state: True
```

Even though it's possible to generate a thread-safe collection, enumerators are still troublesome. .NET enumerators are backed by the underlying collection, and any changes to the elements can cause problems. .NET takes the approach—in common with Java—of throwing an exception if the elements are changed during the life of an enumerator.

Custom Collections

Like Java, .NET makes it difficult to subclass concrete collection classes to provide specialized behavior without implementing large amounts of functionality. There always seems to be some vital method or inner class that is not accessible. Both languages provide abstract classes as the mechanism for custom designs, but we think that the .NET classes are better thought out.

The abstract classes in .NET are listed in Table 9-7.

Table 9-7   Abstract .NET Collection Classes

Class	Description
CollectionBase	Provides a basis for strongly typed collections.
ReadOnlyCollectionBase	Provides a basis for strongly typed collections that don't permit elements to be modified.
DictionaryBase	Provides a basis for strongly typed collections of key/value pairs.

The most interesting aspect of these classes is that none of the collections detailed in this chapter are derived from them. There is no specific reason why custom collections have to be subclassed from one of these bases, but it is generally good practice to do so.

Summary

This chapter has illustrated that collections in .NET are broadly similar to those in Java, although less comprehensive in nature. The most frequently used classes (*Hashtable* and *ArrayList*) are almost identical, allowing for basic differences between the Java and C# language.

There are some striking omissions from the .NET class library, most notably support for sets and the base classes for providing least recently used (LRU) maps, such as the *LinkedHashMap* Java class. However, the ability to treat arrays as collections is a useful feature.

10

Streams, Files, and I/O

This chapter discusses the facilities the Microsoft .NET Framework provides for input/output. Most programs require the ability to store persistent data in the file system or to communicate with another process. With one exception, the topics discussed in this chapter are familiar to the Java programmer. Concepts such as streams, working with the file system, serialization, and using the console have been staple elements of Java for some time. The only aspect of the .NET I/O support that will be new is known as *isolated storage*, which allows data to be easily stored on a per-user basis.

Working with the Console

Reading from and writing to the console are two of the most fundamental uses of I/O, especially for server-side applications. Despite improvements in logging and debugging tools, writing to the console is still a prevalent means of tracking activity and problems in code. During development we still find console output to be the quickest and simplest means of getting a handle on a tricky problem. Reading from the console is less common but is still an important tool. A good UI goes a long way, but sometimes there is no substitute for grabbing a keystroke straight from the user.

In Java, the console is exposed to the programmer as a set of streams obtained through the *java.lang.System* class. The .NET Framework puts all of the console functions in the *System.Console* class. The *Console* class is a wrapper around three streams, which are accessible via read-only properties. These are shown alongside their Java equivalents in Table 10-1.

Table 10-1 **Comparison Between the Java and .NET Standard Streams**

Java	.NET	Comments
System.out	*Console.Out*	The standard output stream
System.in	*Console.In*	The standard input stream
System.err	*Console.Error*	The standard error output stream

The *Error* and *Out* properties return *System.IO.TextWriter* streams, whereas the *In* property returns an instance of *System.IO.TextReader*. These classes are covered in more detail later in this chapter in the "Readers and Writers" section, but for now it's enough to know that they provide much the same support as the streams available in the *java.lang.System* class.

Writing to the Console

The *System.IO.TextWriter* class returned by the *Out* and *Error* properties is similar in functionality to the *java.io.PrintStream* class that is used for the *System.out* and *System.err* streams in Java. The *TextWriter.Write* method is overloaded to accept a wide range of simple types and formatted strings for display on the console. The *WriteLine* method offers the same overloads but appends a line terminator to the output. By default, the line terminator is the *\r\n* sequence, but it can be changed using the *TextWriter.NewLine* property.

The *Console* class also provides two convenience methods that offer the same overloads and write to the *Out* stream, making the following pairs of statements equivalent:

```
Console.Out.WriteLine("This is a message");
Console.WriteLine("This is a message");

Console.Out.Write("This is a message");
Console.Write("This is a message");
```

The *Console* class doesn't provide these convenience methods for the standard error stream, so error messages must be written using the *Console.Error.Write* and *Console.Error.WriteLine* methods directly.

> **More Info** All *Write* and *WriteLine* methods discussed in this section offer overloads that will generate formatted strings as discussed in Chapter 7, "Strings and Regular Expressions."

Reading from the Console

Input can be read from the console either through the convenience methods in the *Console* class or through the *System.IO.TextReader* instance accessible via the *Console.In* property. In keeping with the model for writing to the console, the following pairs of statements are equivalent:

```
Console.In.ReadLine();
Console.ReadLine();

Console.In.Read();
Console.Read();
```

The *ReadLine* method reads the next line of characters from the input stream, stripping out the line terminator. The *Read* method returns a single character of input but will do so only after a read operation has been terminated, typically because the user has pressed the Enter key. Java provides the ability to read a complete line from the standard input by wrapping *System.in* in either a *java.io.BufferedReader* or a *java.io.DataInputStream*, but it doesn't provide this feature directly in the console stream.

Changing the Console Streams

In common with Java, the .NET console class allows new streams to be substituted for the default instances. This is useful for redirecting console output to a file or filtering the output before displaying it to the user. The *In*, *Out*, and *Error* properties are read-only, but the *SetIn*, *SetOut*, and *SetError* methods of *Console* can be used to install new instances of *TextReader* and *TextWriter* as required.

Console Summary

Table 10-2 provides a summary of the Java-to-.NET mappings for using the console. All members are static.

Table 10-2   Comparison Between the Java and .NET *Console* Classes

Java	.NET
System.in	*Console.In*
System.out	*Console.Out*
System.err	*Console.Error*
System.out.println()	*Console.WriteLine()* *Console.Out.WriteLine()*

(continued)

Table 10-2   Comparison Between the Java and .NET *Console* Classes   *(continued)*

Java	.NET
System.out.print()	*Console.Write()*
	Console.Out.Write()
System.in.read()	*Console.Read()*
	Console.In.Read()
N/A	*Console.ReadLine()*
	Console.In.ReadLine()
System.err.print()	*Console.Error.Write()*
System.err.println()	*Console.Error.WrintLine()*
System.setIn()	*Console.SetIn()*
System.setOut()	*Console.SetOut()*
System.setErr()	*Console.SetError()*

The File System

This section covers the classes that provide access to the file system. Creating, copying, and deleting files and directories are handled in Java by the *java.io.File* class. A slightly different approach is taken by .NET, but the end result is much the same. We end this section with a comparison of the Java and .NET file system methods.

Paths

The *System.IO.Path* class contains a series of static utility methods used to manipulate strings representing file and directory paths. With the exception of the *GetTempFileName* method, the *Path* class does not interact with the file system.

Although the *Path* class provides little functionality that can't be achieved using string parsing and regular expressions, it is designed to provide cross-platform support. When the .NET Framework is ported to other platforms, applications that utilize the *Path* class should work seamlessly.

> **Note**   When using the *Path* class to formulate file paths, bear in mind that although the class ensures that paths do not contain illegal characters, no checks are made to ensure that the path is valid on the local system.

Table 10-3 summarizes the methods and fields of the *Path* class.

Table 10-3   The *Path* Class

Member	Comments
DirectorySeparatorChar	The platform-specific separator character. Defaults to \ for Windows.
InvalidPathChars	Provides a platform-specific array of characters that are illegal in path names.
PathSeparator	Provides a platform-specific path separator character. Defaults to ; for Windows.
VolumeSeparatorChar	Provides a platform-specific volume separator character. Defaults to : for Windows.
ChangeExtension()	Changes the extension of a path string.
Combine()	Concatenates two path strings.
GetDirectoryName()	Gets the contents of a path string between the first and last instances of *DirectorySeparatorChar*.
GetExtension()	Returns the extension of a path string, including the period.
GetFileName()	Returns the contents of a path string after the last instance of *DirectorySeparatorChar*.
GetFileNameWithoutExtension()	Returns the contents of a path string after the last instance of *DirectorySeparatorChar* and before the last period.
GetFullPath()	Returns a fully qualified path for a partial path string. If the partial path begins with the directory separator character, the result will be prepended with *<default drive>:*; otherwise, the result will be the current working directory plus the partial path name.
GetPathRoot()	Returns the root for a path string.
GetTempFileName()	Creates a zero-length temporary file with a unique path, which is returned as the result.

(continued)

Table 10-3 **The *Path* Class**   *(continued)*

Member	Comments
GetTempPath()	Returns the path of the current system's temporary directory.
HasExtension()	Returns *true* if the path string contains the period character followed by at least one other character.
IsPathRooted()	Returns *true* if the path is fully qualified.

Files and Directories

Java handles interrogating the file system through a single class, *java.io.File*. .NET breaks the same functionality up into four separate classes, which provides some flexibility. We feel, however, that this results in an overly complex approach that can be frustrating to work with.

Two classes contain static methods for managing the file system. The *System.IO.Directory* class provides methods to create, move, and manage directories, while the *System.IO.File* class offers the same services for files. Every call to a method in one of these classes requires a string containing the name of the desired file or directory.

These classes are supplemented by *System.IO.DirectoryInfo* and *System.IO.FileInfo*, which offer largely the same functionality as *Directory* and *File* but require instantiation prior to use. Instances of *DirectoryInfo* and *FileInfo* are created by passing a path string into the constructor, resulting in better efficiency if multiple operations are performed on the same file or directory.

The following example demonstrates how to write out the creation time for a file using a *FileInfo* instance and with the static methods of the *File* class:

```
FileInfo x_fileinfo = new FileInfo("myfile.txt");
Console.WriteLine(x_fileinfo.CreationTime);

Console.WriteLine(File.GetCreationTime("myfile.txt"));
```

Differentiating Between Files and Directories

Our principal complaint about these classes is that it's difficult to determine whether a path represents a file or a directory. The Java *java.io.File* class provides the *isDirectory* method, but the .NET classes don't offer anything so simple.

There are two approaches to determining the status of a path: the first relies on the behavior of the *Exists* methods in the *File, FileInfo, Directory*, and *DirectoryInfo* classes, and the second uses a bitwise operation on the attribute sets exposed by *FileInfo* and *DirectoryInfo*.

Using the *Exists* methods   The *Exists* method in the *Directory* class will return *true* only if a path represents a directory in the file system. The *Exists* method in the *File* class will return *true* only if the path represents a file in the file system. These behaviors can be combined to determine whether a path represents a file, represents a directory, or doesn't exist in the file system. The following code fragment demonstrates this approach:

```
string x_path = "C:\\mypath\\myfile.txt";
if (Directory.Exists(x_path)) {
    Console.WriteLine("{0} is a directory", x_path);
} else if (File.Exists(x_path)) {
    Console.WriteLine("{0} is a file", x_path);
} else {
    Console.WriteLine("{0} does not exist", x_path);
}
```

Using bitwise operations   Using bitwise operations is slightly more complicated than the foregoing approach. The *FileInfo* and *DirectoryInfo* classes provide an *Attributes* property, which is a bit flag enumeration containing file attributes, as listed in the *System.IO.FileAttributes* enumeration. This approach looks for the presence of the *FileAttributes.Directory* flag to differentiate between a file and a directory.

```
string x_path = "C:\\mypath\\myfile.txt";

FileInfo x_info = new FileInfo(x_path);

if ((ulong)x_info.Attributes == UInt64.MaxValue) {
    Console.WriteLine("{0} does not exist", x_path);
} else if ((x_info.Attributes & FileAttributes.Directory)
    == FileAttributes.Directory) {
        Console.WriteLine("{0} is a directory", x_path);
} else {
    Console.WriteLine("{0} is a file", x_path);
}
```

This fragment detects paths that relate to nonexistent files by checking to see whether the unsigned integer value of the attributes is the same as that of the *UInt64.MaxValue* field. The Microsoft documentation on the file attributes is a little hazy, and we're not sure whether this is a bug or an expected behavior. For obvious reasons, we suggest using the *Exists* methods to tell files and directories apart.

Getting Streams from Files

As with Java, data is read from and written to files through use of a streams model. (See the "Streams" section later in this chapter for more details.) This section demonstrates how to get streams to access files. .NET provides several means to get a stream, but all result in the creation of a *System.IO.FileStream* instance. The *FileStream* class is the default stream for operations that are backed by a file. In .NET, streams can typically read and write data, so this class is roughly equivalent to a combination of *java.io.FileOutputStream* and *java.io.FileInputStream.*

Creating a stream directly   The most direct way to create a stream is to create a new instance of *FileStream,* passing in a path string to the constructor. Because .NET streams can be used to read and write data, details must be supplied about how the file is opened. The basic *FileStream* constructor takes the following form:

```
FileStream(string path, FileMode mode, FileAccesss access);
```

The *FileMode* enumeration argument indicates how the file should be opened. Table 10-4 describes the different *FileMode* enumeration members.

Table 10-4   Available Modes When Creating a New *FileStream*

System.IOFileStream Member	Description
Append	Opens the file and seeks to the end, creating the file if it doesn't exist. Can be used for write operations only.
Create	Creates a new file if one doesn't exist. Overwrites the file if it does exist.
CreateNew	Creates a new file. If the file already exists, an *IOException* is thrown.
Open	Opens a file. Throws a *FileNotFoundException* if the file doesn't exist.
OpenOrCreate	Opens a file if one exists; creates a new file otherwise.
Truncate	Sets the file size to 0 and opens the file for writing. Can be used for write operations only.

The *FileAccess* argument specifies whether the file should be opened for reading, writing, or both, using values from the *System.IO.FileAccess* enumeration, which consists of *Read*, *Write*, and *ReadWrite*. The following statements demonstrate how these arguments can be combined:

```
// open an existing file for reading and writing
FileStream("myfile.txt", FileMode.Open, FileAccess.ReadWrite);

// truncate an existing file
FileStream("myfile.txt", FileMode.Truncate, FileAccess.Write);

// create a new file for reading
FileStream("mynewfile.txt", FileMode.CreateNew, FileAccess.Read);
```

The most comprehensive constructor takes the following form:

```
FileStream(string path, FileMode mode, FileAccesss access,
    FileShare share, int buffer, bool async);
```

The new elements are detailed next. In between the basic and comprehensive forms are several overloaded constructors that provide defaults for certain values. These are described in Table 10-5.

Table 10-5   Available *FileStream* Constructor Arguments

Constructor Argument	Description
FileShare access	Specifies how other processes access the file that has been opened. This argument provides a mapping onto the file lock. Valid values are contained in the *System.IO.FileShare* enumeration.
int buffer	The size of the buffer for the stream.
bool async	When set to *true*, asynchronous I/O will be enabled on the stream. See the "Asynchronous I/O" section later in this chapter for details.

Creating a stream indirectly   Instances of *FileStream* can also be created indirectly via the *File* and *FileInfo* classes. Both classes provide the same range of methods for this task, the difference being that the path name for the file must be passed into the static *File* methods. These classes can also be used to create instances of *System.IO.StreamReader*, which is covered in the "Readers and Writers" section later in this chapter. Table 10-6 lists the methods available in the *File* and *FileInfo* classes.

Table 10-6   Methods in the _File_ and _FileInfo_ Classes

Method	Description
File.Open() _FileInfo.Open()_	Creates a _FileStream_ using _FileMode_ and _FileAccess_. Equivalent to using the _FileStream_ constructor.
File.OpenRead() _FileInfo.OpenRead()_	Opens a read-only stream. Equivalent to specifying the _FileMode.Open_ and _FileAccess.Read_ arguments.
File.OpenText() _FileInfo.OpenText()_ _File.AppendText()_ _FileInfo.AppendText()_ _File.CreateText()_ _FileInfo.CreateText()_	Creates a _StreamReader_. See the "Readers and Writers" section later in this chapter for a description of this class.
File.OpenWrite() _FileInfo.OpenWrite()_	Opens a write-only stream. Equivalent to using the _FileMode.Open_ and _FileAccess.Write_ arguments.

Comparison with Java

Although the class structure is different, most of the file system features from the _java.io.File_ class can be found in the _System.IO_ namespace. Table 10-7 provides the mapping between Java and the .NET classes. Where a method is listed from the _File_ and _Directory_ classes, there is typically a similar method in the _FileInfo_ and _DirectoryInfo_ classes.

Table 10-7   Comparison Between the Java and .NET File System Support Classes

Java	.NET	Comments
File(string path)	_FileInfo(path)_ _DirInfo(path)_	File system support is also provided by the static utility classes _Directory_ and _File_.
canRead()	N/A	
canWrite()	N/A	
compareTo()	N/A	
createNewFile()	_File.Create()_ _Directory.Create()_	
createTempFile()	_Path.GetTempFileName()_	
delete()	_File.Delete()_ _Directory.Delete()_	
deleteOnExit()	N/A	

Table 10-7   **Comparison Between the Java and .NET File System Support Classes**   *(continued)*

Java	.NET	Comments
exists()	*File.Exists()* *Directory.Exists()*	
getAbsolutePath() *getAbsoluteName()*	N/A	
getCanonicalPath() *getCanonicalName()*	*Path.GetFullPath()*	
getName()	*Path.GetFileName()*	
getParent()	*Path.GetDirectoryName()* *Directory.GetParent()*	
isAbsolute()	*Path.IsPathRooted()*	
isFile() *isDirectory()*	*File.Exists()* *Directory.Exists()*	See the "Differentiating Between Files and Directories" section earlier for more details.
isHidden()	*File.GetAttributes().Hidden* *Directory.GetAttributes().Hidden*	
lastModified()	*File.GetLastWriteTime()* *Directory.GetLastWriteTime()*	
length()	*FileInfo.Length*	
listFiles()	*Directory.GetFileSystemEntries()* *Directory.GetFiles()* *Directory.GetDirectories()*	
listRoots()	*Directory.GetLogicalDrives()*	
mkdir() *mkdirs()*	*Directory.CreateDirectory()*	
renameTo()	*Directory.Move()* *File.Move()*	
setLastModified()	*File.SetLastWriteTime()* *Directory.SetLastWriteTime()*	
isReadOnly()	*File.Attributes.ReadOnly*	
N/A	*File.Copy()*	Copies a file to a new location.
N/A	*File.GetAttributes()* *Directory.GetAttributes()*	Returns the set of attributes for a file or directory.
N/A	*File.SetAttributes()* *Directory.SetAttributes()*	Sets the attributes for a file or directory.

(continued)

Table 10-7 Comparison Between the Java and .NET File System Support Classes *(continued)*

Java	.NET	Comments
N/A	*File.SetCreationTime()* *File.GetCreationTime()* *File.SetLastAccessTime()* *File.GetLastAccessTime()* *Directory.SetCreationTime()* *Directory.GetCreationTime()* *Directory.SetLastAccessTime()* *Directory.GetLastAccessTime()*	Gets or sets the time that a file or directory was created or accessed.
N/A	*Directory.GetCurrentDirectory()* *Directory.SetCurrentDirectory()*	Available in Java through the *user.dir* system property.

Streams

Using streams for I/O is a familiar model for Java programmers. The .NET Framework embraces the same approach, with a number of subtle differences. The most important change is that a stream can be used for both reading and writing data, in contrast with Java, which separates these operations by using input and output streams (and readers and writers since Java version 1.1).

The .NET stream classes are fewer in number than the Java equivalents, partly because of the bidirectional support and partly because .NET doesn't offer the same range of specialized streams found in the *java.io* package. Java version 1.1 introduced the reader and writer classes, and this has further increased the number of choices for the programmer.

The Foundation of Streams

The abstract *System.IO.Stream* class is the basis for streaming in .NET. Similar to the *java.io.InputStream* and *java.io.OutputStream* classes, *System.IO.Stream* reads and writes bytes. The class also defines the methods required for asynchronous I/O.

Table 10-8 summarizes the methods of the *Stream* class. Bear in mind that stream implementations aren't required to support all methods and might throw a *NotSupportedException*. Some of the methods and properties listed have particular reference to accessing streamed data randomly. Although the Java base classes don't support these features, random access to files is available through the *java.io.RandomAccessFile* class.

Table 10-8   Comparison of .NET and Java Stream Classes

Java Streams	System.IO.Stream	Comments
InputStream.close() *OutputStream.close()*	*Close()*	
OutputStream.flush()	*Flush()*	
InputStream.read()	*Read()*	Reads a sequence of bytes.
InputStream.read()	*ReadByte()*	Reads a single byte.
OutputStream.write()	*Write()*	Writes a sequence of bytes to the stream.
OutputStream.write()	*WriteByte()*	Writes a single byte.
N/A	*CanRead*	Returns *true* if a stream can be used for reading.
N/A	*CanSeek*	Returns *true* if a stream supports seeking to a specific location.
N/A	*CanWrite*	Returns *true* if a stream can be used for writing.
N/A	*Length*	Gets the number of bytes in the stream.
N/A	*Position*	Gets the current seek position within the stream.
N/A	*BeginRead()* *EndRead()* *BeginWrite()* *EndWrite()*	Provide support for asynchronous I/O, detailed later in this chapter in "Asynchronous I/O."
N/A	*Seek()*	Indirectly available in Java through the *mark*, *reset*, and *skip* methods in *InputStream*.

The *Stream* class also defines the static property *Null*, which is an analog of the */dev/null* UNIX device. The result of getting this property is a stream in which calls to a read method will return without any data, and data written to this stream will be quietly discarded.

Base Streams

Streams representing a backing store are known as base streams. Examples of backing stores include a disk file, memory, and a network connection. Base stream classes have constructors that are used to configure the relationship between the backing store and the data stream; for example, the *FileStream* classes detailed earlier in this chapter accept constructor arguments that specify which file should be opened and which file modes will be used.

Three base stream classes are included in the .NET Framework, providing support for backing stores based on files, network connections, and bytes held in memory. These classes, and their Java counterparts, are described in Table 10-9.

Table 10-9   **Comparison of the Base Stream Classes Provided by Java and .NET**

Java	.NET	Backing Store
FileInputStream *FileOutputStream*	*System.IO.FileStream*	Disk file
ByteArrayInputStream *ByteArrayOutputStream*	*System.IO.MemoryStream*	Array of bytes held in memory
N/A	*System.Net.Sockets.NetworkStream*	Network connection

The Java *java.net.Socket* class exposes streams backed by network connections using the basic *InputStream* and *OutputStream* classes. In .NET, instances of network streams can be created using a *System.Net.Sockets.Socket* as a constructor argument but are more typically obtained indirectly through the *Socket* instance.

> **More Info**   See Chapter 14, "Networking," for more information about using sockets.

Creating instances of the *FileStream* class is discussed in the preceding section of this chapter, leaving only the *MemoryStream* class. The following example demonstrates a simple use of this class:

```
MemoryStream x_write_stream = new MemoryStream();
x_write_stream.WriteByte((byte)'.');
x_write_stream.WriteByte((byte)'N');
x_write_stream.WriteByte((byte)'E');
x_write_stream.WriteByte((byte)'T');
Console.WriteLine(Encoding.Default.GetString(x_write_stream.ToArray()));
```

The example creates a *MemoryStream* instance with the default constructor, which creates a stream with no initial stream data and no initial capacity. The overloaded constructor *MemoryStream(int)* creates a new instance with the specified capacity. The capacity refers to the size of the array in which byte information will be stored. When data is written to streams created with these constructors, the underlying array will be resized as needed to accommodate new bytes. The example writes 4 bytes into the stream and then uses the *ToArray* method to extract the data from the class and writes the contents to the console, using the *Encoding* class, which converts *byte* arrays to strings.

The next example demonstrates how to create a stream with initial data:

```
MemoryStream x_read_stream
    = new MemoryStream(Encoding.Default.GetBytes("Java"));

int x_byte;
while ((x_byte = x_read_stream.ReadByte()) != -1) {
    Console.Write((char)x_byte);
}
```

The stream is created with an array of bytes representing the word *Java*. Then each byte is read from the stream and written to the console. Instances of *MemoryStream* created with initial data do not resize the underlying array, and attempting to append more data will result in an exception. However, it's possible to create a fixed-size stream that allows the array contents to be changed (where the *CanWrite* property returns *true*) by using different constructor forms. The following example demonstrates how this can be done:

```
byte[] x_initial_content = Encoding.Default.GetBytes("Java");
MemoryStream x_stream = new MemoryStream(x_initial_content, true);

byte[] x_new_content = Encoding.Default.GetBytes(".NET");
foreach (byte x_byte in x_new_content) {
    x_stream.WriteByte(x_byte);
}
        Console.WriteLine(Encoding.Default.GetString(x_stream.ToArray()));
```

The *MemoryStream* is created using the *byte* array representing the word *Java*. The second argument in the constructor indicates that the stream should allow write operations. A series of write operations alters the content of the stream, replacing *Java* with *.NET*. Finally the contents of the stream are written to the console.

Pass-Through Streams

Stream implementations that are backed by another stream are known as *pass-through* streams and take instances of *System.IO.Stream* as constructor arguments. Pass-though streams can transform data that is read or written or provide some additional functionality to the programmer. Several pass-though streams can be chained to combine specialized functionality for a base stream.

The *java.io* package contains several examples of pass-through streams, including *LineNumberInputStream* (which keeps track of line numbers) and *PushbackInputStream* (which provides the ability to push back or un-read a single *byte* of data). Java pass-through streams are derived from either *FilterInputStream* or *FilterOutputStream*. By contrast, the .NET *System.IO* namespace contains only one pass-though stream, *BufferedStream*, which buffers read and write operations.

The *BufferedStream* class is equivalent to the *java.io.BufferedInputStream* and *java.io.BufferedOutputStream* classes (because .NET streams can be used for reading and writing). The default constructor accepts an instance of *System.IO.Stream* to buffer against and will create a default buffer of 4096 bytes; a different buffer size can be specified as an integer argument.

> **Tip**   The *System.IO.FileStream* class is already buffered and doesn't benefit from being used with *BufferedStream*. The *System.Net.Sockets.NetworkStream* class isn't buffered.

Readers and Writers

The .NET reader and writer classes are functionally similar to those in Java. The Java classes were introduced to provide character-based streams to better support internationalization, and implementations include both base and pass-through streams. The .NET reader and writer classes are also character oriented but can't be used as pass-through streams. No base classes exist for the .NET readers and writers; each implementation stands alone, meaning that the programmer can't cast to a single abstract type. The classes described in this section most closely resemble the Java I/O model, implementing a division of responsibility between reading and writing data.

BinaryReader and BinaryWriter

The *BinaryReader* and *BinaryWriter* classes read and write primitive data types and strings to a stream as binary data; however, they are not able to serialize object graphs. The following example demonstrates writing a series of integers, from 0 to 9, to a *MemoryStream* using a *BinaryWriter* and then using a *Binary-Reader* to read the data back and write it to the console, one integer per line.

```
MemoryStream x_stream = new MemoryStream();

BinaryWriter x_writer = new BinaryWriter(x_stream);
for (int i = 0; i < 10; i++) {
    x_writer.Write(i);
}

x_stream.Seek(0, SeekOrigin.Begin);

BinaryReader x_reader = new BinaryReader(x_stream);
for (int i = 0; i < 10; i++) {
    int x_result = x_reader.ReadInt32();
    Console.WriteLine(x_result);
}
```

TextReader and TextWriter

The abstract *TextReader* and *TextWriter* classes are responsible for providing character-based I/O. The members provided by these classes are listed in Table 10-10.

Table 10-10   **The *TextReader* and *TextWriter* Classes**

Member	Description
TextReader.Null	Provides a *TextReader* with no data to read.
TextWriter.Null	Provides a *TextWriter* that acts as a data sink.
TextReader.Close() *TextWriter.Close()*	Closes the reader or writer.
TextReader.Peek()	Returns the next character that will be returned with a *Read* method call.
TextReader.Read()	Reads either a single character or an array of characters.
TextReader.ReadBlock()	Performs a blocking read operation to obtain a specified number of characters.
TextReader.ReadLine()	Reads a line of text, returned as a string.

(continued)

Table 10-10 **The *TextReader* and *TextWriter* Classes** *(continued)*

Member	Description
TextReader.ReadToEnd()	Reads all of the characters from the current position to the end of the reader, returned as a string.
TextReader.Synchronized *TextWriter.Synchronized*	Creates a thread-safe wrapper around the reader or writer.
TextWriter.Encoding	Returns the *Encoding* that is used to write character data.
TextWriter.FormatProvider	Returns the object used to control formatting. See Chapter 7 for more information on formatting.
TextWriter.NewLine	Gets or sets the line separator string.
TextWriter.Flush()	Flushes any buffered data.
TextWriter.Write()	Writes a range of types, including primitives and strings. Although there is an overloaded form that accepts an object argument, the object isn't serialized. The data written is the result of calling *ToString* on the argument value.
TextWriter.WriteLine()	Writes a range of types, including primitives and strings, followed by the line terminator string.

These classes provide the basis for character-oriented I/O, and the .NET Framework contains two sets of implementation classes, detailed in the following sections.

StreamReader and StreamWriter   The *StreamReader* and *StreamWriter* classes implement the functionality of the *TextReader* and *TextWriter* classes against streams, making character-based I/O available for all of the base stream types. As a convenience, overloaded constructors for these classes will accept file paths for input or output, allowing the programmer to use character I/O without having to explicitly create instances of *FileStream*. The following example demonstrates a simple use of these classes, following the model of the preceding example.

```
MemoryStream x_stream = new MemoryStream();

StreamWriter x_writer = new StreamWriter(x_stream);

x_writer.WriteLine("C# for Java Developers");
x_writer.Flush();

x_stream.Seek(0, SeekOrigin.Begin);

StreamReader x_reader = new StreamReader(x_stream);
Console.WriteLine(x_reader.ReadLine());
```

StringReader* and *StringWriter   The *StringReader* and *StringWriter* classes use strings held in memory as the backing store. The *StringReader* class takes a string as the constructor argument, and calls to *Read* return characters sequentially from the string. The *StringWriter* class uses an instance of *System.Text.StringBuilder* to store characters processed using the *Write* method. The contents of the string are available through the *ToString* method. These classes represent character-based implementation of the broad functionality provided by the *System.IO.MemoryStream* class.

Synchronizing Streams

The .NET stream classes do not provide synchronization support for instance members; the programmer must assume the responsibility for ensuring safe access to stream instances. Members that are *public* and *static* are guaranteed to be safe.

Streams Summary

Although the .NET stream classes are few in number, they manage to provide the majority of the features available in Java. Some of the specialized streams and readers are missing, but the ability of the same *stream* instance to both read and write data belies the sparse appearance of the class set. The implementation of the reader and writer classes seems out of keeping with the slick design of the stream classes, and the lack of a common base class leads to a lack of abstraction. The mixed model of defining classes that are both base and pass-through implementations is far from ideal.

Asynchronous I/O

The preceding section was concerned with using streams to perform synchronous I/O operations, in which a call to a read or write method blocks until the operation completes. This section discusses the .NET support for asynchronous I/O, which allows read and write operations to be performed without blocking. Version 1.4 of the Java platform includes support for asynchronous, or non-blocking, I/O, but the .NET model differs so much that we see little benefit in providing a comparison.

Asynchronous I/O is byte-oriented, not character-oriented. All classes derived from *System.IO.Stream* can be used in asynchronous I/O. Importantly, none of the reader and writer classes detailed in the preceding section can be used. To demonstrate asynchronous I/O, we'll concentrate on using the

FileStream class. Since all streams can be used for asynchronous I/O, the model laid out in this section can be applied to any of the stream classes.

At the heart of all asynchronous operations is the *System.AsyncCallback* delegate, which will be invoked when an asynchronous operation has completed. The signature for this delegate is a method that accepts an instance of *System.IAsyncResult* and returns *void*. The following example demonstrates reading an English transcript of the *Magna Carta* using asynchronous calls:

```
using System;
using System.IO;
using System.Text;
using System.Threading;

namespace MagnaCarta {

    class MagnaCartaDemo {
        private byte[] o_byte_arr;
        private FileStream o_stream;
        private AsyncCallback o_callback;

        MagnaCartaDemo() {
            o_byte_arr = new byte[100];
            o_stream = new FileStream("magnacarta.txt",
                FileMode.Open, FileAccess.Read,
                FileShare.Read, 100, true);

            o_callback = new AsyncCallback(readFinished);

            o_stream.BeginRead(o_byte_arr, 0,
                o_byte_arr.Length, o_callback, null);

            Console.WriteLine(">>>> Current thread is " +
                "not blocking!");
        }

        private void readFinished(IAsyncResult p_result) {
            int x_bytes_read = o_stream.EndRead(p_result);
            if (x_bytes_read > 0) {
                Console.Write(Encoding.Default.GetString(
                    o_byte_arr,
                    0,
                    x_bytes_read));

                o_stream.BeginRead(o_byte_arr, 0,
                    o_byte_arr.Length, o_callback,
                    null);
            } else {
```

```
        o_stream.Close();
    }
}
public static void Main() {
    new MagnaCartaDemo() ;
}
```

In the class constructor, we define a byte array that will be used to read data from the stream; since we are dealing with *FileStream*, we are limited to byte, rather than character, operations. The next step is to create the stream that will be used to read from the file. Notice that we use the constructor form, which explicitly enables asynchronous operations.

> **Warning**   It's important to specify that the *FileStream* should allow asynchronous operations in the constructor. If the default method of invoking the constructor is used, the *BeginRead* and *BeginWrite* methods will still function but will be working synchronously.

We then create the callback delegate and call the *BeginRead* method to start the asynchronous read. The *BeginRead* method accepts a *byte* array, offsets and lengths to store data in the array, the *delegate* that should be called when an operation is complete, and an *object* that the programmer can use to differentiate between I/O operations. Since we are working with only one file in this example, we have set the reference object to *null*. The remaining statement in the class constructor prints out a message indicating that the current thread isn't blocking on the I/O operations.

After calling the *BeginRead* method, the current thread is free to do other things. When a read operation is complete, the method specified by *delegate* (*readFinished* in the example) will be called. In this method, we need to call *EndRead* to find out how many bytes have been read. If the number of bytes is 0, we have reached the end of the stream, and we close the *FileStream* instance. If there are bytes to be processed, we translate them into a string and write the result to the console. In order to continue reading from the file, we need to invoke *BeginRead* after each delegate callback until no bytes remain. Because the *BeginRead* method needs to be called repeatedly, it's important to keep a local reference to the *delegate* and the data array. Creating an instance of this class leads to the following output:

```
>>>> Current thread is not blocking!
Magna Carta

A translation of Magna Carta as confirmed by Edward I with his seal in
  1297

[Preamble] EDWARD by the grace of God, King of England, Lord of Irelan
d, and Duke of Guyan, to all Archbishops, Bishops, etc. We have seen t
he Great Charter of the Lord HENRY, sometimes King of England, our fat
her, of the Liberties of England, in these words: Henry by the grace o
f God, King of England, Lord of Ireland, Duke of…
```

We have trimmed the output for brevity. The important part to note is that the message appears before the document text. If the stream had not been opened for asynchronous operations, this message would have appeared at the end of the output, indicating that the thread is, contrary to the message, blocking after all.

Asynchronous I/O Summary

The .NET model for asynchronous operations is simple to use and can provide significant performance improvements over synchronous I/O. The callback delegate is used in various places in the .NET Framework, including the networking classes, and once you've mastered asynchronous I/O, it's a simple matter to apply the knowledge to perform asynchronous network operations. The limitation of asynchronous I/O is that the character-based support of the reader and writer classes is not available.

Isolated Storage

Isolated storage allows applications to store data on a per-user basis in a safe and consistent way. The .NET Framework uniquely identifies applications or assemblies and uses this identity to create a directory where the application can safely write data.

> **Caution**   Isolated storage is not suitable for storing secure or confidential data. The .NET Framework enforces isolation for managed code, but unmanaged code and code with high system trust are able to access the files in the store.

The isolated storage mechanism is the cross-platform equivalent of storing data in the Windows registry. The programmer doesn't have to be aware of the identity of the current user or the details of where application data will be stored. This section explores the *System.IO.IsolatedStorage* namespace and explains how the .NET Framework can help the programmer isolate data easily.

Obtaining and Managing the Isolated Stores

At the heart of this isolated stores mechanism is the misleadingly named *IsolatedStorageFile* class. Rather than representing a file, this class represents the storage area that contains files and directories. This class can be used to manage the contents of the storage area and to obtain different levels of isolation.

The static factory method *IsolatedStorageFile.GetStore* is used to obtain instances of the *IsolatedStorageFile* class. As a parameter, this method takes a bit mask, which defines the level of isolation required. Valid values are members of the *IsolatedStorageScope* enumeration. These include the values described in Table 10-11.

Table 10-11   Valid Values in the *IsolatedStorageScope* Enumeration

Isolation Level	Description
IsolatedStorageScope.Assembly	Isolation is scoped to the identity of the assembly. If multiple applications share the same assembly, all applications will be able to access the data in the isolated store.
IsolatedStorageScope.Domain	Isolation is scoped to the identity of the application domain. Multiple applications that share the same assembly will each access different isolated stores.
IsolatedStorageScope.None	No isolated storage. Currently not used.
IsolatedStorageScope.Roaming	The isolated storage can be placed in a location that will be available to roaming users.
IsolatedStorageScope.User	Isolation is scoped by the identity of the user.

The permutations accepted by *GetStore* are as follows:

- *User | Assembly*
- *User | Assembly | Domain*
- *Roaming | User | Assembly*
- *Roaming | User | Assembly | Domain*

In practice, it's much easier to obtain an *IsolatedStorageFile* instance by using one of the two static factory methods included in the class than to use the *GetStore* method. The following statements demonstrate how to easily obtain stores isolated by assembly and by application domain:

```
// Obtain store isolated by assembly
IsolatedStorageFile x_assembly_iso =
    IsolatedStorageFile.GetUserStoreForAssembly();

// Obtain store isolated by application domain
IsolatedStorageFile x_domain_iso   =
    IsolatedStorageFile.GetUserStoreForDomain();
```

Once obtained, *IsolatedStorageFile* can be used to manage the contents of the store, and the programmer can create and delete directories, delete files, and enumerate the contents. Creating files and obtaining content from them is discussed in the next section. The members of the *IsolatedStorageFile* class are listed in Table 10-12.

Table 10-12 The *IsolatedStorageFile* .NET Class

Member	Description
AssemblyIdentity	Gets an assembly identity that is used to set the scope for isolation.
DomainIdentity	Gets an application domain identity that is used to set the scope for isolation.
CurrentSize	The number of bytes of data in the store. Administrators can define quotas for storage.
MaximumSize	The maximum number of bytes that can be written to the store.
Scope	The scope of the store.
Close()	Closes a store.
CreateDirectory()	Creates a new directory within the store.
DeleteDirectory()	Deletes a directory within the store.
DeleteFile()	Deletes a file from the store.
GetDirectoryNames()	Enumerates the directories in the store that match a specified search pattern.
GetFileNames()	Enumerates the files in the store that match a specified search pattern.
GetStore()	Obtains an *IsolatedStorageFile* based on the specified scope.
GetUserStoreForAssembly()	Obtains an *IsolatedStorageFile* that is isolated by assembly.

Table 10-12   **The *IsolatedStorageFile* .NET Class**   *(continued)*

Member	Description
GetUserStoreForDomain()	Obtains an *IsolatedStorageFile* that is isolated by application domain.
Remove()	Removes the storage area and all contents.

Reading and Writing Isolated Data

The *IsolatedStorageFileStream* class is used to read and write isolated data. This class is derived from *System.IO.FileStream* and is the only mechanism available to stream isolated data. With the exception of the constructors, the members of this class are the same as those of *FileStream*. Where the constructor signature matches one of the *FileStream* members, the specified file will be opened in a store that is isolated by application domain.

Additional constructors are provided that allow the programmer to specify a store (which may have a different level of isolation) obtained through the *IsolatedStorageFile.GetStore* method or one of the factory methods in the same class.

All path names used in the constructor are relative to the root of the isolated storage area. The following example demonstrates using the *IsolatedStorageFileStream* class to create a new file, write out some simple data, and then read it back in. Because the *IsolatedStorageFileStream* inherits from *FileStream*, asynchronous I/O is supported and reader and writer classes can be used for synchronous operations.

Executing these statements leads to the string "*C# for Java Developers*" being displayed on the console. However, we also have an isolated storage area that contains a single file, named *sample.txt*. Because we didn't specify an isolation store to use in the stream constructor, the default will ensure that the data is isolated for the application domain.

```
using System;
using System.IO;
using System.IO.IsolatedStorage;

public class IsolatedDemo {

public IsolatedDemo() {
        // create the file
        IsolatedStorageFileStream x_stream =
            new IsolatedStorageFileStream("sample.txt",
            FileMode.Create);
        StreamWriter x_writer = new StreamWriter(x_stream);
```

(continued)

```
        // write the data
        x_writer.WriteLine("C# for Java Developers");
        x_writer.Close();

        // read the data back in
        x_stream = new IsolatedStorageFileStream("sample.txt",
            FileMode.Open);
        StreamReader x_reader = new StreamReader(x_stream);
        Console.WriteLine(x_reader.ReadLine());
        x_reader.Close();
    }
}
```

Isolated Storage Summary

Isolated storage is a simple mechanism that allows programmers to store data on a per-user basis. Where possible, users should use isolated storage in preference to using the Windows registry or attempting to manage a directory hierarchy manually. While not suitable for storing secure or confidential data, the isolated storage mechanism is incredibly useful and allows assemblies that have low security requirements to store data persistently.

Object Serialization

Object serialization is the process of rendering an object into a state that can be stored persistently. The Java platform has included serialization support since version 1.1, and while there have been additional enhancements, the model has proved sufficiently flexible to meet the needs of most developers.

In .NET, the way in which serialized data is stored is controlled by formatters, which are classes that implement the *System.Runtime.Serialization.IFormatter* interface. Two implementations are available in the .NET Framework:

- *System.Runtime.Serialization.Formatters.Binary.BinaryFormatter*

- *System.Runtime.Serialization.Formatters.Soap.SoapFormatter*

The *BinaryFormatter* produces a compact and efficient binary representation of the state of an object. The *SoapFormatter* produces an XML SOAP document that can be parsed like any other XML document. Both formatters accept an instance of *System.IO.Stream* to read from or write to and so can be used to serialize to a range of backing stores, including files and network connections.

Simple Serialization

Java classes are not serializable by default and are required to implement the *java.io.Serializable* interface before they can be persisted. .NET classes require annotation with the *Serializable* attribute before they can be processed by the formatter.

The following class demonstrates the use of this attribute:

```
[Serializable]
class SimpleClass {
    private int o_int;
    private string o_string;

    public int SimpleInt {
        get {
            return o_int;
        }
        set {
            o_int = value;
        }
    }

    public String SimpleString {
        get {
            return o_string;
        }
        set {
            o_string = value;
        }
    }
}
```

This class maintains two private members, which are accessible via public properties. Because the class is annotated, it can be serialized and restored as shown next. We use these statements to serialize all of the example classes in this section:

```
using System;
using System.IO ;
using System.Runtime.Serialization ;
using System.Runtime.Serialization.Formatters.Binary ;

class Test {
    public static void Main() {
        SimpleClass x_simple = new SimpleClass();
        x_simple.SimpleInt = 20172;
        x_simple.SimpleString = "C# for Java Developers";
```

(continued)

```
        FileStream x_stream = new FileStream("serial.bin",
            FileMode.OpenOrCreate, FileAccess.Write);

        IFormatter x_formatter = new BinaryFormatter();
        x_formatter.Serialize(x_stream, x_simple);
        x_stream.Close();

        FileStream x_in_stream = new FileStream("serial.bin",
            FileMode.Open, FileAccess.Read);
        x_simple = (SimpleClass)x_formatter.Deserialize(x_in_stream);
        x_in_stream.Close();

        Console.WriteLine("String value: " + x_simple.SimpleString);
        Console.WriteLine("Int value: " + x_simple.SimpleInt);
    }
}
```

We start by creating an instance of the serializable class, named *Simple-Class*, and set the values for the private variables. We then create a *FileStream* that will be used to store the serialized data, followed by a *BinaryFormatter*. The formatter is created with this statement:

```
IFormatter x_formatter = new BinaryFormatter();
```

Alternatively, if we wanted a *SoapFormatter*, the syntax would be

```
IFormatter x_formatter = new SoapFormatter();
```

Finally we call the *IFormatter.Serialize* method, passing in the stream and the object to persist.

Restoring the object is just as easy. We create a new *FileStream* that will read from the file that we created and then call the *IFormatter.Deserialize* method passing in the stream. In common with the Java serialization support, the *Deserialize* method returns an *object*, which must be cast to *SimpleClass* before we can print the values of the *int* and *string* members.

This example demonstrates the basic serialization of an object. The following sections illustrate how the programmer can exert more control over the serialization process and select which elements should be persisted.

Selective Serialization

In the preceding section, both the *int* and *string* fields were serialized. .NET provides support for selecting fields to be omitted from the persistent data. Fields marked with the *NonSerialized* attribute will not be persisted.

The following code fragment demonstrates the use of this attribute to indicate that the *int* field should not be serialized for the *SimpleClass* type:

```
[Serializable]
class SimpleClass {

[NonSerialized] private int o_int;
private string o_string;
```

Using the formatter as shown results in the following output:

```
String value: C# for Java Developers
Int value: 0
```

When the instance is restored from the file, there is no persisted value for *o_int*, so the default value (0) is displayed.

Custom Serialization

By implementing the *System.Runtime.Serialization.ISerializable* interface, a developer can manually control which fields a class serializes. This is the functional equivalent of *java.io.Externalizable*, allowing the programmer to take responsibility for the serialization process.

The *ISerializable* interface contains a single method, *GetObjectData*, which is called when the object is written to a formatter. Classes that implement the interface must also provide a constructor that accepts the same arguments as the *GetObjectData* method. Note that types that implement *ISerializable* must still be annotated with the *Serializable* attribute. Here is *SimpleClass*, modified to implement the interface and the constructor:

```
[Serializable]
class SimpleClass : ISerializable {
    private int o_int;
    private string o_string;

    public SimpleClass() {
    }

    protected SimpleClass(SerializationInfo p_info,
        StreamingContext p_context) {
```

(continued)

```
            o_int = p_info.GetInt32("int");
            o_string = p_info.GetString("string");
        }

    public int SimpleInt {
        get {
            return o_int;
        }
        set {
            o_int = value;
        }
    }

    public String SimpleString {
        get {
            return o_string;
        }
        set {
            o_string = value;
        }
    }

    public virtual void GetObjectData(SerializationInfo p_info,
        StreamingContext p_context) {

        p_info.AddValue("int", o_int);
        p_info.AddValue("string", o_string);
    }
}
```

The changes appear in boldface, the first being a default constructor, required because we have added the protected form for the *ISerializable* support. The *GetObjectData* method takes two arguments, a *SerializationInfo* and a *StreamingContext*.

The *StreamingContext* represents the scope of the serialized data. When either a *BinaryFormatter* or a *SoapFormatter* is created, it's possible to specify a value from the *StreamingContext* enumeration, which will be made available as the argument to *GetObjectData*. The default context state is *All*, indicating that the data can be transmitted to any other context or application domain. Setting different values for this scope allows the programmer to selectively serialize data based on where it will be used—for example, omitting fields when the data will cross to another process but ensuring that all fields are serialized when the object is persisted to a local file.

The *SerializationInfo* type is used to serialize and restore fields. In the example *GetObjectData* method, we use the *AddValue* method to store an integer and a string. Overloaded forms of this method accept all primitive data types and all objects, which will in turn be serialized. Each value added with *AddValue* is stored as a key/value pair, and the programmer is able to specify any string as the key. These keys are then used in the special constructor to retrieve the values and restore the object state.

> **Important**   Classes that are derived from types that implement *ISeri-alizable* must implement the *GetObjectData* and the special construc-tor and must ensure that the base versions of these members are invoked.

Summary

The model of using streams for I/O is well understood, and the .NET imple-mentation doesn't differ much from the Java approach. Although the C# exam-ples may look different, the underlying mechanisms are the same, and the Java programmer has little to adjust to. In other areas, the differences are more apparent, and this is especially clear with object serialization. The deep integra-tion of attributes in .NET is evident and is far removed from the Java approach of interface implementation. Overall, the Java programmer should adapt to the .NET I/O classes quickly and find the majority of functionality available, albeit in a slightly different manner.

11

XML Processing

There are many third-party Java tools for the direct manipulation of XML. In addition, many new Java APIs are currently in early release as part of the Java Community Process. However, Java version 1.4 includes only basic XML processing features, providing support for the Document Object Model (DOM), Simple API for XML (SAX), and Extensible Stylesheet Language Transformations (XSLT) standards, detailed in Table 11-1.

Table 11-1 The Three XML Standards Supported by Java

Standard	Description
Document Object Model Level 2	A standardized interface for accessing and updating XML documents as a hierarchical tree of nodes. See *www.w3.org/DOM/* for details.
Simple API for XML 2.0	An event-driven interface for the efficient parsing of XML documents. See *www.saxproject.org/* for details.
XSL Transformations 1.0	A language for transforming XML documents into other XML documents. See *www.w3.org/Style/XSL/* for details.

This chapter explores the Microsoft .NET XML processing features that are comparable to those provided by Java version 1.4. We will also discuss features for which Java version 1.4 provides no equivalent, including support for XPath, and a mechanism that simplifies the writing of well-formed XML documents. Throughout this chapter, we assume the reader has knowledge of XML and related technologies.

In addition to explicit manipulation, the designers of .NET have factored implicit XML support into many aspects of the .NET Framework. Table 11-2 highlights the extent of XML integration within the .NET Framework and includes references to relevant chapters.

Table 11-2 XML Integration into .NET

Feature	Usage	Reference
Serialization	Objects can be serialized as Simple Object Access Protocol (SOAP) messages using a *SoapFormatter*.	Chapter 10, "Streams, Files, and I/O"
ADO.NET	Communication with SQL databases, database schema, XPath queries on data sets.	Chapter 16, "Database Connectivity"
Remoting	*HttpChannels* transmit data encoded as SOAP messages.	Chapter 15, "Remoting"
XML Web services	SOAP, Web Service Definition Language (WSDL), Universal Description, Discovery, and Integration (UDDI).	Chapter 19, "Introduction to XML Web Services"
Configuration files	Configuration files affecting many parts of the .NET Framework are specified using XML.	Appendix C, "Configuring Applications"

XmlNameTable

One of the most frequent tasks when parsing XML is comparing strings; comparing the contents of strings is significantly more expensive than comparing object references. The .NET XML classes such as *XmlDocument*, *XmlReader*, and *XPathNavigator*—all discussed later in this chapter—use the *System.Xml.NameTable* class—derived from *System.Xml.XmlNameTable*—to reduce the overhead of repeatedly comparing string values.

The *NameTable* class maintains a table of strings stored as objects. As strings are parsed from an XML document, the parser calls the *NameTable.Add* method. *Add* takes a *String* or *char* array, places it in the *string* table, and returns a reference to the contained *object*; if the *string* already exists, on subsequent calls the previously created *object* reference is returned. String values added to the *NameTable* are referred to as *atomized* strings.

The *NameTable.Get* method returns a reference to an atomized string based on the *String* or *char* array argument provided; *null* is returned if the string has not been atomized.

Classes such as *XmlDocument* and *XmlReader* provide a *NameTable* property that returns a reference to the internal *NameTable*. The programmer can use an existing *NameTable* instance in the constructor of other XML classes. A populated *NameTable* can be used to prime a new XML class and improve efficiency where element and attribute commonality exists across XML documents.

XmlReader

The .NET Framework does not provide a SAX parser implementation. While the SAX API is the de facto standard for event-driven XML processing in Java, Microsoft has chosen a fundamentally different approach for .NET.

As a SAX parser processes XML input, application callbacks are used to signal events such as the start or end of an XML element; this approach is considered a *push* model.

The .NET approach, based on the abstract *System.Xml.XmlReader* class, provides a *pull* model, wherein the application invokes *XmlReader* members to control how and when the parser progresses through the XML document. This is analogous to a forward-only cursor that provides read-only access to the XML source. As with SAX, *XmlReader* is a noncaching parser.

The .NET Framework provides three concrete implementations of the *XmlReader* class: *XmlTextReader*, *XmlValidatingReader*, and *XmlNodeReader*. All classes are members of the *System.Xml* namespace.

XmlTextReader

The *XmlTextReader* class provides the most direct .NET alternative to a Java nonvalidating *SAXParser*. The *XmlTextReader* ensures that an XML document is well formed but will not perform validation against a DTD or an XML schema.

The *XmlTextReader* is a concrete implementation of the abstract *XmlReader* class but also provides a number of nonoverridden members, which we highlight as they are discussed.

Opening an XML Source

The *XmlTextReader* class provides a set of overloaded constructors offering flexibility for specifying the source of the XML document to be parsed. For example, the following statement creates a new *XmlTextReader* using the SomeXmlFile.xml file located in the assembly directory as a source:

```
XmlTextReader xmlReader = new XmlTextReader("SomeXmlFile.xml");
```

Alternatively, if the XML data were contained in a *String* variable named *SomeXml*, we could use a *StringReader* as the *XmlTextReader* source, as in the following example:

```
XmlTextReader xmlReader = new XmlTextReader(new StringReader(SomeXml));
```

The principal *XmlTextReader* constructors are summarized in Table 11-3.

Table 11-3   The Principal *XmlTextReader* Constructors

Constructor	Comment
XmlTextReader(Stream)	Creates an *XmlTextReader* pulling XML from a *System.IO.Stream* derivative such as *FileStream, MemoryStream,* or *NetworkStream.* Streams are discussed in Chapter 10.
XmlTextReader(String)	Creates an *XmlTextReader* pulling XML from a file with the specified URL.
XmlTextReader(TextReader)	Creates an *XmlTextReader* pulling XML from a *System.IO.TextReader* such as *StreamReader* or *StringReader.* Readers are discussed in Chapter 10.

Following creation, the *XmlTextReader* cursor is positioned before the first XML node in the source.

XmlTextReader Properties

The *XmlTextReader* class exposes properties that both control the behavior of the reader and give the programmer access to the state of the reader; these properties are discussed in the following sections.

Reader state   The *XmlTextReader.ReadState* property provides read-only access to the current state of the *XmlTextReader.* Upon creation, the *XmlTextReader* has a state of *Initial.* The state changes to *Interactive* once read operations are performed. The *XmlTextReader* will maintain an *Interactive* state until the end of the input file is reached or an error occurs. The *ReadState* property returns one of the following values from the *System.Xml.ReadState* enumeration, listed in Table 11-4.

Table 11-4   The *System.Xml.ReadState* Enumeration

Value	Comment
Closed	The *XmlTextReader* has been closed using the *Close* method.
EndOfFile	The end of the input source has been reached. This state can also be tested using the *XmlTextReader.EOF* property.
Error	An error has occurred that prevents further read operations.
Initial	The *XmlTextReader* has been created, but no read operations have been called.
Interactive	Read operations have been called at least once, and further read operations can be attempted.

If a source stream contains more than one XML document, the *ResetState* method must be used to reinitialize the *XmlTextReader* prior to parsing the second and subsequent documents; the *ResetState* method sets the *ReadState* property to *ReadState.Initialized*.

Controlling parsing behavior   The *XmlTextReader* has a number of properties that control the way XML files are parsed. Table 11-5 summarizes these properties.

Table 11-5   The *XmlTextReader* Properties

Property	Comments
Namespaces	Controls whether the *XmlTextReader* supports namespaces in accordance with the W3C "Namespaces in XML" recommendation. The default value is *true*.
WhitespaceHandling	Controls how the *XmlTextReader* handles white space. The property must be set to a value of the *System.Xml.WhitespaceHandling* enumeration. Valid values are
	■ *All*—returns *Whitespace* and *SignificantWhitespace* nodes.
	■ *None*—returns no *Whitespace* or *SignificantWhitespace* nodes.
	■ *Significant*—returns *SignificantWhitespace* nodes only.
	The *Whitespace* and *SignificantWhitespace* node types are described later in the "Working with XML Nodes" section. The default value is *All*. Not inherited from *XmlReader*.
Normalization	Controls whether the *XmlTextReader* normalizes white space and attribute values in accordance with the "Attribute-Value Normalization" section of the W3C XML 1.0 specification.
	The default value is *false*.
	Not inherited from *XmlReader*.
XmlResolver	Controls the *System.Xml.XmlResolver* to use for resolving DTD references. By default, an instance of the *System.Xml.XmlUrlResolver* is used.
	Not inherited from *XmlReader*.

The *Namespaces* property must be set before the first read operation (when the *ReadState* property is *ReadState.Initial*), or an *InvalidOperationException* will be thrown; the other properties can be set at any time while the *XmlTextReader* is not in a *ReadState.Closed* state and will affect future read operations.

Working with XML Nodes

The XML source represents a hierarchy of nodes that the *XmlTextReader* retrieves sequentially. Progress through the XML is analogous to the use of a cursor that moves through the XML nodes. The node currently under the cursor is the *current node*.

The *XmlTextReader* exposes information about the current node through the properties of the *XmlTextReader* instance, although not all properties apply to all node types.

Node types   As the *XmlTextReader* reads a node, it identifies the node type. Each node type is assigned a value from the *System.Xml.XmlNodeType* enumeration. The *XmlTextReader.NodeType* property returns the type of the current node.

The node types include those defined in the W3C "DOM Level 1 Core" specification and five nonstandard extension types added by Microsoft. Node type values that can be returned by *XmlTextReader.NodeType* include the following—those that are not defined in DOM are italicized: Attribute, CDATA, Comment, DocumentType, Element, *EndElement*, EntityReference, *None*, ProcessingInstructions, *SignificantWhitespace*, Text, *Whitespace*, and *XmlDeclaration*. The additional node types defined by Microsoft are summarized in Table 11-6.

Table 11-6   The Microsoft-Specific Node Types

XmlNodeType	Description
None	Indicates that there is no current node. Either no read operations have been executed or the end of the XML input has been reached.
EndElement	Represents the end tag of an XML element—for example, *</book>*.
SignificantWhitespace	Represents white space between markup in a mixed content mode or white space within an *xml:space= 'preserve'* scope.
Whitespace	Represents white space in the content of an element.
XmlDeclaration	Represents the declaration node *<?xml version="1.0"...>*.

Node names   The *Name* and *LocalName* properties of the *XmlTextReader* return names of the current node. The *Name* property returns the qualified node name, including any namespace prefix. The *LocalName* property returns the node name with any namespace prefix stripped off. The name returned by the *Name* and *LocalName* properties depends on the current node type, summarized by the following list:

- **Attribute**   The name of the attribute
- **DocumentType**   The document type name
- **Element**   The tag name
- **EntityReference**   The entity reference name
- **ProcessingInstruction**   The processing instruction target
- **XmlDeclaration**   The string literal *xml*
- **Other node types**   *String.Empty*

The *XmlTextReader.Prefix* property returns the namespace prefix of the current node, or *String.Empty* if it doesn't have one.

Node values and contents   The *XmlTextReader.Value* property returns the text value of the current node. The value of a node depends on the node type and is summarized in the following list:

- **Attribute**   The value of the attribute
- **CDATA**   The content of the CDATA section
- **Comment**   The content of the comment
- **DocumentType**   The internal subset
- **SignificantWhitespace**   The white space within an *xml:space='preserve'* scope
- **Text**   The content of the text node
- **Whitespace**   The white space between markup
- **ProcessingInstruction**   The entire content excluding the target
- **XmlDeclaration**   The content of the declaration
- **Other node types**   *String.Empty*

The *XmlTextReader.HasValue* property returns *true* if the current node is a type that returns a value; otherwise, it returns *false*.

Other node properties   Other information about the current node available through *XmlTextReader* properties is summarized in Table 11-7.

Table 11-7   Other Node Properties Available Through *XmlTextReader*

Property	Comments
AttributeCount	Gets the number of attributes on the current node.
	Valid node types: *Element, DocumentType, XmlDeclaration*.
BaseURI	Gets a *String* containing the base Uniform Resource Identifier (URI) of the current node.
	Valid node types: All.
CanResolveEntity	Always returns *false* for an *XmlTextReader*. See the "Unimplemented Members" section later in this chapter for details.
Depth	Gets the depth of the current node in the XML source.
	Valid node types: All.
HasAttributes	Returns *true* if the current node has attributes. Will always return *false* for element types other than *Element, DocumentType*, and *XmlDeclaration*.
IsEmptyElement	Returns *true* if the current node is an empty *Element* type ending in /> (for example: <*SomeElement/>*). For all other node types and nonempty *Element* nodes, *IsEmptyElement* returns *false*.
LineNumber	Gets the current line number of the XML source. Line numbers begin at 1.
	Not inherited from *XmlReader*; provides implementation of the *System.Xml.IXmlLineInfo.LineNumber* interface member.
	Valid node types: All.
LinePosition	Gets the current line position of the XML source. Line positions begin at 1.
	Not inherited from *XmlReader*; provides implementation of the *System.Xml.IXmlLineInfo.LinePosition* interface member.
	Valid node types: All.
NamespaceURI	Gets the namespace URI of the current node.
	Valid node types: *Element* and *Attribute*.
QuoteChar	Gets the quotation mark character used to enclose the value of an *Attribute* node. For nonattribute nodes, *QuoteChar* always returns a double quotation mark (").

Read operations   Operations that change the location of the cursor are collectively referred to as *read* operations. All read operations move the cursor relative to the current node. Note that while attributes are nodes, they are not returned as part of the normal node stream and never become the current node using the read operations discussed in this section; accessing attribute nodes is covered in the following section.

The simplest cursor operation is the *XmlTextReader.Read* method, which attempts to move the cursor to the next node in the XML source and returns *true* if successful. If there are no further nodes, *Read* returns *false*. The following code fragment visits every node in an *XmlTextReader* and displays the node name on the console:

```
XmlTextReader rdr = new XmlTextReader("MyXmlFile.xml");
while (rdr.Read()) {
    System.Console.WriteLine("Inspecting node : {0}", rdr.Name);
}
```

Using the *Read* method is the simplest way to process the nodes in an XML document but is often not the desired behavior because all nodes, including noncontent and *EndElement* nodes, are returned.

The *MoveToContent* method determines whether the current node is a *content* node. Content nodes include the following node types: *Text*, *CDATA*, *Element*, *EndElement*, *EntityReference*, and *EndEntity*. If the current node is a noncontent node, the cursor skips over all nodes until it reaches a content node or the end of the XML source. The *MoveToContent* method returns the *XmlNodeType* of the new current node (*XmlNodeType.None* if the end of the input is reached).

The *Skip* method causes the cursor to be moved to the next sibling of the current node; all child nodes will be ignored. For nodes with no children, the *Skip* method is equivalent to calling *Read*.

The *IsStartElement* method calls *MoveToContent* and returns *true* if the current node is a start tag or an empty element. Overloaded versions of the *IsStartElement* method support the provision of a name or local name and a namespace URI; if names are specified, the method will return *true* if the new current node name matches the specified name. The following code fragment demonstrates the use of *IsStartElement* to display the name of each element start tag:

```
XmlTextReader rdr = new XmlTextReader("MyXmlFile.xml");
while (rdr.Read()) {
    if (rdr.IsStartElement()) {
        System.Console.WriteLine("Inspecting node : {0}", rdr.Name);

    }
}
```

The *ReadStartElement* method calls *IsStartElement* followed by the *Read* method; if the result of the initial call to *IsStartElement* is *false*, an *XmlException* is thrown. *ReadStartElement* provides the same set of overloads as *IsStartElement,* allowing an element name to be specified.

The *ReadEndElement* method checks that the current node is an end tag and then advances the cursor to the next node; an *XmlException* is thrown if the current node is not an end tag.

The *XmlTextReader* also includes a number of methods to return content from the current node and its descendants; these are summarized in Table 11-8.

Table 11-8 *XmlTextReader* **Methods That Return Content from the Current Node**

Method	Comments
ReadInnerXml()	Returns a *String* containing the raw content (including markup) of the current node. The start and end tags are excluded.
ReadOuterXml()	The same as *ReadInnerXml* except that the start and end tags are included.
ReadString()	Returns the contents of an element or text node as a *String*. Nonelement and text nodes return *String.Empty*. The cursor is not moved.
ReadChars()	Reads the text contents (including markup) of an element node into a specified *char* array a section at a time and returns the number of characters read. Subsequent calls to *ReadChars* continue reading from where the previous call finished. *ReadChars* returns 0 when no more content is available. Nonelement nodes always return 0. The cursor is not moved.
ReadBase64()	Like *ReadChars* but reads and decodes Base64-encoded content.
ReadBinHex()	Like *ReadChars* but reads and decodes BinHex-encoded content.

Accessing Attributes

Three types of node support attributes: *Elements*, *XmlDeclarations*, and *DocumentType* declarations. The *XmlTextReader* doesn't treat attributes as normal nodes; attributes are always read as part of the containing node.

The *XmlTextReader* class offers two mechanisms to access the attributes of the current node; we discuss both approaches in the following sections.

Direct attribute value access   The attribute values of the current node can be accessed through the *XmlTextReader* class using both methods and indexers; the attribute is specified either by name or by index position. A URI can be specified for attributes contained in a namespace. The members used to access attribute values are summarized in Table 11-9.

Table 11-9 *XmlTextReader* **Members Used to Access Attribute Values**

Member	Comment
<XmlTextReader>[int]GetAttribute(int)	Indexer and method alternative that get the value of an attribute based on its index.
<XmlTextReader>[String]Get-Attribute(String)	Indexer and method alternative that get the value of an attribute by name.
<XmlTextReader>[String, String]Get-Attribute(String, String)	Indexer and method alternative that get the value of an attribute in a specific namespace by name.

Attribute node access   The *XmlTextReader* class provides support for accessing attributes as independent nodes, allowing attribute information to be accessed using the *XmlTextReader* class properties described earlier in this section.

If the current node has attributes, the *XmlTextReader.MoveToFirstAttribute* method returns *true* and moves the cursor to the first attribute of the current node; the first attribute becomes the current node. If the current node has no attributes, the method returns *false* and the cursor remains unmoved.

Once the cursor is positioned on an attribute node, calling *MoveToNextAttribute* will move it to the next attribute node. If another attribute exists, the method will return *true*; otherwise, the method returns *false* and the position of the cursor remains unchanged. If the current node is not an attribute, but a node with attributes, the *MoveToNextAttribute* method has the same effect as *MoveToFirstAttribute*.

The *MoveToAttribute* method provides three overloads for moving the cursor directly to a specific attribute node. These overloads are summarized in Table 11-10.

Table 11-10   **The Overloaded Versions of the** *MoveToAttribute* **Method**

Method	Comments
MoveToAttribute(int)	Moves the cursor to the attribute node at the specified index. If there is no attribute at the specified index, an *ArgumentOutOfRangeException* is thrown and the cursor is not moved.
MoveToAttribute(String)	Moves the cursor to the attribute node with the specified name. This method returns *true* if the named attribute exists; otherwise, it returns *false* and the cursor doesn't move.
MoveToAttribute(String, String)	Same as *MoveToAttribute(String)* but also allows a namespace URI to be specified for the target attribute.

The *MoveToElement* method moves the cursor back to the node containing the attributes.

The following example demonstrates attribute access using both direct and node access. The example class parses an XML file loaded from the *http://localhost/test.xml* URL and determines whether any element type node contains an attribute named *att1*. If the *att1* attribute is present, the program displays its value on the console; otherwise, the program displays a list of all attributes and values of the current element.

XML Input (assumed to be located at *http://localhost/test.xml*):

```
<?xml version='1.0'?>
<root>
    <node1 att1='abc' att2='def'/>
    <node2 att2='ghi' att3='jkl' att4='mno'/>
    <node3 att1='uvw' att2='xyz'/>
</root>
```

Example code:

```csharp
using System;
using System.Xml;

public class xmltest {

    public static void Main () {

        String myFile = "http://localhost/test.xml";
        XmlTextReader rdr = new XmlTextReader(myFile);

        while (rdr.Read()) {
            if (rdr.NodeType == XmlNodeType.Element) {
                Console.WriteLine("Inspecting node : {0}",rdr.Name);

                if (rdr["att1"] != null){
                    Console.WriteLine("\tatt1 =  {0}",rdr["att1"]);
                } else {
                    while(rdr.MoveToNextAttribute()) {
                        Console.WriteLine("\t{0} = {1}",
                            rdr.Name, rdr.Value);
                    }
                    rdr.MoveToElement();
                }
            }
        }
    }
}
```

Output:

```
Inspecting node : root
Inspecting node : node1
        att1 =  abc
Inspecting node : node2
        att2 = ghi
        att3 = jkl
        att4 = mno
Inspecting node : node3
        att1 =  uvw
```

Closing an *XmlTextReader*

The *XmlTextReader.GetRemainder* method returns a *System.IO.TextReader* containing the remaining XML from a partially parsed source. Following the *GetRemainder* call, the *XmlTextReader.ReadState* property is set to *EOF*.

Instances of *XmlTextReader* should be closed using the *Close* method. This releases any resources used while reading and sets the *ReadState* property to the value *ReadState.Closed*.

Unimplemented Members

Because *XmlTextReader* doesn't validate XML, the *IsDefault*, *CanResolveEntity*, and *ResolveEntity* members inherited from *XmlReader* exhibit default behavior as described in Table 11-11.

Table 11-11 The Default Behavior of Unimplemented *XmlReader* Methods in *XmlTextReader*

Member	Comments
IsDefault	Always returns *false*. *XmlTextReader* doesn't expand default attributes defined in schemas.
CanResolveEntity	Always returns *false*. *XmlTextReader* cannot resolve entity references.
ResolveEntity()	Throws a *System.InvalidOperationException*. *XmlTextReader* cannot resolve general entity references.

XmlValidatingReader

The *XmlValidatingReader* class is a concrete implementation of *XmlReader* that validates an XML source against one of the following:

- Document type definitions as defined in the W3C Recommendation "Extensible Markup Language (XML) 1.0"

- MSXML Schema specification for XML-Data Reduced (XDR) schemas

■   XML Schema as defined in the W3C Recommendations "XML Schema Part 0: Primer," "XML Schema Part 1: Structures," and "XML Schema Part 2: Datatypes," collectively referred to as XML Schema Definition (XSD)

The functionality of *XmlValidatingReader* is predominantly the same as *XmlTextReader*, described in the *"XmlTextReader"* section earlier in this chapter. However, *XmlValidatingReader* includes a number of new members and some members that operate differently than in *XmlTextReader*; these differences are the focus of this section.

Creating an *XmlValidatingReader*

The most commonly used *XmlValidatingReader* constructor takes an *XmlReader* instance as the source of XML. The following statements demonstrate the creation of an *XmlValidatingReader* from an *XmlTextReader*:

```
XmlTextReader rdr = new XmlTextReader("SomeXmlFile.xml");
XmlValidatingReader vRdr = new XmlValidatingReader(rdr);
```

Specifying a Validation Type

The *XmlValidatingReader.ValidationType* property gets and sets the type of validation the reader will perform. This property must be set before execution of the first read operation; otherwise, an *InvalidOperationException* will be thrown.

The *ValidationType* property must be set to a value from the *ValidationType* enumeration; Table 11-12 summarizes the available values.

Table 11-12   The *ValidationType* Enumeration

Value	Comments
Auto	Validates based on the DTD or schema information the parser finds. This is the default value.
DTD	Validates according to a DTD.
None	Performs no validation. The only benefit of *XmlValidatingReader* in this mode is that general entity references can be resolved and default attributes are reported.
Schema	Validates according to an XSD schema.
XDR	Validates according to an XDR schema.

Validation Events

If the *ValidationType* is set to *Auto, DTD, Schema,* or *XDR* and validation errors occur when parsing an XML document, an *XmlSchemaException* is thrown and parsing of the current node stops. Parsing cannot be resumed once an error has occurred.

Alternatively, the *ValidationEventHandler* member of *XmlValidating-Reader* allows the programmer to specify a delegate that is called to handle validation errors, suppressing the exception that would be raised. The arguments of the delegate provide access to information about the severity of the validation error, the exception that would have occurred, and a textual message associated with the error.

Use of the *ValidationEventHandler* member allows the programmer to determine whether to resume or terminate the parser.

Cached Schemas

The read-only *XmlValidatingReader.Schemas* property can be used in conjunction with the *XmlSchemaCollection* class to cache XSD and XDR schemas in memory, saving the reader from having to reload schema files. However, *XmlValidatingReader* doesn't automatically cache schemas; any caching must be explicitly performed by the programmer. Once cached, schemas cannot be removed from an *XmlSchemaCollection*.

The *XmlValidatingReader* maintains an *XmlSchemaCollection* that is accessed via the *Schemas* property; the most common way to add new schema files to the collection is by using the *Add* method. The *XmlSchemaCollection* class implements the *ICollection* and *IEnumerable* interfaces and provides indexer access to schemas based on a namespace URI.

An important feature of the *XmlSchemaCollection* is the *Validation-EventHandler* event; this member is unrelated to the *ValidationEventHandler* member of the *XmlValidatingReader* class. This event specifies a method called to handle errors that occur when validating a schema loaded into the collection. *XmlSchemaCollection* throws an *XmlSchemaException* if no event handler is specified.

The following example demonstrates the steps necessary to configure the *XmlSchemaCollection* validation event handler and to cache a schema.

```
using System;
using System.Xml;
using System.Xml.Schema;

public class schematest {
    public static void Main() {
```

(continued)

```
// Create the validating reader
XmlTextReader rdr = new XmlTextReader("MyXmlDocument.xml");
XmlValidatingReader valRdr = new XmlValidatingReader(rdr);

// Get the schema collection from the validating reader
XmlSchemaCollection sCol = valRdr.Schemas;

// Set the validation event handler for the schema collection
sCol.ValidationEventHandler +=
    new ValidationEventHandler(ValidationCallBack);

// Cache a schema in the schema collection
sCol.Add("urn:mynamespace","myschema.xsd");

}

// Create handler for validation events
public static void ValidationCallBack(object sender,
    ValidationEventArgs args) {
        Console.WriteLine("Schema error : "
+ args.Exception.Message);
    }
}
```

Differences from *XmlTextReader*

As mentioned at the start of this section, *XmlValidatingReader* has a number of new members or members with behavior different from that of the members in *XmlTextReader*; these members are summarized in Table 11-13.

**Table 11-13 Differences Between *XmlValidatingReader*
and *XmlTextReader***

Member	Comments
Different	
CanResolveEntity	Always returns *true*.
IsDefault	Returns *true* if the current node is an attribute whose value was generated from a default specified in a DTD or a schema.
LineNumber	While *XmlValidatingReader* implements the *IXmlLineInfo* interface, explicit interface implementation has been used to implement the *LineNumber* property. The *XmlValidatingReader* must be explicitly cast to an *IXmlLineInfo* type before *LineNumber* can be called.
LinePosition	Same as *LineNumber*.
ResolveEntity()	This method resolves the entity reference if the current node is an *EntityReference*.

Table 11-13   Differences Between *XmlValidatingReader* and *XmlTextReader* *(continued)*

Member	Comments
New	
Reader	Returns the *XmlReader* used to instantiate the *XmlValidatingReader*.

XmlNodeReader

The *System.Xml.XmlNodeReader* class is a concrete implementation of *XmlReader* that provides read-only, forward-only cursor style access to a Document Object Model (DOM) node or subtree.

The *XmlNodeReader* provides predominantly the same behavior and functionality as the *XmlTextReader* described in the "*XmlTextReader*" section earlier in this chapter. However, *XmlNodeReader* offers a single constructor with the following signature:

```
public XmlNodeReader(XmlNode node);
```

The *node* argument provides the root element of the *XmlNodeReader*. Given that *XmlDocument* derives from *XmlNode*, the *XmlNodeReader* can be used to navigate a partial or full DOM tree.

The following code fragment demonstrates the creation of an *XmlNodeReader* using an *XmlDocument* as the source. We then iterate through the nodes and display the names of any *Element* type nodes on the console.

```
XmlDocument doc = new XmlDocument();
doc.Load("SomeXmlFile.xml");
XmlNodeReader rdr = new XmlNodeReader(doc);

while (rdr.Read()) {
    if (rdr.NodeType == XmlNodeType.Element) {
        System.Console.WriteLine("Node name = {0}", rdr.LocalName);
    }
}
```

XmlWriter

.NET provides a useful feature to simplify the creation of XML without using DOM. The abstract *System.Xml.XmlWriter* class defines the functionality for a fast, noncached mechanism to generate streams or files containing well-formed XML; *XmlTextWriter* provides a concrete implementation of this functionality.

XmlTextWriter

Although the *XmlTextWriter* class is primarily an implementation of *XmlWriter*, it also contains a number of noninherited members. We highlight these members as they are discussed.

XmlTextWriter Creation

XmlTextWriter provides three constructors; the constructor arguments identify the destination where the *XmlTextWriter* should write to as well as the encoding to use. These constructors are summarized in Table 11-14.

Table 11-14 The *XmlTextWriter* Constructors

Constructor	Comments
XmlTextWriter(TextWriter)	Creates an *XmlTextWriter* that writes to the specified *System.IO.TextWriter*. Uses the encoding configured on the *TextWriter* instance.
XmlTextWriter(Stream, Encoding)	Creates an *XmlTextWriter* that writes to a *System.IO.Stream* using the specified *System.Text.Encoding*. If the *Encoding* argument is *null*, the default is UTF-8 encoding.
XmlTextWriter(string, Encoding)	Creates an *XmlTextWriter* that writes to the file with the name specified in the *string* argument using the *System.Text.Encoding* provided. If the *Encoding* argument is *null*, the default is UTF-8 encoding. The *XmlTextWriter* overwrites the file if it exists.

The *XmlTextWriter.BaseStream* property returns the underlying *Stream* used for output. If the *XmlTextWriter* was created from a *TextWriter* that doesn't derive from *System.IO.StreamWriter*, *null* is returned.

XmlTextWriter Status

The *WriteState* property returns a value from the *System.Xml.WriteState* enumeration indicating the current state of the writer; valid values are summarized in Table 11-15.

Table 11-15 The *System.Xml.WriteState* Enumeration

Value	Comment
Attribute	The *XmlTextWriter* is currently writing an attribute value.
Closed	The *XmlTextWriter.Close* method has been called.
Content	The *XmlTextWriter* is currently writing element content.
Element	The *XmlTextWriter* is currently writing an element tag.

Table 11-15   **The *System.Xml.WriteState* Enumeration**   *(continued)*

Value	Comment
Prolog	The *XmlTextWriter* is currently writing the XML prolog.
Start	The *XmlTextWriter* is in the initial state; no write methods have been called.

Writing XML Documents

The *XmlTextWriter* provides methods for writing all types of XML nodes. Use of the *XmlTextWriter* methods is straightforward, and complete coverage is included in the .NET documentation. The following example demonstrates the use of many of these methods:

```
using System;
using System.Xml;

public class xmlwritetest {

    public static void Main () {
        XmlTextWriter wtr = new XmlTextWriter("output.xml", null);

        // Write the XML declaration
        wtr.WriteStartDocument();

        // Write white space to start a new line followed by a comment
        wtr.WriteWhitespace("\r\n");
        wtr.WriteComment("An XmlTextWriter example.");

        // Write the <root> start tag and an attribute
        wtr.WriteStartElement("root");
        wtr.WriteAttributeString("anAttribute", "an attribute value");

        // Write a complete element in a single call. Special
        // symbols are automatically replaced with entity references
        wtr.WriteElementString("node1", "The contents of <node1>");

        // Write <node2> start tag, CData section and </node2> end tag
        wtr.WriteStartElement("node2");
        wtr.WriteCData("This CData is contained in the <node2> node");
        wtr.WriteEndElement();

        // Write the <node3> start tag with two attributes
        wtr.WriteStartElement("node3");
        wtr.WriteStartAttribute("", "Attribute1", "");
        wtr.WriteString("Attribute value 1");
```

(continued)

```
        wtr.WriteEndAttribute();
        wtr.WriteAttributeString("Attribute2", "Attribute value 2");

        // Write an element with some text content
        wtr.WriteStartElement("node4");
        wtr.WriteString("The content of node4");
        wtr.WriteEndElement();

        // Write raw XML
        wtr.WriteRaw("<node5>Manually formatted XML</node5>");

        // Write a complete element in a single call
        wtr.WriteElementString("node6", "The contents of <node6>");

        // WriteEndDocument automatically closes any open elements
        // In this case <root> and <node3> are closed.
        wtr.WriteEndDocument();
        wtr.Close();
    }
}
```

The output from the preceding code is as follows:

```
<?xml version="1.0"?>
<!An XmlTextWriter example.><root anAttribute="an attribute value"><no
de1>The contents of &lt;node1&gt;<node1><node2><![CDATA[This CData is
contained in the <node2> node]]><node2><node3 Attribute1="Attribute va
lue 1" Attribute2="Attribute value 2"><node4>The content of node4</
node4><node5>Manually formatted XML<node5><node6>The contents of &lt;n
ode6&gt;</node6></node3></root>
```

Output Formatting

As can be seen from the preceding example, the *XmlTextReader* output is
unformatted and difficult to read. However, *XmlTextWriter* provides four properties that enable the programmer to control the indentation of XML output as
well as the quotation mark used for attribute values. Indentation affects only the
following node types: *DocumentType*, *Element*, *Comment*, *ProcessingInstruction*, and *CDATASection*.

XmlTextWriter doesn't inherit these properties from *XmlWriter*; we sum-
marize them in Table 11-16.

Table 11-16   The *XmlTextWriter* Properties

Property	Comments
Formatting	Controls how the XML output by *XmlTextWriter* is formatted by using a value from the *System.Xml.Formatting* enumeration. Valid values are ■ *Indented*—where *XmlTextWriter* uses the *Indentation* and *Indent-Char* properties (described next) to format XML output. ■ *None*—where no formatting is used. This is the default value.
Indentation	When *Indented Formatting* is used, *Indentation* specifies the number of *IndentChar* characters to use as indentation for each level of the XML hierarchy (specified as an *int*).
IndentChar	The *char* to use for indenting; default to a space.
QuoteChar	The quotation mark to use with attribute values; must be either a single quotation mark or a double quotation mark.

In the preceding example, the output was one long string. If instead we configure the formatting of the *XmlTextWriter* with the following statements:

```
XmlTextWriter wtr = new XmlTextWriter("output.xml", null);
wtr.Formatting = Formatting.Indented;
wtr.Indentation = 2;
wtr.QuoteChar = '\u0027';
```

the output will look as follows:

```
<?xml version='1.0'?>

<!--An XmlTextWriter example.-->
<root anAttribute='an attribute value'>
  <node1>The contents of &lt;node1&gt;</node1>
  <node2><![CDATA[This CData is contained in the <node2> node]]></node2>
  <node3 Attribute1='Attribute value 1' Attribute2='Attribute value 2'>
    <node4>The content of node4</node4><node5>Manually formatted XML</
node5><node6>The contents of &lt;node6&gt;</node6></node3>
</root>
```

Caution   Note that the output written with *WriteRaw* is not affected by the formatting configurations and in fact breaks the ability of the *XmlTextWriter* to indent future output correctly.

Namespace Support

The *XmlTextWriter.Namespaces* property controls whether the *XmlTextWriter* supports XML namespaces; by default, namespace support is enabled. If namespace support is enabled, the *XmlTextWriter* maintains a namespace stack that tracks the namespaces defined by elements. The *LookupPrefix* method is used to find the namespace prefix based on a Uniform Resource Name (URN).

The *XmlTextWriter* methods demonstrated in the preceding example that write elements and attributes offer overloaded versions accepting strings to define and use namespaces and prefixes.

Closing the *XmlTextWriter*

The *Close* method automatically calls any *WriteEndXXX* methods necessary to close document nodes created with a matching *WriteStartXXX* method, where *XXX* identifies a node type. The *Close* method then closes the *XmlTextWriter* and the underlying output stream. If *Close* isn't called, output buffers won't be flushed correctly. An *InvalidOperationException* is thrown if further write methods are invoked after the *Close* method is called.

> **Note** To flush the *XmlTextWriter* and underlying stream buffers without closing the writer, use the *Flush* method.

Document Object Model

.NET provides an implementation of the Document Object Model (DOM) that offers broadly the same functionality as that provided by Java. Instead of undertaking a detailed description of the complete DOM API, we'll restrict our discussion to highlighting some of the key differences between the Java and .NET implementations. A Java developer familiar with the use of DOM will find few problems working with the .NET implementation.

Key Classes

The Java DOM API is specified almost exclusively by using interfaces, whereas .NET uses predominantly classes. However, apart from three new node types defined by Microsoft, there is a direct mapping between the .NET classes, the Java interfaces, and the node types specified in the DOM specification. These are summarized in Table 11-17.

Table 11-17   Comparison Between Java and .NET DOM APIs

DOM Node	Java Interface	.NET Class
N/A	*Node*	*XmlNode*
Document	*Document*	*XmlDocument*
DocumentFragment	*DocumentFragment*	*XmlDocumentFragment*
DocumentType	*DocumentType*	*XmlDocumentType*
EntityReference	*EntityReference*	*XmlEntityReference*
Element	*Element*	*XmlElement*
Attr	*Attr*	*XmlAttribute*
ProcessingInstruction	*ProcessingInstruction*	*XmlProcessingInstruction*
Comment	*Comment*	*XmlComment*
Text	*Text*	*XmlText*
CDataSection	*CDataSection*	*XmlCDataSection*
Entity	*Entity*	*XmlEntity*
Notation	*Notation*	*XmlNotation*
N/A	N/A	*XmlDeclaration*
N/A	N/A	*XmlSignificantWhitespace*
N/A	N/A	*XmlWhitespace*

Document Creation

Java provides the *DocumentBuilderFactory* to create validating and nonvalidating *DocumentBuilder* parsers. Empty *Document* instances are created using the *DocumentBuilder.newDocument* factory method, whereas an existing XML document is parsed into a *Document* instance using one of the overloaded *DocumentBuilder.parse* methods.

.NET *XmlDocument* instances, on the other hand, are created using standard constructors and always result in an empty document. An *XmlNameTable*, discussed in the "*XmlNameTable*" section earlier in this chapter, can be provided as an argument to the constructor.

XML is parsed into the *XmlDocument* using the *Load* and *LoadXml* methods. *LoadXml* loads from a *String* containing an XML document without performing any validation. The *Load* method has four overloaded versions that take a stream, a URL (contained in a *String*), a *TextReader*, or an *XmlReader*, respectively as the XML source. To perform validation on the input to an *XmlDocument*, pass an *XmlValidatingReader* as the argument to the constructor.

Other Key Differences

Other key differences between the Java and the .NET implementation of the DOM API include the following:

■ .NET frequently makes use of properties, events, and delegates, whereas Java uses get/set accessors and methods to implement the DOM API.

■ The only way to output a Java DOM *Document* is to use the *Transformer* class, discussed in the "XSL Transformations" section later in this chapter, as a conduit to a stream. The .NET *XmlDocument* class provides the *Save*, *WriteTo*, and *WriteContentTo* methods to simplify the output of DOM trees.

XPath

The .NET Framework provides an API through which components can support XPath queries against underlying data stores. To use the XPath API, it's necessary to understand the XPath language, a discussion of which is beyond the scope of this book. The W3C Recommendation "XML Path Language (XPath) Version 1.0," which is available at *www.w3.org/TR/xpath*, contains a complete definition of XPath.

This section discusses the .NET Framework classes provided to support XPath. Unless specifically stated otherwise, all XPath classes discussed in this section are members of the *System.Xml.XPath* namespace.

IXPathNavigable

Components provide XPath support by implementing the *IXPathNavigable* interface, which defines a single method with the following signature:

```
XPathNavigator CreateNavigator();
```

The *XPathNavigator* class defines members that support read-only random access to data using XPath expressions.

The classes in the .NET Framework that directly implement *IXPathNavigable* are *System.Xml.XmlNode* and *System.Xml.XPath.XPathDocument*. *XmlNode* is the root class from which some members of the *System.Xml* namespace are derived, including *XmlDocument*. The *XmlDocument* class provides a base class for the *System.Xml.XmlDataDocument* class, providing XPath access to the data stored in an ADO *DataSet*.

> **More Info**   We discuss the *XmlDocument* and *XmlNode* classes in the "Document Object Model" and "XPath" sections of this chapter, respectively, and the *XmlDataDocument* class in Chapter 16.

XPathDocument

The *XPathDocument* class implements *IXPathNavigable* and provides simple and efficient read-only access to an XML document. Optimized for XSLT and XPath manipulation, *XPathDocument* provides no direct navigation or node management functionality. The primary purpose of the *XPathDocument* class is to provide an XML cache for access via the *XPathNavigator* class.

XPathDocument instances can be constructed from XML contained in any of the following sources: *System.IO.Stream*, URI (contained within a *String*), *System.IO.TextReader*, or *XmlReader*. Preservation of white space from the XML source is controlled with the provision of a value from the *System.Xml.XmlSpace* enumeration.

XPathNavigator

XPathNavigator provides read-only access to an underlying data store as if it were a hierarchy of nodes, conceptually similar to the Document Object Model. The members of *XPathNavigator* provide the means to navigate through the nodes, obtain information about nodes, and, most important, evaluate XPath expressions against the node set.

Navigation through the nodes is via a cursor similar to that provided by *XmlReader*; the node under the cursor is the *current node*. Unlike *XmlReader*, *XPathNavigator* works against a cached node tree and so supports both backward and forward cursor movements.

Using XPath expressions means that sets of nodes meeting specified criteria can be identified and accessed directly.

Node Types

The *XPathNavigator.NodeType* property returns the node type of the current node, returning a value from the *XPathNodeType* enumeration. While there is some overlap with DOM and *XmlReader*, the XPath specification defines a different set of node types. The values contained in the *XPathNodeType* enumeration are summarized in the following list; those values that are .NET specific and do not form part of the XPath specification are italicized: Root, Element, Attribute, Namespace, Text, ProcessingInstruction, Comment, *Significant-Whitespace*, *Whitespace*, and *All*.

Node Navigation

The *XPathNavigator* provides a similar, if simplified, set of members to *XmlReader* to navigate the nodes of the data store. These are summarized in Table 11-18.

Table 11-18 The *XPathNavigator* Members Used to Navigate Nodes

Method	Comments
MoveTo()	Takes another *XPathNavigator* instance as an argument and moves the cursor to point to the current node of the *XPathNavigator* provided. The success of this method depends on the *XPathNavigator* implementation and the underlying data store.
MoveToNext()	Moves the cursor to the next sibling of the current node.
MoveToPrevious()	Moves the cursor to the previous sibling of the current node.
MoveToFirst()	Moves the cursor to the first sibling of the current node.
MoveToFirstChild()	Moves the cursor to the first child node of the current node.
MoveToParent()	Moves the cursor to the parent of the current node.
MoveToRoot()	Moves the cursor to the root node.
MoveToId()	Moves the cursor to a node with the specified ID. This is valid only if the XML document declares attributes of type ID using a DTD.

Attribute and Namespace Node Navigation

Although attributes and namespaces are considered nodes, they are not navigable using the node navigation methods discussed in the preceding section. Instead, *XPathNavigator* implements methods specifically for navigating the attributes and namespaces contained in the current node. Using these methods makes an attribute or namespace node the current node and makes information available through the properties of the *XPathNavigator* instance as with any other node. Table 11-19 summarizes the method of *XPathNavigator* for navigating attributes and namespaces.

Table 11-19 *XPathNavigator* **Methods for Navigating Attributes and Namespaces**

Method	Comment
Attributes	
MoveToAttribute()	Moves the cursor to the attribute of the current element node that has the specified name.
MoveToFirstAttribute()	Moves the cursor to the first attribute of the current element node.
MoveToNextAttribute()	Moves the cursor to the next attribute of the containing element. If not positioned on an attribute node, the cursor will not move.
Namespaces	
MoveToNamespace()	Moves the cursor to the specified namespace of the current element node.
MoveToFirstNamespace()	Moves the cursor to the first namespace of the current element node.
MoveToNextNamespace()	Moves the cursor to the next namespace of the containing element. If not positioned on a namespace node, the cursor will not move.
Other	
MoveToParent()	After working with attribute or namespace nodes, returns the cursor to the parent element node.

The following example demonstrates the use of the foregoing methods to navigate across the namespaces and attributes of a node and print information for each.

XML Input (stored in file named test.xml):

```
<?xml version='1.0'?>
<root>
    <node1 xmlns:a='someNamespaceUri' att1='abc' att2='cde'>
    <node2 xmlns:b='someOtherNamespaceUri' att1='xyz'/>
    </node1>
</root>
```

Code:

```
using System;
using System.Xml;
using System.Xml.XPath;

public class xmltest {
```

(continued)

```
    public static void Main () {

        XPathNavigator myNav =
            new XPathDocument("test.xml").CreateNavigator();
        XPathNodeIterator myIt =
            myNav.SelectDescendants(XPathNodeType.Element,true);

        while (myIt.MoveNext()) {
            XPathNavigator curNode = myIt.Current;
            Console.WriteLine("Inspecting node : {0}",
                curNode.LocalName);

            if (curNode.MoveToFirstAttribute()) {
                do {
                    Console.WriteLine("\tAttribute: {0} = {1}",
                        curNode.LocalName, curNode.Value);
                } while (curNode.MoveToNextAttribute());
                curNode.MoveToParent();
            }

            if (curNode.MoveToFirstNamespace()) {
                do {
                    Console.WriteLine("\tNamespace: {0} = {1}",
                        curNode.LocalName, curNode.Value);
                } while (curNode.MoveToNextNamespace());
                curNode.MoveToParent();
            }
        }
    }
}
```

Output:

```
Inspecting node : root
        Namespace: xml = http://www.w3.org/XML/1998/namespace
Inspecting node : node1
        Attribute: att1 = abc
        Attribute: att2 = cde
        Namespace: a = someNamespaceUri
        Namespace: xml = http://www.w3.org/XML/1998/namespace
Inspecting node : node2
        Attribute: att1 = xyz
        Namespace: b = someOtherNamespaceUri
        Namespace: a = someNamespaceUri
        Namespace: xml = http://www.w3.org/XML/1998/namespace
```

Node Properties

As with *XmlReader*, the information about the current node is available through the properties of the *XPathNavigator* instance. The properties available are a subset of those available through *XmlReader* and include the following: *BaseURI, HasAttributes, HasChildren, IsEmptyElement, LocalName, Name, NamespaceURI, NodeType, Prefix, Value,* and *XmlLang*. We won't discuss these properties in detail here; refer to the .NET documentation for complete details.

Queries

The primary benefit of *XPathNavigator* is the support for querying the contained data by using XPath expressions. The XPath expression can be passed to *XPathNavigator* methods either as a string or as an instance of *System.Xml.XPath.XPathExpression*.

The *XPathExpression* class encapsulates a precompiled XPath expression. Instances are created using the *XPathNavigator.Compile* method passing a *String* argument containing the XPath expression. There are three key benefits to using instances of *XPathExpression* over using strings:

■   It is more efficient to compile an XPath expression if it is to be used repeatedly.

■   The *XPathExpression.AddSort* method enables the configuration of sorting characteristics for node sets selected by the expression.

■   The *XPathExpression.ReturnType* property returns a member of the *XPathResultType* enumeration that identifies which result type the encapsulated XPath expression will return.

The *XPathNavigator* doesn't provide individual methods that map to the different types of expressions defined in the XPath specification. Instead, XPath expressions are evaluated primarily through three methods of *XPathNavigator*: *Select, Evaluate,* and *Matches*.

The difficulty with using a standard set of methods for all expressions is that different XPath expressions return different data types. These are

■   Node Set, an unordered collection of nodes without duplicates. The *XPathNodeIterator* class encapsulates a node set.

■   boolean, *true* or *false*

■   number, a floating-point number

■   string, a sequence of UCS characters

The XPath navigator takes two approaches to work around this problem:

■ Limiting the types of expressions that can be submitted through each method

■ Returning an *Object* that must be cast to the appropriate type, depending on the expression submitted

In both instances, the programmer must either know in advance or determine at run time which result type the expression will return. The *XPathExpression.ReturnType* property returns a value from the *XPathResultType* enumeration identifying the result type of an expression. This can be used to determine the right method to use or to which type the result should be cast.

We discuss the specifics of the *Select*, *Evaluate*, and *Matches* methods in the following sections.

Select   The *Select* method takes only XPath expressions that result in node sets and returns an instance of *XPathNodeIterator*. If the XPath expression argument is invalid or doesn't return a node set, *XPathNavigator* throws an *ArgumentException*.

Evaluate   The *Evaluate* method takes any XPath expression and returns an *Object*. The programmer must cast the returned *Object* to the appropriate type, depending on the result type of the XPath expression.

Matches   The *Matches* method takes any XPath expression and returns a *bool* indicating whether the current node matches the expression.

Optimized Queries

XPathNavigator also provides optimized convenience methods that perform common XPath queries more quickly than using an explicit XPath expression. These methods do not affect the position of the cursor and are summarized in Table 11-20.

Table 11-20   *XPathNavigator* **Methods for Performing Optimized XPath Queries**

Method	Comment
SelectChildren()	Returns an *XPathNodeIterator* containing the child nodes of the current node. Overloads allow names and node types to be provided, filtering the child nodes returned.
SelectAncestors()	Returns an *XPathNodeIterator* containing the ancestor nodes of the current node. Overloads allow for the provision of names and node types, filtering the ancestor nodes returned.
SelectDescendants()	Returns an *XPathNodeIterator* containing the descendant nodes of the current node. Overloads allow for the provision of names and node types, filtering the descendant nodes returned.
IsDescendant()	Takes another *XPathNavigator* instance as an argument and returns *true* if the current node of that *XPathNavigator* is a descendant of the current node.

XSL Transformations

Java and .NET both provide comparable support for XSLT. An understanding of XSL is necessary to use these features; the W3C Recommendation "Extensible Stylesheet Language (XSL) Version 1.0" contains a full definition of XSL.

The .NET *System.Xml.Xsl.XslTransform* class encapsulates an XSLT processor providing functionality comparable to that of the *javax.xml.Transformer* class. The use of both classes follows roughly the same pattern. For the .NET *XslTransform* class, this can be summarized as follows:

- Create an *XslTransform* instance.

- Load a style sheet into the *XslTransform* using the *Load* method.

- Execute the transformation against an XML source using the *Transform* method.

Creating a Transformer

Java provides the static *javax.xml.transform.TransformerFactory.newTransformer* method to create instances of *javax.xml.transform.Transformer*. The *TransformerFactory* provides a vendor-neutral mechanism, allowing different *Tranformer* implementations to be easily plugged into the generic framework.

.NET provides a single concrete *XslTranform* implementation that is instantiated using a default constructor. The following statement instantiates a new *XslTransform*:

```
XslTransform myTransform = new XslTransform();
```

Loading a Style Sheet

The Java *Transformer* class is the primary mechanism for writing XML SAX and DOM sources to files. However, if it's used to perform XSL Transformations, an XSL style sheet must be provided as a parameter to the *newTransformer* factory method. Once the *Tranformer* is created with a given style sheet, it can be reused but cannot load a new style sheet.

The .NET *XslTransform* class provides the *Load* method to load a style sheet into an existing *XslTranform* instance. Separating the style sheet loading from the transformer creation allows new style sheets to be loaded into existing *XslTransform* instances as required.

Overloaded versions of the *Load* method support the loading of the style sheet from a variety of sources, including instances of *IXPathNavigable*, URL (contained in a *String*), *XmlReader*, and *XPathNavigator*. For example, the following statements load a style sheet from a file named test.xsl in the assembly directory:

```
XslTransform myTransformer = new XslTransform();
myTransformer.Load("test.xsl");
```

Additional overloaded *Load* methods take a *System.Xml.XmlResolver* instance as a second argument. The *XmlResolver* is used to load any style sheets referenced by *xsl:import* or *xsl:include* statements contained within the loaded style sheet. If an *XmlResolver* is not specified, a *System.Xml.XmlUrlResolver* instance with default credentials is used.

Transforming XML Data

The Java *Transformer.transform* method takes a *javax.xml.transform.Source* instance, which provides the XML to be transformed, and a *javax.xml.transform.Result* instance, which provides a destination for the output of the transformation process. Both *Source* and *Result* are interfaces; implementations are provided to support input from and output to DOM, SAX, and stream instances.

.NET provides a series of overloaded *Transform* methods that take a wide variety of source and destination references. Many of the *Transform* methods also take an instance of *XsltArgumentList* that contains arguments that can be used by the style sheet performing the transformation.

The following code fragment demonstrates the simplest *Transform* overload, which takes the names of an input and an output file:

```
XslTransform myTransformer = new XslTransform();
myTransformer.Load("test.xsl");
myTransformer.Transform("input.xml", "output.xml");
```

More commonly, the source would be an *XmlReader* or *XmlDocument* passed to *Transform* as an *IXPathNavigable* or *XPathNavigator* reference, and the output would be a stream, a *TextWriter*, an *XmlWriter*, or an *XmlReader*.

Extensibility

Java and .NET take fundamentally different approaches to the provision of XML parsing and transformation technologies.

Java implements factory classes through which concrete parsers are created; parsers themselves are defined by a set of interfaces. This allows the programmer to use any compliant parser or transformer implementation that can be plugged into the generic XML framework.

The .NET implementations are based on a set of abstract classes; customizing the parsers involves deriving new functionality from the existing base classes. The use of a custom parser requires the explicit instantiation of the customized class.

Summary

This chapter has shown the extensive support provided in .NET for the direct manipulation of XML. *XmlReader* provides a simple and logical alternative to SAX, while the DOM and XSLT implementations in .NET are comparable to those in Java version 1.4. Moreover, the addition of *XmlWriter* and XPath support provides features with no native Java equivalent.

IV

Advanced Topics

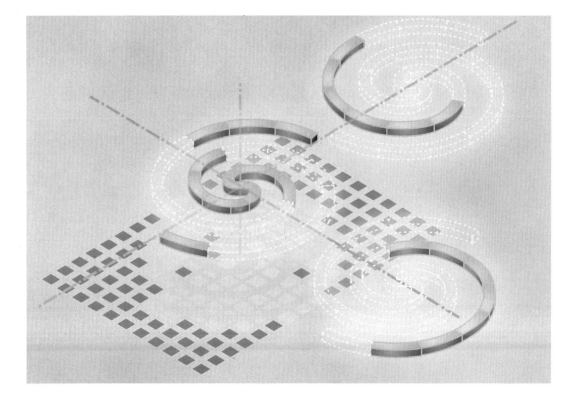

12

Reflection

Reflection exposes type information at run time, supporting powerful scripting technologies and applications that allow *plug-in* modules, such as application servers. This chapter details the .NET support for reflection, demonstrating how to gain type information and programmatically instantiate and manipulate types.

Dealing with Types

Java and .NET both encapsulate the details of a type in a single class: Java relies on *java.lang.Class*, and .NET defines *System.Type*. The following sections describe how to obtain *System.Type* instances.

Local Types

Local types are those that are directly available within the scope of an application. In Java, local types are those that can be found in the classpath; in .NET, local types are those that are contained in the application assemblies and the assemblies referenced at compile time. For more information about assemblies and references, see Chapter 3, "Creating Assemblies."

Table 12-1 shows the intrinsic support available in both platforms for obtaining local type details.

Table 12-1 **Comparison Between the Java and .NET Intrinsic Local Type Support**

Java	.NET	Comments
Object.getClass()	*Object.GetType()*	Returns details of a type from an instance of the type
<ClassName>.class	*typeof(<ClassName>)*	Returns type information from the type name
Class.forName(string)	*Type.GetType(string)*	Return details of a type specified by a string representing the type name

For example, the *System.String* class is a local type because the assembly that contains it, mscorlib.dll, is automatically referenced by the C# compiler. The following example demonstrates how to obtain type information for this class:

```
String myString = "this is my string";
System.Type stringType1 = myString.GetType();
System.Type stringType2 = typeof(System.String);
System.Type stringType3 = Type.GetType("System.String");
```

Foreign Types

Foreign types are those that are not directly available to an application. Java foreign types are those whose class files are not included in the application classpath; .NET foreign types are those contained in assemblies that were not referenced at compilation.

The Java *java.lang.Class* class includes an overloaded form of the *forName* method, which accepts a *java.lang.ClassLoader* as an argument. The .NET Framework makes similar functionality available through the *System.Reflection.Assembly* class.

The *Assembly* class defines several static methods that can be used to obtain *Assembly* instances, as detailed in Table 12-2.

Table 12-2 **Static Methods Available from the *Assembly* Class**

Assembly Method	Description
GetAssembly()	Returns the assembly in which a specified type is contained.
GetCallingAssembly()	Returns the assembly that invoked the method that is currently being executed.
GetEntryAssembly()	Returns the first assembly that was executed by the common language runtime.
GetExecutingAssembly()	Returns the assembly that contains the currently executing code.

Table 12-2   Static Methods Available from the *Assembly* Class   *(continued)*

Assembly Method	Description
Load()	Loads an assembly from a file by name or from a *byte* array held in memory. File-based assemblies must be locatable in the application search path. See Appendix B, "Shared Assemblies," for more details about assembly search paths.
LoadFrom()	Loads an assembly from a specified file.

The *Assembly.GetType* method returns an instance of *System.Type* for a named type; the *GetTypes* method returns an array of *System.Type* objects containing all of the types contained within the assembly.

The following example shows how to list the names of all of the types contained in the mscorlib assembly:

```
Assembly x_assembly = Assembly.Load("mscorlib");
Type[] x_types = x_assembly.GetTypes();
foreach (Type x_type in x_types) {
    Console.WriteLine("Name: " + x_type.Name);
}
```

Inspecting Types

Central to reflection is the abstract *System.Reflection.MemberInfo* class. Concrete classes are derived from *MemberInfo* to form representations of each member type, including constructors, methods, properties, and fields. For general information about each of the .NET member types, see Chapter 5, "Data Types."

Instances of classes derived from *MemberInfo* are obtained through the methods of the *System.Type* class; these methods are grouped by the member type they reflect and follow a clear pattern, each offering three forms, as shown in the following list:

- GetXXX(System.Type[])

- GetXXXs(System.Reflection.BindingFlags)

- GetXXXs()

The *XXX* indicates a member type—for example, *GetConstructor(Type[])*, *GetConstructors(BindingFlags)*, and *GetConstructors()*. The types returned from these methods are derived implementations of *MemberInfo* named to reflect the member that has been reflected: for example, the *GetConstructors* method returns instances of *ConstructorInfo*, and the *GetFields* method returns instances of *FieldInfo*.

The first form searches for a member that accepts arguments that match the types specified in the argument array. The following example demonstrates obtaining the *System.String* constructor that accepts a character array:

```
Type x_string_type = typeof(System.String);
ConstructorInfo x_constructor =
    x_string_type.GetConstructor(new Type[] {typeof(char[])});
```

The second form accepts a *System.Reflection.BindingFlags* value, which specifies attributes that the member must possess in order to be included in the search results. The *BindingFlags* enumeration is annotated with the *Flags-Attribute* attribute, so the values can be combined using bitwise operations.

The most commonly used values from the *BindingFlags* enumeration are

- Public
- NonPublic
- Instance
- Static

The following example demonstrates how to combine *BindingFlags* values to obtain a list of the public instance constructors for a type, in this case the *System.String* class:

```
Type x_string_type = typeof(System.String);
BindingFlags x_flags = BindingFlags.Public | BindingFlags.Instance;
ConstructorInfo[] x_constructors =
    x_string_type.GetConstructors(x_flags);
```

To obtain information about all of the members of a type, the following combination of *BindingFlags* values must be used:

```
BindingFlags.Public | BindingFlags.NonPublic | BindingFlags.Instance |
    BindingFlags.Static
```

The final *GetXXX* method form takes no arguments and is equivalent to specifying the *Public* and *Instance* binding flags, as shown in the preceding example.

Table 12-3 lists the methods of the *System.Type* class that can be used to obtain instances of *MemberInfo* or derived classes, contrasted against the comparable Java reflection functionality.

Table 12-3   Comparison Between Java Reflection and .NET *System.Type* Class Methods

java.lang.Class	*System.Type*
N/A	*GetMember()* *GetMembers()*
getConstructor() *getConstructors()* *getDeclaredConstructor()* *getDeclaredConstructors()*	*GetConstructor()* *GetConstructors()*
getField() *getFields()* *getDeclaredField()* *getDeclaredFields()*	*GetField()* *GetFields()*
getMethod() *getMethods()* *getDeclaredMethod()* *getDeclaredMethods()*	*GetMethod()* *GetMethods()*
N/A	*GetEvent()* *GetEvents()*
N/A	*GetProperty()* *GetProperties()*

Once a *MemberInfo* class has been obtained, several methods, detailed in Table 12-4, are available to obtain type information.

Table 12-4   Methods Available from the *MemberInfo* Class

Member	Description
DeclaringType	Returns the type that contains the member.
MemberType	Returns a value from the *System.Reflection.MemberTypes* enumeration indicating the type of member represented (constructor, method, field, and so on).
Name	Returns the name of the member.
ReflectedType	Returns the instance of *System.Type* that was used to obtain the *MemberInfo* instance.
GetCustomAttributes()	See the "Inspecting Attributes" section later in this chapter for more information.
IsDefined()	See the "Inspecting Attributes" section for more information.

Inspecting Constructors and Methods

The *System.Reflection.MethodBase* class is an abstract derivation of *MemberInfo* that contains additional functionality to reflect on methods. Two concrete subclasses of *MethodBase* exist: *ConstructorInfo* and *MethodInfo*. The following example demonstrates how to obtain the public instance method and constructor information for the *System.String* class:

```
Type x_string_type = typeof(System.String);

ConstructorInfo[] x_constructors = x_string_type.GetConstructors();
foreach (ConstructorInfo x_into in x_constructors) {
    Console.WriteLine("Constructor: " + x_into);
}

Console.WriteLine();

MethodInfo[] x_methods = x_string_type.GetMethods();
foreach (MethodInfo x_info in x_methods) {
    Console.WriteLine("Method: " + x_info);
}
```

The first few lines of the output are listed next; the *String* class contains too many members to list completely:

```
Constructor: Void .ctor(Char*)
Constructor: Void .ctor(Char*, Int32, Int32)
Constructor: Void .ctor(SByte*)
Constructor: Void .ctor(SByte*, Int32, Int32)
Constructor: Void .ctor(SByte*, Int32, Int32, System.Text.Encoding)
Constructor: Void .ctor(Char[], Int32, Int32)
Constructor: Void .ctor(Char[])
Constructor: Void .ctor(Char, Int32)

Method: System.String ToString(System.IFormatProvider)
Method: System.TypeCode GetTypeCode()
Method: System.Object Clone()
Method: Int32 CompareTo(System.Object)
Method: Int32 GetHashCode()
Method: Boolean Equals(System.Object)
Method: System.String ToString()
```

The .NET *ConstructorInfo* class is equivalent to the Java *java.lang.reflect.Constructor* class. Table 12-5 compares these two classes.

Table 12-5   **Comparison Between the Java *Constructor* Class and the .NET *ConstructorInfo* Class**

Java *Constructor* Class	.NET *ConstructorInfo* Class	Comments
getDeclaringClass()	*DeclaringType*	
getExceptionTypes()	N/A	
getModifiers()	*Attributes*	The *Attributes* property returns a value from the *MethodAttributes* enumeration.
getName()	*Name*	In .NET applications, normal constructors are denoted by *.ctor*, while static constructors are denoted by *.cctor*.
getParameterTypes()	*GetParameters()*	See the "Inspecting Parameters" section later in this chapter for more information.
newInstance()	*Invoke()*	See the "Late Binding" section later in this chapter for more information.

The .NET *MethodInfo* class is equivalent to the *java.lang.reflect.Method* class. These two classes are compared in Table 12-6.

Table 12-6   **Comparison Between the Java *Method* Class and the .NET *MethodInfo* Class**

Java *Method* Class	.NET *MethodInfo* Class	Comments
getDeclaringClass()	*DeclaringType*	
getExceptionTypes()	N/A	
getModifiers()	*Attributes*	The *Attributes* property returns a value from the *MethodAttributes* enumeration.
getName()	*Name*	
getParameterTypes()	*GetParameters()*	See the "Inspecting Parameters" section for more information.
getReturnType()	*ReturnType*	
invoke()	*Invoke()*	See the "Late Binding" section for more information.

The *MethodBase* class defines convenience members implemented by *ConstructorInfo* and *MethodInfo* that provide more details about method-type members. These details can also be derived from inspecting the contents of the *Attributes* property of *ConstructorInfo* and *MethodInfo*. These methods are summarized in Table 12-7.

Table 12-7 The *MethodBase* Convenience Members

MethodBase Member	Description
IsAbstract	Returns *true* if the method is *abstract*.
IsAssembly	Returns *true* if the method can be called by other types in the same assembly.
IsConstructor	Returns *true* if the method is a constructor.
IsPrivate	Returns *true* if the method is private.
IsPublic	Returns *true* if the method is public.
IsStatic	Returns *true* if the method is static.
IsVirtual	Returns *true* if the method is virtual.

Inspecting Properties

Properties are represented by the *System.Reflection.PropertyInfo* class; the members of this class are listed in Table 12-8.

Table 12-8 The *PropertyInfo* Members

PropertyInfo Member	Description
CanRead	Returns *true* if the property has a get accessor.
CanWrite	Returns *true* if the property has a set accessor.
PropertyType	Returns a *System.Type* instance representing the type handled by the property.
GetAccessors()	Returns a *MethodInfo* array representing the get and set accessors for the property.
GetGetMethod()	Returns a *MethodInfo* representing the property get accessor.
GetSetMethod()	Returns a *MethodInfo* representing the property set accessor.
GetIndexParameters()	Returns a *ParameterInfo* array representing the arguments to the property. See the "Inspecting Parameters" section for more information about the *ParameterInfo* class.

Table 12-8 The *PropertyInfo* Members   *(continued)*

PropertyInfo Member	Description
GetValue()	Gets the value of the property for a given instance of the declaring type. See the "Late Binding" section for more information.
SetValue()	Sets the value of the property for a given instance of the declaring type. See the "Late Binding" section for more information.

Inspecting Events

Events are represented by the *EventInfo* class; Table 12-9 details the members of this class.

Table 12-9 The *EventInfo* Members

EventInfo Member	Description
EventHandlerType	Returns a *System.Type* representing the underlying delegate
IsMulticast	Returns *true* if the underlying delegate is a multicast delegate
AddEventHandler()	Adds an event handler to a specified instance of the event type
GetAddMethod()	Returns a *MethodInfo* representing the add method of the event
GetRaiseMethod()	Returns a *MethodInfo* representing the raise method of the event
GetRemoveMethod()	Returns a *MethodInfo* representing the remove method of the event
RemoveEventHandler()	Removes an event handler from a specified instance of the type

Inspecting Parameters

The *ParameterInfo* class is used to represent the definition of parameters that are passed into member functions. Table 12-10 details the methods used to obtain parameter information.

Table 12-10 Methods Used to Obtain Parameter Information

Member Type	Method
Constructor	*ConstructorInfo.GetParameters()*
Method	*MethodInfo.GetParameters()*
Property	*PropertyInfo.GetIndexParameters()*

The *ParameterInfo* class is required to represent the modifiers that can be applied to parameters, such as *out* and *ref*. Java does not support parameter modifiers and thus has no equivalent class.

> **More Info** For details of parameter modifiers, see Chapter 4, "Language Syntax and Features."

Table 12-11 lists the members available in the *ParameterInfo* class.

Table 12-11 The *ParameterInfo* Members

ParameterInfo Member	Description
IsOut	Returns *true* if the parameter is annotated with the *out* modifier
Name	Returns the name of the parameter
ParameterType	Returns the *System.Type* of the parameter
Position	Returns the position of the parameter in the parameter list

Inspecting Fields

Fields are represented by the *FieldInfo* class, the equivalent of the *java.lang.reflect.Field* class. Table 12-12 contrasts these two classes.

Table 12-12 Comparison Between the Java *Field* and .NET *FieldInfo* Classes

Field	*FieldInfo*	Comments
get() *getBoolean()* *getByte()* *getChar()* *getDouble()* *getFloat()* *getInt()* *getLong()* *getShort()*	*GetValue()*	Gets the value of a field from a specific instance of the declaring type.
getModifiers()	*IsAssembly* *IsInitOnly* *IsLiteral* *IsNotSerialized* *IsPrivate* *IsPublic* *IsStatic*	Java encapsulates the modifiers for a field in the *java.lang.reflect.Modifiers* class. The *FieldInfo* class makes the same information available through a series of properties.

**Table 12-12   Comparison Between the Java *Field*
and .NET *FieldInfo* Classes**   *(continued)*

Field	*FieldInfo*	Comments
getName()	*Name*	Returns the name of the field.
getType()	*FieldType*	Returns the type of the field.
set() *setBoolean()* *setByte()* *setChar()* *setDouble()* *setFloat()* *setInt()* *setLong()* *setShort()*	*SetValue()*	Sets the value of a field for a specific instance of the declaring type.

Inspecting Attributes

Reflection is available only on custom attributes; it isn't possible to determine whether a type or a member is annotated with one of the system attributes, such as *Serializable*. The *System.Type* class includes properties that go some way toward exposing system properties (such as *IsSerializable*), but the methods that expose attributes via reflection will return custom attributes only.

The *MemberInfo* class defines the *GetCustomAttributes* method, which returns an *object* array; each element in the array can be cast to an instance of an attribute that has been applied to the member. Once an instance of a custom attribute has been obtained, the values that were declared in the attribute annotation are available through direct member calls; it isn't necessary to use reflection to work with attributes.

The *System.Attribute* class defines the static *IsDefined* method, which allows the programmer to determine whether a specific type of custom attribute has been applied to a member.

Late Binding

Late binding is the instantiation and manipulation of types at run time. This is most often used by scripting engines and applications that accept pluggable modules—for example, an application server that allows modules to be loaded dynamically.

Instantiation

Instances of types can be created either by using the *System.Activator* class or by calling the *Invoke* method of a *ConstructorInfo* instance obtained from *System.Type.GetConstructor*. The methods are the equivalents of the *java.lang.Class.newInstance* and *java.lang.reflect.Constructor.newInstance* methods.

The *Activator* class accepts an array of objects that will be used as constructor arguments and attempts to locate a constructor that offers the best possible match. Using the *ConstructorInfo* class ensures that a specific constructor is used for instantiation.

The following example demonstrates how to instantiate a *StringBuilder* using the *Activator* and *ConstructorInfo* classes:

```
Type x_type = typeof(System.Text.StringBuilder);

object first_instance = Activator.CreateInstance(x_type,
    new object[] {"C# for Java Developers"});

ConstructorInfo x_constructor = x_type.GetConstructor(
    new Type[] {typeof(System.String)});
object x_second_instance = x_constructor.Invoke(
    new object[] {"C# for Java Developers"});
```

Manipulation

In the preceding example, we could have cast the instantiated object to *StringBuilder* and called the members as for a normally instantiated type. This is the approach usually adopted if types are required to implement a specific interface to provide functionality.

However, it's also possible to call members using the reflection classes described in the preceding section. Table 12-13 details the methods available.

Table 12-13   Important .NET Reflection Methods

Method	Description
ConstructorInfo.Invoke()	Creates a new instance of the declaring type
MethodInfo.Invoke()	Calls the method
PropertyInfo.SetValue() *PropertyInfo.GetValue()*	Gets or sets the value of a property

Table 12-13   **Important .NET Reflection Methods**   *(continued)*

Method	Description
EventInfo.AddEventHandler() *EventInfo.RemoveEventHandler()* *EventInfo.GetAddMethod()* *EventInfo.GetRemoveMethod()* *EventInfo.GetRaiseMethod()*	Directly adds and removes handlers and exposes the methods that are used to add and remove handlers and raise the event
FieldInfo.GetValue() *FieldInfo.SetValue()*	Gets or sets the value of a field

The following example demonstrates how to invoke a method via the *MethodInfo* class:

```
Type x_string_type = typeof(System.Text.StringBuilder);

object first_instance = Activator.CreateInstance(x_string_type,
    new object[] {"C# for "});

MethodInfo x_method = x_string_type.GetMethod("Append",
    new Type[] {typeof(String)});

x_method.Invoke(first_instance, new object[] {"Java Developers"});
```

The example uses the *Activator* class to create a new instance of *StringBuilder* and then locates and invokes the *Append* method.

Summary

Java and .NET implement reflection in slightly different ways, but the basic principles will be familiar to the experienced Java developer. The differences that do exist reflect the differences between the platforms, including the .NET use of assemblies and the modifiers that can be applied to parameters.

13

Threading and Synchronization

Although Java has been a threaded language from inception, support for multi-threaded programming in the base language has benefited from little innovation in recent years. Furthermore, while significant achievements have been made outside the base language—for example, *Concurrent Programming in Java*, by Doug Lea—the base language itself still supports only the lowest available common denominator because of the platform portability requirements of Java Byte-Code.

By contrast, Microsoft .NET and the common language runtime (CLR) expose many of the rich threading features available in Microsoft Windows and provide fine-grain control over the thread life cycle. .NET applications can also benefit from the many lessons learned in developing robust multithreaded Java applications, including the techniques discussed in Doug Lea's innovative concurrent programming library, available at *www.gee.cs.oswego.edu/dl/cpj*.

With threading, richness equates to complexity, and complexity leads to problems that are difficult to track down and fix. The first part of this chapter will cover the areas where .NET and Java overlap, highlighting the more complex and dangerous features. The second part of this chapter explores the *Thread-Pool* class, which is significantly different from the Java *ThreadGroup* class. In .NET, this class provides access to a pool of threads that will take work items from a queue, and it can be used to simplify threading for some applications. The remainder of the chapter is given over to synchronization. As with threading, there is commonality between .NET and Java, but closer inspection reveals that .NET provides a more sophisticated and complete approach.

Threads

This section discusses the .NET support for threading and illustrates the differences between the Java and .NET approaches.

Creating and Starting Threads

In Java, threading operations are centered on the *java.lang.Thread* class. .NET has the equivalent *System.Threading.Thread* class. Unlike Java, .NET doesn't allow classes to be derived from *Thread*, so creating a thread is more like the use of the Java *Runnable* interface, where the code to be executed is contained in another class. In .NET, threads are created by passing an instance of the *ThreadStart* delegate to the constructor of a new *Thread* instance. Here's a simple threading example in Java using the *Runnable* interface:

```java
public class Example implements Runnable {

    public void run() {
        for (int i = 0; i < 10; i++) {
            System.out.println("Counter: " + i);
        }
    }

    public Example() throws Exception {
        Thread x_thread = new Thread(this);
        x_thread.start();
    }
}
```

The *Example* class implements the *Runnable* interface, which is passed as a parameter to a new instance of *Thread*. When the *Thread* is started, it calls the *Example.run* method.

Here's the equivalent in C#:

```csharp
using System;
using System.Threading;

namespace Example {

    class Example {

        public void run() {
            for (int i = 0; i < 10; i++) {
                Console.WriteLine("Counter " + i);
            }
        }
    }
```

```
    public Example() {
        Thread x_thread = new Thread(new ThreadStart(run));
        x_thread.Start();
    }
}
}
```

Key points worth highlighting include the following:

■ The *System.Threading* namespace must be imported into each class file that uses the threading classes.

■ The *ThreadStart* delegate will accept any method that has no arguments and returns type *void*.

■ The method that is passed to the delegate doesn't have to be called *run* and doesn't need to be public.

■ .NET doesn't define a functional equivalent of the *ThreadGroup* class in Java.

Suspending and Resuming Threads

Another difference between .NET and Java is that the methods *suspend* and *resume* are available for use in a C# application. In Java, these methods (and the *stop* method) have been deprecated because they are considered inherently unsafe. While the same potential problems with the *Suspend* and *Resume* methods exist in a .NET application, Microsoft decided not to eliminate this functionality but rather to allow developers to take their own precautions.

It's recommended that Java threads be controlled by modifying a variable that is periodically checked during execution, a process known as polling. This is commonly achieved by setting the thread reference to null and checking that the reference matches the current thread during iteration:

```
private volatile Thread o_blinker;

public void stop() {
    o_blinker = null;
}

public void run() {
    Thread x_this_thread = Thread.currentThread();
    while (o_blinker == x_this_thread) {
        // perform some operations
    }
}
```

Besides reducing flexibility and introducing complexity, this approach has one major consequence: for methods that take a long time to complete, the responsiveness of the thread is dependent on the frequency with which the thread reference is checked. The programmer has to decide between checking the state frequently and accepting that the call to *stop* might not result in the thread being halted immediately.

By contrast, .NET supports almost immediate thread control using the *Suspend* and *Resume* methods. These methods work as their names indicate. Resuming a thread that has been suspended causes execution to continue from the point at which it stopped. Watch out for the exceptions that can be thrown; it's easy to forget about them since C# doesn't enforce declaring exceptions on method signatures.

Both methods will throw a *ThreadStateException* if the thread hasn't been started or because the thread is dead. In addition, *Resume* will throw this exception if the thread hasn't been suspended. Checking the thread state before making one of these calls can help minimize these exceptions. See the "Thread States" section later in this chapter.

Also note that these calls will throw a *SecurityException* if the caller doesn't have the required permission. See Chapter 17, "Security and Cryptography," for more information on security.

Stopping Threads

The .NET *Thread* class provides an overloaded method, named *Abort*, for stopping the execution of a thread. Calling this method causes a *ThreadAbortException* to be raised in the method that was passed to the *ThreadStart* instance when the thread was instantiated.

There are two overloads on this method:

```
public void Abort();
public void Abort(object);
```

The first version takes no parameters, causes the exception to be thrown, and begins the process of terminating the thread. The second overload takes an object as an argument, which is made available through the exception, and can be used to tidy up.

It's possible to catch a *ThreadAbortException*, but this doesn't prevent the thread from being killed. The exception will be thrown again at the end of the *try...catch* block, but only after any *finally* blocks have been executed. This presents an opportunity to clean up any incomplete state and to ensure that any resources are correctly released.

The following fragment shows how this may be done:

```
public void run() {
    try {
        while (true) {
            try {
                // do some important operation that can result
                // in state problems if stopped suddenly
            } catch (ThreadAbortException) {
                Console.WriteLine("Got inner abort exception.");
            } finally {
                Console.WriteLine("Tidy up.");
            }
        }
    } catch (ThreadAbortException) {
        Console.WriteLine("Got outer abort exception.");
    }
}
```

The results of passing a method into a *ThreadStart* delegate and then calling *Abort* on the running thread are shown below:

```
Got inner abort exception.
Tidy up.
Got outer abort exception.
```

The opportunity to tidy up occurs at each point in the code where the *ThreadAbortException* is caught. If the exception is not caught, it will unwind up the stack to the thread class instance and will not be seen again. The *try...catch...finally* block is not required since there is no state to maintain and notifications about thread deaths are not required.

Although calling *Abort* seems neater and more intuitive than the Java approach detailed earlier, there is no way to determine where the exception will be thrown. It falls to the developer to ensure that no unusual state is left behind if, for example, the exception is thrown during iteration.

Although calls to *Abort* usually result in threads being stopped, the CLR makes no guarantees. An unbounded computation (one that will never complete) can be started in the catch block for *ThreadAbortException*. For this reason, it's important to use the catch block only as intended and not to perform further calculations. If the caller of the *Abort* method needs to ensure that the thread has stopped, the *Join* method can be used, which will block until the thread has been unraveled and stopped.

Another reason that a thread might not stop is that *Thread.ResetAbort* might be called in the *catch* statement. This doesn't stop the exception from being thrown again but does prevent the thread from terminating. This method should be used with care because any other threads blocking through the *Join* method won't return as expected. Time should be taken to consider why a thread should refuse to die when asked.

> **Caution**   We can understand why the *ResetAbort* method has been added, but we feel that it's too dangerous for general use and recommend that you use it as little as possible.

We have seen the *Abort* and *ResetAbort* methods used to try to build a cleaner version of the Java approach to stopping threads, by which an internal flag is used to cause the thread to stop naturally after the current iteration. This approach is problematic because it's impossible to continue the current iteration correctly without knowing where the exception is thrown. If it's important that a thread finish the current iteration before stopping, we recommend using the Java approach, although other threads might still call the *Abort* method and cause unexpected results.

Finally, if a thread is blocking because a call has been made to *Wait*, the *ThreadAbortException* won't be raised until the thread returns from the call or is interrupted, meaning that the target thread won't be stopped immediately. It's possible to determine in advance whether this is likely to be the case by examining the state of the thread, which is discussed later in this chapter in the "Thread States" section.

Setting Thread Priorities

Thread priorities in .NET are handled in much the same way as in Java. The .NET *Thread* class has a property named *Priority*, which controls the thread's priority level using the enumeration *System.Threading.ThreadPriority*. Five priority levels are defined in .NET, vs. 10 in Java, and they are (in descending priority): *Highest*, *AboveNormal*, *Normal*, *BelowNormal*, and *Lowest*. By default, threads are created with *Normal* priority.

As with Java, the scheduling of threads is driven by the underlying operating system. The operating system is not required to honor thread priorities.

There is no direct equivalent of the Java *yield* method in .NET. To ensure that threads of equal priority execute in a .NET application, use *Thread.Sleep(0)*.

Thread States

.NET threads have a defined set of states that demarcate their life cycle. These states are defined in the *System.Threading.ThreadState* enumeration and are described in Table 13-1.

Table 13-1   The *Thread.ThreadState* Enumeration

Thread State	Description
Aborted	The thread is in the *Stopped* state.
AbortRequested	The *Abort* method has been called for this thread, but the *ThreadAbortException* hasn't been dispatched yet.
Background	The thread is running as a background thread. This is similar to the Java *daemon* thread.
Running	The thread has been started. It isn't blocked, and no call has been made to *Abort*.
Stopped	The thread has stopped.
StopRequested	This is for internal use only.
Suspended	The thread has been suspended via the *Suspend* method.
SuspendRequested	The thread is being requested to suspend.
Unstarted	The thread has been created but not started via the *Start* method.
WaitSleepJoin	The thread is blocked because of a call to one of the following methods: *Wait*, *Sleep*, or *Join*.

These states are accessible through the read-only *Thread.ThreadState* property. Threads can be in more than one state, so it's important to check the state carefully. For example, if a thread is blocked because of a call to the *Monitor.Wait* class and another thread calls *Abort*, the blocked thread will be in both the *WaitSleepJoin* and *AbortRequested* states. (See the "Synchronization" section later in this chapter for an explanation of the *Monitor.Wait* class.) When the blocked thread returns from the *Wait* call or is interrupted, the state will be just *AbortRequested* and the *ThreadAbortException* will be thrown, leading to an *Aborted* state.

Key points worth highlighting include the following:

- The *IsAlive* property returns *true* if the thread state doesn't include *Unstarted*, *Stopped*, and *Aborted*.

- The *IsBackground* property returns *true* if the thread is running in the background. This is similar to the Java *isDaemon* method. Background threads are identical to normal threads except that they don't prevent a process from terminating. If a process has no active foreground threads, *Abort* calls will be dispatched to any running background threads and the process will then terminate.

Table 13-2 lists actions and the effect they have on thread state.

Table 13-2 **Effect of Actions on Thread State**

Action Performed	Thread State Becomes...
A new thread is started.	*Unstarted*
A thread calls *Start*.	*Running*
The thread begins running.	*Running*
The thread calls *Sleep*.	*WaitSleepJoin*
The thread calls *Wait* on another *Object*.	*WaitSleepJoin*
Another thread calls *Interrupt*.	*Running*
Another thread calls *Suspend*.	*SuspendRequested*
The thread is suspended.	*Suspended*
Another thread calls *Resume*.	*Running*
Another thread calls *Abort*.	*AbortRequested*
The thread responds to an abort request.	*Stopped*
A thread is terminated.	*Stopped*

When using the thread states, bear in mind that they can change quickly and might be altered before subsequent calls are made. Just because the thread has a state of *Suspended* when checked doesn't necessarily mean that it will remain that way for long before another thread calls *Resume*. For this reason, it's important to check for the possible exceptions when using the thread calls.

Interrupting a Thread

Both Java and .NET provide similar means to interrupt a thread that is blocking. In .NET, a thread is blocked when it's sleeping (via the *Sleep* method), waiting for another thread to end (through the *Join* method), waiting to obtain access to a synchronized code block, or waiting to be signaled by an event.

There are two significant differences when interrupting a thread with .NET. The first is that since C# doesn't require exceptions to be declared in the way that Java does, it's easy to miss instances of *ThreadInterruptedException*—the .NET equivalent of the Java *InterruptedException*—being thrown. These exceptions roll up the call stack of the target thread and can disappear without a trace. If threading code shouldn't terminate when the thread is interrupted, it's vital that these exceptions be caught.

The second difference is more dangerous. With Java, calling *Interrupt* on a thread that isn't blocking has no effect. In .NET, however, calling *Interrupt* on a thread that isn't blocking will cause the thread to be interrupted the next time it blocks. This means that calls to interrupt a thread can have unexpected results long after *Interrupt* is called, creating a problem that can be difficult to track down. We advise caution in the use of this method in .NET.

Local Thread Data

Since version 1.2, Java has provided the *ThreadLocal* class, representing a specialized variable type in which each thread that sets or gets the value modifies its own independent copy of the variable. .NET makes some broadly similar features available, but in contrast with Java, the calls that drive these features are integrated directly into the *Thread* class and are based on the idea of data slots.

There is also a metadata annotation using attributes that allows for a similar effect without directly using the *Thread* class.

Data Slots

Dealing with data slots is a two-stage process, first allocating the slot (akin to creating a new instance of *ThreadLocal* in Java) and then getting or setting the associated data (just like the *get* and *set* methods in *ThreadLocal*).

There are two approaches to allocating slots that affect access to them and the way in which they are garbage collected. The first kind, known as an *unnamed* slot, is most like Java in that to access the slot a thread must have a handle on the reference to the slot itself (an instance of the *System.LocalData-StoreSlot* type). If no threads are referencing the slot, it will be garbage collected automatically.

The second approach is to create a *named* slot, which is available to any thread that knows the name assigned during construction. Named slots aren't automatically garbage collected when they fall out of use and must be explicitly freed using the *FreeNamedDataSlot* method.

Accessing the data is the same for both approaches since the result of the allocate operations is the same data type, and this is the argument that is passed into the accessor methods in the *Thread* class.

Here's a code fragment that illustrates how to create the two kinds of slot:

```
LocalDataStoreSlot x_named_slot =
    Thread.AllocateNamedDataSlot("my slot");
LocalDataStoreSlot x_unnamed_slot = Thread.AllocateDataSlot();
```

Both calls return the same type. The method to set the variable data is the same for both types of slot:

```
Thread.SetData(x_named_slot, "data");
Thread.SetData(x_unnamed_slot, "data");
```

The method to get the variable data is the same, but with the named slot it's possible to get a reference to the *LocalDataStoreSlot* instance by knowing the name:

```
// get the data
object x_unnamed_data = Thread.GetData(x_unnamed_slot);
object x_named_data =
    Thread.GetData(Thread.GetNamedDataSlot("my slot"));
```

To release a named slot, call *Thread.FreeNamedDataSlot*, passing in the name of the slot as the only argument.

Unlike Java, .NET doesn't provide a means for child threads to inherit the slot values from the parent, provided in Java via the *InheritableThreadLocal* class.

Metadata Annotation

The extensive .NET support for metadata can also be used to achieve local thread data in a way that is more familiar in implementation to Java programmers. Static variables annotated with the *ThreadStatic* attribute aren't shared among threads. Each thread has a separate instance of the variable, and modifications affect a copy local to the thread.

An annotated class variable looks like this:

```
[ThreadStatic] static int S_COUNTER;
```

Once annotated, the variable can be used as normal. It's important to ensure that the *static* keyword is used. An annotated instance variable acts as an ordinary variable and will be shared between threads.

Timers

Many threads sleep for most of the time, waking periodically to perform some system or background task—for example, clearing a cache or updating a window. Creating threads consumes system resources, so a common approach to addressing this issue is to provide timers that will signal a callback after a given time period to perform the background task. The advantage of this approach is that the operating system or runtime platform can optimize the way that these signals are managed and use fewer resources to attain the same effect as a pool of programmer-created threads.

.NET provides three different timers to programmers: *System.Threading.Timer*, *System.Timers.Timer*, and *System.Windows.Forms.Timer*. Broadly speaking, the *Forms.Timer* class should be used only for UI applications, as its precision is limited to around 55 ms; for high-performance applications, this level of granularity can be a problem.

The *System.Threading.Timer* class uses the *ThreadPool* class, discussed in "The *ThreadPool* Class" section later in this chapter, to periodically call delegates.

This approach is more accurate than the *Forms.Timer* approach and is suitable for general use.

The *System.Timers.Timer* class provides the greatest accuracy and flexibility. Time ticks are generated by the operating system and place the lowest demand on system resources.

We'll ignore the *Forms.Timer* class—also known as the Windows timer—and focus on the more accurate implementations, which are useful in server-side programming.

System.Threading.Timer

The *System.Threading.Timer* class is simple to use and relies on a state object and a *TimerCallback* delegate to signal. The state object is optional. Here's an example that uses a timer to print a message:

```
class ThreadTimer {
    Timer o_timer;

    public ThreadTimer() {
        // create the timer
        o_timer = new Timer(new TimerCallback(TimerCallbackHandler),
            null, 1000, 2000);
    }

    void TimerCallbackHandler(object p_state) {
        DateTime x_now = DateTime.Now;
        Console.WriteLine("Timer Called: {0}:{1}:{2} ", x_now.Hour,
            x_now.Minute, x_now.Second);
    }
}
```

In this example, we create a *Timer*, specifying a new *TimerCallback*, a delegate that requires a method with a *void* return and a single *object* parameter. The first numeric argument specifies the number of milliseconds before the timer first signals the callback, and the second argument specifies how frequently the timer should subsequently signal the callback, again in milliseconds. The *null* argument represents a state object that's passed into the callback method; we don't use this feature in the example.

As soon as the timer is created, it will begin waiting for the initial delay to elapse. We keep an instance reference to the timer in the class that created it because the timer will continue to signal the delegate until it is disposed of. If we do not have a reference, we cannot make that call. A timer is terminated by calling the *Dispose* method.

Another reason that we kept a reference to the *Timer* instance is that it's possible to change the details of the timer after it has been created, in effect restarting the timer. This can be done with the *Change* method, which takes two *long* arguments. The first argument specifies how many milliseconds should pass before the delegate is signaled again, and the second argument specifies how many milliseconds should elapse between subsequent signals.

The output from this example will be something similar to the following:

```
Timer Called: 14:23:10
Timer Called: 14:23:12
Timer Called: 14:23:14
Timer Called: 14:23:16
```

System.Timers.Timer

The *System.Timers.Timer* class is more sophisticated than the other timers but is as easy to use. Here's a version of the preceding example using this timer:

```
class TimerExample {

    public TimerExample() {
        System.Timers.Timer x_timer = new System.Timers.Timer(2000);
        x_timer.Elapsed += new ElapsedEventHandler(onElapsed);
        x_timer.AutoReset = true;
        x_timer.Enabled = true;
    }

    public static void onElapsed(
        object p_source,
        ElapsedEventArgs p_event) {

        DateTime x_now = DateTime.Now;
        Console.WriteLine("Timer Called: {0}:{1}:{2} ",
            x_now.Hour, x_now.Minute, x_now.Second);
    }
}
```

Although this timer is more flexible than the *System.Threading.Timer* class, it doesn't have support for delaying the initial signal to the handler. However, the timer doesn't start automatically; and it can be started, stopped, and restarted using the *Enabled* property.

An event is raised each time the timer fires. The signature for the event handler requires a source *object* (which is the timer that invoked the event) and an *event* argument. The source reference can be used to control the timer without needing a reference to be kept as with the first example. The *ElapsedEventArgs* argument contains the *SignalTime* property, which indicates the time at which the signal was raised—this can differ from when the signal is received.

The additional flexibility available when working with a *System.Timers.Timer* comes from the way that these timers can be stopped and started and also from their *AutoReset* property, which allows an instance of this timer to represent an event that should be repeated or should no longer be fired. Because the timer instance is passed into the event handler, this can be controlled on the fly. In addition, being aware of which timer has raised a signal is better suited to complex code, which can maintain a number of timers. Since this class raises signals via events, multiple handlers can be attached to a single timer, although we advise caution if attempting to modify the timer settings since the other listeners may then produce unexpected results.

This is the timer class that we tend to use when defining systemwide events, such as the start of a batch process or rolling log files. By having all actions that should occur together tied to a single timer, we can vary the period between actions in a single place and have the effect propagate through the code seamlessly. For other tasks, we favor *System.Threading.Timer*.

Basic Threading Summary

Table 13-3 summarizes the basic threading members for Java and .NET.

Table 13-3 Comparison Between the Basic Threading Members for Java and .NET

Java	.NET	Comments
Runnable	*ThreadStart*	Delegate.
Thread.currentThread	*Thread.CurrentThread*	Property.
Thread.getName	*Thread.Name*	Property.
Thread.getPriority	*Thread.Priority*	Property. .NET uses an enumera-
Thread.setPriority		tion to define thread states.
Thread.getThreadGroup	N/A	
Thread.interrupt	*Thread.Interrupt*	Method.
Thread.interrupted	N/A	
Thread.isInterrupted	N/A	
Thread.isDaemon	*Thread.IsBackGround*	Property.
N/A	*Thread.IsAlive*	Property.
N/A	*Thread.IsThreadPoolThread*	Property.
Thread.join	*Thread.Join*	Method.
Thread.suspend (dep)	*Thread.Suspend*	Method.
Thread.resume (dep)	*Thread.Resume*	Method.

(continued)

Table 13-3   **Comparison Between the Basic Threading Members for Java and .NET**   *(continued)*

Java	.NET	Comments
Thread.run	N/A	.NET uses the *ThreadStart* delegate to define threads.
Thread.sleep	*Thread.Sleep*	Method.
Thread.start	*Thread.Start*	Method.
Thread.stop	*Thread.Abort*	Method.
N/A	*Thread.ResetAbort*	Method.
N/A	*Thread.SpinWait*	Method.
Thread.yield	*Thread.Sleep(0)*	Method.

The *ThreadPool* Class

Many threads spend most of their time waiting for user interaction, such as a user logging in, a key being pressed, or the availability of data on an I/O stream. In its *ThreadPool* class, .NET has provided an event-driven model that can replace these threads.

The .NET *ThreadPool* class has a fixed number of threads available for each processor—normally 50 (25 worker threads and 25 threads for asynchronous I/O). This number is fixed by the CLR and cannot be changed. This pool of threads can monitor several wait operations and notify a delegate when they become free.

Explicit Thread Alternative

The *ThreadPool* class can be used to offload an asynchronous task without using a thread directly. This is not as useful as it sounds since one of the available threads from the *ThreadPool* will be assigned the task and there are only 25 threads available for tasks in the first place. Furthermore, additional *Thread-Pools* cannot be created, and any code running in the process space has equal access to this resource. We can see some advantages to this approach, but since there is so little control over the way that work is handled inside a *ThreadPool*, we think a low-priority thread is usually a better approach. Nonetheless, for completeness, we include an example of how to use this feature:

```
class ThreadPoolExample {

    public ThreadPoolExample() {
        ThreadPool.QueueUserWorkItem(
            new WaitCallback(doCount), "mystate");
    }
```

```
public void doCount(object p_status) {
    for (int i = 0; i < 10; i++) {
        Console.WriteLine("Count: " + i);
    }
}
}
```

The *WaitCallBack* delegate is used to pass in the method that should be executed. The method signature requires a state object that can be used to differentiate between different operations. The call to *QueueUserWorkItem* causes the request to be added to the queue immediately, although the elapsed time before the delegate is called is driven by the workload of the pool.

> **Important**   Once a request has been queued, it cannot be stopped or canceled.

While this approach can be used to achieve threading without having to create the threads manually, we think that this achieves short-term simplicity at a high long-term price.

Waiting for an Event

We feel that waiting for an event is the real strength of the *ThreadPool* class. It's possible to register a callback for a delegate that will be signaled when an event is triggered. We find ourselves using this for all sorts of tasks, especially for handling logging and auditing operations. The following is a simple example:

```
class ThreadPoolExample {

    public ThreadPoolExample() {
        // create the reset event
        AutoResetEvent x_event = new AutoResetEvent(false);
        WaitOrTimerCallback x_callback
            = new WaitOrTimerCallback(this.CallbackHandler);
        object x_status = "my status";

        // add to thread pool
        ThreadPool.RegisterWaitForSingleObject(x_event, x_callback,
            x_status, -1, false);

        x_event.Set();
    }
```

```
public void CallbackHandler(object p_status, bool p_timeout) {
    Console.WriteLine("STAT: " + p_status);
    Console.WriteLine("SIG: " + p_timeout);
}
}
```

The first step is to create an *AutoResetEvent* instance. This is an *event* that will reset after being signaled and is the key to triggering the threaded code. As with most .NET threading operations, we are required to pass in a *delegate* to the *WaitOrTimerCallback* constructor, defining the method that will be called when the *event* is signaled and taking an *object* argument (which contains the user-defined state) and a *bool* that will be *true* if the timer expires before the code is triggered.

The last step is to register with the *ThreadPool*. We do this by calling *RegisterWaitForSingleObject*, passing in the *event*, the callback *delegate*, the status *object* that we want passed to the delegate (in this case a *String*), a timeout value, and a *bool* indicating whether the event should be reset after it's signaled.

In our example, we specify a timeout of -1, meaning that nothing should be done until the event is signaled. There are overloaded forms of this method that take various sizes of timeout and one that takes a *System.TimeSpan*.

We then set the event signal. This would be done in response to something changing (a user clicking a button, a new connection, and so forth), but in our example, we simply set the signal after registering with the *ThreadPool*. The effect of this is that our *CallbackHandler* method will be called immediately.

If we had set the timeout to be greater than -1, we would receive periodic notification to indicate that the timer had expired (indicated by the *bool* in the delegate signature).

The real power of this class is that the code can be notified if the event isn't fired within a given time period. The addition of the state object means that one handler can be responsible for processing the events for several registrations, thus providing further flexibility.

Synchronization

The basic synchronization support in .NET is similar to that in Java. For advanced functionality, .NET goes into areas not covered by Java, exposing some sophisticated tools and fine-grain controls.

Basic Locking

In Java, the keyword *synchronized* is used to ensure that only one thread will enter a specific section of code at a time. In the following example, Java ensures that a thread will not enter the code block containing the comment until an exclusive lock has been obtained on the *this* object.

```
public void doSomething() {
    synchronized (this) {
        // some synchronized operation
    }
}
```

When the thread exits the code section, Java will automatically release the lock so that another thread can attempt to acquire it and enter the synchronized code block.

C# provides the keyword *lock*, which does the same thing. The Java fragment above is translated to C# as follows:

```
public void doSomething() {
    lock (this) {
        // some synchronized operation
    }
}
```

C# doesn't provide a direct analog of using the Java *synchronized* keyword as a method modifier, but the same effect can be achieved by annotating the method with the *MethodImpl(MethodImplOptions.Synchronized)* attribute.

So a synchronized method in Java:

```
private synchronized void doLock() {
    // do something
}
```

looks like this in C#:

```
[MethodImpl(MethodImplOptions.Synchronized)]
private void doLock() {
    // do something
}
```

The *MethodImpl* attribute is defined in the *System.Runtime.CompilerServices* namespace, so this must be imported before the method can be annotated. Key points worth highlighting include the following:

■ No implicit boxing is performed on the *lock* object, so value types, such as an integer or a floating-point number, cannot be used to perform locking. Attempting to use a value type will result in a compile-time error.

■   To protect a *static* method or variable, the use of *this* is not available, but it's possible to use the return from *typeof(MyClass)*.

Waiting and Notifying

In Java, the *Object* class contains the methods *wait*, *notify*, and *notifyAll*. The .NET *Object* class doesn't contain the equivalent methods, but the *System.Threading.Monitor* class exposes the required functionality, as detailed in Table 13-4.

Table 13-4   Mapping the Java *Object* Class Threading Methods to .NET

Java	.NET
Object.wait()	*Monitor.Wait(object)*
Object.notify()	*Monitor.Pulse(object)*
Object.notifyAll()	*Monitor.PulseAll(object)*

The only significant difference is that the *Monitor* class requires the programmer to pass in an object on which to acquire a lock. Like Java, C# requires these calls to be performed within a synchronized section of code, which is accomplished using the *lock* keyword.

The *Monitor* class also provides some functionality that Java doesn't have, giving the programmer more control over how locks are acquired and released.

Enter, TryEnter, and Exit

The *Enter* and *Exit* methods in the .NET *Monitor* class provide the same basic support as the *lock* keyword, albeit with additional flexibility. Locks acquired with the *Enter* call can be released in different methods (or classes) by calling the *Exit* method.

A call to *Monitor.Enter* will cause .NET to either acquire a lock on the *Object* passed in as the argument or block until the lock can be acquired.

When blocking, the thread is in the *WaitSleepJoin* thread state and can be interrupted by another thread calling *Interrupt*. This will cause the thread to unblock and will throw a *ThreadIntrerruptedException*.

Once acquired, a lock can be released by calling *Monitor.Exit*. A thread can request the lock for an object repeatedly without blocking, but Microsoft recommends that *Exit* be called the same number of times as *Enter*. Calling *Exit* to release a lock that isn't held by the current thread will result in an instance of *SynchronizationLockException* being thrown.

The *Monitor* class also provides the ability to attempt to acquire a lock on an object without blocking, akin to checking to see whether a lock is available, acquiring if available and returning if not.

This feature is made available through the *TryEnter* method. If only an *object* is supplied as an argument, an attempt will be made to acquire the lock for the object and the success of the attempt is returned as a *bool*. If an *int* is supplied as well as the object, the CLR will try to acquire the lock for the specified number of milliseconds before returning.

ReaderWriterLock

Although most of the synchronization support in .NET works based on acquiring a lock on a target *Object*, a different model is available in the *ReaderWriterLock* class. This class maintains two levels of lock, an exclusive lock for writers and a nonexclusive one for readers. Many readers are allowed to acquire the read lock simultaneously, but only if the write lock isn't held. One writer can acquire the write lock, but only if there are no active readers. Readers can upgrade to get a handle on the write lock.

We won't cover this class in detail because its use is simple and obvious. This class is ideal for implementing custom collections.

> **Note**   Requests for locks are handled on a first come–first served basis. This means that no more readers will be let through once a writer has requested a lock.

The Java language specification guarantees that any operation on a 32-bit or smaller value will be atomic, without the need to explicitly synchronize access to the variable. With its richer set of data types, .NET takes a different approach, allowing the developer to use the *Interlocked* class to implement atomic access to variables. *Interlocked* allows *int* and *long* types to be exchanged, incremented, and decremented in a thread-safe manner, with the same effect as wrapping the operations in a *lock* block. For example:

```
private void incrementCounter() {
    lock (this) {
        o_counter++;
    }
}
```

This fragment can be rewritten to use *Interlocked* as follows:

```
private void incrementCounter() {
    Interlocked.Increment(ref o_counter);
}
```

Using the *Interlocked* class introduces tidier code and removes the need to use *typeof* to protect *static* variables. The variable must be annotated with the *ref* keyword to ensure that the target variable is modified. Omitting the annotation causes the value of the instance to r be copied and modified without affecting the original instance, in which case simultaneous calls to *Interlocked* will be dealing with different values.

WaitHandle

The *WaitHandle* class is used as a base class for synchronization classes that interoperate with the native operating system. The class defines a signaling mechanism that is used to indicate that a shared resource has been acquired or released. The significance of this class comes from the static methods that allow callers to block until one or more instances of *WaitHandle* are signaled. Three methods are available:

- ■ **WaitOne**   Waits for a single *WaitHandle* to be signaled.

- ■ **WaitAny**   Static method; waits for any one of an array of *WaitHandle* objects to be signaled.

- ■ **WaitAll**   Static method; waits for all of the *WaitHandles* in an array to be signaled.

The three classes in the namespace that are derived from *WaitHandle* are discussed in the following sections.

Mutex

The *Mutex* class can be used to provide synchronization between processes. Here's a simple example of using the *Mutex* class:

```
Mutex x_mutex = new Mutex(false, "shared");
Console.WriteLine("Created mutex");

while (true) {
    string x_str = Console.ReadLine();
    if (x_str.Equals("a")) {
        Console.WriteLine("Attempting to acquire...");
        x_mutex.WaitOne();
        Console.WriteLine("Acquired the mutex");
    } else if (x_str.Equals("r")) {
```

```
        Console.WriteLine("Releasing");
        x_mutex.ReleaseMutex();
        Console.WriteLine("Released");
    }
}
```

Running two instances of this code on a machine demonstrates a shared *Mutex*. Typing *a* causes the class to attempt to acquire the lock. Typing *r* will release the lock. If a process dies when holding the lock, the resource becomes available for acquisition.

The example illustrates a *named Mutex*. Processes that know the name of the *Mutex* can share named instances. Instances can also be created without names. With an *unnamed Mutex*, an object reference must be passed to enable another thread or process to synchronize against it.

> **Tip**   Any process that knows the name of the instance can share a named *Mutex*. Choose names that are project specific. Be aware that other programmers may attempt to acquire the lock for reasons that were not intended, leading to deadlocks.

AutoResetEvent and *ManualResetEvent*

The final classes that we'll cover in this chapter are *AutoResetEvent* and *Manual-ResetEvent*. Threads calling the *waitOne* method of these classes will block until the event is signaled through a call to the *Set* method.

The *AutoResetEvent* is constructed with a single argument that dictates the initial signal state. Using *true* as the argument will result in the first call to *waitOne* not blocking the thread. This class provides a simpler approach to using the *Monitor* class in order to coordinate access to shared resources driven by external events.

In the following example, once started the thread will block on the *waitOne* method until the user types the *s* key, when the default thread will set the event signal. This releases the thread, which writes a message to the console. The *AutoResetEvent* resets automatically—hence the name—and subsequent calls to *waitOne* will also block:

```
class AutoEvent {
    AutoResetEvent o_event = new AutoResetEvent(false);

    public AutoEvent() {
        Thread x_thread = new Thread(new ThreadStart(run));
        x_thread.Start();
```

```
        while (true) {
            if (Console.Read() == 's') {
                o_event.Set();
            }
        }
    }

    public void run() {
        while (true) {
            o_event.WaitOne();
            Console.WriteLine("Event signalled");
        }
    }
}
```

There is also a *ManualResetEvent* class that remains signaled after the *Set* method is used (meaning that calls to *waitOne* will not block). To reset the signal state, the *Reset* method must be used, causing *waitOne* calls to block until the event is signaled again.

Summary

This chapter illustrates that the Java programmer has nothing to fear from the threading and synchronization support in .NET. Most of the constructs and approaches available in Java have at least one analog in .NET.

We end the chapter with a note of caution. When Java was first released, all of the calls in the *java.lang.Thread* class were available for use. Over the years, several have been deprecated because they were found to be unsafe. C# and the CLR are new products, and it's possible that over time the same thing will happen. We think that this is less likely than with Java because the CLR threading model is so closely based on Windows.

14

Networking

This chapter covers the Microsoft .NET Framework networking classes, showing how they work and where there are differences from the *java.net* package. Table 14-1 shows the tiers of service provided by the classes in the *java.net* package alongside their .NET equivalents.

Table 14-1 Three Network Tiers of Service

Service Tier	Java	.NET
Request/response	*URLConnection*	*System.Net.WebClient*
		System.Net.WebRequest
		System.Net.WebResponse
Protocol	*Socket*	*System.Net.Sockets.TcpClient*
	ServerSocket	*System.Net.Sockets.TcpListener*
	DatagramSocket	*System.Net.Sockets.UdpClient*
	MulticastSocket	
Native socket access	N/A	*System.Net.Sockets.Socket*

The first section of this chapter discusses the *WebClient*, *WebRequest*, and *WebResponse* classes that support the request/response tier. The request/response tier supports HTTP-type requests, whereby a client initiates a connection, sends a message to the server, and blocks until the server returns a response via the open connection.

The protocol tier exposes more control to the programmer and can be used for streams-based programming. The programmer can develop custom clients and servers and can send and receive both point-to-point and broadcast messages. The protocol tier consists of a set of convenience classes that make using underlying sockets easier; these classes are discussed in the second part of the chapter.

Finally, the .NET Framework provides a managed code wrapper around the WinSock32 sockets API and provides the programmer with fine-grain control of networking, albeit at the cost of additional complexity. The native socket classes are discussed in the final part of this chapter.

Accessing the Internet

This section discusses the classes that make it possible to make Internet requests. We cover the underlying classes that deal with host names, network addresses, Uniform Resource Identifiers (URIs), and Uniform Resource Locators (URLs), and we conclude this section with the different ways that Internet requests can be handled.

URLs and URIs

Java version 1.4 includes the new *java.net.URI* class. This class coexists alongside *java.net.URL*, but the *URL* class doesn't inherit from the *URI* class. The .NET Framework includes the *System.Uri* class, which is an overarching representation of all URIs and therefore URLs.

Java and .NET both use *pluggable* protocol handlers to abstract URLs from the network protocol implementations. A protocol handler is a class that can service requests for one or more URI schemes. These handlers are registered with a factory class that will create instances in response to calls to a static method ensuring that new types of URI support can be added in the future. The .NET Framework includes protocol handlers for the *http*, *https*, and *file* schemes.

> **Note** Unlike *java.net.URLConnection*, the .NET Framework classes do not provide support for the *ftp* protocol.

The contents of a *System.Uri* instance are immutable. To manipulate URI strings, the programmer must use the *System.UriBuilder* class, which allows the segments of the URI string to be changed.

Constructors

The Java *URL* class contains overloaded constructors that support the specification of individual elements of a URL. The .NET *Uri* class is constructed using strings that are parsed into individual elements and can take arguments representing a base URL and the resource name to target.

This example demonstrates how to create instances of the *Uri* class:

```
Uri x_uri1 = new Uri("http://www.microsoft.com/ms.htm");
Uri x_base = new Uri("http://www.microsoft.com");
Uri x_uri2 = new Uri(x_base, "ms.htm");
```

The *Uri* class also provides constructors that allow the programmer to specify whether escape characters should be substituted in the URL. Here's an example of creating a new URI using a string that is already escaped:

```
Uri x_uri = new Uri("http://www.microsoft.com/
Hello%20World.htm", true);
```

Setting the second argument to *true* indicates that the string should not be escaped, preventing the *Uri* string from being escaped twice, which would cause the percentage symbol to be mapped out of the string.

Methods

Table 14-2 contrasts the *java.net.URI* and *java.net.URL* classes against the .NET *System.Uri* class.

Table 14-2   Comparison Between the Java *URI* and *URL* Classes and the .Net *Uri* Class

java.net.URI & *java.net.URL*	*System.Uri*	**Comments**
URI.create(String)	*new Uri(string)*	Parses the string argument to create a new *Uri*.
URI.getAuthority() *URL.getAuthority()*	*Authority*	Gets the authority for the URI. The authority is the fully qualified host name or Domain Name System (DNS) address of the server plus the port number if the port is not the default for the scheme.
URL.getContent() *URL.getContent(Class[])*	N/A	
URI.getFragment()	*Fragment*	*System.Uri* does not include the fragment in equality checks.
URI.getHost() *URL.getHost()*	*Host*	

(continued)

Table 14-2 **Comparison Between the Java *URI* and *URL* Classes and the .Net *Uri* Class** *(continued)*

java.net.URI & java.net.URL	System.Uri	Comments
N/A	HostNameType	Returns the type of host name specified in the URI—for example, a DNS name or an IP address. Both versions 4 and 6 are supported.
URI.getPath() URL.getPath()	AbsolutePath	
URI.getQuery() URL.getQuery()	Query	
N/A	PathAndQuery	Gets the *AbsolutePath* and *Query* properties, separated by a question mark.
URI.getPort() URL.getPort()	Port	
URL.getDefaultPort()	N/A	
N/A	IsDefaultPort	Returns *true* if the port is the default for the URI scheme.
URI.getScheme() URL.getProtocol()	Scheme	
N/A	IsFile	Returns *true* if the URI references a file.
N/A	IsLoopback	Returns *true* if the URI references the local host.
N/A	IsUNC	Returns *true* if the URI is a UNC path (*server**folder**file*).
URI.getUserInfo()	UserInfo	
URI.isAbsolute()	N/A	
URI.isOpaque()	N/A	
URI.normalize()	N/A	
URL.openConnection() URL.openStream()	N/A	See "The *WebClient* Class" section coming up for information on the *WebClient* class.
URI.parseServerAuthority()	N/A	
URI.relativize(URI)	MakeRelative(Uri)	
URI.resolve(URI)	new Uri(Uri, string)	
URI.toURL()	N/A	The .NET Framework doesn't provide a separate class representation for URLs.
N/A	Segments	Returns a *String* array containing all of the elements that make up the URI.

**Table 14-2 Comparison Between the Java *URI* and *URL* Classes and
the .Net *Uri* Class**   *(continued)*

java.net.URI & *java.net.URL*	*System.Uri*	**Comments**
N/A	*CheckHostName* *(string)*	Checks a host name to ensure that it is valid. The name is not resolved but simply checked to ensure that it meets the requirements for validity.
N/A	*CheckSchemeName* *(string)*	Checks a URI scheme name for compliance with RFC 2396.

The *WebClient* Class

The easiest way to perform Web requests is with the *System.Net.WebClient* class. This class provides functionality similar to that of the Java *URLConnection* class for sending and receiving data. *WebClient* supports requests to URIs using the *https*, *http*, and *file* schemes.

The *WebClient* class provides a simplified networking model that is easy to use and sufficient for many purposes. However, the cost of this simplicity is a loss of functionality and flexibility. For example, with HTTP requests, *WebClient* doesn't support cookies or credentials, doesn't provide access to the result code sent back by the server, and will throw an exception if the code isn't *OK*, which is indicated by result code 200.

Downloading Data

The following example shows the Java *URLConnection* class used to download the Microsoft home page writing the content to the console:

```
URLConnection x_connection
    = new URL("http://www.microsoft.com").openConnection();

BufferedReader x_reader = new BufferedReader(
    new InputStreamReader(x_connection.getInputStream()));
String x_str;
while ((x_str = x_reader.readLine()) != null) {
    System.out.println(x_str);
}
x_reader.close();
```

Here's a C# implementation using the .NET *WebClient* class:

```
WebClient x_client = new WebClient();

StreamReader x_reader =
    new StreamReader(x_client.OpenRead("http://www.microsoft.com"));
```

(continued)

```
string x_str;
while ((x_str = x_reader.ReadLine()) != null) {
    Console.WriteLine(x_str);
}
x_reader.Close();
```

The two approaches are similar, hiding the complexities of the underlying network protocols and providing the programmer with a stream containing the results of the download request. The key difference with *WebClient* is that the target URI is passed as an argument to the *OpenRead* method, not the constructor as with *URLConnection*, allowing *WebClient* instances to be reused across multiple URIs.

The *WebClient* class also provides two convenience methods for downloading data into *byte* arrays and directly into local files. To download data into a *byte* array, use the *DownloadData* method, as in the following example:

```
WebClient x_client = new WebClient();
byte[] x_data = x_client.DownloadData("http://www.microsoft.com");
```

To download data and store it directly in a local file, use the *DownloadFile* method. The following example downloads the Microsoft home page and stores it in *homepage.html*:

```
WebClient x_client = new WebClient();
x_client.DownloadFile("http://www.microsoft.com", "homepage.html");
```

Uploading Data

Sending data to a server with the *WebClient* is similar to receiving data. Four methods can be used; they are listed in Table 14-3.

Table 14-3   The *WebClient* Methods Used to Send Data to a Server

Method	Description
OpenWrite()	Returns a stream that can be used to write data to the server
UploadData()	Writes a *byte* array to the server and returns a *byte* array representing the response
UploadFile()	Uploads the contents of a specified file and returns a *byte* array representing the server response
UploadValues()	Uploads a series of name/value pairs

Each of these four methods is overloaded to accept an HTTP method argument. The default method is *POST*, but any method can be used. Note that the value of the HTTP method isn't validated against values allowed by the HTTP specification.

Configuring *WebClient*

The *WebClient* class has various properties that can be used to configure the request and get information about the response.

Request headers   By default, all requests contain the following headers:

■ *Connection: Keep-Alive*

■ *Host: <name of host derived from the URL used to create the request>*

Requests to send data to the server also contain the following headers:

■ *Content-Length: <length of data being sent>*

■ *Expect: 100-continue*

Headers can be set through the *Headers* property, specifying key/value pairs through an indexer. The default headers just listed don't appear in the *WebHeaderCollection* that the property returns. *WebHeaderCollection* is derived from *System.Collections.Specialized.NameObjectCollectionBase*. For more information, see Chapter 9, "Collections."

Setting a header for an instance of *WebClient* affects all subsequent requests to the server. If requests to the same server require different headers, different instances of *WebClient* should be used, or the headers should be modified between requests.

Response headers   After each call to send or receive data, the *ResponseHeaders* property will return a *WebHeaderCollection* that contains name/value pairs for each of the headers contained in the response. The response headers reflect the result of the most recent request and are overwritten with each subsequent request.

Setting a base address   The *WebClient* class allows a base address to be set. The request strings passed to the upload and download methods will be appended to the base address to form fully qualified URLs. If passed a fully formed request string, the *WebClient* base address is not used but remains in place for future requests.

The following example demonstrates the use of the *BaseAddress* property. First the base address is set to *http://www.microsoft.com*. A subsequent *DownloadData* call specifying *ms.htm* results in a call to the URI *http://www.microsoft.com/ms.htm*:

```
WebClient x_client = new WebClient();
x_client.BaseAddress = "http://www.microsoft.com";
byte[] x_data = x_client.DownloadData("ms.htm");
```

WebRequest and *WebResponse*

The *WebRequest* and *WebResponse* classes represent the next level down in the network class hierarchy, placing the programmer closer to the protocol implementation. The main advantage of using the *WebRequest* and *WebResponse* classes over the *WebClient* class is the level of control available to the programmer. Instances of these abstract types can be cast to protocol-specific concrete types, taking advantage of the methods and properties that expose more control over the request. For example, the *WebResponse* class can be cast to *HttpWebResponse*, which supports features such as cookies and protocol versions.

Here's a simple example using the *WebRequest* and *WebResponse* classes to write the contents of the Microsoft homepage to the console:

```
WebRequest x_req = WebRequest.Create("http://www.microsoft.com");
WebResponse x_response = x_req.GetResponse();
StreamReader x_reader
    = new StreamReader(x_response.GetResponseStream());
String x_str;
while ((x_str = x_reader.ReadLine()) != null) {
    Console.WriteLine(x_str);
}
x_reader.Close();
```

WebRequest

WebRequest is an abstract class that encapsulates functionality common to all Internet requests. Implementation classes that represent a specific protocol are not required to deal with all of the features, so many of the properties in the class can throw a *System.NotSupportedException* to indicate that the feature has no meaning for the protocol that will be used to handle the request.

Creating a request   Instances of *WebRequest* are created using the static *WebRequest.Create* factory method. The *Create* method takes either a *System.Uri* or a *String* containing a URI that specifies the destination of the request.

The factory method approach enables the *Create* method to return a subclass of *WebRequest* designed to handle the protocol specified in the URI argument. Currently only two protocol-specific handlers are provided, *HttpWebRequest* for *http* and *https* scheme requests and *FileWebRequest* for *file* scheme requests.

Configuring a request   Table 14-4 lists the properties of the *WebRequest* class. Not all of these properties apply to all protocol implementations, and many of the following items are clearly derived from an HTTP-centric view of Internet requests.

Table 14-4 The *WebRequest* Properties

Property	Description
ContentType	Gets or sets the type of content being sent to the server.
ConnectionName	Sets a name for the connection. Connections with different names will use a different *ServicePoint*, discussed in the "HTTP Connection Features" section later in this chapter.
Credentials	Gets or sets the security credentials that will be used in the request. See the "Request Credentials" section coming up for more information.
Headers	Gets or sets the collection of name/value pairs that will be used as the headers for the request.
Method	Gets or sets the protocol method to use in the request.
PreAuthenticate	Specifies whether the available authentication information should always be sent with the request or only in response to an authorization challenge.
Proxy	Gets or sets the *System.Net.IWebProxy* that will be used for the request.
RequestUri	Returns the URI of the request.
Timeout	Gets or sets the amount of time that will elapse before the request times out.

Setting Proxies

The default proxy for all *WebRequest* instances is configured using the *System.Net.GlobalProxySelection* class. The *WebRequest.Proxy* property enables the proxy to be set on a per-request basis, overriding the global default. The following example demonstrates the setting of a default proxy:

```
Uri x_uri = new Uri("http://myproxy:8080");
GlobalProxySelection.Select = new WebProxy(x_uri);
```

Request Credentials

The *System.Net.CredentialCache* class stores credentials used to access Internet resources, typically applied to HTTP requests. A single cache of credentials supports authentication information for multiple Internet resources but is intended for supporting a single user. Here is an example of defining credentials:

```
CredentialCache x_cache = new CredentialCache();
x_cache.Add(new Uri("http://www.microsoft.com"), "Basic",
    new NetworkCredential("adam", "adams_password"));
x_cache.Add(new Uri("http://www.java.sun.com"), "Digest",
    new NetworkCredential("adam", "adams_other_password"));
```

The code fragment defines two different credentials, both of which are associated with the user *adam*. Although account names may differ from system to system, the *CredentialCache* class is not intended to track different users. Credentials are associated with a request using the *Credentials* property, and the *PreAuthenticate* property controls whether the credentials are always set with a request or only in response to an authorization challenge. The *WebRequest* class and the concrete implementations are responsible for determining the best credential to use from the cache.

WebResponse

Instances of *WebResponse* cannot be instantiated directly but are obtained when the *WebRequest.GetResponse* method is called. Calling *GetResponse* causes the *WebRequest* instance to send the request to the server; nothing is sent across the network until *GetResponse* is invoked.

As with *WebRequest*, *WebResponse* provides an abstract view of a server response and does not expose protocol-specific functionality. For protocol-specific functionality, cast the *WebResponse* instance to an *HttpWebResponse* or a *FileWebResponse*. Table 14-5 lists the properties available in the *WebResponse* class.

Table 14-5 The *WebResponse* Properties

Property	Description
ContentLength	Gets the content length of the data returned from the server, excluding any headers.
ContentType	Gets the Multipurpose Internet Mail Extensions (MIME) content type of the data returned from the server.
Headers	Gets a collection of name/value pairs that represent the headers returned by the server.
ResponseUri	Gets the URI of the server that responded to the request.

Getting response data   *WebResponse* defines the *GetResponseStream* method, which returns a stream that is used to read the content returned by the server. See the example at the start of this section for a demonstration of reading content with the response stream.

Protocol-Specific Request and Response Classes

Two sets of protocol implementation classes are available in the .NET Framework. The *HttpWebRequest* and *HttpWebResponse* classes are responsible for the *http* and *https* URI schemes, while *FileWebRequest* and *FileWebResponse* are responsible for the *file* scheme.

These protocol-specific classes aren't available for direct instantiation. The static *Create* and instance *GetResponse* methods in the *WebRequest* class always return one of the abstract base classes. If the programmer requires more specific access, the types returned from these methods can be cast to the appropriate protocol-handler class.

File protocol classes   The *FileWebRequest* and *FileWebResponse* classes service requests for the *file* scheme. These classes don't expose any additional information about the file that matches the request, and there is little value in casting to these types when using the request/response classes.

HTTP protocol classes   The *HttpWebRequest* and *HttpWebResponse* classes are responsible for servicing requests using the HTTP and SSL/TLS protocols, represented by the *http* and *https* URI schemes. The classes extend the abstract *WebRequest* and *WebResponse* classes to expose features that are specific to the HTTP protocols and provide a lot of the functionality that is available in the *java.net.URLConnection* class. These classes provide many HTTP-specific features, including the following:

- Selecting between versions 1.0 and 1.1 of the HTTP protocol

- Setting HTTP request headers

- Managing cookies

- Configuring connection persistence and request pipelining

- Support for automatically following redirection directives

Here's the example we used at the start of this section for downloading the Microsoft home page. This time we cast the request and response to the HTTP protocol classes:

```
HttpWebRequest x_req =
    (HttpWebRequest)WebRequest.Create("http://www.microsoft.com");
HttpWebResponse x_response = (HttpWebResponse)x_req.GetResponse();
StreamReader x_reader =
    new StreamReader(x_response.GetResponseStream());
String x_str;
while ((x_str = x_reader.ReadLine()) != null) {
    Console.WriteLine(x_str);
}
x_reader.Close();
```

Table 14-6 details the members of the *HttpWebRequest* and *HttpWebResponse* classes.

**Table 14-6   Members of the *HttpWebRequest* and *HttpWebResponse*
Classes**

Property/Method	Description
Accept	Represents the value of the *Accept* HTTP header.
AddRange()	Adds an HTTP *Range* header to the request.
Address	Gets the URI of the server that responded to the request. The HTTP request and response classes will follow redirection instructions. This property returns the URI of the server after redirections have been performed. The *ResponseUri* property in the base class does not take into account redirections.
AllowAutoRedirect	If set to *true*, redirection directives issued by servers will be followed automatically. If set to *false*, a redirection message is considered to be a response.
AllowWriteStreamingBuffer	If set to *true*, write operations to the server will be buffered in memory. This is useful when redirection directives are received and *AllowAutoRedirect* is enabled.
Connection	Represents the value of the *Connection* HTTP header.
ContinueDelegate	Allows a delegate to be set that will be executed when a server returns an HTTP *Continue* response.
CookieContainer	Represents the cookies associated with the request.
Expect	Represents the value of the HTTP *Expect* header.
HaveResponse	Returns *true* if the server has returned a response to the request.
IfModifiedSince	Represents the value of the HTTP *If-Modified-Since* header.
KeepAlive	Used to determine whether a connection to a server should be persistent, via the *Connection: KeepAlive* header.
MaximumAutomaticRedirections	Specifies the number of redirection directives that will be followed when *AllowAutoRedirect* is enabled. Defaults to 50 redirections.
Pipelined	When *true*, indicates that connections should be pipelined in accordance with version 1.1 of the HTTP protocol, whereby multiple requests and responses are handled in series over a single connection.
ProtocolVersion	Sets the version of HTTP that will be used in the request. Versions 1.0 and 1.1 are supported.
Referer	Represents the value of the *Referer* HTTP header.
SendChunked	When *true*, data will be sent to the server encoded in chunked segments.

Table 14-6   Members of the *HttpWebRequest* and *HttpWebResponse* Classes   *(continued)*

Property/Method	Description
ServicePoint	See the "HTTP Connection Features" section coming up for information about service points.
TransferEncoding	Represents the value of the *Transfer-encoding* HTTP header.
UserAgent	Represents the value of the *User-agent* HTTP header.

HTTP Connection Features

The .NET Framework provides support for controlling the number of open network connections to each HTTP server. Large numbers of connections have a performance impact at both the server and the client. The connection persistence and request pipelining features of the HTTP protocol are used to allow a small number of open connections to service a large number of requests.

This support is provided by the *System.Net.ServicePoint* class, which applies a basic set of constraints for each remote server that an application is using. A new *ServicePoint* instance is instantiated when a request to a new server is created, applying the default limits contained in the *System.Net.ServicePointManager* class.

The *ServicePoint* class has an idle time limit. If no requests are made to the server associated with the service point within this limit, the instance is freed and is available for garbage collection. While an instance of *ServicePoint* is valid, all connections to the server will be governed by the service point settings.

When a *ServicePoint* times out, any settings that are different from the defaults in *ServicePointManager* will be lost. It isn't possible to create an instance of *ServicePoint* and manually associate it with an HTTP request. To ensure that a host retains specific settings, the *ServicePoint* instance needs to be manually configured for each request.

Setting Defaults for All Hosts

The *ServicePointManager* class manages a collection of *ServicePoint* instances. This class is responsible for creating new *ServicePoint* instances as required and applying default values. Changes to the defaults are not applied to previously created *ServicePoint* instances.

Table 14-7 lists the features defined in the *ServicePointManager* class.

Table 14-7   **The *ServicePointManager* Class**

Method/Property	Description
DefaultNonPersistentConnectionLimit	The default number of concurrent connections allowed to an HTTP/1.0 server, currently set to 4.
DefaultPersistentConnectionLimit	The default number of concurrent connections allowed to an HTTP/1.1 server, currently set to 2.
DefaultConnectionLimit	Gets or sets the default number of connections that will be set for new instances of *ServicePoint*.
MaxServicePointIdleTime	Specifies the number of milliseconds that a *ServicePoint* can remain disconnected from the server before being considered expired.
MaxServicePoints	The maximum number of *ServicePoint* instances allowed. The default value (0) indicates that there is no limit. Setting a limit will cause an exception to be thrown if the limit is exceeded by requests to new servers.
FindServicePoint()	Returns the *ServicePoint* associated with a URI. New instances will be created as required.

Configuring a Specific Host

Instances of *ServicePoint* aren't created until the *GetResponse* method is called in the *HttpWebRequest* class or until the *FindServicePoint* method is used for a server that has not previously been contacted.

The first method of configuring the settings for a host is to ensure that the service point is created before any requests are made. Here's an example:

```
Uri x_uri = new Uri("http://www.microsoft.com");
ServicePoint x_sp = ServicePointManager.FindServicePoint(x_uri);
x_sp.ConnectionLimit = 10;

WebRequest x_req = WebRequest.Create(x_uri);
WebResponse x_resp = x_req.GetResponse();
```

In this code fragment, we call the *FindServicePoint* method before we make any requests to the HTTP server and change the limit for concurrent connections. Since no calls have yet been made to the URI, a new instance will be created. When we call the *GetResponse* method in the *WebRequest* class, the *ServicePoint* we have configured will be located and used.

The second approach involves making an initial connection and configuring the *ServicePoint* that is automatically created when the *GetResponse* method is called. Here's an example:

```
Uri x_uri = new Uri("http://www.microsoft.com");
WebRequest x_req = WebRequest.Create(x_uri);
WebResponse x_resp = x_req.GetResponse();

ServicePoint x_sp = ((HttpWebRequest)x_req).ServicePoint;
x_sp.ConnectionLimit = 10;
```

For the first request, the *ServicePointManager* default values will be applied. Subsequent requests will be subject to the configured values.

  ServicePoint instances will be released for garbage collection if a connection isn't made to the server within the time limit. Subsequent connections will result in a new *ServicePoint* being created with the defaults from *ServicePoint-Manager*. We recommend changing the default values where possible to avoid incorrect settings being accidentally applied.

  Table 14-8 lists the methods and properties defined in the *ServicePoint* class.

Table 14-8   The *ServicePoint* Class

Method/Property	Description
Address	Gets the URI of the server that the *ServicePoint* connects to.
ConnectionLimit	The maximum number of concurrent connections that will be allowed to the server. This defaults to the *ServicePointManager* property *Default-ConnectionLimit* when the instance is created.
ConnectionName	Gets the connection name set by the *WebRequest* that caused the *Service-Point* to be created. Only *WebRequest* objects with the same name can use a single *ServicePoint*.
CurrentConnections	Gets the number of connections open to the server.
IdleSince	Gets the date and time that the *ServicePoint* was last used. Any *Service-Point* objects that are unused for longer than *MaxIdleTime* are released for garbage collection.
ProtocolVersion	Gets the version of HTTP used to communicate with the server. This is set automatically based on the response from the server.
SupportsPipelining	Indicates whether requests will be pipelined over a connection. This is set automatically based on the response from the server.

Names and Addresses

Most of the time, it's sufficient to rely on the default behavior of the networking classes to correctly resolve host names to IP addresses. However, there are times when the developer needs to work directly with IP addresses and host names. Both Java and the .NET Framework provide support for creating and managing classes that represent IP addresses and support for resolving details directly using DNS.

Java takes the approach of bundling the support for IP addresses and resolving names into one class, *java.net.InetAddress*. With version 1.4, Java adds support for version 6 of the IP protocol (IPv6) and provides two derived classes, *Inet4Address* and *Inet6Address*, representing addresses for versions 4 and 6 of IP. The .NET Framework breaks out the functionality into several classes, representing conceptual elements for handling names and addresses. There is also a special class, *System.Net.EndPoint*, that represents a network resource or service.

Using the Domain Name System

The Java support for DNS is contained in the *InetAddress* class, and all methods to resolve host information return an instance of *InetAddress*. The .NET Framework includes the *System.Net.Dns* class, which is responsible for resolving names and addresses; the methods of the *Dns* class return the *System.Net.IPHostEntry* type, which represents a DNS record. Table 14-9 summarizes the *IPHostEntry* class.

Table 14-9 The *IPHostEntry* Class

Method/Property	Description
HostName	The primary name of a host
Aliases	A *String* array representing any aliases associated with the host
AddressList	An array of the *IPAddress* type associated with the host

The use of the *IPHostEntry* class to represent all of the DNS entry details available for a host provides a clean class structure. The Java *InetAddress* class provides methods that will return either one IP address or all addresses, while the .NET *Dns* class requires less complexity to achieve the same goals. The *IPHostEntry* type always contains all of the DNS information available.

> **Note** The Java support for name resolution caches successful results indefinitely. Changes in DNS records will not be reflected during the life of an application. The .NET DNS support is hooked directly into the Windows operating system and will reflect changes as they propagate down the DNS hierarchy, subject to the operating system settings.

Here is an example of resolving the name *www.microsoft.com*. The methods of the *System.Net.Dns* class are listed later in this section.

```
IPHostEntry x_entry = Dns.GetHostByName("www.microsoft.com");
Console.WriteLine("Host name: " + x_entry.HostName);
foreach (string x_str in x_entry.Aliases) {
    Console.WriteLine("Alias: " + x_str);
}
foreach (IPAddress x_addr in x_entry.AddressList) {
    Console.WriteLine("IP Address: " + x_addr.ToString());
}
```

The result of this fragment is shown here. Note that the results may change because a large number of servers host the Microsoft site.

```
Host name: www.microsoft.akadns.net
Alias: www.microsoft.com
IP Address: 207.46.230.219
IP Address: 207.46.197.100
IP Address: 207.46.197.102
IP Address: 207.46.230.218
IP Address: 207.46.197.113
IP Address: 207.46.230.220
```

We like this approach. We feel that the model of always getting all of the available information is cleaner and simpler, and the .NET classes expose more details from DNS than Java.

Table 14-10 shows the mapping between DNS support in the Java *InetAddress* and .NET *Dns* classes.

Table 14-10   **The Mapping Between the Java *InetAddress* Class and the .NET *Dns* Class**

java.net.InetAddress	*System.Net.Dns*
getByName()	*GetHostByName()*
getAllByName()	
getByAddress()	*GetHostByAddress()*
getAllByAddress()	
getLocalHost()	*GetHostName()*

IP Addresses

The main purpose of *java.net.InetAddress* is to represent an instance of an Internet Protocol address, and the additions for DNS resolution are a bolt-on feature. The .NET Framework relies on the *System.Net.IPAddress* class to do the same thing. Table 14-11 shows the mapping between these two classes.

Table 14-11   The Mapping Between the Java *InetAddress* Class and the .NET *IPAddress* Class

java.net.InetAddress	*System.Net.IPAddress*	**Comments**
getAddress()	*Address*	The *IPAddress* type returns a *long* instead of a *byte* array
getHostAddress()	*ToString()*	
getHostName()	*Dns.getHostByAddress(IPAddress).HostName*	
N/A	*Parse()*	Parses a *String* representing an IP address into an instance of *IPAddress*
N/A	*IsLoopback()*	Indicates whether an *IPAddress* is the loop-back address

Application Endpoints

The final class in this discussion is *System.Net.IPEndPoint*. This class represents a combination of a host address and port that can be used to contact a service on a remote computer. This class is used extensively with the lower-level networking classes discussed in "Programming with Native Sockets" later in this chapter. Instances of *IPEndPoint* are created using an *IPAddress* to represent the host and an integer to represent the port number, as follows:

```
IPAddress x_addr = IPAddress.Parse("207.46.230.219");
IPEndPoint x_endpoint = new IPEndPoint(x_addr, 80);
```

The example demonstrates how to parse a *String* into an instance of an IP address and then create the *IPEndPoint*. The address we used is from the list registered for *www.microsoft.com*, so this *IPEndPoint* represents the default port for HTTP on the Microsoft Web server. The same result can be achieved directly by using the results of a DNS lookup, as shown here:

```
IPHostEntry x_hostentry = Dns.GetHostByName("www.microsoft.com");
IPAddress x_addr = x_hostentry.AddressList[0];
IPEndPoint x_endpoint = new IPEndPoint(x_addr, 80);
```

Sockets

The *System.Net.Sockets* namespace contains classes used to create applications that work directly with the Transmission Control Protocol (TCP) and the User Datagram Protocol (UDP). These classes build on the native socket classes discussed in the "Programming with Native Sockets" section later in this chapter.

Creating a TCP Client

To illustrate the use of the TCP client classes, we'll read the index page from the Microsoft Web site. Here is a Java example using the *Socket* class:

```java
import java.net.*;
import java.io.*;

public class SocketClient {

    public SocketClient() throws IOException, UnknownHostException {
        Socket x_socket = new Socket("www.microsoft.com", 80);
        PrintWriter x_writer =
            new PrintWriter(x_socket.getOutputStream(), true);
        x_writer.println("GET / HTTP/1.0");
        x_writer.println();
        BufferedReader x_reader = new BufferedReader(
            new InputStreamReader(x_socket.getInputStream()));
        String x_str;
        while ((x_str = x_reader.readLine()) != null) {
            System.out.println(x_str);
        }
        x_writer.close();
        x_reader.close();
        x_socket.close();
    }

    public static void main(String[] p_args) throws Exception {
        new SocketClient();
    }
}
```

This example opens a connection to the HTTP server, sends a message requesting the index page, and then prints the response from the server. After all of the response has been processed, the streams and the socket are closed. This represents a basic HTTP client but doesn't have any of the knowledge of

HTTP that's available in the *WebClient*, *WebRequest*, and *WebResponse* classes described at the start of this chapter. Here's the equivalent functionality written in C#:

```
using System;
using System.Net.Sockets;
using System.IO;

namespace SimpleTCPClient {

    class Client {

        Client() {
            TcpClient x_client
                = new TcpClient("www.microsoft.com", 80);
            NetworkStream x_stream = x_client.GetStream();
            StreamWriter x_writer = new StreamWriter(x_stream);
            StreamReader x_reader = new StreamReader(x_stream);
            x_writer.WriteLine("GET / HTTP/1.0");
            x_writer.WriteLine();
            x_writer.Flush();
            string x_str;
            while ((x_str = x_reader.ReadLine()) != null) {
                Console.WriteLine(x_str);
            }
            x_writer.Close();
            x_reader.Close();
            x_stream.Close();
            x_client.Close();
        }

        static void Main(string[] p_args) {
            new Client();
        }
    }
}
```

The C# and Java examples are very similar, and the *System.Net.Sockets.TcpClient* class can be considered as a direct replacement for *java.net.Socket*. Table 14-12 shows the member mapping between these two classes.

Table 14-12   **The Mapping Between the Java *Socket* Class and the .NET *TcpClient* Class**

java.net.Socket	TcpClient	Comments
bind()	N/A	
close()	Close()	
connect()	Connect()	Both classes will automatically connect to the server if the host name and port number are provided as arguments to the constructor.
getChannel()	N/A	
getInetAddress()	N/A	
getLocalAddress()		
getLocalPort()		
getLocalSocketAddress()		
getPort()		
getInputStream()	GetStream()	The *NetworkStream* class is responsible for both input and output.
getOutputStream()		
getKeepAlive()	N/A	
getOOBInline()		
getReuseAddress()		
getSoTimeout()		
getReceiveBufferSize()	ReceiveBufferSize	
setReceiveBufferSize()		
getSendBufferSize()	SendBufferSize	
setSendBufferSize()		
getSoLinger()	LingerState	
setSoLinger()		
getTcpNoDelay()	NoDelay	
setTcpNoDelay()		
isClosed()	N/A	
isConnected()	Active	This property is protected.
isInputShutdown()	N/A	Input is shut down with the *Close* method.
isOutputShutdown()		
shutdownInput()		
shutdownOutput()		

Creating a TCP Server

The *System.Net.Sockets.TcpListener* class is used to create server applications. Like the *TcpClient* class, *TcpListener* provides a simple wrapper around the socket classes and provides a substitute for the *java.net.ServerSocket* class. Here is a simple TCP server that accepts a single client connection and writes the current time to the server console:

```
using System;
using System.Net.Sockets;
using System.IO;

namespace SimpleTcpServer {

    class Server {

        Server() {
            TcpListener x_listener = new TcpListener(20172);
            x_listener.Start();
            Console.WriteLine("Waiting for a connection");

            TcpClient x_client = x_listener.AcceptTcpClient();
            Console.WriteLine("Accepted connection");
            StreamWriter x_writer =
                new StreamWriter(x_client.GetStream());
            x_writer.WriteLine("The time is {0}",
                DateTime.Now.ToShortTimeString());
            x_writer.Flush();
            Console.WriteLine("Sent time to client");

            x_client.Close();
            x_listener.Stop();
            Console.WriteLine("Finished");
        }

        static void Main(string[] args) {
            new Server();
        }
    }
}
```

The *TcpListener* constructor accepts a port number, which will be used to receive client connections. The *Start* method begins listening for connections, and the class will continue to do so until the *Stop* method is called.

New client connections are accepted using either the *AcceptTcpClient* or *AcceptSocket* method. The *AcceptTcpClient* method returns an instance of *TcpClient*, discussed in the preceding section. The *AcceptSocket* method returns an instance of *System.Net.Sockets.Socket*, which is covered in the "Programming with Native Sockets" section of this chapter.

> **Note**   The *Stop* method ensures that *TcpListener* won't accept new client connections but it won't terminate connections already accepted with the *AcceptTcpClient* and *AcceptSocket* methods. *Socket* and *TcpClient* instances must be closed explicitly before the underlying socket can be released.

Once a connection has been accepted, the resulting type can be used to communicate with the client. These operations can be handed off to threaded delegates, but the process of accepting new connections is synchronous. The *Socket* class allows connections to be accepted asynchronously; see the "Programming with Native Sockets" section for more details.

Table 14-13 illustrates the mapping between *java.net.ServerSocket* and *System.Net.Sockets.TcpListener*.

Table 14-13   The Mapping Between the Java *ServerSocket* Class and the .NET *TcpListener* Class

Java *ServerSocket* Class	.NET *TcpListener* Class	Comments
accept()	*AcceptTcpClient()* *AcceptSocket()*	*TcpListener* won't begin to listen for client connections until the *Start* method is called.
bind()	N/A	
N/A	*Start()*	Starts listening for client connections.
close()	*Stop()*	
isClosed()	N/A	
getChannel()	N/A	
getInetAddress() *getPort()*	*LocalEndpoint*	Returns the *EndPoint* instance for the *TcpListener* that contains the address and port details.
getLocalSocketAddress()	N/A	
getReceiveBufferSize() *getReuseAddress()* *getSoTimeout()*	N/A	
N/A	*Pending()*	Returns *true* if there are pending client connection requests.

Using UDP

The *UdpClient* is responsible for handling both point-to-point and multicast messages with the UDP protocol; since UDP is a connectionless protocol, the *UdpClient* class is used by all endpoints. This provides functionality equivalent to that of the *java.net.DatagramSocket* and *java.net.MulticastSocket* classes from the Java API.

The *UdpClient* can be constructed with details of a default host, and the programmer has the choice of supplying host details for each message or using the default by invoking different forms of the *Send* method. The class provides a *Receive* method that blocks until a datagram is received. The mapping between the Java *DatagramSocket* and *MulticastSocket* classes and the .NET *UdpClient* class is shown in Table 14-14.

Table 14-14 **The Mapping Between the Java *DatagramSocket* and *MulticastSocket* Classes and the .NET *UdpClient* Class**

Java *DatagramSocket* and *MulticastSocket* Classes	.NET *UdpClient* Class	Comments
DatagramSocket.bind()	N/A	
DatagramSocket.isBound()		
DatagramSocket.close()	*Close()*	
DatagramSocket.connect()	*Connect()*	Binds the *UdpClient* to a specific host and port.
DatagramSocket.disconnect()	N/A	
DatagramSocket.getChannel()	N/A	
DatagramSocket.getInetAddress()	N/A	
DatagramSocket.getLocalAddress()		
DatagramSocket.getLocalPort()		
DatagramSocket.getLocalSocketAddress()		
DatagramSocket.getReceiveBufferSize()		
DatagramSocket.getRemoteSocketAddress()		
DatagramSocket.getReuseAddress()		
DatagramSocket.getSoTimeout()		
DatagramSocket.send()	*Send()*	
DatagramSocket.receive()	*Receive()*	
MulticastSocket.joinGroup()	*JoinMulticastGroup()*	
MulticastSocket.leaveGroup()	*DropMulticastGroup()*	

Programming with Native Sockets

The native sockets interface is a managed code wrapper around the WinSock32 API, exposing the underlying socket system of the Windows operating system. For the most part, the .NET socket classes simply provide a one-to-one wrapper around the unmanaged code.

Java programmers are used to working with sockets at a higher level. The .NET socket classes allow for absolute control over Windows-based network programming but achieve this with increased complexity and demand a deeper understanding of network programming from the developer.

Creating Sockets

Sockets are created by specifying an address family, a socket type, and a protocol type. The address family is the address format that will be used to construct packets. The *System.Net.Sockets.AddressFamily* contains a large range of families, but the most commonly used is *InterNetwork*, representing IP version 4 (IPv4). The socket type represents the communication mode of the socket, represented by a value from the *System.Net.Sockets.SocketType* enumeration. The final element is the protocol type, represented by a value from the *System.Net.Sockets.ProtocolType* enumeration. Here is an example of creating a TCP and a UDP socket:

```
Socket x_tcp_socket = new Socket(
    AddressFamily.InterNetwork,
    SocketType.Stream,
    ProtocolType.Tcp);

Socket x_udp_socket = new Socket(
    AddressFamily.InterNetwork,
    SocketType.Dgram,
    ProtocolType.Udp);
```

Client Sockets

The following example demonstrates how to use the socket classes to request the index page from the Microsoft HTTP server:

```
Socket x_socket = new Socket(
    AddressFamily.InterNetwork,
    SocketType.Stream,
    ProtocolType.Tcp);

IPHostEntry x_hostentry = Dns.GetHostByName("www.microsoft.com");
```

(continued)

```
IPEndPoint x_endpoint =
    new IPEndPoint(x_hostentry.AddressList[0], 80);
x_socket.Connect(x_endpoint);

x_socket.Send(Encoding.ASCII.GetBytes("GET / HTTP/1.0\r\n\r\n"));

byte[] x_byte = new byte[100];
int x_read;
while ((x_read = x_socket.Receive(x_byte)) > 0) {
    Console.Write(Encoding.ASCII.GetString(x_byte, 0, x_read));
}

x_socket.Shutdown(SocketShutdown.Both);
x_socket.Close();
```

The obvious changes between using the *Socket* class instead of *TcpListener* have largely to do with convenience:

■   Connections must be made using an *EndPoint*.

■   Sending and receiving data is done using *byte* arrays. There is no stream support in the *Socket* class.

■   Data cannot be buffered.

■   There are no convenience methods for configuring the socket connection.

Once connected, data can be sent to the server using the *Send* or *SendTo* method. The *SendTo* method is useful only for connectionless protocols, such as UDP, in which the target for the message needs to be specified. To receive data from the server, a *byte* array must be passed into the *Receive* or *ReceiveFrom* method, which returns the number of bytes read.

When a socket is no longer required, the *Shutdown* method must be called, followed by *Close*. Shutdown specifies whether the socket I/O should be closed for reading, writing, or both, based on values contained in the *SocketShutdown* enumeration.

Server Sockets

The following example demonstrates a native socket implementation of the simple *time* server from earlier in this chapter. A client connects, and the server writes out the current time:

```
Socket x_server_socket = new Socket(AddressFamily.InterNetwork,
    SocketType.Stream, ProtocolType.Tcp);
```

```
IPHostEntry x_hostentry = Dns.Resolve(Dns.GetHostName());
IPEndPoint x_endpoint = new IPEndPoint(x_hostentry.AddressList[0],
    20172);

x_server_socket.Bind(x_endpoint);
x_server_socket.Listen(5);

while (true) {
    Socket x_socket = x_server_socket.Accept();

    byte[] x_msg = Encoding.ASCII.GetBytes("The time is "
        + DateTime.Now.ToShortTimeString());

    x_socket.Send(x_msg);
    x_socket.Shutdown(SocketShutdown.Both);
    x_socket.Close();

}
```

This example demonstrates that the connections are handled in much the same way as with *java.net.ServerSocket*. The *Bind* method indicates that this socket will be used to receive client connections, and the *Listen* method signals that the socket should be placed in a listening mode. Connections are accepted with the *Accept* method and return a *Socket* representing the connection to the client.

Configuring Sockets

The *Socket* class exposes options that can be set for a connection. A treatise on socket programming is outside the scope of this book, but we will explain how options are set, using some commonly understood examples. Setting socket options requires three elements:

- The level at which the option applies, defined by the *SocketOption-Level* enumeration:

    ❑ *IP*, affecting all IP sockets

    ❑ *Socket*, affecting individual socket instances

    ❑ *Tcp*, affecting TCP sockets

    ❑ *Udp*, affecting UDP sockets

- The name of the socket option, from the set in the *SocketOption-Name* enumeration. Consult the .NET documentation for a complete listing.

- The value of the options, which can be expressed as a *byte* array, an *int*, or an *object*. We recommend consulting the WinSock32 reference guide for more details.

The following example demonstrates how to set an option:

```
x_socket.SetSocketOption(SocketOptionLevel.Tcp,
    SocketOptionName.SendTimeout, 2000);
```

This option sets the amount of time the socket will wait for the other party to acknowledge data sent with the *Send* method.

Asynchronous Sockets

The main advantage of using the *Socket* class is that almost all operations can be performed asynchronously, which is useful for large-scale applications. The details of asynchronous I/O are covered in Chapter 10, "Streams, Files, and I/O," but the *Socket* class also allows connections to be made and received in this manner.

Table 14-15 details the methods that are available for asynchronous programming in the *Socket* class.

Table 14-15 The Asynchronous Methods in the *Socket* Class

Method	Synchronous Method	Description
BeginAccept()	*Accept()*	Accepts a connection from a client
EndAccept()		
BeginConnect()	*Connect()*	Creates a connection to a server
EndConnect()		
BeginReceive()	*Receive()*	Reads data from a socket into a *byte* array
BeginReceiveFrom()	*ReceiveFrom()*	
EndReceive()		
EndReceiveFrom()		
BeginSend()	*Send()*	Sends data to a connected socket
BeginSendTo()	*SendTo()*	
EndSend()		
EndSendTo()		

Summary

The networking classes in the .NET Framework are broadly comparable to their Java equivalents. The *TcpListener*, *TcpClient*, and *UdpClient* classes are all easy to use but don't expose asynchronous features. The *Socket* class allows complete control over the connection but is difficult to use and requires a deeper knowledge of socket programming, often exposing the WinSock32 API in a confusing manner.

Overall, the networking classes are well designed, and we feel that they are better thought out than the Java equivalents, but there is a gap where the partially abstracted functionality of the Java *Socket* class would be useful.

15

Remoting

.NET Remoting is the functional equivalent of the Java Remote Method Invocation (RMI) framework. Both systems allow applications to communicate between processes and machines, enabling objects in one application to manipulate objects in another. RMI was added to Java after the original release of the platform, while the remoting system in .NET has clearly been factored into the platform design from the start. The deep integration into the .NET Framework makes the remoting system easier to use than RMI. Some key differences are:

- Remoting doesn't rely on a registry to locate instances of remote classes. Services must be *well known*, implying that the client must know the location of the remote service at run time.

- Remoting doesn't require remote operations to be handled via interfaces.

- Remoting doesn't require stub classes to be compiled. The support for handling remote operations is intrinsic to the CLR.

First Steps

The best way of demonstrating remoting is by example. In this section, we'll build a simple remote service that adds a series of integer values to a running total. The client sends the server an array of integers and receives back a state object that contains the running total. There is little purpose in such contrived functionality, but the simplicity of this remote service will allow us to illustrate the features of the remoting system.

All of the code files that we'll create in the following sections should be saved in a single directory.

For these examples, the references for the application must include the *System.Runtime.Remoting* namespace included in the *System.Runtime.Remoting.dll* assembly. For more information about compiling with assemblies, see Chapter 3, "Creating Assemblies."

Creating the Server

First we define a server class to sum the array of integers sent from the client, accumulating a running total. The class is listed here and should be saved to a file named CountServer.cs.

```
using System;

public class CountServer : MarshalByRefObject {
    private CountState o_state;

    public CountServer() {
        o_state = new CountState();
    }

    public CountState SumNumbers(params int[] p_values) {
        foreach (int x_value in p_values) {
            o_state.AddNumber(x_value);
        }
        return o_state;
    }

    public CountState State {
        get {
            return o_state;
        }
    }
}
```

The parts of this class that relate to remoting are marked in boldface. We indicate that the class can be made available remotely by deriving the class from *System.MarshalByRefObject*. *MarshalByRefObject* is discussed in the "Copies and References" section later in this chapter.

We keep track of the running total with the *CountState* class. *CountState* provides methods to add new values to the total, clear the total, and return the current total. We have annotated *CountState* with the *Serializable* attribute, meaning that it will be passed by value across the network. For general information about this attribute, consult Chapter 10, "Streams, Files, and I/O"; see the "Copies and References" section in this chapter for details of the impact on remoting. The *CountState* class should be saved to a file named CountState.cs in the same directory as the CountServer.cs file.

```
using System;

[Serializable]
public class CountState {
    private int o_total;

    public void AddNumber(int p_value) {
        o_total += p_value;
    }

    public void Clear() {
        o_total = 0;
    }

    public int GetTotal() {
        return o_total;
    }
}
```

The *CountState* and *CountServer* classes define the functionality for the remoting example, but we still need to define the remoting service. We have created the *Start* class, shown here, which makes the *CountServer* type available to remote clients. This class should be saved to a file named Start.cs in the same directory as the previous two files.

```
using System;
using System.Runtime.Remoting;
using System.Runtime.Remoting.Channels;
using System.Runtime.Remoting.Channels.Http;

class Start {

    static void Main(string[] p_args) {

        // create and register the channel
        HttpChannel x_channel = new HttpChannel(20172);
        ChannelServices.RegisterChannel(x_channel);

        // register the count server for remoting
        RemotingConfiguration.RegisterWellKnownServiceType(
            typeof(CountServer), "CountServer",
            WellKnownObjectMode.Singleton);

        Console.WriteLine("Press return to exit.");
        Console.ReadLine();
    }
}
```

This example introduces the concept of *channels*. Channels are the means by which clients are able to access the remote service. By using the *HttpChannel* class and setting the constructor argument to *20172*, we're stating that the service will accept client requests via the HTTP protocol on port 20172. We then register the new channel with the *ChannelServices* class to activate the network settings and make the channels available for use. Channels are discussed in detail in the "Channels" section later in this chapter.

After creating the channels, we need to register the *CountServer* type; until the type is registered, the remoting system won't accept client requests. This is known as *publishing* and is achieved with the *RegisterWellKnownService-Type* method of the *RemotingConfiguration* class. For the details of publishing objects, see the section entitled "Publishing and Activation" later in this chapter.

Creating the Client

Now that the server side of the remote service is complete, the next step is to build a client. The client will obtain a remote reference to the server and send over an array of integers to be added, returning the total. The result from the *SumNumbers* method is an instance of *CountState*. Finally the *GetTotal* method is called to print the total.

```
using System;
using System.Runtime.Remoting;
using System.Runtime.Remoting.Channels;
using System.Runtime.Remoting.Channels.Http;

class CountClient {

    CountClient() {
        // create and register the remoting channel
        HttpChannel x_channel = new HttpChannel();
        ChannelServices.RegisterChannel(x_channel);

        // local member to initialize the remoting system
        InitRemoteServer();

        DoRemoteSummation(new CountServer());
    }

    private void InitRemoteServer() {
        RemotingConfiguration.RegisterWellKnownClientType(
            typeof(CountServer),
            "http://localhost:20172/CountServer");
    }
```

```
private void DoRemoteSummation(CountServer p_server) {
    // send some numbers to be added to the total
    CountState x_state = p_server.SumNumbers(1, 2, 3, 4, 5);

    // print out the total
    Console.WriteLine("Sum: {0}", x_state.GetTotal());
}

static void Main(string[] args) {
    new CountClient();
}
}
```

Remoting clients also need to create a channel. We create and register a client channel using the same approach as in the *Start* class of the server. We must create the same type of channel for the client as was created for the server, in this case an *HttpChannel*. However, if no port number is specified, a random port is used.

We have isolated in the *InitRemoteServer* method the code responsible for defining the relationship with the server, thus allowing us to demonstrate changes later in the chapter without having to detail the entire class each time. The statement in the *InitRemoteServer* method tells the CLR that when the client instantiates new *CountServer* instances, the remoting service should be used. The details of this are explained in the "Publishing and Activation" section later in this chapter. For now we'll focus on the URL passed as the second argument to the *RegisterWellKnownClientType* method. This URL defines the location where the remoting system can find the server; in the example, we specify *http://localhost:20172/CountServer*. Table 15-1 lists the URL elements.

Table 15-1   The URL Elements

Element	Derivation
http://	Specifies that an HTTP channel should be used to connect to the server. The channel created and registered in the *CountClient* constructor will be used. See the "Channels" section in this chapter for more details.
localhost:20172/	The port number must match the one defined by the constructor argument used by the server class when instantiating the *HttpChannel* instance. See the "Channels" section in this chapter for more details.
CountServer	This is the service name specified by the server in the call to *RegisterWellKnownServiceType*. See the "Publishing and Activation" section later in this chapter for more information.

After the call to *InitRemoteServer*, the *CountClient* calls the *SumNumber* method to request that the server add the values of an array of integers to the running total, which returns an instance of *CountState*. The client then prints the value of the *CountState.GetTotal* method.

Building and Testing the Example

Now that we have created the four C# source files that the example comprises, we can use the C# compiler (csc.exe) to build the executable client and server applications. The first step is to compile the CountServer.cs and CountState.cs files into a DLL/library that can be used by both the client and the server. The following statement shows how this is done using csc.exe:

```
csc /target:library CountServer.cs CountState.cs
```

The compiler creates a file named CountServer.dll that we will use in the following steps when creating the client and server executables. The following statement illustrates how to compile the Start.cs file, including the Count-Server.dll library:

```
csc Start.cs /reference:CountServer.dll
```

The compiler will create a file named Start.exe, which is the server-side executable for our example. The final compilation step creates the client and creates a file named CountClient.exe:

```
csc CountClient.cs /reference:CountServer.dll
```

The server is started by typing Start.exe from a command prompt; the client is started by typing CountClient.exe The server must be instantiated before the client can be run. Each time the client is executed, the server total will be incremented. Here's the output from the client for two separate executions:

```
Sum: 15
Sum: 30
```

We have now created a simple distributed application using remoting. The following sections will move on to the detail of how remoting works and the options available to the programmer.

Copies and References

In common with RMI, remoting provides the distinction between classes that will be referenced remotely and classes that will be copied across the network via serialization. In the example, the *CountState* class is annotated with the *Serializable* attribute, indicating that it will be copied and sent to the client as the result of a call to the *CountServer.SumNumbers* method; all of the .NET primitive types are annotated with the *Serializable* attribute. We can see the effect of serialization if we modify the *CountClient.DoRemoteSummation* method:

```
private void DoRemoteSummation(CountServer p_server) {
    for (int i = 0; i < 2; i++) {
        // clear the state total
        Console.WriteLine("Clearing state.");
        p_server.State.Clear();
        // send some numbers to be added to the total
        CountState x_state = p_server.SumNumbers(1, 2, 3, 4, 5);
        // print out the total
        Console.WriteLine("Sum: {0}", x_state.GetTotal());
    }
}
```

In this version, we invoke *Clear* on the *CountState* instance returned by the *CountServer.State* method before sending the array of integers to be summed. The output from this follows:

```
Clearing state.
Sum: 15
Clearing state.
Sum: 30
```

Although the *Clear* method is being invoked on the *CountState* type, the *Serializable* attribute means that the instance that receives the *Clear* method call is contained in the local process, copied from the instance of the server, and returned as the result of the *SumNumbers* method.

By contrast, classes that inherit from *System.MarshalByRefObject* will be handled as references and the remoting system will ensure that a proxy is used to dispatch method calls to the instance hosted by the server.

A proxy class is one that appears as the remote type to the client but that dispatches member calls across the network to the remoting server; the client isn't aware that the remoting system is being used to service the type. The *CountServer* type is presented to the client via a proxy; all of the members of the type are available to the client, but when a method is invoked, the remoting system will be used to transparently perform the operation on the instance hosted by the server. See the "Publishing Limitations and Scope" section later in this chapter for details of members that will not be invoked remotely.

By removing the *Serializable* attribute and deriving the *CountState* class from *System.MarshalByRefObject*, we change the way that the remoting system handles the *CountState* type; instead of creating serialized copies of the class and sending them to the client, a proxy will transparently dispatch member calls to the instance maintained on the remote server. The revised declaration for the class is shown here:

```
public class CountState : MarshalByRefObject {
```

These changes result in the *Clear* method behaving as expected and resetting the total on the server, as shown by the following output:

```
Clearing state.
Sum: 15
Clearing state.
Sum: 15
```

For more information about attributes, see Chapter 6, "Advanced Language Features." For more information about serialization, see Chapter 10.

Channels

One of the first actions performed by both the client and the server is to create an instance of *HttpChannel*. Here is the server-side statement:

```
HttpChannel x_channel = new HttpChannel(20172);
```

Channels are the mechanism used to transport messages between distributed applications. Channels don't handle the transmission directly, but they act as a binding between a URL scheme and the means by which a remoting operation can be serialized and transmitted.

Channels are defined by three interfaces contained in the *System.Runtime.Remoting.Channels* namespace:

- *IChannel* defines the basis for channels and is used to define common properties.

- *IChannelSender* denotes a channel that is capable of emitting a message.

- *IChannelReceiver* denotes a channel that will listen for messages of a specific protocol on a specific port.

The .NET Framework provides two bidirectional channel implementations:

- System.Runtime.Remoting.Channels.Http.HttpChannel
- System.Runtime.Remoting.Channels.Tcp.TcpChannel

HttpChannel sends messages over HTTP, while *TcpChannel* sends messages using TCP sockets. By default, the *HttpChannel* class encodes messages using Simple Object Access Protocol (SOAP), whereas the *TcpChannel* class uses a binary stream. In most cases, *TcpChannel* offers better performance because encoding and decoding SOAP messages can be a time-consuming process. On the other hand, SOAP forms the basis for XML Web services and allows clients and servers on different platforms written in different languages to communicate seamlessly.

Both the *HttpChannel* and *TcpChannel* classes are convenience wrappers around unidirectional channels; *HttpChannel* combines *HttpServerChannel* and *HttpClientChannel*; *TcpChannel* combines *TcpServerChannel* and *Tcp-ClientChannel*.

Caution   Although *HttpChannel* and *TcpChannel* both rely on TCP/ IP for communication, messages sent from one kind of channel cannot be processed by the other because *TcpChannel* uses binary and *HttpChannel* uses text. It's important to ensure that messages are sent and received by the same type of channel.

Creating a Channel

Both *HttpChannel* and *TcpChannel* offer the same overloaded constructors as detailed in Table 15-2.

Table 15-2   Channel Constructors

Constructor	Description
HttpChannel()	Creates a channel using default values.
TcpChannel()	Locates an available port and binds to it.
	Creates only a client-side channel (that is, this channel cannot be used to publish remoting services).
HttpChannel(int) *TcpChannel(int)*	Creates a channel that binds to the specified port number.
	Creates a channel that can be used to initiate client requests and publish object services. Using *0* (zero) as a port number allows the channel to select an unused port at random and bind to it.
HttpChannel(IDictionary, IClientChannel-SinkProvider, IServerChannelSinkProvider) *TcpChannel(IDictionary, IClientChannel-SinkProvider, IServerChannelSinkProvider)*	Creates a channel that is configured by the entries in *IDictionary* and that uses the specified sinks for processing outbound and inbound messages. If either of the sink provider arguments is set to *null*, the default providers will be used instead.

Using the default constructor creates a channel that is suitable only for remoting clients. Requests can be initiated through the channel, but services cannot be published. If a channel is created with any other constructor, it is able to initiate client requests as well as listen for inbound messages, allowing an application to publish a service for clients and consume services from elsewhere.

The last constructor in the list allows for the greatest control over the channel. Setting aside the sink provider, which is outside the scope of this book, the properties contained in *IDictionary* can be used to configure a channel before it's used.

Most of the channel properties are outside the scope of this book and relate to advanced remoting operations. The only relevant property for this section is *port*, which applies only to server channels, those channels that can be used to publish an object service.

Here's an example of creating a channel using the *port* property:

```
IDictionary x_props = new Hashtable();
x_props["port"] = "20172";
HttpChannel x_channel = new HttpChannel(x_props, null, null);
```

This is equivalent to

```
HttpChannel x_channel = new HttpChannel(20172);
```

> **Important**   The properties of a channel are accessible via the *Properties* property. Changing the value of these properties has no effect on the channel configuration. Properties must be defined and passed in via the constructor.

Registering a Channel

A channel cannot be used until it's registered. At least one channel must be registered before remoting operations can be performed. Channels are registered in the following way:

```
ChannelServices.RegisterChannel(mychannel);
```

The *ChannelServices* class is used to register, unregister, and locate channels. Once a channel has been registered, it becomes available for use. A channel can be withdrawn from use with the *UnregisterChannel* method of the *Channel-Services* class.

Using More than One Channel

Applications can register more than one channel; for example, a server application can offer services via HTTP and TCP. Different types of clients can have different network requirements, and the programmer can decide which channel is best suited to the task at hand.

The *HttpChannel* class is better suited to clients that are located on different networks. Using SOAP over HTTP makes traversing Internet proxies easier, and the *HttpChannel* class provides specific support for using proxies. By contrast, *TcpChannel* uses a binary encoding that is transmitted directly using sockets. This combination of format and transport is less likely to pass through proxies, but it does offer a performance advantage. For applications that need to offer a service to both internal and external clients, multiple concurrent channels give the best of both worlds, providing compatibility for remote clients and performance for local clients.

Here's a variation of the *Start* class from the preceding example, shown without the necessary *using* statements, which registers both a *TcpChannel* and an *HttpChannel*. The changes are marked in boldface:

```
class Start {
    static void Main(string[] p_args) {
        // create the count server instance
        CountServer x_server = new CountServer();
```

(continued)

```
        // create and register the channel
        HttpChannel x_channel = new HttpChannel(20172);
        ChannelServices.RegisterChannel(x_channel);

        // create the tcp channel
        TcpChannel x_tcp_channel = new TcpChannel(20173);
        ChannelServices.RegisterChannel(x_tcp_channel);

        // register the count server for remoting
        RemotingConfiguration.RegisterWellKnownServiceType(
            typeof(CountServer), "CountServer",
            WellKnownObjectMode.Singleton);

        Console.WriteLine("Press return to exit.");
        Console.ReadLine();
    }
}
```

We can now redefine the client-side *InitRemoteServer* method to use TCP as follows:

```
private void InitRemoteServer() {
    RemotingConfiguration.RegisterWellKnownClientType(
        typeof(CountServer), "tcp://localhost:20173/CountServer");
}
```

Notice that the protocol scheme for the client URL has changed to *tcp*. Using the *HttpChannel* class requires clients to use the *http* scheme, while the *TcpChannel* class requires the *tcp* scheme. Using the wrong scheme (for example, *tcp* for a URL that should map to an *HttpChannel*) will result in an exception at run time.

Clients with this new definition can coexist alongside the original version without any problems. The appropriate channel will receive requests, and the object that is targeted by a remote request is not aware of which protocol and transport were used.

Multiple instances of the same type of channel can also coexist, although care must be taken to ensure that the remoting system can tell them apart. This is achieved using the *name* property. The following example demonstrates how to create two channels of the same type with different names:

```
using System.Collections;
using System.Runtime.Remoting.Channels;
using System.Runtime.Remoting.Channels.Tcp;
using System.Runtime.Remoting.Channels.Http;

public class MultipleChannelTest {
```

```
public MultipleChannelTest() {
    IDictionary x_props1 = new Hashtable();
    x_props1["port"] = "20174";
    x_props1["name"] = "http-20174";
    HttpChannel x_channel1 =
        new HttpChannel(x_props1, null, null);
    ChannelServices.RegisterChannel(x_channel1);

    IDictionary x_props2 = new Hashtable();
    x_props2["port"] = "20175";
    x_props2["name"] = "http-20175";
    HttpChannel x_channel2 =
        new HttpChannel(x_props2, null, null);
    ChannelServices.RegisterChannel(x_channel2);
}

public static void Main() {
    new MultipleChannelTest();
}
}
```

Channels have a default name, which is *http* for instances of *HttpChannel* and *tcp* for *TcpChannel*. The naming scheme is left to the programmer to define; any valid string value can be used. To create multiple channels of the same type without unique names, the *name* property should be set to the empty string, which allows any number of channels to be registered without conflict. For clarity, however, we recommend using meaningful names.

Publishing and Activation

When publishing an object service to the remoting system, the programmer needs to be aware of the different activation and life cycle models that are available. There are two types of activation—client activation and server activation—both of which are handled by the *System.Runtime.Remoting.RemotingConfiguration* class.

- When a server publishes a service, the activation type defines how and when the object will be created, and how the life cycle of the object will be controlled.

- When a client registers for an activated service, the runtime is provided with information about how to create new proxies to represent the remote type. Calls to create instances of the registered type using the *new* keyword will be translated into the appropriate remoting operations.

Client Activation

With client activation, a new instance of the published object is created on the server when the client instantiates a local reference. Each new instance on a client will lead to the creation of a new instance of the published object on the server, resulting in a one-to-one mapping between client proxies and instances of the server object.

The client controls the life cycle of the server object. The server won't free the object until the client has finished with it or the client has exited.

We would register the example service in the following way to support client activation:

```
RemotingConfiguration.RegisterActivatedServiceType(typeof(Server));
```

Clients register a mapping for the type as follows:

```
RemotingConfiguration.RegisterActivatedClientType(
    typeof(Server), "http://localhost:20172");
```

After the client has registered for the activated type, calls to *new Server()* will cause a new instance of the *Server* class to be created at the server and a proxy representing this instance to be created at the client. Once a type has been registered for remoting, local instances (those that will not be remoted) can no longer be created.

Key points worth highlighting include the following:

- The URL used by clients to register for a client-activated service doesn't contain the service name.

- Because the remote object is created in response to the *new* keyword, constructors with arguments can be used to instantiate remote objects.

Server Activation

The lifetime of a server-activated object is controlled directly by the server. When the client creates a new instance of the remote type, a proxy is created local to the client, but the instantiation of the remote type at the server is deferred until the client invokes a remote type member via the proxy. Key points worth highlighting include the following:

- No network call is made when the remote type is instantiated.

- Only default constructors can be used because the construction of the remote object is deferred until the client has invoked a method and there are no means to pass constructor arguments.

There are two variations of server activation, which are defined in the *System.Runtime.Remoting.WellKnownObjectMode* enumeration: *Singleton* and *SingleCall*.

Clients register for both kinds of server-activated type in the same way, as shown in the example at the start of this chapter:

```
RemotingConfiguration.RegisterWellKnownClientType(
    typeof(Server), "http://localhost:20172/CountServer");
```

The URL that is passed as an argument is a composite of a channel URL and the name of the service, specified in the server registration. Because the server controls the lifetime of the remote object, the client doesn't need to be aware of the server-activation model used.

Singleton

The first variant of server activation is *Singleton*, wherein the remoting system directs all remote method requests to a single instance of the activated class. The runtime guarantees zero or one instance of the published class will be in existence and that a single instance will be created and shared as required to service client requests. By default, a type instance used as a *Singleton* will be released if no clients make a request for 5 minutes. When this happens, there will be no instances of the published class until the next client invokes a method via a proxy, at which time a new instance will be created.

Overriding the *MarshalByRefObject.InitializeLifetimeService* method to return *null* creates a *Singleton* that never expires. See the section on lifetime leases for more information.

The original example (on page 343) demonstrated a *Singleton* type; the key statement from the *Start* class follows:

```
RemotingConfiguration.RegisterWellKnownServiceType(
    typeof(Server), "CountServer", WellKnownObjectMode.Singleton);
```

The first argument is the type that should be created in response to client invocations, the second argument is the name of the service to be published, and the final argument is the *Singleton* flag.

SingleCall

The *SingleCall* server-activation variation creates a new instance of the published type for each member invocation from a remote client. The instance is released for garbage collection after the member has completed execution.

Servers register a *SingleCall* type as follows:

```
RemotingConfiguration.RegisterWellKnownServiceType(
    typeof(Server), "CountServer", WellKnownObjectMode.SingleCall);
```

Publishing an Existing Instance

Because both *Singleton* and *SingleCall* activation types create instances using the default constructor, the programmer cannot configure instances of the class by passing in arguments during construction. However, it is possible to publish an already created and configured instance of the class as a *Singleton* using the following call:

```
RemotingServices.Marshal(myObjectInstance,"myServiceName");
```

Instances published in this way have an idle time of 5 minutes. Override the *MarshalByRefObject.InitializeLifetimeService* to return *null* if the instance should be available indefinitely. If this method isn't overridden, client attempts to perform operations on the remoting service will throw exceptions because the remoting system is unable to create new instances after the original has expired.

Individual instances can be made unavailable to remote clients by calling the *RemotingServices.Disconnect* method. The argument for this method is the instance that was published, so it's important to keep a reference to published instances if the instance needs to be withdrawn at a later time. When an instance is withdrawn from service, client attempts to perform operations will throw an exception.

Using Configuration Files

The foregoing examples demonstrate how to publish and activate remote objects programmatically. The remoting system also allows remoting to be controlled via XML configuration files. For general information about using .NET configuration files, see Appendix C, "Configuring Applications."

The configuration file requires that channels and published types be declared separately; this reflects the fact that all channels within an application can be used for all published types. All remoting information is contained in the *configuration/system.runtime.remoting/application* section of the configuration file.

Configuration information can be stored in the same file as other application settings but must be loaded explicitly using the *Configure* method in the *System.Runtime.Remoting.RemotingConfiguration* class; other configuration settings are loaded automatically by the common language runtime, but this is not the case for remoting settings.

Defining Channels

Channels are defined using the *<channels>* element, as shown in the following example:

```
<configuration>
    <system.runtime.remoting>
```

```
        <application>
          <channels>
              <channel ref="http" port="0"/>
          </channels>
        </application>
      </system.runtime.remoting>
</configuration>
```

Using this file, we can update the *CountClient* constructor to load the configuration information in order to define the client HTTP channel, as shown here:

```
CountClient() {
    // load the remoting configuration file
    RemotingConfiguration.Configure("RemotingConfig.xml");

    // local member to initialize the remoting system
    InitRemoteServer();

    DoRemoteSummation(new CountServer());
}
```

The statement marked in boldface loads the configuration information, assuming that the details have been saved to a file named RemotingConfig.xml. The contents of the configuration file are equivalent to the following programmatic statements:

```
HttpChannel x_channel = new HttpChannel();
ChannelServices.RegisterChannel(x_channel);
```

Server Configuration

Types are published for remoting using the *<service>* element. The following example demonstrates how to publish a server-activated type:

```
<configuration>
    <system.runtime.remoting>
        <application>

            <service>
                <wellknown mode="Singleton"
                    type="CountServer.Server, CountServer"
                    objectUri="CountServer" />
            </service>

            <channels>
                <channel ref="http" port="20172"/>
            </channels>
```

(continued)

```
        </application>
    </system.runtime.remoting>
</configuration>
```

The *<well-known>* element defines the activation mode (*Singleton* or *SingleCall*), the type, and the URI that will be used to access the service. The *type* attribute is a combination of the fully qualified type name and the name of the assembly that the type is contained in, separated by a comma. The preceding configuration example is equivalent to the following C# statements:

```
HttpChannel x_channel = new HttpChannel(20172);
ChannelServices.RegisterChannel(x_channel);

RemotingConfiguration.RegisterWellKnownServiceType(
    typeof(CountServer.Server), "CountServer",
    WellKnownObjectMode.Singleton);
```

Client-activated types are defined as in the following example:

```
<configuration>
    <system.runtime.remoting>
        <application>
            <service>
                <activated type="CountServer.Server, CountServer"/>
            </service>

            <channels>
                <channel ref="http" port="20172"/>
            </channels>

        </application>
    </system.runtime.remoting>
</configuration>
```

The previous configuration file is equivalent to the following C# statements:

```
HttpChannel x_channel = new HttpChannel(20172);
ChannelServices.RegisterChannel(x_channel);

RemotingConfiguration.RegisterActivatedServiceType(
    typeof(CountServer.Server));
```

Client Configuration

Client configuration is similar to the foregoing examples. The following configuration file demonstrates registering settings for a client-activated type:

```
<configuration>
```

```
<system.runtime.remoting>
    <application>

        <client url="http://localhost:20172">
            <activated type="CountServer.Server, CountServer"/>
        </client>

        <channels>
            <channel ref="http"/>
        </channels>

    </application>
</system.runtime.remoting>
</configuration>
```

The *URL* attribute of the client element is used to indicate the server details. This configuration file is equivalent to the following C# statements:

```
HttpChannel x_channel = new HttpChannel();
ChannelServices.RegisterChannel(x_channel);
RemotingConfiguration.RegisterActivatedClientType(
    typeof(CountServer.Server),
    "http://localhost:20172");
```

The following configuration file demonstrates settings for a server-activated type:

```
<configuration>
    <system.runtime.remoting>
        <application>

            <client>
                <wellknown
                    type="CountServer.Server, CountServer"
                    url="http://localhost:20172/CountServer"/>
            </client>

            <channels>
                <channel ref="http"/>
            </channels>

        </application>
    </system.runtime.remoting>
</configuration>
```

This configuration file is equivalent to the following C# statements:

```
HttpChannel x_channel = new HttpChannel();
ChannelServices.RegisterChannel(x_channel);
```

(continued)

```
RemotingConfiguration.RegisterWellKnownClientType(
    typeof(Server),
    "http://localhost:20172/CountServer");
```

Publishing Limitations and Scope

For the most part, dealing with remote objects is just like dealing with local objects, but in some situations this is not the case.

Methods in the *Object* Class

Calls to the following methods will be sent to the remote object only if the published type overrides the default implementation in the *System.Object* class:

- GetHashCode

- Equals

- ToString

- MemberwiseClone

Calls to the static version of *Object.Equals* will never be sent to the remote object.

Private Methods and Delegates

Private methods cannot be used remotely. With a local object, it's possible to use a delegate to pass a reference to a private method to another class. The remoting system doesn't allow private methods to be used in this manner. Where delegates are used, the object passed to the delegate must be a valid remote type, either annotated with the *Serializable* attribute or derived from *System.MarshalByRefObject*.

Static Fields and Methods

Static members are never remoted. When a static method or field is called, the local class definition is used to satisfy the request. This can be problematic, especially in multithreaded environments, when instance members rely on static fields that are changed as a result of static method calls.

Lifetime Leases

Objects that derive from *System.MarshalByRef* don't live in memory forever. We stated earlier in this chapter that these objects have a default idle period of 5 minutes, after which time the instance will be released. A new instance will be created to service future client requests. The .NET remoting system uses a system of *leases* to control the lifetime of *MarshalByRefObject* (MBR) objects.

A lease defines the amount of time that an MBR object will be held in memory before the .NET remoting system releases the instance freeing the resources it consumes. Leases are used by the remoting server to ensure that objects not currently in use are marked for garbage collection.

When a new instance of a server-activated type is created, the server side of the remoting system will call the *InitializeLifetimeService* method (inherited from the *MarshalByRefObject* class) on the new instance. The return type of this method is the *System.Runtime.Remoting.Lifetime.ILease* interface, which represents an object's lifetime lease.

The *ILease* instance defines the period for which the MBR object will be active. Each time a client makes a remote request to the instance, the lease will be extended. Leases can also be extended by a *sponsor*; a sponsor is a class that implements the *System.Runtime.Remoting.Lifetime.ISponsor* interface. When the lease for an MBR object has expired, the lease manager will query sponsors that have registered with the lease to see whether the lease period should be extended.

Server-activated types aren't required to implement the *ILease* interface; the interface is a representation of a lease, which is maintained separately from the activated instance and managed by the server side of the remoting system.

Configuring a Lease

Table 15-3 lists the properties defined in the *ILease* interface.

Table 15-3   The Properties Defined in the *ILease* Interface

Property	Description
CurrentLeaseTime	Returns a *System.Timespan* representing the amount of time left before the lease expires.
CurrentState	Returns a *LeaseState* describing the state of the lease. (See Table 15-4.)
InitialLeaseTime	Gets or sets the initial lease period.
RenewOnCallTime	Gets or sets the period by which a client request extends the lease.
SponsorshipTimeout	Gets or sets the amount of time that the lease manager will wait for a sponsor to renew a lease.

The *ILease.CurrentState* property returns a *LeaseState* value, an enumeration whose defined states are listed in Table 15-4.

Table 15-4 **The *LeaseState* Enumeration**

Value	Description
Active	The lease is active and has not expired.
Expired	The lease has expired. Expired leases cannot be renewed.
Initial	A lease has been created but is not yet active.
None	The lease is not initialized.
Renewing	The lease has expired, and the lease manager is asking sponsors for renewal.

MBR objects can configure their own leases by overriding the *InitializeLifetimeService* method. The following fragment demonstrates increasing the *RenewOnCallTime* to 5 minutes and the *InitialLeaseTime* to 1 hour:

```
public override object InitializeLifetimeService() {
    ILease x_lease = (ILease)base.InitializeLifetimeService();

    x_lease.InitialLeaseTime = TimeSpan.FromHours(2);
    x_lease.RenewOnCallTime = TimeSpan.FromMinutes(5);

    return x_lease;
}
```

Classes that override the *InitializeLifetimeService* method must call the base class implementation to create the lease; the resulting *ILease* can be used to modify the properties of the lease.

For remote objects that should never expire, override the *InitializeLifetimeService* method to return *null*. Alternatively, setting the value of the *InitialLeaseTime* lease property to *TimeSpan.Zero* has the same result.

Renewing a Lease

With the exception of *ILease.CurrentLeaseTime*, lease properties can be changed only when the lease is in the *LeaseState.Initial* mode. Once a lease is activated, property changes will be ignored. Leases can be renewed either by calling *ILease.Renew* directly or by the lease manager requesting a renewal from a sponsor. Leases are automatically extended by the period defined in the *ILease.RenewOnCallTime* period each time a client performs a remote operation on the MBR object.

Renewing a Lease Directly

Leases are obtained via the *GetLifetimeService* method, which is declared as a static member in the *System.Runtime.Remoting.RemotingServices* class or as an instance member in MBR objects. Once a lease has been obtained, the *Renew* method can be called to increase the lease life. The lease can be directly renewed by any class that has a reference to the MBR object, including a client. The following example shows the *CountClient* example class constructor updated to create a remote instance of the *Server* class and then renew the lease for 5 hours:

```
using System;
using System.Runtime.Remoting;
using System.Runtime.Remoting.Channels;
using System.Runtime.Remoting.Channels.Http;
using System.Runtime.Remoting.Lifetime;

class CountClient {

    CountClient() {
        // create and register the remoting channel
        HttpChannel x_channel = new HttpChannel();
        ChannelServices.RegisterChannel(x_channel);

        InitRemoteServer();

        CountServer x_server = new CountServer();

        ILease x_lease =
            (ILease)RemotingServices.GetLifetimeService(x_server);
        x_lease.Renew(TimeSpan.FromHours(5));

        DoRemoteSummation(x_server);
    }
    // other methods
}
```

Sponsorship Renewal

Sponsors register an interest with the lease of an MBR object through the *ILease.Register* method. Leases are obtained via the *GetLifetimeService* method declared as a static member in *System.Runtime.Remoting.RemotingServices* class or as an instance member in MBR objects. The following fragment demonstrates how to obtain the lease and register as a sponsor. The calling class must implement the *ISponsor* interface.

```
ILease x_lease =
    (ILease)RemotingServices.GetLifetimeService(myRemoteObject);
x_lease.Register(this);
```

Once registered, a sponsor waits for the lease manager to call the *ISponsor.Renewal* method, returning a *TimeSpan* indicating how much longer the lease should be extended for. Lease instances are themselves MBR objects, so clients are able to act as sponsors through the proxy mechanism. Note that if multiple sponsors are registered for an MBR instance, the lease manager will query the sponsors only until one responds with a numeric value representing a positive period of extension.

Leases can be renewed or sponsored only by using a reference to the type instance that has been published for remoting; for types that are activated by the server, the reference can be a client proxy to the remote service. If the lease for an activated type expired, sponsors aren't automatically transferred to instances that are subsequently activated.

Setting Lease Defaults

The default values for new leases can be set using the static properties in the *LifetimeServices* class. Table 15-5 describes these properties.

Table 15-5   The *LifetimeServices* Class Properties

Property	Description
LeaseManagerPollTime	Gets or sets the period between each attempt by the lease manager to detect expired leases
LeaseTime	Gets or sets the initial lease period for new leases
RenewOnCallTime	Gets or sets the amount of time that a lease is extended each time a client makes a request to a server object
SponsorshipTimeout	Gets or sets the amount of time that the lease manager will wait for a response from a lease sponsor

Setting the defaults through the *LifetimeServices* class applies only to new leases; existing leases aren't affected, and objects can specify different values in the *InitializeLifetimeService* method.

Summary

The basis and structure of the .NET remoting service are very different from those of RMI, but the .NET remoting service is easy to use and provides closer integration with the underlying platform. Although lacking interoperability support, the remoting service is a strong offering and quickly allows programmers to develop distributed applications.

16

Database Connectivity

Microsoft ADO.NET is the .NET equivalent of the JDBC API and provides the programmer with consistent access to a variety of data sources. Most commonly, these will be SQL-based relational databases, but they can also be other tabular data sources, such as flat files and spreadsheets. ADO.NET consists of two major components:

- **Data Provider** The Data Provider includes the functionality required to manage a data source, including connection management, transaction support, and data retrieval and manipulation. The Data Provider also acts as a source of data to higher-level data manipulation components such as the *DataSet*.

- ***DataSet*** The *DataSet* is a disconnected, in-memory cache of data. The *DataSet* provides a simplified relational data model in which data from multiple sources can be loaded and manipulated. Data can be written from a *DataSet* back to the original data source or forwarded to another component for further processing.

The functionality of the core JDBC API is most directly comparable with the Data Provider. Although the JDBC *RowSet* interface provides functionality similar to that of a *DataSet*, the exact capabilities of a *RowSet* are implementation specific, and Java version 1.4 doesn't include a concrete implementation. Therefore, we won't provide a direct comparison of *DataSet* and *RowSet*.

> **Note**   References to JDBC in this chapter are to JDBC 3.0 as distributed with Java 2 Standard Edition (J2SE) version 1.4; this includes the *javax.sql* package that was formerly available as the JDBC 2.0 Optional Package. Throughout this chapter, we assume you have a good understanding of relational databases and structured query language (SQL).

Data Providers

An ADO.NET Data Provider is a set of components that encapsulate the basic mechanisms for connecting to and interacting with a data source. Table 16-1 describes the key architectural elements of a Data Provider.

Table 16-1   Elements of an ADO.NET Data Provider

Element	Comments
Connection	Provides connectivity to the data source, connection pooling, transaction control, and factory methods to create Command components. Comparable to the JDBC *java.sql.Connection* interface.
Command	Encapsulates data manipulation and query commands. Provides support for parameter configuration and management, as well as command execution. Comparable to the JDBC *Statement*, *PreparedStatement*, and *CallableStatement* interfaces from the *java.sql* package.
Data Reader	Provides a lightweight, forward-only reader to access the results of an executed command. Comparable to the JDBC *ResultSet* interface.
Data Adapter	Provides a bridge between a Data Provider and a *DataSet*. Data Adapters are closely affiliated with *DataSet* objects, which are discussed in the "*DataSet*" main section later in this chapter.

Interfaces and Implementations

As with JDBC, the components of an ADO.NET Data Provider are defined by a set of interfaces. Table 16-2 provides a comparison of the key JDBC and Data Provider interfaces. The Java interfaces are all from the *java.sql* package, while the .NET interfaces are from the *System.Data* namespace.

Table 16-2   Comparison of Key JDBC and .NET Data Provider Interfaces

Java Interface	.NET Interface	.NET Class
Connection	*IDbConnection*	*OleDbConnection*
		SqlConnection
Statement	*IDbCommand*	*OleDbCommand*
PreparedStatement		*SqlCommand*
CallableStatement		
ResultSet	*IDataReader*	*OleDbDataReader*
		SqlDataReader

Table 16-2 also lists classes from the *System.Data.SqlClient* and *System.Data.OleDb* namespaces of the .NET class libraries that provide concrete implementations of each interface; these are components of the following Data Provider implementations provided with .NET:

■ **OLE DB.NET Data Provider**   Provides connectivity to any data source that implements an OLE DB interface. All class names in this Data Provider implementation are prefixed with the string *OleDb*.

■ **SQL Server.NET Data Provider**   Provides optimized connectivity to Microsoft SQL Server 7.0 and later versions. All class names in this Data Provider implementation are prefixed with the string *Sql*.

There is also a Data Provider implementation for connectivity to ODBC data sources, which requires a separate download from the Microsoft Web site.

Although a Data Provider is defined by interfaces, much of the .NET documentation focuses on the use of the concrete Data Provider implementations. Our approach is to focus predominantly on the use of the Data Provider interfaces; this provides a more accurate comparison with the JDBC model and results in more portable and data source–independent code.

We'll use the SQL Server Data Provider as the basis for implementation discussions and examples. And we'll highlight only key features and differences of the OLE DB Data Provider; for complete details, consult the .NET and OLE DB documentation.

Data Provider Sample Code

The *DBDemo* class, listed below, is a fully functional, if simplistic, application that demonstrates the Data Provider functionality we discuss in this chapter. *DBDemo* manipulates a simple SQL table containing the name, age, and sex of different people. Specifically, when executed, the *DBDemo* application does the following:

1.   Creates a connection to a SQL Server.

2.   Creates three records: one each for Bob, Fred, and Betty.

3.   Sets Fred's age to 28.

4.   Retrieves and displays the name, sex, and age of each person in the SQL table and displays them on the console, producing the following output:

```
Bob is 32 years old; Bob is male.
Fred is 28 years old; Fred is male.
Betty is 43 years old; Betty is female.
```

5.   Deletes the records of all people.

6.   Closes the SQL Server connection.

DBDemo doesn't attempt to exhibit good design or best practice; it's purely a vehicle to demonstrate how to use a .NET Data Provider. We have listed *DBDemo* in its entirety here, and we'll also use appropriate excerpts throughout this chapter to demonstrate the current feature we're discussing. Before executing the *DBDemo* application, the reader must

■   Have access to a Microsoft SQL Server. The SQL Server Desktop Engine (MSDE) that ships with Visual Studio .NET is sufficient for this example.

■   Create a database on the SQL Server named MyDataBase, which can be done using the SQL Server Enterprise Manager.

■   Create a *people* table in the newly created MyDataBase, which can easily be done with the SQL Server Query Analyzer, using the following SQL script:

```
CREATE TABLE people (
    name varchar (20) NOT NULL,
    age int NOT NULL,
    sex varchar (10) NOT NULL)
```

■   Modify the *DBDemo* code by changing the value of the private *DBDemo.sqlServerName* field to the name of the SQL Server being accessed. For example, if your SQL Server instance is running on the mySqlHost.com server, you should do the following:

```
private string sqlServerName = "mySqlHost.com" ;
```

■   Build *DBDemo* using the C# compiler; instructions on using the compiler are available in Chapter 3, "Creating Assemblies."

```
using System;
using System.Data;
using System.Data.SqlClient;

public class DBDemo {

    // Private field to hold DB connection reference
    private IDbConnection sqlCon = null;
    // Private field to hold the SQL Server Name
    private string sqlServerName = "MySQLServer";

    private void Connect() {
        // Create a connection to the specified SQL Server using
        // a database named MyDatabase
        // and integrated Windows security
        string conStr = "Data Source=" + sqlServerName +
            " ; Database=MyDataBase;" +
            " Integrated Security=SSPI";
        sqlCon = new SqlConnection(conStr);
        // Open the SQL Server Connection
        sqlCon.Open();
    }

    private void Disconnect() {
        // Close the SQL Server connection
        sqlCon.Close();
    }

    private void InsertPeople() {
        // Create and start a transaction
        IDbTransaction sqlTx = sqlCon.BeginTransaction();

        // Create the SQL command and assign it to
        // participate in the local transaction
        IDbCommand sqlCmd = sqlCon.CreateCommand();
        sqlCmd.CommandType = CommandType.Text;
```

(continued)

```
            sqlCmd.Transaction = sqlTx;

            try {
                // Insert three records into the "people" table
                sqlCmd.CommandText
                    = "INSERT INTO people (name,age,sex)" +
                    " VALUES ('Bob', 32, 'male')";
                sqlCmd.ExecuteNonQuery();
                sqlCmd.CommandText
                    = "INSERT INTO people (name,age,sex)" +
                    " VALUES ('Fred', 27, 'male')";
                sqlCmd.ExecuteNonQuery();
                sqlCmd.CommandText
                    = "INSERT INTO people (name,age,sex)" +
                    " VALUES ('Betty', 43, 'female')";
                sqlCmd.ExecuteNonQuery();

                // Commit the transaction
                sqlTx.Commit();
            } catch {
                // An exception has occurred,
                // rollback the transaction
                sqlTx.Rollback();
            }
        }

        private void DeletePeople() {
            // Create the SQL command to delete all records from
            // the "people" table
            IDbCommand sqlCmd = sqlCon.CreateCommand();
            sqlCmd.CommandType = CommandType.Text;
            sqlCmd.CommandText = "DELETE FROM people";

            // Execute the DELETE command
            sqlCmd.ExecuteNonQuery();
        }

        private void ListPeople() {
            // Create and configure the SQL command
            IDbCommand sqlCmd = sqlCon.CreateCommand();
            sqlCmd.CommandType = CommandType.Text;
            sqlCmd.CommandText = "SELECT name, sex, age FROM people";

            // Execute the SQL command and create the IDataReader
            IDataReader sqlRdr = sqlCmd.ExecuteReader();

            // Loop through the results and display each record
```

```
    while (sqlRdr.Read()) {
        Console.WriteLine("{0} is {1} years old; {0} is {2}.",
            sqlRdr.GetString(0),      // Typed get
            sqlRdr["age"],            // Named indexer
            sqlRdr[1]);               // Integer indexer
    }

    // Close the IDataReader
    sqlRdr.Close();
}

public void SetAge(string p_name, int p_age) {
    // Create a Text command to perform an UPDATE
    // the age of a specified person
    IDbCommand sqlCmd = sqlCon.CreateCommand();
    sqlCmd.CommandType = CommandType.Text;
    sqlCmd.CommandText = "UPDATE people SET age = @age" +
        " WHERE name = @name";

    // Instantiate and add parameters, order is irrelevant
    IDbDataParameter nameParam = sqlCmd.CreateParameter();
    nameParam.ParameterName = "@name";
    nameParam.DbType = DbType.String;
    nameParam.Value = p_name;
    sqlCmd.Parameters.Add(nameParam);

    IDbDataParameter ageParam = sqlCmd.CreateParameter();
    ageParam.ParameterName = "@age";
    ageParam.DbType = DbType.Int32;
    ageParam.Value = p_age;
    sqlCmd.Parameters.Add(ageParam);

    // Execute the command
    sqlCmd.ExecuteNonQuery();
}

public static void Main() {
    // Instantiate new DBDemo object
    DBDemo dbDemo = new DBDemo();

    // Open database connection
    dbDemo.Connect();

    // Create the demo people records
    dbDemo.InsertPeople();

    // Set the age of "Fred"
```

(continued)

```
                    dbDemo.SetAge("Fred", 28);

                    // List the people records
                    dbDemo.ListPeople();

                    // Delete the people records
                    dbDemo.DeletePeople();

                    // Close the database connection
                    dbDemo.Disconnect();
                }
            }
```

Connections

In both JDBC and ADO.NET, a connection to the underlying data source is represented by a *Connection* object, which provides the starting point for all subsequent interaction with the data source.

Creating and Opening Connections

The *IDbConnection* interface is the ADO.NET equivalent of the JDBC *Connection* interface. An explicit instance of the JDBC *Connection* interface is obtained via the *getConnection* factory method of the *java.sql.DriverManager* or *javax.sql.DataSource* interface. *IDbConnection* instances are created using constructors; the programmer must explicitly instantiate the appropriate implementation for the underlying data source.

The *IDbConnection* implementation classes accept a *connection string* as a constructor argument containing connection configuration parameters in the form of name/value pairs separated by semicolons, similar in nature to a JDBC URL. The connection string can be passed as an argument to the *IDbConnection* implementation class constructor or set via the *ConnectionString* property after construction. Invalid or missing values in the connection string cause a *System.ArgumentException* to be thrown.

Once the *IDbConnection* has been created, it's prepared for use by calling the *Open* method. This method should be called only once for each connection; repeated calls to the *Open* method cause a *System.InvalidOperationException* to be thrown. The state of a *Connection* can be determined using the *IDb-Connection.State* property. *State* returns one of the following values from the *System.Data.ConnectionState* enumeration: *Broken*, *Open*, or *Closed*.

The *DBDemo.Connect* method creates and opens an *IDbConnection* to a Microsoft SQL Server with the name contained in the *sqlServerName* field.

```
private void Connect() {
```

```
    // Create a connection to the specified SQL Server using
    // a database named MyDatabase and integrated Windows security
    string conStr = "Data Source=" + sqlServerName +
        " ; Database=MyDataBase;" +
        " Integrated Security=SSPI";
    sqlCon = new SqlConnection(conStr);
    // Open the SQL Server Connection
    sqlCon.Open();
}
```

Table 16-3 contains a summary of the commonly used parameters for the *SqlConnection* class.

Table 16-3   Common *SqlConnection* Configuration Parameters

Parameter	Comments
Application Name	The application name to use for the connection. Defaults to *.Net SqlClient Data Provider*.
Connect Timeout	The number of seconds the connection will try to connect to the data source before failing and generating an error. Defaults to 15 seconds.
Data Source	The name or address of the Microsoft SQL Server instance with which to connect.
Database	The name of the database to use.
Integrated Security	Determines whether the connection is secure. Valid values are *true*, *false*, and *sspi*, which is equivalent to *true*. Defaults to *false*.
Packet Size	Size in bytes of the network packets used to communicate with SQL Server. Defaults to 8192.
Password	The user password to use to connect to the SQL Server.
User ID	The user name to use to connect to the SQL Server.
Workstation ID	The workstation name to use for the connection. Defaults to the local computer name.

Connection Pooling

If implemented by the data source vendor, JDBC Connection instances obtained via the *DataSource.getConnection* method will be pooled, meaning that a small number of connections will be shared to service requests from a larger number of clients.

All connections obtained through the .NET SQL and OLE Data Provider implementations are pooled by default. The native OLE DB implementation provides connection pooling for the OLE Data Provider, and the SQL Provider implements pooling directly in the .NET classes; consult the .NET documentation for details of the pooling strategy.

Table 16-4 summarizes the connection string parameters that can be used to specify the default connection pooling behavior of the *SqlConnection* class.

Table 16-4 *SqlConnection* **Parameters for Connection Pooling**

Property	Comments
Connection Lifetime	A connection is destroyed if it is older than this value in seconds when it is returned to the pool. The default value of 0 (zero) seconds prevents connections from being destroyed.
Connection Reset	If *true*, the connection is reset when taken from the pool; if *false*, it is not reset, avoiding the additional communication with the server. Defaults to *true*.
Max Pool Size	The maximum number of connections allowed in the pool. Defaults to 100.
Min Pool Size	The minimum number of connections allowed in the pool. Defaults to 0 (zero).
Pooling	When *true*, the new connection object is taken from or created in an appropriate pool; otherwise, the connection is created independent of pooling. Defaults to *true*.

Closing a Connection

Connections should always be closed using the *IDbConnection.Close* method or the *Dispose* method inherited from the *IDisposable* interface. If connection pooling is disabled, the underlying connection to the server will be closed; otherwise, the connection is maintained and the *IDbConnection* instance will be returned to the connection pool for future use. The *DBDemo.Disconnect* method demonstrates the use of *IDbConnection.Close* to close a database connection.

```
private void Disconnect() {
    // Close the SQL Server connection
    sqlCon.Close();
}
```

Changing the Active Database

The *IDbConnection.ChangeDatabase* method can be used to change the current database without the need to close and reopen a connection.

Transactions

In JDBC, transactions can be managed through the *Connection* interface using the *setAutoCommit*, *setTransactionalIsolation*, *commit*, and *rollback* methods. By default, JDBC utilizes autocommit mode, in which every database communication is handled in a separate transaction. To maintain explicit transaction control, a JDBC application must disable autocommit mode, which is done by passing *false* to the *setAutoCommit* method in the *Connection* interface.

In ADO.NET, a transaction is initiated via the *IDbConnection.BeginTransaction* method, which returns an *IDbTransaction* instance through which all transaction management is performed.

Table 16-5 provides a comparison of the classes and methods used to initiate and control transactions in both JDBC and ADO.NET.

Table 16-5 Transaction Control Classes and Methods

JDBC Connection Methods	ADO.NET Equivalent
Connection.setAutoCommit(false)	*IDbConnection.BeginTransaction()*
Connection.setTransactionIsolation-IsolationLevel)	*IDbConnection.BeginTransaction(IsolationLevel)*
Connection.getTransactionIsolation()	*IDbTransaction.IsolationLevel*
Connection.commit()	*IDbTransaction.Commit()*
Connection.rollback()	*IDbTransaction.Rollback()*
Connection.save()	Not supported by generic interfaces, but the SQL implementation provides an equivalent *SqlTransaction.Save* method.

The same levels of transactional isolation are supported in both JDBC and ADO.NET. In ADO.NET, these are specified using members of the *System.Data.IsolationLevel* enumeration, which includes the following values: *ReadCommitted*, *ReadUncommitted*, *RepeatableRead*, and *Serializable*.

JDBC defines optional support for distributed transactions through the *XAConnection* and *XADataSource* interfaces. For both the SQL and OLE Data Provider implementations, the *IDbTransaction* functionality maps directly to the transactional capabilities of the underlying data source and is not integrated with any distributed transaction manager.

The *DBDemo.InsertPeople* method creates an *IDbTransaction* instance to ensure that all records are inserted into the *people* table atomically. Note that the transaction is created with no arguments, resulting in the default isolation level (*ReadCommitted*) being utilized. Also, the *IDbTransaction* instance must be assigned to the *Transaction* property of the *IDbCommand* prior to execution to enlist the command in the active transaction. If an exception occurs during the insertion of any of the records, the *catch* clause will execute and the partially executed transaction will be rolled back by the code contained in the *catch* clause calling the *IDbTransaction.Rollback* method.

```
private void InsertPeople() {
    // Create and start a transaction
    IDbTransaction sqlTx = sqlCon.BeginTransaction();

    // Create the SQL command and assign it to
    // participate in the local transaction
    IDbCommand sqlCmd = sqlCon.CreateCommand();
    sqlCmd.CommandType = CommandType.Text;
    sqlCmd.Transaction = sqlTx;

    try {
        // Insert three records into the "people" table
        sqlCmd.CommandText = "INSERT INTO people (name,age,sex)" +
            " VALUES ('Bob', 32, 'male')";
        sqlCmd.ExecuteNonQuery();
        sqlCmd.CommandText = "INSERT INTO people (name,age,sex)" +
            " VALUES ('Fred', 27, 'male')";
        sqlCmd.ExecuteNonQuery();
        sqlCmd.CommandText = "INSERT INTO people (name,age,sex)" +
            " VALUES ('Betty', 43, 'female')";
        sqlCmd.ExecuteNonQuery();

        // Commit the transaction
        sqlTx.Commit();
    } catch {
        // An exception has occurred, rollback the transaction
        sqlTx.Rollback();
    }
}
```

Commands

JDBC provides three interfaces to represent SQL commands:

- **Statement**   Used to issue SQL commands against the data source

- **PreparedStatement**   A SQL statement that supports parameter substitution

- **CallableStatement**   Provides support for calling SQL stored procedures

ADO.NET consolidates the major functionality of these three interfaces into a single interface named *IDbCommand*.

Creating Commands

In both JDBC and ADO.NET, connection objects act as factories for creating command objects. The JDBC *Connection* interface defines methods for creating instances of the *Statement*, *PreparedStatement*, and *CallableStatement* interfaces: the *createStatement*, *prepareStatement*, and *prepareCall* methods, respectively. The ADO.NET equivalent is the *IDbConnection.CreateCommand* method; *CreateCommand* takes no arguments and returns an *IDbCommand* instance. Use of the *CreateCommand* method can be seen at the start of the *InsertPeople*, *DeletePeople*, and *SetAge* methods of *DBDemo*.

Both the SQL and OLE Data Provider implementations of *IDbCommand* can be instantiated using constructors; however, use of the *CreateCommand* factory method ensures that the correct implementation of *IDbCommand* is always instantiated, provides default configuration for *IDbCommand*, and improves code portability.

Configuring Commands

Once *IDbCommand* is instantiated, it must be configured using the properties detailed in Table 16-6. If *IDbCommand* is created via the *IDbConnection.CreateCommand* method, the *Connection* property will be set to the correct value for the current *IDbConnection*. The key properties for any *IDbCommand* are *CommandText* and *CommandType*; the text contained in *CommandText* must be compatible with the *CommandType* value.

Table 16-6 **Properties of *IDbCommand***

Property	Comments
CommandText	Gets or sets the text of the command to execute against the data source. The syntax of this text depends on the *CommandType* property.
CommandTimeout	Gets or sets the time (in seconds) that the executing command waits for a response before terminating and throwing an error. The default value is 30 seconds.
CommandType	Gets or sets the command type represented by this *IDbCommand* instance. Specified using the following members of the *System.Data.CommandType* enumeration:
	■ *StoredProcedure*—command text represents the name of a stored procedure.
	■ *TableDirect*—supported only by *OleDbCommand*. Command text represents one or more table names for which the entire contents should be returned.
	■ *Text*—command text represents an SQL command.
	The default value is *Text*.

(continued)

Table 16-6   Properties of *IDbCommand*   *(continued)*

Property	Comments
Connection	Gets or sets the *IDbConnection* instance used by this command.
Transaction	Gets or sets the *IDbTransaction* instance in which this command executes.

Configuring an *IDbCommand* to execute a direct SQL statement   When executing a direct SQL statement such as a *SELECT* or a *DELETE* command, the *CommandType* must be set to *System.Data.CommandType.Text* (the default value), and the *CommandText* property must be set to the text of the SQL statement. The *DBDemo.DeletePeople* method demonstrates the configuration of an *IDbCommand* to execute a *SQL DELETE* statement:

```
private void DeletePeople() {
    // Create the SQL command to delete all records from
    // the "people" table
    IDbCommand sqlCmd = sqlCon.CreateCommand();
    sqlCmd.CommandType = CommandType.Text;
    sqlCmd.CommandText = "DELETE FROM people";

    // Execute the DELETE command
    sqlCmd.ExecuteNonQuery();
}
```

The *CommandText* can also include parameter identifiers that are substituted with values at run time. The syntax for parameter substitution is implementation specific. The SQL Data Provider supports named parameters prefixed with the @ symbol, as demonstrated in the following excerpt from the *DBDemo.SetAge* method:

```
IDbCommand sqlCmd = sqlCon.CreateCommand();
sqlCmd.CommandType = CommandType.Text;
sqlCmd.CommandText = "UPDATE people SET age = @age" +
    " WHERE name = @name";
```

However, the OLE Data Provider supports only positional parameter substitution using the *?* symbol, the same as the JDBC *PreparedStatement*. The preceding code fragment would appear as follows if implemented using an OLE Data Provider:

```
IDbCommand sqlCmd = sqlCon.CreateCommand();
sqlCmd.CommandType = CommandType.Text;
sqlCmd.CommandText = "UPDATE people SET age = ?" +
    " WHERE name = ?";
```

For both positional and named parameters, an *IDbDataParameter* instance must be provided for each parameter included in the command string. See the "Parameters" section coming up for details.

Configuring an *IDbCommand* to execute a stored procedure   When calling a stored procedure, you must set *CommandType* to *System.Data.Command-Type.StoredProcedure* and the *CommandText* must be set to the name of the stored procedure. Later in the "Parameters" section we provide an alternative *DBDemo.SetAge* implementation that calls a stored procedure to update the age of a person. For now, the following code fragment demonstrates the configuration of an *IDbCommand* to execute a stored procedure named *SetAge*. *IDbData-Parameter* instances must be provided for each input and output parameter specified by the stored procedure as well as the stored procedure's return value.

```
// Create a command to call the Stored Procedure SetAge
IDbCommand sqlCmd = sqlCon.CreateCommand();
sqlCmd.CommandType = CommandType.StoredProcedure;
sqlCmd.CommandText = "SetAge";
```

Parameters

Parameters for use with stored procedures or for substitution into text commands are represented by *IDbDataParameter* instances. An *IDbDataParameter* object must be instantiated and configured to satisfy each parameter specified in an *IDbCommand*. The *IDbCommand.Parameters* property contains an *IData-ParameterCollection* in which the parameter objects are placed before the command is executed. *IDataParameterCollection* inherits from *IList*, *ICollection*, and *IEnumerable* and thus provides flexibility for adding, retrieving, and manipulating the contained *IDbDataParameter* instances.

If the *IDbCommand* uses positional parameters (as with the OLE Data Provider implementation), the *IDbDataParameter* instances must be placed in the collection in the same order they occur in the statement. Named parameters can be added in any order and will be mapped correctly during command execution. If a stored procedure provides a return value, the parameter to receive the return value must always be the first *IDbDataParameter* in the collection.

Table 16-7 summarizes the members of *IDbDataParameter*.

Table 16-7 **Members of *IDbDataParameter***

Member	Comments
DbType	Gets or sets the data type of the parameter using a value from the *System.Data.DbType* enumeration. The *DbType* property and the implementation-specific *SqlDbType* and *OleDbType* properties are linked such that setting the *DbType* changes the implementation property to an equivalent implementation-specific data type.
Direction	Gets or sets a value from the *System.Data.ParameterDirection* enumeration that indicates the type of parameter. Valid values are: ■ *Input*—an input parameter ■ *InputOutput*—capable of both input and output ■ *Output*—an output parameter ■ *ReturnValue*—a stored procedure or function return value
IsNullable	Gets or sets a *bool* value indicating whether the parameter accepts *null* values; the default value is *false*.
ParameterName	Gets or sets a *String* value representing the name of the parameter; the default is an empty string.
Precision	Gets or sets the maximum number of digits used to represent numeric *Value* properties; the default value is 0 (zero).
Scale	Gets or sets the number of decimal places that should be used for numeric *Value* properties; the default value is 0 (zero).
Size	Gets or sets the maximum size in bytes of the data within the parameter.
Value	Gets or sets the value of the parameter. This property accepts a *System.Object* instance that the implementation will attempt to convert to the appropriate data source type when used. See *DbType*, *SqlDbType*, and *OleDbType* for details.

The *DBDemo.SetAge* method demonstrates the creation and configuration of an *UPDATE* command that uses parameters to change the age of a specified person:

```
public void SetAge(string p_name, int p_age) {
    // Create a Text command to perform an UPDATE
    // the age of a specified person
    IDbCommand sqlCmd = sqlCon.CreateCommand();
    sqlCmd.CommandType = CommandType.Text;
    sqlCmd.CommandText = "UPDATE people SET age = @age" +
        " WHERE name = @name";

    // Instantiate and add parameters, order is irrelevant
    IDbDataParameter nameParam = sqlCmd.CreateParameter();
    nameParam.ParameterName = "@name";
    nameParam.DbType = DbType.String;
```

```
nameParam.Value = p_name;
sqlCmd.Parameters.Add(nameParam);

IDbDataParameter ageParam = sqlCmd.CreateParameter();
ageParam.ParameterName = "@age";
ageParam.DbType = DbType.Int32;
ageParam.Value = p_age;
sqlCmd.Parameters.Add(ageParam);

// Execute the command
sqlCmd.ExecuteNonQuery();
}
```

We can replace this *DBDemo.SetAge* implementation with a version that calls a stored procedure to update the person's age. First create a stored procedure in MyDatabase named *SetAge*, which can be done with the SQL Server Query Analyzer, using the following *CREATE PROCEDURE* script.

```
CREATE PROCEDURE SetAge
    (@name varchar(20), @age int, @sex varchar(10) OUTPUT)
AS
    DECLARE @oldAge int
    SELECT @oldAge = age, @sex = sex
        FROM people WHERE name = @name
    UPDATE people SET age = @age
        WHERE name = @name
    RETURN (@oldAge)
```

Note that the stored procedure returns the person's original age as its return value, so the *IDbDataParameter* instance to receive this value must be added to the *IDbCommand.Parameters* property first. With these changes in mind, here's the revised *DBDemo.SetAge* method:

```
public void SetAge(string p_name, int p_age) {

    // Create a command to call the Stored Procedure SetAge
    IDbCommand sqlCmd = sqlCon.CreateCommand();
    sqlCmd.CommandType = CommandType.StoredProcedure;
    sqlCmd.CommandText = "SetAge";

    // Instantiate and add parameters, return value must be first
    IDbDataParameter returnParam = sqlCmd.CreateParameter();
    returnParam.ParameterName = "@oldAge";
    returnParam.DbType = DbType.Int32;
    returnParam.Direction = ParameterDirection.ReturnValue;
    sqlCmd.Parameters.Add(returnParam);
```

(continued)

```
IDbDataParameter nameParam = sqlCmd.CreateParameter();
nameParam.ParameterName = "@name";
nameParam.DbType = DbType.String;
nameParam.Direction = ParameterDirection.Input;
nameParam.Value = p_name;
sqlCmd.Parameters.Add(nameParam);

IDbDataParameter ageParam = sqlCmd.CreateParameter();
ageParam.ParameterName = "@age";
ageParam.DbType = DbType.Int32;
ageParam.Direction = ParameterDirection.Input;
ageParam.Value = p_age;
sqlCmd.Parameters.Add(ageParam);

IDbDataParameter sexParam = sqlCmd.CreateParameter();
sexParam.ParameterName = "@sex";
sexParam.DbType = DbType.String;
sexParam.Direction = ParameterDirection.Output;
sexParam.Size = 10;
sqlCmd.Parameters.Add(sexParam);

// Execute the stored procedure
sqlCmd.ExecuteNonQuery();

// Display the return information
Console.WriteLine("{0} was {1} years old and is a {2};" +
    " {0} is now {3} years old.",
    ((IDbDataParameter)sqlCmd.Parameters["@name"]).Value,
    ((IDbDataParameter)sqlCmd.Parameters["@oldAge"]).Value,
    ((IDbDataParameter)sqlCmd.Parameters["@sex"]).Value,
    ((IDbDataParameter)sqlCmd.Parameters["@age"]).Value);
}
```

Running *DBDemo* with the new *SetAge* method generates the following output:

```
Fred was 27 years old and is a male; Fred is now 28 years old.
Bob is 32 years old; Bob is male.
Fred is 28 years old; Fred is male.
Betty is 43 years old; Betty is female.
```

Notice the first line, which is generated by the new *DBDemo.SetAge* method. It contains Fred's original age obtained from the stored procedure return value, as well as his sex, which was specified as an *OUTPUT* parameter.

The process of creating, adding, and accessing parameters is a little long-winded when working with the generic interfaces. Both the SQL and OLE Data

Provider implementations provide typed convenience methods that simplify parameter management at the cost of code portability. To demonstrate this, we can cast *sqlCon* to an instance of *SqlConnection* (because *DBDemo* is built using the SQL Server Data Provider) and replace the *SetAge* method with the following implementation:

```
public void SetAge(string p_name, int p_age) {

    // Cast sqlCon to a SqlConnection
    SqlConnection newCon = (SqlConnection)sqlCon;

    // Create a command to call the Stored Procedure SetAge
    SqlCommand sqlCmd = newCon.CreateCommand();
    sqlCmd.CommandType = CommandType.StoredProcedure;
    sqlCmd.CommandText = "SetAge";

    // Instantiate and add parameters, return value must be first
    sqlCmd.Parameters.Add("@oldAge", SqlDbType.Int).Direction =
        ParameterDirection.ReturnValue;
    sqlCmd.Parameters.Add("@name", SqlDbType.VarChar).Value = p_name;

    sqlCmd.Parameters.Add("@age", SqlDbType.Int).Value = p_age;
    sqlCmd.Parameters.Add("@sex", SqlDbType.VarChar, 10).Direction =
        ParameterDirection.Output;

    // Execute the stored procedure
    sqlCmd.ExecuteNonQuery();

    // Display the return information
    Console.WriteLine("{0} was {1} years old and is a {2};" +
        "{0} is now {3} years old.",
        sqlCmd.Parameters["@name"].Value,
        sqlCmd.Parameters["@oldAge"].Value,
        sqlCmd.Parameters["@sex"].Value,
        sqlCmd.Parameters["@age"].Value);
}
```

Executing Commands and Processing Results

Once the properties and parameters of the *IDbCommand* are configured, the command can be executed; this has been demonstrated many times in the preceding examples. As with JDBC, the method used to execute a command depends on the contents of the command and the type of result expected or desired. Table 16-8 summarizes the methods available for executing a command.

Table 16-8   Command Execution Methods

Member	Comments
IDbCommand	
ExecuteNonQuery()	Returns an *int* that contains the number of rows affected by an *UPDATE*, *INSERT*, or *DELETE* SQL command; for other statements, -1 is returned.
ExecuteReader()	Returns an *IDataReader* instance containing the result sets generated by the executed *SELECT* query or stored procedure. A discussion of *IDataReader* follows this table.
ExecuteScalar()	Returns an *Object* representing the data item from the first column in the first row of a result set returned by a statement, database function, or stored procedure.
SqlCommand	
ExecuteXmlReader()	Supported only by SQL Server 2000 and later versions. Executes a command that has a *FOR XML* clause and returns the results in a *System.Xml.XmlReader* object. While the *XmlReader* is open, the *IDbConnection* cannot be accessed other than to close the connection, at which point the *XmlReader* is also closed. See Chapter 11, "XML Processing," for details of the *XmlReader* class.

IDataReader

The *IDataReader* provides functionality similar to that of a JDBC *ResultSet*. However, the *IDataReader* is a forward-only, read-only mechanism for accessing the results of a SQL query; it provides none of the advanced updating, backward scrolling, or sensitivity features of the JDBC *ResultSet* interface.

> **Important**   The columns returned in a Java *ResultSet* are numbered from 1, while the columns returned in a .NET *IDataReader* are numbered from 0 (zero).

Table 16-9 summarizes the commonly used members of the *IDataReader* interface.

Table 16-9 *IDataReader* **Members**

Member	Comments
IdataReader[key]	Returns an *Object* representing the value of the specified column in the current row. Columns can be specified using a 0-based integer index or a *String* containing the column name.
FieldCount	Gets the number of columns in the current row.
IsClosed	Returns *true* if the *IDataReader* is closed; *false* if it is open.
RecordsAffected	Returns an *int* indicating the number of rows inserted, updated, or deleted by the SQL statement. *SELECT* statements always return -1.
Close()	Closes the *IDataReader* and frees the *IDbConnection* for other uses.
GetDataTypeName()	Gets the name of the data source data type for a specified column.
GetFieldType()	Gets a *System.Type* instance representing the data type of the value contained in the column specified using a 0-based integer index.
GetName()	Gets the name of the column specified using a 0-based integer index.
GetOrdinal()	Gets the 0-based column ordinal for the column with the specified name.
GetSchemaTable()	Returns a *System.Data.DataTable* instance that contains metadata describing the columns contained in the *IDataReader*.
IsDBNull()	Return *true* if the value in the specified column contains a data source *null*; *false* otherwise.
NextResult()	If the *IDataReader* includes multiple result sets because multiple statements were executed, *NextResult* moves to the next result set in the collection of result sets. By default, the *IDataReader* is positioned on the first result set.
Read()	Advances the reader to the next record. The reader starts prior to the first record.

In addition to those members listed in Table 16-9, the *IDataReader* provides a set of methods for retrieving typed data from the current row of an *IData-Reader*. Each of the following methods takes an integer argument that identifies the 0-based index of the column from which the data should be returned: *GetBoolean, GetByte, GetBytes, GetChar, GetChars, GetDateTime, GetDecimal, GetDouble, GetFloat, GetGuid, GetInt16, GetInt32, GetInt64, GetString, GetValue,* and *GetValues*. The *GetValue* and *GetValues* methods return the column data as instances of *Object*.

In both the SQL and OLE Data Provider implementations, if the data type of the column value doesn't match the method used to retrieve it, an *InvalidCastException* is thrown; no data conversion is attempted.

The *DBDemo.ListPeople* method demonstrates the use of an *IDataReader* to display the contents of a result set by using various methods to access the returned data fields.

```
private void ListPeople() {
    // Create and configure the SQL command
    IDbCommand sqlCmd = sqlCon.CreateCommand();
    sqlCmd.CommandType = CommandType.Text;
    sqlCmd.CommandText = "SELECT name, sex, age FROM people";

    // Execute the SQL command and create the IDataReader
    IDataReader sqlRdr = sqlCmd.ExecuteReader();

    // Loop through the results and display each record
    while (sqlRdr.Read()) {
        Console.WriteLine("{0} is {1} years old; {0} is {2}.",
            sqlRdr.GetString(0),      // Typed get
            sqlRdr["age"],            // Named indexer
            sqlRdr[1]);               // Integer indexer
    }
}
```

The individual fields of the current row can be accessed repeatedly and in any order. As we've shown previously, the *DBDemo.ListPeople* method generates the following output:

```
Bob is 32 years old; Bob is male;
Fred is 28 years old; Fred is male;
Betty is 43 years old; Betty is female;
```

While the *IDataReader* is open, no operation can be performed using the *IDbConnection* other than to close it; closing the connection also closes the *IDataReader*.

DataSet

ADO.NET supports a disconnected data access strategy through the use of *DataSet* objects. A *DataSet* is an in-memory cache of data that is data source independent. In effect, a *DataSet* provides a simple relational data store in memory. Although the source of data for a *DataSet* is usually a relational database, a *DataSet* can be populated from any source that's accessible via an ADO.NET Data Provider. A *DataSet* has no inherent functionality to communicate with a data source; the Data Adapter element of the Data Provider is responsible for moving data between the *DataSet* and the data source. A *DataSet* can also be configured and populated manually and includes extensive support for importing XML data.

When working with data from a relational database, a *DataSet* doesn't maintain an active connection to the database; the cached data isn't synchronized with the contents of the database. Data is usually loaded into the *DataSet* and manipulated programmatically, and if necessary, changes are written back to the source. The *DataSet* and Data Adapter provide extensive functionality to simplify the loading and storing of data as well as the merging of changes.

Depending on the application, disconnected data manipulation can provide a more scalable solution than a connection-based approach; however, locking database records while they're in use isn't always feasible. Without locks, database records are subject to change by another application while the disconnected copy is simultaneously being manipulated in the *DataSet*. To handle these situations, a *DataSet* supports the use of an optimistic concurrency strategy by maintaining a copy of both the original and updated data; concurrency errors are identified and handled as updates are written to the database.

> **Note**   A detailed discussion of *DataSet* functionality is beyond the scope of this book. This section of the chapter provides an overview of the *DataSet*, highlights some key features, and demonstrates the simple creation and use of a *DataSet*.

DataSet Component Classes

A *DataSet* consists of set of classes that are analogous to the components found in a relational database. A programmer with relational database experience should have little trouble visualizing the relationship between these classes. The constituent classes of a *DataSet* are summarized in Table 16-10; these classes are all members of the *System.Data* namespace.

Table 16-10 **Constituents of a *DataSet***

Class	Comments
DataTable	A table of data. A *DataTable* normally represents the data from a single database table.
DataTableCollection	A collection of *DataTable* objects accessible through the *DataSet.Tables* property.
DataColumn	Represents a column in a *DataTable*.
DataColumnCollection	A collection of *DataColumn* objects accessible via the *DataTable.Columns* property.
DataRow	Represents a row of data in a *DataTable*. If the row data is changed, the *DataRow* object maintains both a copy of the original data and the new, changed data. These dual versions are maintained until the changes are explicitly accepted, at which point the duplicate is discarded. This feature allows changes to be rolled back and helps support the data merging and updating processes.
DataRowCollection	A collection of *DataRow* objects accessible via the *DataTable.Rows* property.
DataRelation	Represents a relationship between two *DataTable* objects analogous to a parent/child or primary/foreign key relationship. Provides simplified access from a *DataRow* to all other related *DataRow* objects.
DataRelationCollection	A collection of *DataRelation* objects accessible via the *DataSet.Relations* property.
ForeignKeyConstraint	Enforces a foreign/primary key constraint between two *DataTable* objects. Controls the effect on the related data when a value or row is either updated or deleted.
UniqueConstraint	Represents a unique key constraint on a *DataColumn*.
ConstraintCollection	A collection of *Constraint* objects accessible via the *DataTable.Constraints* property.
DataView	Represents a customizable view of a *DataTable* supporting filtering and sorting of the data.

Creating a *DataSet*

A new *DataSet* is created using a constructor that takes the *DataSet* name as an argument; using an empty constructor creates a *DataSet* with the default name *NewDataSet*. For example:

```
DataSet myDataSet1 = new DataSet();
DataSet myDataSet2 = new DataSet("MyDataSet");
```

A new *DataSet* can also be created using the methods of an existing *DataSet* instance; these methods are summarized in Table 16-11.

Table 16-11 *DataSet* **Creation Methods**

Method	Description
Clone()	Copies the data structure (including tables, relationships, and constraints) into a new *DataSet* but doesn't copy any data
Copy()	Copies both the data structure and the data into a new *DataSet*
GetChanges()	Extracts only the modified rows and copies them into a new *DataSet*

Managing a *DataSet* with a Data Adapter

The simplest way to populate a *DataSet* from a database that's accessible via an ADO.NET Data Provider is to use a Data Adapter. A Data Adapter is defined by the *System.Data.IDbDataAdapter* interface; all complete Data Provider implementations should provide a Data Adapter implementation.

As well as populating the *DataSet*, the Data Adapter contains functionality to simplify the ongoing synchronization of data between the *DataSet* and the database. Table 16-12 summarizes the members of *IDbDataAdapter*. Consult the .NET documentation for complete details.

Table 16-12 **Members of** *IDbDataAdapter*

Member	Description
Properties	
DeleteCommand	Gets or sets an *IDbCommand* used for deleting records from the underlying database.
InsertCommand	Gets or sets an *IDbCommand* used for inserting records into the underlying database.
SelectCommand	Gets or sets an *IDbCommand* used for selecting records from the underlying database.
UpdateCommand	Gets or sets an *IDbCommand* used for updating records in the underlying database.
MissingMappingAction	Determines how the Data Adapter handles data from the data source that doesn't have a matching table or column in the *DataSet*.
MissingSchemaAction	Determines how the Data Adapter handles schema information coming from the data source that is different from the *DataSet*.
TableMappings	Determines how source tables are mapped to *DataTable* instances in the *DataSet*.
Members	
Fill()	Executes the *IDbCommand* contained in the *SelectCommand* property and fills the *DataSet* with the results.

(continued)

Table 16-12 **Members of *IDbDataAdapter*** *(continued)*

Member	Description
FillSchema()	Executes the *IDbCommand* contained in the *SelectCommand* property and builds the relational structure of the *DataSet* without populating it with data.
Update()	The Data Adapter inspects each row of the specified *DataSet* to determine whether changes have occurred. The appropriate *IDbCommand* held in the *InsertCommand*, *UpdateCommand*, or *DeleteCommand* property is used to apply the changes to the database. Updates from the database are read and integrated into the *DataSet*.

The following example demonstrates the population of a *DataSet* from the *people* table (used earlier in this chapter) using a *SqlDataAdapter*. The *name*, *age*, and *sex* fields of the records in the *people* table are read and copied into a *DataTable* named *People*, which is automatically created in the *DataSet*.

```
using System;
using System.Data;
using System.Data.SqlClient;

public class DataSetDemo {

    // Private field to hold the SQL Server Name
    private static string sqlServerName = "MySqlServer";

    public static void Main() {

        // Create a connection to the specified SQL Server using
        // a database named MyDatabase and integrated Windows security
        string conStr = "Data Source=" + sqlServerName +
            " ; Database=MyDataBase;" +
            " Integrated Security=SSPI";
        SqlConnection sqlCon = new SqlConnection(conStr);

        // Create a Data Adapter
        SqlDataAdapter sqlAdapter = new SqlDataAdapter();
        sqlAdapter.SelectCommand = sqlCon.CreateCommand();
        sqlAdapter.SelectCommand.CommandText =
            "SELECT name, age, sex FROM people";

        // Create and populate the DataSet
        DataSet myDataSet = new DataSet("MySampleDataSet");
        sqlAdapter.Fill(myDataSet, "People");
```

```
        // Dump the contents of the DataSet to the console
        Console.WriteLine(myDataSet.GetXml());
    }
}
```

We'll discuss the *DataSet.GetXml* method later, in the "XML Support" section; we're using it now as a simple mechanism to dump the contents of the *DataSet* in a human-readable form. If the *DBDemo* example from the "Data Providers" section of this chapter is modified so that it doesn't delete all records from the *people* table, running the preceding code after running *DBDemo* will produce the following output:

```
<MySampleDataSet>
    <People>
        <name>Bob</name>
        <age>32</age>
        <sex>male</sex>
    </People>
    <People>
        <name>Fred</name>
        <age>28</age>
        <sex>male</sex>
    </People>
    <People>
        <name>Betty</name>
        <age>43</age>
        <sex>female</sex>
    </People>
</MySampleDataSet>
```

Note in this example that we don't explicitly open or close the database connection. If the connection is closed when the *Fill*, *FillSchema*, or *Update* method is called, the Data Adapter will automatically open and close the connection. If the connection is already open, the connection's state will not be changed.

Manually Managing a *DataSet*

The constituent components of a *DataSet* provide full capabilities to manually create and manipulate the contents of the *DataSet*. Table 16-13 provides a summary of the classes and methods used to create and manage some of the structural components most commonly contained within a *DataSet*.

Table 16-13 **Common *DataSet* Actions**

Action	Comments
Table Actions	
Add a table	*DataSet.Tables.Add(TableName);*
Get a specified table	*DataSet.Tables[TableName];*
	DataSet.Tables[TableIndex];
Remove all tables	*DataSet.Tables.Clear();*
Remove a specified table	*DataSet.Tables.Remove(TableName);*
	DataSet.Tables.RemoveAt(TableIndex);
Column Actions	
Add a column	*DataTable.Columns.Add(ColumnName);*
	DataTable.Columns.Add(DataColumn);
Get a specified column	*DataTable.Columns[ColumnName];*
	DataTable.Columns[ColumnIndex];
Remove all columns	*DataTable.Columns.Clear();*
Remove a specified column	*DataTable.Columns.Remove(ColumnName);*
	DataTable.Columns.RemoveAt(ColumnIndex);
Row Actions	
Add or insert a row	*DataTable.Rows.Add(DataRow);*
	DataTable.Rows.InsertAt(DataRow, RowIndex);
	The new *DataRow* to be added or inserted must be created using the *DataTable.NewRow* method.
Get a specified row	*DataTable.Rows[RowIndex];*
Remove all rows	*DataTable.Rows.Clear();*
Remove a specified row	*DataTable.Rows.Remove(DataRow);*
	DataTable.Rows.RemoveAt(RowIndex);
Work with column data in a row	*DataRow[ColumnName];*
	DataRow[ColumnIndex];

XML Support

One of the most powerful features of the *DataSet* is the extensive support for XML. The internal format of the *DataSet* is not XML, but its public members and integration with other XML classes provide support for the management and manipulation of the *DataSet* contents and structure via XML and related technologies.

Table 16-14 summarizes the XML-oriented features provided by the public methods of the *DataSet* class.

Table 16-14   XML-Oriented Methods of the *DataSet*

Method	Comments
GetXml()	Returns a *String* containing the XML representation of the data held in the *DataSet*; this does not include schema information.
GetXmlSchema()	Returns a *String* containing the XML Schema Definition (XSD) schema for the XML representation of the data contained in the *DataSet*.
InferXmlSchema()	Infers the XML schema from a specified *Stream*, file, *TextReader*, or *XmlReader* into the *DataSet*. A *String* array argument contains a list of namespace URIs to exclude from the inference.
ReadXml()	Reads XML schema and data into the *DataSet* from a specified *Stream*, file, *TextReader*, or *XmlReader*. The method optionally takes one of the following values from the *System.Data.XmlReadMode* enumeration as an argument: ■ *Auto*—evaluates the source XML and applies the most appropriate option from *DiffGram*, *ReadSchema*, or *InferSchema*, listed here. ■ *DiffGram*—reads a *DiffGram* and applies any changes to the data in the *DataSet*; relies on the *DiffGram* source having the same schema as the *DataSet*. See the section "*DiffGram*" coming up for more information. ■ *Fragment*—reads XML fragments and loads data that matches the existing *DataSet* schema; unmatched data is discarded. ■ *IgnoreSchema*—reads XML data into the existing *DataSet*, ignoring any inline schema. Any data that does not match the existing *DataSet* schema is discarded. ■ *InferSchema*—infers schema from the XML data and loads both into the *DataSet*. ■ *ReadSchema*—reads an inline schema and loads the XML data. Creates new tables where necessary but will not change or update existing ones. The default value is *Auto*.
ReadXmlSchema()	Reads an XSD schema from a *Stream*, a file, a *TextReader*, or an *XmlReader* and uses it to configure the *DataReader* schema.

(continued)

Table 16-14 XML-Oriented Methods of the *DataSet* *(continued)*

Method	Comments
WriteXml()	Writes an XML representation of the contents of the *DataSet* to a *Stream*, a file, a *TextWriter*, or an *XmlWriter*. The method optionally takes one of the following values from the *System.Data.XmlWriteMode* enumeration as an argument: ■ *DiffGram*—writes the contents as a *DiffGram*. See the section "*DiffGram*" coming up for more information. ■ *IgnoreSchema*—the data is written without schema information. ■ *WriteSchema*—the XSD schema is written inline along with the data. The default value is *WriteSchema*.
WriteXmlSchema()	Writes the XSD schema for the XML representation of the contents of the *DataSet* to a *Stream*, a file, a *TextWriter*, or an *XmlWriter*.

DiffGram

A *DiffGram* is an XML format used to describe the contents (but not the schema) of a *DataSet*. When a *DataSet* is written as a *DiffGram*, the XML contains both the current and original versions of data row information as well as row order and error information.

The *DiffGram* format is ideal for sending details of *DataSet* updates across the network and for merging content changes between multiple *DataSet* objects with the same schema. The *DiffGram* format can also be used to send updates to SQL Server 2000.

> **More Info** Consult the .NET and SQL Server documentation for complete details of the structure and use of a *DiffGram*.

XmlDataDocument Synchronization

In addition to the XML features presented in Table 16-14, a *DataSet* can be synchronized with an *XmlDataDocument*. The utility of this relationship stems from the *XmlDataDocument* support for Document Object Model (DOM) manipulation as well as XPath queries and XSL Transformations. This provides both relational and hierarchical access to the same underlying data. Changes made through either the *DataSet* or the *XmlDataDocument* are immediately reflected in the corresponding view.

To synchronize a *DataSet* with an *XmlDataDocument*, pass the *DataSet* instance as an argument to the *XmlDataDocument* constructor. For example:

```
// Assume existing DataAdapter instance called myDataAdapter
DataSet myDataSet = new DataSet();
myDataAdapater.Fill(myDataSet);

// Create a new XmlDataDocument and synchronize with myDataSet
XmlDataDocument myDataDoc = new XmlDataDocument(myDataSet);
```

Alternatively, to create a *DataSet* from the contents of an *XmlDataDocument*, use the *DataSet* property. For example:

```
// Assume existing XmlDataDocument instance called myDataDoc
DataSet myDataSet = myDataDoc.DataSet;
```

> **More Info**   Consult Chapter 11 for details of DOM, XPath, and XSLT support in .NET.

Summary

This chapter has provided an overview of the data access capabilities provided by ADO.NET. The ADO.NET Data Provider architecture provides functionality comparable to that of JDBC. Although the .NET *DataReader* lacks some of the more advanced functionality of the *ResultSet*, the consolidation of the *Command* classes and the use of C# properties and indexers often results in cleaner code, in our opinion.

The ADO.NET *DataSet* offers functionality similar to that of the JDBC *RowSet* interface. A *DataSet* can place heavy demands on the memory of a system and can be complex to configure correctly; however, the disconnected data management capabilities and extensive support for XML integration of a *DataSet* make it a valuable tool to simplify the development of any data-oriented application.

17

Security and Cryptography

This chapter details the support for security and cryptography in the Microsoft .NET platform. The support for cryptographic operations and role-based security should be easily understood by experienced Java developers, but the .NET Code Access Security (CAS) model has no direct parallel in Java. Although some of the concepts may seem awkward, the system does offer significant benefits, especially for those programmers who write code to be used by third parties.

Code Access Security

The .NET Framework CAS model is similar to an expanded implementation of the Java security manager. CAS controls access to protected resources (such as the file system) and can be used to prevent applications from performing certain operations (such as opening a network connection or reading a file). We say that CAS is similar to an *expanded* Java security manager because the .NET Framework provides very fine grain controls for protected resources and the security model is tightly integrated into the runtime model.

When a .NET application is started, the common language runtime (CLR) checks to see which permissions should be granted to the code; the CLR will throw a *System.Security.SecurityException* if an application attempts to perform an operation requiring a permission that has not been granted.

The rules determining the set of permissions that should be granted are applied at the assembly level. Each assembly is evaluated individually to determine the policies that should be applied using a technique known as *evidence-based security*, by which characteristics of an assembly (such as the publisher or source URL) are assessed to determine which permission policies are relevant.

The permissions defined by the policies that apply are then granted to the assembly.

Programming for CAS

Programmers aren't required to make explicit use of CAS in code, although there are benefits in doing so, especially for assemblies that are shipped to third parties. The benefits of CAS include the following:

■ CAS allows administrators to easily assess the security requirements of an assembly, allowing an informed decision to be made when determining the level of trust to grant an application or library.

■ CAS allows programmers to tailor the behavior of an assembly to work within a security policy by requesting optional permissions; for example, a CD player can provide song lists to the user, but only if the security policy allows Internet connections to be made so that the player can look up the CD details.

■ CAS allows programmers to protect their code against subversion; assemblies that never need access to a protected resource can be written to ensure that the code isn't tricked into performing a task that wasn't intended by a programmer.

Ignoring the CAS support doesn't exempt an assembly from security policies; administrators can still apply restrictions to an assembly. Code that has been written without taking CAS into consideration can behave unexpectedly: security exceptions may be thrown, and the applications will have no means of recovering.

CAS permissions are defined by a set of attribute classes that implement the abstract *System.Security.CodeAccessPermissionClass*. Table 17-1 details the most commonly used attributes.

Table 17-1 CAS Permission Classes

Attribute Class Name	Permission Represented
System.Net.DnsPermission	Accessing the DNS
System.Security.Permissions.EnvironmentPermission	Reading and writing environment variables
System.Diagnostics.EventLogPermission	Reading and writing to event log services

Table 17-1 CAS Permission Classes *(continued)*

Attribute Class Name	Permission Represented
System.Security.Permissions.FileDialogPermission	Accessing files that are selected by the user via a file dialog window
System.Security.Permissions.FileIOPermission	Reading, appending, or writing files or directories
System.Security.Permissions.IsolatedStorageFilePermission	Accessing private virtual file systems
System.Drawing.Printing.PrintingPermission	Accessing printing services
System.Security.Permissions.RegistryPermission	Reading or modifying the Windows registry
System.Net.SocketPermission	Opening socket connections to remote machines
System.Data.SqlClient.SqlClientPermission	Accessing SQL servers
System.Security.Permissions.UIPermission	Creating user interfaces
System.Net.WebPermission	Accessing HTTP Internet resources

Declarative CAS Statements

Declarative statements—also known as *soft* statements—are a means of indicating the permissions that an assembly requires. The CLR reads the declarative statements from an assembly prior to execution; if the required permissions cannot be granted, a *System.Security.SecurityException* will be thrown and the code will not be executed.

Declarative CAS statements fall into three categories—minimum permissions, optional permissions, and denied permissions—as described here:

- Minimum permissions are those that an application needs in order to provide core services and cannot function without.

- Optional permissions are those that the application would like to have (perhaps in order to offer additional features) but that are not essential.

- Denied permissions are those that the application should never be granted, even if they're permitted by the CAS security policies.

Statement Scope

Declarative statements can be applied to an assembly, a class, or a method; this approach allows the programmer to limit the scope of permissions. Declarative CAS statements cannot be applied to other member types, such as properties or indexers. The following example demonstrates the three statement scopes, which appear in boldface:

```
using System;
using System.Security.Permissions;

[assembly:FileIOPermissionAttribute(SecurityAction.RequestMinimum,
    Unrestricted = true)]

[EnvironmentPermission(SecurityAction.Demand, Unrestricted=true)]
class MyClass {

    [System.Net.WebPermission(SecurityAction.Demand, Unrestricted=true)]
    public void myMethod() {
        // method statements
    }

    public void myOtherMethod() {
        // methods statements
    }

    public static void Main() {
    }
}

class MyOtherClass {
    // class definition statements
}
```

The syntax of these statements is explained here:

■ The first statement, prefixed with *assembly*, requests access to the file system for the entire assembly; any method contained in *MyClass* and *MyOtherClass* can make calls that access the file system.

■ The second statement requests permission for all methods of *MyClass* to be able to read and write environment variables. This permission will not be available to methods of *MyOtherClass*.

■ The third statement requests access to HTTP Internet servers for the *MyClass.myMethod* method; this permission will not be available to *MyClass.myOtherMethod* or to any method of *MyOtherClass*.

Declarative Statement Syntax

The first argument for a declarative attribute is a value from the *System.Security.Permissions.SecurityAction* enumeration; this value allows the programmer to specify the kind of CAS request that the statement represents. Not all values can be applied for all permission scopes. Table 17-2 details these values.

Table 17-2 *SecurityAction* **Values**

Value	Scope	Action
RequestMinimum	Assembly	A request for the minimum permissions required for the code to run.
RequestOptional	Assembly	A request for additional permissions that are optional (not required to run).
RequestRefuse	Assembly	A request that permissions that might be misused should not be granted to the calling code.
Demand	Class, method	All callers higher in the call stack are required to have been granted the permission specified by the current permission object.
Assert	Class, method	The calling code can access the resource identified by the current permission object, even if callers higher in the stack haven't been granted permission to access the resource.
Deny	Class, method	The ability to access the resource specified by the current permission object is denied to callers, even if they have been granted permission to access it.

The second argument represents a property that will be used to control the way that the permission restricts access to the protected resource. The statements in the preceding example all used the *Unrestricted=true* argument, which specifies that the declarative statement applies to all aspects of the protected resource—for example, allowing access to all HTTP servers.

The *Unrestricted* property is the only one that is common to all permission classes; each class defines a unique set of properties that reflect how the permission is applied. For example, the *WebPermission* class shown in the preceding example defines the *Connect* property that specifies the URL to which the permission applies. The following statement demonstrates how to combine the *SecurityAction.Deny* value with the *WebPermission.Connect* property to prevent access to a specific URL:

```
[System.Net.WebPermission(SecurityAction.Deny,
    Connect="http://www.mycompany.com/index.html")]
```

More Info   Consult the .NET documentation on each permission attribute for details of the properties that are available.

Using Optional Permissions

Requesting optional permissions allows an application to gracefully reduce functionality when CAS permissions are not granted. Consider an HTML browser; the core function of the browser is to read and display HTML files from Web servers. The browser may offer additional features such as caching the HTML file to disk to improve performance for future requests.

Some customers might trust the company that produces the browser and configure the CAS policy to allow access to the file system; other customers might not want the browser to access the file system at all. By requesting optional permissions, the browser can operate in both environments. Customers who allow cached files might benefit from improved performance; customers who don't allow cached files can still view HTML pages.

The following code fragment demonstrates how optional permissions can be used. Note that the CLR throws a *SecurityException* when an operation that requires an optional permission is attempted and the permission hasn't been granted; it's the responsibility of the programmer to catch this exception.

```
using System.Security;
using System.Security.Permissions;

[assembly:FileIOPermissionAttribute(SecurityAction.RequestOptional,
    Unrestricted = true)]

class OptionalPermissionDemo {

    public void loadHTMLFile(string p_url) {
        if (isPageCached(p_url)) {
            // statements to process the cached data
        } else {
            // statements to connect to the server
            // and obtain the web page
        }
    }

    private bool isPageCached(string p_url) {
        try {
            // code to determine if there is a
            // cached version of the HTML page
        } catch (SecurityException) {
            // the optional file system permission
            // has not been granted
            return false;
        }
    }
}
```

Refusing Permissions

The benefit of refusing permissions is to reduce the likelihood of code being subverted into performing tasks that the programmer didn't intend. Consider the following example, which prints the contents of a URL to the console:

```
using System;
using System.Net;
using System.Text;
using System.Security.Permissions;

class MyClass {

    [FileIOPermission(SecurityAction.Deny, Unrestricted=true)]
    public void printURL(string p_target) {
        WebClient x_client = new WebClient();
        byte[] x_data_array = x_client.DownloadData(p_target);
        String x_data_string = Encoding.Default.GetString(x_data_array);
        Console.WriteLine(x_data_string);
    }

    static void Main(string[] p_args) {
        new MyClass().printURL(p_args[0]);
    }
}
```

The CAS statement requests that the *printURL* method never be allowed access to the file system; without this statement, the method could be used to read files from the disk using URLs of the form *file://c:\myfilename*. With this statement, the programmer can be sure that the code won't be subverted into reading the contents of files when the intended purpose of the code is to read the contents of remote URLs.

Although the example shown in this section is contrived, the impact of refusing permissions is significant and can be a considerable help in ensuring that code shipped to customers and other third parties is less likely to be subverted to compromise security.

Assessing Declarative Statements

The Permission Viewer tool (permview.exe) is used to view the permissions that an assembly has requested via declarative statements. By default, the output of permview displays only the permission statements requested for the entire assembly; the */DECL* switch includes class and method scope permission requests.

The example listed previously in the "Statement Scope" section of this chapter produces the following output from permview:

```
Microsoft (R) .NET Framework Permission Request Viewer.  Version 1.0.3705.0
Copyright (C) Microsoft Corporation 1998-2001. All rights reserved.

Assembly RequestMinimum permission set:
<PermissionSet class="System.Security.PermissionSet" version="1">
   <IPermission class="System.Security.Permissions.FileIOPermission,
       mscorlib, Version=1.0.3300.0, Culture=neutral,
       PublicKeyToken=b77a5c561934e089"
       version="1"
       Unrestricted="true"/>
</PermissionSet>

Class MyClass Demand permission set:
<PermissionSet class="System.Security.PermissionSet" version="1">
   <IPermission class="System.Security.Permissions.EnvironmentPermission,
       mscorlib, Version=1.0.3300.0, Culture=neutral,
       PublicKeyToken=b77a5c561934e089"
       version="1"
       Unrestricted="true"/>
</PermissionSet>

Method MyClass::myMethod() Demand permission set:
<PermissionSet class="System.Security.PermissionSet" version="1">
   <IPermission class="System.Net.WebPermission, System,
       Version=1.0.3300.0, Culture=neutral, PublicKeyToken=b77a5c561934e089"
       version="1"
       Unrestricted="true"/>
</PermissionSet>
```

The output shows the permission set requested at each level, including the details of the assembly that contains the permission class that has been used.

Imperative Security Demands

Imperative statements—also known as *hard* statements—request CAS permissions at run time, in contrast with declarative statements, which can be assessed before the code in an assembly is executed. Imperative statements are useful when the details of the resource to be accessed aren't available ahead of execution—for example, writing to a file that the user has specified via a dialog box. The disadvantage of imperative statements is that the specific security demands of an assembly can be determined only at run time, so a system administrator cannot assess the security demands of an assembly in order to determine a suitable level of trust.

Imperative statements are made by creating a new instance of a permission class and then calling the *Assert*, *Deny*, or *Demand* method; these methods relate to the values of the *SecurityAction* enumeration described in the preceding section. Each permission class provides different constructor forms; consult the

.NET documentation for more information. The following example demonstrates how to make a simple imperative statement using the *FileIOPermission* class:

```
public void readFile(string p_file_name) {

    FileIOPermission x_perm = new FileIOPermission(
        FileIOPermissionAccess.Read,
        new string[] {p_file_name});

    x_perm.Demand();

    // statements to operate on the file
    // specifed in the method argument
}
```

The example demands permission to read the file that is passed in by name as a method argument; this would not be possible to implement using declarative statements. The *Demand* method returns *void*; if the permission is not granted, an instance of *System.Security.SecurityException* will be thrown.

CAS Policies

The .NET Framework determines the CAS permissions to grant to an assembly by inspecting a hierarchy of security information, known as the *CAS security policy*. The permissions described in the preceding section are grouped into *permission sets*. One or more permission sets can be associated in a *code group*, which also includes a name and a membership condition. A permission set can be included in multiple code groups. The membership condition specifies a characteristic to look for in an assembly; if the assembly displays the characteristic, the permissions contained in the code group should be applied and the assembly is said to be a *member* of the code group. Table 17-3 describes the most commonly used membership characteristics.

Table 17-3   Code Group Membership Conditions

Membership Condition	Description
All Code	Applies to every .NET assembly; used to specify default policies.
Application Directory	Applies to assemblies installed alongside the current application.
Cryptographic Hash	Applies to assemblies that have a specific hash value. See the "Hash Codes" section later in this chapter for more information.
Site Membership	Applies to assemblies that were obtained from a specific FTP or HTTP server.
Strong Name	Applies to assemblies that have a specific strong name. See Appendix B, "Shared Assemblies," for more information.

At the top of the hierarchy are *policy levels*, which contain a set of code groups. The policy levels are as follows:

- **Enterprise**   Applies to all machines in an enterprise, where the policy details may be automatically distributed.

- **Machine**   Applies to a single machine.

- **User**   Applies to the current user.

A security policy is determined by examining the code groups contained in each policy level and establishing whether an assembly is a member of each one; the sum of the permissions included in all code groups of which the assembly is a member will be granted. Note that the policy levels are searched in the sequence just listed and that lower policy levels can restrict only the permissions granted at higher levels; for example, the *User* policy level cannot grant more permissions to an assembly than the *Machine* level.

The programmer isn't responsible for determining security policies, only for using CAS statements to declare the permissions that an assembly requires. The system administrator uses the CAS information (via the permview tool) to assess security requirements and determine an appropriate level of trust.

The simplest way to manage CAS policies is through the .NET Framework Configuration tool, which can be found in the Administrative Tools section of the Windows Control Panel. This tool allows the administrator to graphically configure policies and assess assemblies to see which permissions or code groups will be applied. The .NET Framework also includes the caspol.exe tool to manage CAS policies from the command line; this tool uses XML files to express permission settings. Consult the .NET documentation for more details on using these tools.

Role-Based Security

Role-based security allows the programmer to specify that a class or member can be called only if the user making the call has a specific username or role. Products such as HTTP and application servers will implement custom models for identifying users, but the .NET Framework provides default support for identifying Windows Users and Groups, which is the topic of this section. Unlike the Code Access Security model, role-based restrictions can be applied to classes and any class member, including properties and events.

The following fragment shows how to make a declarative statement to ensure that only the *MyDomain\MyUser* user account can invoke a method:

```
using System;
using System.Security.Permissions;
using System.Security.Principal;

class RoleBasedDemo {

    RoleBasedDemo() {
        AppDomain.CurrentDomain.SetPrincipalPolicy(
            PrincipalPolicy.WindowsPrincipal);
    }

    [PrincipalPermission(SecurityAction.Demand, Name=@"MyDomain\MyUser")]
    private void MyMethod() {
        // statements
    }
}
```

The statement marked in boldface determines that Windows accounts should be used to identify users; this call should be made only once and should not be made when using applications that provide custom identification systems. The declarative statement prior to the *MyMethod* definition applies the role-based security policy in a manner similar to CAS statements. Roles can also be enforced using imperative statements, as shown in the following example:

```
using System;
using System.Security.Permissions;
using System.Security.Principal;

class RoleBasedDemo {

    RoleBasedDemo() {
        AppDomain.CurrentDomain.SetPrincipalPolicy(
            PrincipalPolicy.WindowsPrincipal);
    }

    private void MyMethod() {
        PrincipalPermission x_perm =
            new PrincipalPermission("MyUser", "Administrator");
        x_perm.Demand();

        // statements
    }
}
```

The statements in boldface create a new *PrincipalPermission* that specifies the account name *MyUser*, who is an administrator. The *PrincipalPermission* class is used in the same way as the permissions described previously in the "Code Access Security" section of this chapter. Unlike CAS permissions, user identities can also be obtained without using the permissions class; the following example demonstrates how to obtain the identity of the current user and ensure that the user is part of the Administrators group:

```
using System;
using System.Security.Permissions;
using System.Security.Principal;
using System.Threading;

class RoleBasedDemo {

    RoleBasedDemo() {
        AppDomain.CurrentDomain.SetPrincipalPolicy(
            PrincipalPolicy.WindowsPrincipal);
    }

    private void MyMethod() {
        WindowsPrincipal x_principle
            = (WindowsPrincipal)Thread.CurrentPrincipal;
        if (x_principle.IsInRole(WindowsBuiltInRole.Administrator)) {
            // user can execute code
        } else {
            // user cannot execute code
        }
    }
}
```

The first statement marked in boldface obtains the identity of the current user from the *System.Threading.Thread* class, casting the result to an instance of *WindowsPrincipal*. The second statement checks to see that the user is an administrator. The *WindowsBuiltInRole* enumeration provides values representing the default Windows groups, as listed in Table 17-4.

Table 17-4 Default Windows Groups

Group	Description
AccountOperator	Account operators manage the user accounts on a computer or domain.
Administrator	Administrators have complete and unrestricted access to the computer or domain.
BackupOperator	Backup operators can override security restrictions for the sole purpose of backing up or restoring files.
Guest	Guests are more restricted than users.
PowerUser	Power users possess most administrative permissions, with some restrictions. Thus, power users can run legacy applications, in addition to certified applications.

Table 17-4 Default Windows Groups   *(continued)*

Group	Description
PrintOperator	Print operators can take control of a printer.
Replicator	Replicators support file replication in a domain.
SystemOperator	System operators manage a particular computer.
User	Users are prevented from making accidental or intentional systemwide changes. Thus, users can run certified applications but not most legacy applications.

Cryptography

This section describes how the .NET Framework supports common cryptographic tasks. The reader should be familiar with the basics of cryptography, a description of which is outside the scope of this book. There is only a surface-level similarity between the cipher support in .NET and the Java Cryptographic Extension (JCE); however, the basic principles behind both are the same.

Encrypting and Decrypting Data

The .NET Framework supports encryption algorithms that can be broken down into two groups: symmetric and asymmetric. Symmetric algorithms use the same key to encrypt and decrypt data, whereas asymmetric algorithms use a public and a private key.

Symmetric algorithms are usually used to encrypt large amounts of data; the processing requirements are less than for asymmetric encryption but are considered to be less secure because both the originator and the recipient of the encrypted data must possess a copy of the same key. Asymmetric encryption requires more computation, but the originator and the recipient don't have to use the same key; asymmetric encryption is often used to encrypt the keys for symmetric schemes.

Symmetrical Encryption

The .NET Framework supports the following symmetrical encryption algorithms:

- DES
- TripleDES
- RC2
- Rijndael (also known as AES)

The base class for all symmetrical algorithms is *System.Security.Cryptography.SymmetricAlgorithm*. This class provides the basic members for encrypting data as well as creating keys and initialization vectors (IVs), which are nonsecret binary inputs to the algorithms. Each of the supported algorithms is represented by an abstract class and a default implementation class; the abstract class allows alternative implementations of algorithms to be used, such as those that accelerate encryption by using hardware. Table 17-5 lists the abstract and default implementation classes for each algorithm; all classes are members of the *System.Security.Cryptography* namespace.

Table 17-5 Symmetric Encryption Classes

Abstract Class	Implementation Class
DES	*DESCryptoServiceProvider*
RC2	*RC2CryptoServiceProvider*
Rijndael	*RijndaelManaged*
TripleDES	*TripleDESCryptoServiceProvider*

The key and IV can be generated using the *GenerateKey* and *GenerateIV* methods or set using the *Key* and *IV* properties. Reading and writing encrypted data are supported through the streams model using the *System.Security.Cryptography.CryptoStream* class. See Chapter 10, "Streams, Files, and I/O," for general information on streams. The *CryptoStream* constructor takes three arguments, as detailed in Table 17-6.

Table 17-6 *CryptoStream* Constructor Arguments

Constructor Argument Type	Description
System.IO.Stream	The *Stream* that should be used for reading or writing.
System.Security.Cryptography.ICryptoTransform	A class that can perform cryptographic transformations (encrypting and decrypting data). Transformers can be obtained using the *CreateDecryptor* and *CreateEncryptor* methods from the *SymmetricAlgorithm* class.
System.Security.Cryptography.CryptoStreamMode	An enumeration value that specifies whether the *CryptoStream* instance will be used to read or write data.

The following example demonstrates how to write encrypted data to a *MemoryStream* and then read it back, using the Triple DES algorithm:

```
using System;
using System.Security.Cryptography;
using System.IO;
using System.Text;

class DESExample {

    DESExample() {
        byte[] x_secret_message
            = Encoding.Default.GetBytes("C# for Java Developers");

        // create the provider and generate the key and IV
        TripleDESCryptoServiceProvider x_3des
            = new TripleDESCryptoServiceProvider();
        x_3des.GenerateKey();
        x_3des.GenerateIV();

        // create the memory stream to hold the encrypted data
        MemoryStream x_memory_stream = new MemoryStream();

        // create the cryto stream
        CryptoStream x_crypto_stream = new CryptoStream(
            x_memory_stream,
            x_3des.CreateEncryptor(x_3des.Key, x_3des.IV),
            CryptoStreamMode.Write);

        // write the data to the crypto stream
        x_crypto_stream.Write(x_secret_message, 0,
            x_secret_message.Length);
        x_crypto_stream.Flush();

        // create a crypto stream to read the data
        x_crypto_stream = new CryptoStream(
            x_memory_stream,
            x_3des.CreateDecryptor(x_3des.Key, x_3des.IV),
            CryptoStreamMode.Read);

        // read and print the secret message
        x_crypto_stream.Read(x_secret_message, 0, x_secret_message.Length);
        Console.WriteLine(Encoding.Default.GetString(x_secret_message));
    }

    static void Main(string[] args) {
        new DESExample();
    }
}
```

Asymmetrical Encryption

The .NET Framework provides support for the asymmetrical encryption algorithms DSA and RSA. The class hierarchy for asymmetrical encryption follows the same model as for symmetrical algorithms. The abstract class *System.Security.Cryptography.AsymmetricAlgorithm* provides the basic members, which are accompanied by abstract and concrete implementations for each of the algorithms, as detailed in Table 17-7.

Table 17-7 Asymmetric Encryption Classes

Abstract Class	Implementation Class
System.Security.Cryptography.DSA	*System.Security.Cryptography.DSACryptoServiceProvider*
System.Security.Cryptography.RSA	*System.Security.Cryptography.RSACryptoServiceProvider*

A public/private key pair is generated automatically when the implementation classes are instantiated; the key information can be extracted in the following ways:

- By using the *ExportParameters* method, which returns a class representing the key information (either *DSAParameters* or *RSAParameters*)

- By using the *ToXmlString* method, which returns an XML description of the key pair

Both methods of obtaining the key information take a *bool* argument to specify whether the private key element should be included in the output. *ImportParameters* and *FromXmlString* allow previously generated keys to be imported.

Unlike the symmetrical algorithms, the *RSA* and *DSA* classes do not support encrypting and decrypting data through streams; the asymmetrical algorithm classes work on *byte* arrays. The following example demonstrates how to use the RSA algorithm to encrypt data and then decrypt it:

```
using System;
using System.Security.Cryptography;
using System.Text;

class RSAExample {

    RSAExample() {
        byte[] x_secret_message
            = Encoding.Default.GetBytes("C# for Java Developers");
```

```
    // create the RSA provider
    RSACryptoServiceProvider x_rsa_encryptor
        = new RSACryptoServiceProvider();
    // extract the parameters so we can decrypt the data later
    RSAParameters x_key_info = x_rsa_encryptor.ExportParameters(true);

    // encrypt the data
    byte[] x_encrypted_data
        = x_rsa_encryptor.Encrypt(x_secret_message, false);

    // create the RSA provider
    RSACryptoServiceProvider x_rsa_decryptor
        = new RSACryptoServiceProvider();
    x_rsa_decryptor.ImportParameters(x_key_info);

    // decrypt the data
    x_secret_message
        = x_rsa_decryptor.Decrypt(x_encrypted_data, false);
    Console.WriteLine(Encoding.Default.GetString(x_secret_message));
    }

    static void Main(string[] args) {
        new RSAExample();
    }
}
```

Hash Codes

Hash codes create fixed-length binary strings to uniquely identify a set of binary data; hash codes can be used to determine that the data that has been hashed has not been altered. The .NET Framework supports the following hashing algorithms:

■   MD5

■   SHA-1

■   SHA-256

■   SHA-384

■   SHA-512

The base class for all hash code algorithms is *System.Security.Cryptography.HashAlgorithm*, and following the model for other cryptographic functions, the .NET Framework provides an abstract class and an implementation class for each algorithm. Table 17-8 lists the classes.

Table 17-8 **Hash Code Classes**

Abstract Class	Implementation Class
System.Security.Cryptography.MD5	*System.Security.Cryptography.MD5CryptoServiceProvider*
System.Security.Cryptography.SHA1	*System.Security.Cryptography.SHA1CryptoServiceProvider*
System.Security.Cryptography.SHA256	*System.Security.Cryptography.SHA256Managed*
System.Security.Cryptography.SHA384	*System.Security.Cryptography.SHA384Managed*
System.Security.Cryptography.SHA512	*System.Security.Cryptography.SHA512Managed*

Hash codes are generated using the *ComputeHash* method derived from the *HashAlgorithm* class; this method will generate a hash code either from a *byte* array or by reading data from an instance of *System.IO.Stream*.

There are no class members to verify a hash code directly; to validate a hash code, the *ComputeHash* method must be called with the candidate data and the result compared with the original code. The following example demonstrates how to generate an MD5 hash code and print it to the console:

```
using System;
using System.Security.Cryptography;
using System.Text;

class MD5Demo {

    MD5Demo() {
        byte[] x_message
            = Encoding.Default.GetBytes("C# for Java Developers");

        // create the MD5 hash code provider
        MD5CryptoServiceProvider x_md5_provider
            = new MD5CryptoServiceProvider();

        // generate the hash code for the message
        byte[] x_hashcode = x_md5_provider.ComputeHash(x_message);

        // print out the hashcode
        foreach (byte x_byte in x_hashcode) {
            Console.Write(x_byte);
        }
    }

    static void Main(string[] args) {
        new MD5Demo() ;
    }
}
```

Digital Signatures

Digital signatures provide verification that data has originated from a certain individual; digital signatures rely on asymmetrical cryptography, and the processing that is required to generate a signature means that digital signatures are usually used to sign a hash code generated from the source data. See the preceding section in this chapter for more information on generating hash codes.

The base class for signatures is *System.Security.Cryptography.Asymmetric-SignatureFormatter*. Unlike the other classes in the cryptography library, the signature classes do not provide abstract and implementation classes for each algorithm. The .NET Framework supports the signature formats RSA PKCS #1 version 1.5 and DSA PKCS #1 version 1.5.

For each signature format, the .NET Framework includes a formatter class (to produce a signature) and a deformatter class (to validate a signature). The constructors for the formatter and deformatter classes accept an instance of an asymmetrical algorithm implementation class, as detailed in Table 17-9.

Table 17-9   Digital Signature Formatter Classes

Signature Format	Formatter/Deformatter Class	Constructor Algorithm Class
RSA PKCS #1	*RSAPKCS1SignatureFormatter* *RSAPKCS1SignatureDeformatter*	*RSACryptoServiceProvider*
DSA PKCS #1	*DSASignatureFormatter* *DSASignatureDeformatter*	*DSACryptoServiceProvider*

The following example demonstrates how to produce an RSA digital signature for an MD5 hash code and then verify the signature:

```
using System;
using System.Security.Cryptography;
using System.Text;

class RSASignatureDemo{

    RSASignatureDemo() {
        byte[] x_message
            = Encoding.Default.GetBytes("C# for Java Developers");

        // create the MD5 hash code provider
        MD5CryptoServiceProvider x_md5_provider
            = new MD5CryptoServiceProvider();

        // generate the hash code for the message
        byte[] x_hashcode = x_md5_provider.ComputeHash(x_message);
```

(continued)

```
RSACryptoServiceProvider x_rsa_provider
    = new RSACryptoServiceProvider();
RSAPKCS1SignatureFormatter x_formatter
    = new RSAPKCS1SignatureFormatter(x_rsa_provider);
x_formatter.SetHashAlgorithm("MD5");

byte[] x_signature = x_formatter.CreateSignature(x_hashcode);

// print out the hashcode
foreach (byte x_byte in x_signature) {
    Console.Write(x_byte);
}

RSAPKCS1SignatureDeformatter x_deformatter
    = new RSAPKCS1SignatureDeformatter(x_rsa_provider);
x_deformatter.SetHashAlgorithm("MD5");
bool x_verified = x_deformatter.VerifySignature(x_hashcode,
    x_signature);
Console.WriteLine("Verified: " + x_verified);
    }

    static void Main(string[] args) {
        new RSASignatureDemo () ;
    }
}
```

Note that the *SetHashAlgorithm* method must be called to specify the format of the hash code that is to be signed or verified. Table 17-10 lists the mapping between the hash code algorithms and the string names that can be used with this method.

Table 17-10   String Representations of Hash Code Algorithms

Hash Algorithm	String Name
MD5	*MD5*
SHA-1	*SHA1*
SHA-256	*SHA256* *SHA-256*
SHA-348	*SHA348* *SHA-348*
SHA-512	*SHA512* *SHA-512*

Summary

The support for security in the .NET platform is tightly integrated into the platform and allows a great deal of flexibility. The use of the Code Access Security model allows programmers to provide administrators with the information necessary to implement trust policies. The support for cryptography is well structured and easy to use, offering high-performance cipher implementations for applications that work with sensitive data.

18

Graphics and UI

The aim of this chapter is to provide a brief introduction to Windows Forms and GDI+ graphics through a high-level overview of the relevant .NET libraries and a comparison with the Java classes that provide equivalent functionality. Anything more than an introduction is beyond the scope of this book; both the Windows Forms library and the GDI+ toolkit are sufficiently complex that full coverage would require a dedicated book.

The coverage presented in this chapter provides enough information to allow a Java developer experienced in the Swing/JFC, Java AWT, and Java 2D APIs to quickly use the comparable .NET libraries; the .NET documentation should be consulted for the details of the individual topics discussed.

Windows Forms

The Windows Forms library is a toolkit for building UI applications for the Microsoft Windows operating system, equivalent in purpose to the Java AWT and Swing/JFC libraries.

While Swing and the AWT are intended for cross-platform development, Windows Forms are clearly rooted in the Windows operating system; there is no support for different platform appearances or behaviors.

The experienced Java programmer will have little problem adjusting to Windows Forms but will find the toolkit to be less flexible than Swing and the AWT. Forms provide fewer components, and it can be difficult to implement custom behavior using the provided classes.

Using Windows Forms

The central class in the Forms library is *System.Windows.Forms.Form*. This class represents top-level application windows and is the starting point for a UI application.

Adding and Disposing of Controls

Controls are added to a *Form* by creating the control instance and calling the *Add* method on the *Form.Controls* property. This property returns an instance of *System.Windows.Forms.Control.ControlsCollection*.

When a *Form* is no longer required, the *Dispose* method must be called; it's important to ensure that the *Dispose* method is also called on any controls that the *Form* contains.

The *System.ComponentModel.Container* class can be used to track a group of controls, and calling the *Dispose* method on the *Container* class ensures that *Dispose* is also called on all of the controls that have been added to the container.

The following example demonstrates how to add a *Button* to a *Form* and how to ensure that controls are correctly disposed of; for more information on disposing of objects, see the "Destructors" section in Chapter 5, "Data Types." For an overview of controls included in the .NET Framework, see the "Control Overview" section later in this chapter.

```
using System.Drawing;
using System.Windows.Forms;

public class SimpleForm : Form {

    private System.ComponentModel.Container o_components = null;

    public SimpleForm() {
        o_components = new System.ComponentModel.Container();
        Button x_button = new Button();
        x_button.Text = "My Button";
        Controls.Add(x_button);
        o_components.Add(x_button);
    }

    protected override void Dispose(bool p_disposing) {
        if(p_disposing) {
            if (o_components != null) {
```

```
            o_components.Dispose();
        }
    }
    base.Dispose(p_disposing);
}
}
```

Starting and Stopping a Forms Application

Windows Forms applications are started by calling the static *Run* method of the *System.Windows.Forms.Application* class, normally from the application *Main* method. The following fragment demonstrates how to run an instance of the *SimpleForm* class created earlier:

```
static void Main() {
    Application.Run(new SimpleForm());
}
```

A Forms application can be terminated either by calling the *Application.Exit* method or when the user clicks on the Close icon at the top of a form window.

Compiling

Compiling a Forms application using the command-line compiler is similar to compiling any other C# application. However, you should use the */target:winexe* flag to specify that the output is a UI application. Applications built with the */target:exe* flag will still work but will cause a command prompt to be displayed to the user alongside the main window. The following statement demonstrates how to compile the SimpleForm.cs file:

```
csc /target:winexe /out:MyApp.exe SimpleForm.cs
```

For more information about compiling C# classes, see Chapter 3, "Creating Assemblies."

Control Overview

Table 18-1 describes the Windows Forms controls that are included in the .NET Framework. These classes are found in the *System.Windows.Forms* namespace. Consult the .NET documentation for more information about the controls. This table demonstrates the lack of explicit implementation classes in Java when directly compared with the Windows Forms library.

Table 18-1   **A Comparison Between Windows Forms and Swing Controls**

Windows Forms	Swing	Description
Containers		
TabControl	*JTabbedPane*	A tabbed pane, used to group controls on separate pages.
GroupBox	*JPanel*	A labeled panel, typically used for a related group of controls, such as radio buttons; the equivalent can be achieved in Java using a *JPanel* and the *TitledBorder* class.
Panel	*JPanel*	An unlabeled panel used to group controls.
Button Controls		
Button	*JButton*	A standard button control, which can display an image and/or a text string.
LinkLabel	*JButton*	A button that can display a URL.
NotifyIcon	N/A	Displays an icon in the Windows Task Tray, typically used to represent an application running in the background.
Toolbar	*JToolBar*	A collection of buttons grouped together, typically used to present the user with commonly used commands.
Menu Controls		
MainMenu	*JMenuBar*	The menu for a Windows Form.
MenuItem	*JMenuItem*	An individual element of a *MainMenu*.
ContextMenu	*JPopupMenu*	A menu that appears when the user clicks on a control with the right mouse button.
Value Controls		
CheckBox	*JCheckBox*	Displays a text label and a check box to allow the user to select a property.
CheckedListBox	N/A	Displays a scrollable list of items, each with a check box.
RadioButton	*JRadioButton*	Displays a button that can be turned on or off; typically used in groups to allow mutually exclusive options to be selected.
Trackbar	*JSlider*	Allows a value to be selected by dragging a thumb along a scale.
List Controls		
ComboBox	*JComboBox*	Displays a drop-down list of items.
DomainUpDown	*JSpinner*	Displays a list of text items that the user can scroll through using an up and a down button.

Table 18-1   A Comparison Between Windows Forms and Swing Controls   *(continued)*

Windows Forms	Swing	Description
ListBox	*JList*	Displays a list of text or image items.
ListView	*JTable*	Displays items in one of four different views; the *report* view can be used as a table.
NumericUpDown	*JSpinner*	Displays a list of numeric values that the user can scroll though using an up and a down button.
TreeView	*JTree*	Displays a hierarchical set of nodes, displayed in a tree format.
Text Editing Controls		
TextBox	*JTextArea*	Displays text, which can be edited either by the user or programmatically.
RichTextBox	*JTextPane* *JEditorPane*	Displays formatted text, using the Rich Text Format (RTF).
Text Display Controls		
Label	*JLabel*	Displays a line of text that cannot be edited by the user.
StatusBar	*JProgressBar*	Displays status information about the application to the user; typically docked at the bottom of a form.
Dialog Box Controls		
ColorDialog	*JColorChooser*	Displays a color picker.
FontDialog	N/A	Displays a font picker.
OpenFileDialog	*JFileChooser*	Displays a dialog that allows a user to specify a file to be opened.
SaveFileDialog	*JFileChooser*	Displays a dialog that allows a user to specify a location to save a file.
PrintDialog	N/A	Displays a dialog that allows a user to select and configure a printer.
Date Controls		
DateTimePicker	N/A	Displays a calendar that allows a user to select a date or a time.
MonthCalendar	N/A	Displays a calendar that allows a user to select a range of dates.
Other Controls		
VScrollBar *HScrollBar*	*JScrollBar*	Vertical and horizontal scroll bars.
PictureBox	*ImageIcon*	Displays bitmaps and icons in a frame.

Docking and Anchoring

The Windows Form library doesn't provide the same layout flexibility as Swing or the AWT; the location of controls must be specified relative to their containers, as shown in the following example:

```
using System.Drawing;
using System.Windows.Forms;

public class LayoutDemo : Form {

    public LayoutDemo() {
        Button x_button = new Button();
        x_button.Text = "My Button";
        x_button.Location = new Point(20, 20);

        Controls.Add(x_button);
    }

    // Other methods, such as Dispose, would go here.

    static void Main() {
        Application.Run(new LayoutDemo());
    }
}
```

The position of the button in the form is specified using the *Location* property; this value defaults to the upper left corner of the container. No equivalent of the Java layout manager system exists in the Windows Forms library. This means that controls will overlap unless their locations are explicitly specified.

Anchoring

When a control is anchored to the edge of a container, the distance between the edge of the control and the edge of the container remains constant when the container is resized. A control can be anchored to any combination of edges, which causes the control to be resized as needed to maintain the distance between edges.

The following code demonstrates anchoring a button to the left and right edges of the form; the button will be resized as the form is resized to ensure that the distance from the edge of the button to the edge of the form remains constant:

```
using System.Drawing;
using System.Windows.Forms;
```

```
public class LayoutDemo : Form {

    public LayoutDemo() {
        Button x_button = new Button();
        x_button.Text = "My Button";
        x_button.Location = new Point(20, 20);
        x_button.Anchor = AnchorStyles.Left | AnchorStyles.Right;

        Controls.Add(x_button);
    }

    // Other methods, such as Dispose, would go here.

    static void Main() {
        Application.Run(new LayoutDemo());
    }
}
```

The *Anchor* property is used to specify a value from the *AnchorStyles* enumeration; values can be combined using a bit mask, as shown in the statement marked in boldface. Table 18-2 shows the values in the *AnchorStyle* enumeration.

Table 18-2   The *AnchorStyle* Enumeration

Value	Description
Top	The control is anchored to the top edge of its container.
Bottom	The control is anchored to the bottom edge of its container.
Left	The control is anchored to the left edge of its container.
Right	The control is anchored to the right edge of its container.
None	The control is not anchored to any edge of its container.

Docking

When a control is docked to an edge of its container, it remains in contact with that edge when the container is resized; the control will be resized to ensure that it is the same size as the docked edge. Docking is specified using the *Dock* property, as shown in the following example, which docks a button to the left edge of a form; the button will be resized to be completely in contact with the left edge of the form at all times, so it will be resized horizontally to follow the size of the form:

```
using System.Drawing;
using System.Windows.Forms;
```

(continued)

```
public class LayoutDemo : Form {

    public LayoutDemo() {
        Button x_button = new Button();
        x_button.Text = "My Button";
        x_button.Location = new Point(20, 20);
        x_button.Dock = DockStyle.Left;

        Controls.Add(x_button);
    }

    // Other methods, such as Dispose, would go here.

    static void Main() {
        Application.Run(new LayoutDemo());
    }
}
```

The *Dock* property accepts a value from the *DockStyle* enumeration; Table 18-3 describes the values in this enumeration.

Table 18-3   The *DockStyle* Enumeration

Value	Description
Top	The top edge of the control is docked to the top of the container.
Bottom	The bottom edge of the control is docked to the bottom of the container.
Left	The left edge of the control is docked to the left edge of the container.
Right	The right edge of the control is docked to the right edge of the container.
Fill	All of the control edges are docked to all of the container edges.
None	No control edges are docked.

Handling Events

Windows Forms controls define events that can be used to monitor instances for state changes and interaction with users. For general information on events, see Chapter 5.

The following example demonstrates how to handle an event from a *Button*; for details of the events supported by each control, consult the .NET documentation.

```
using System.Drawing;
using System.Windows.Forms;

public class EventDemo : Form {
```

```
Button o_button;

public EventDemo() {
    o_button = new Button();
    o_button.Text = "Press Me";
    o_button.Click += new System.EventHandler(processButtonEvent);

    Controls.Add(o_button);
}

private void processButtonEvent(object p_source,
        System.EventArgs p_event) {
    o_button.Text = "Press Again";
}

// Other methods, such as Dispose, would go here.

static void Main() {
    Application.Run(new EventDemo());
}
}
```

When the button is pressed, the *processButtonEvent* method is called, and the button's text is changed appropriately.

Drawing with GDI+

GDI+ is responsible for two-dimensional graphics, imaging, and typography for the Windows operating system. The .NET Framework includes classes that act as a managed wrapper around GDI+, providing graphics capabilities for Windows Forms.

The features of GDI+ are similar to those of the Java 2D API included in the Java 2 platform; with some minor exceptions, the principles behind both technologies are the same, and knowledge of Java 2D can easily be translated to GDI+.

The *System.Drawing.Graphics* class represents a container on which GDI+ operations can be performed; this class is the equivalent of the *java.awt.Graphics2D* and *java.awt.Graphics* classes from the Java API.

Obtaining a *Graphics* Instance

The most common approach to obtaining an instance of *System.Drawing.Graphics* is to override the *Control.OnPaint* event handler, which is invoked when a control should repaint itself. The following example demonstrates this approach:

```
using System.Drawing;
using System.Windows.Forms;

public class SimpleForm :Form {

    static void Main() {
        Application.Run(new SimpleForm());
    }

    // Other methods, such as Dispose and a default
    // constructor, would go here.

    protected override void OnPaint(PaintEventArgs p_event) {
        Graphics x_graph = p_event.Graphics;
        // drawing operations
    }
}
```

The *Graphics* property of the *PaintEventArgs* class returns the *System.Drawing.Graphics* instance for the current control, to which GDI+ operations can be applied. The *Paint* event is raised automatically when a component should be redrawn or manually by calling the *Control.RaisePaint-Event* method.

Instances of *System.Drawing.Graphics* can also be obtained by calling the *Control.CreateGraphics* method. Drawing operations applied to the *Graphics* instance that is returned from this method take effect immediately, as opposed to waiting for the component to be repainted.

Lines, Shapes, and Curves

Unlike Java, the GDI+ *Graphics* class doesn't maintain state information for drawing operations. For example, the Java *java.awt.Graphics.setColor* method specifies a color that will be used for subsequent drawing operations; specifying *Color.Red* means that all shapes and lines will be drawn in red until the color is changed.

By contrast, the .NET GDI+ classes require the programmer to specify the color settings as part of each draw method. The *System.Drawing.Brush* class is used to specify fill settings for solid shapes and the *System.Drawing.Pen* class to specify line settings.

The *Brush* class is abstract, and drawing operations are performed using a concrete implementation. Table 18-4 describes the brush implementations included in the .NET Framework.

Table 18-4   Brush Implementations

Brush Implementation	Description
System.Drawing.SolidBrush	A brush that uses a single color to fill the interior of a shape
System.Drawing.TextureBrush	A brush that uses an image to fill the interior of a shape
System.Drawing.Drawing2D.HatchBrush	A brush that uses a hatched-line pattern to fill the interior of a shape
System.Drawing.Drawing2D.LinearGradientBrush	A brush that fills the interior of a shape using a gradient between two or more colors

The following example demonstrates how to use a *SolidBrush* to fill a rectangle. The *SolidBrush* constructor accepts a value from the *System.Drawing.Color* structure, which is equivalent to the *java.awt.Color* class:

```
Graphics x_graphics = CreateGraphics();
Brush x_brush = new SolidBrush(Color.Red);
x_graphics.FillRectangle(x_brush, 10, 10, 50, 50);
```

The sealed *System.Drawing.Pen* class is used to specify properties for drawing lines and shapes. The constructor for the class accepts a *Color* value and an optional line width; the width defaults to 1 pixel if not specified. The following code fragment demonstrates how to use a *Pen* to draw a line:

```
Graphics x_graphics = CreateGraphics();
Pen x_pen = new Pen(Color.Green, 2);
x_graphics.DrawLine(x_pen, 10, 10, 50, 50);
```

The *System.Drawing.Pens* class contains properties that can be used to obtain *Pen* instances for all of the colors specified in the *System.Drawing.Color* structure; each of the instances has a width of 1 pixel. The statements in the following code fragment are equivalent:

```
Pen x_pen = new Pen(Color.Green, 1);
Pen x_pen = Pens.Green;
```

The *Pen* class defines members that allow a great deal of control over how a line is drawn. Table 18-5 summarizes these members; consult the .NET documentation for more information.

Table 18-5   *System.Drawing.Pen* **Members**

Member	Description
Alignment	When a shape is drawn, the *Alignment* property specifies whether the line should be drawn centered or inside the border of the shape; applies to lines more than 1 pixel wide.
Color	The color (from the *System.Drawing.Color* structure) used to draw lines.
DashCap	Specifies the way that the ends of dashed lines will be drawn using the *DashCap* enumeration. Defaults to *DashCap.Flat*.
DashOffset	Specifies the distance from the start of a line to begin dashing.
DashStyle	Specifies the dashing style for a line using the *DashStyle* enumeration. Defaults to *DashStyle.Solid* but also supports dots and dashes.
EndCap *StartCap*	Specifies the *cap* that will be drawn at the start or end of a line. Defaults to *LineCap.Flat* but can also be rounded, triangular, and square.
LineJoin	Specifies the way two lines are joined together when drawn as part of a shape. Defaults to *LineJoin.Miter* but can also be beveled or rounded.
Width	Specifies the width of the line in pixels.

Table 18-6 summarizes the members in the *java.awt.Graphics* and *System.Drawing.Graphics2D* classes used for drawing lines, shapes and curves.

Table 18-6   **Comparison of** *Graphics* **Members**

Java	.NET	Comments
draw3DRect()	N/A	
drawArc()	*DrawArc()*	
N/A	*DrawBezier()*	Draws a Bézier curve using four *System.Drawing.Point* instances. Similar functionality is available in Java through the *java.awt.geom.GeneralPath* class.
N/A	*DrawBeziers()*	Draws a series of Bézier curves using an array of *System.Drawing.Point* structures.
N/A	*DrawClosedCurve()*	Draws a closed curve through an array of *Point* structures.
N/A	*DrawCurve()*	Draws an open curve through an array of *Point* structures.
drawLine()	*DrawLine()*	

Table 18-6 **Comparison of *Graphics* Members** *(continued)*

Java	.NET	Comments
N/A	*DrawLines()*	Draws a series of lines that connect a set of *Point* structures. Similar functionality is available in Java through the *java.awt.geom.GeneralPath* class.
drawOval()	*DrawEllipse()*	
N/A	*DrawPie()*	Draws a pie-shaped segment.
drawPolygon()	*DrawPolygon()*	
drawRect() *drawRoundRect()*	*DrawRectangle()*	The effect of a round rectangle can be achieved by using the *LineJoin* property of the *Pen* class.
N/A	*DrawRectangles()*	Draws a series of rectangles.
fill3DRect()	N/A	
fillArc()	N/A	
fillOval()	*FillEllipse()*	
fillPolygon()	*FillPolygon()*	
N/A	*FillPie()*	
fillRect() *fillRoundRect()*	*FillRectangle()*	The effect of a round rectangle can be achieved by using the *LineJoin* property of the *Pen* class.

Drawing Strings

The GDI+ approach to drawing text follows a model similar to that of the support for lines and shapes. The *System.Drawing.Graphics* class doesn't maintain state information for font or color, so settings must be passed into the drawing method using the *Font* and *Brush* classes with each call. The following example demonstrates how to draw a string using the *Graphics.DrawString* method, which is functionally equivalent to the *java.awt.Graphics.drawString* method:

```
Graphics x_graphics = CreateGraphics();

String x_string = "C# for Java Developers";
Font x_font = new Font("TimesRoman", 14);
SolidBrush x_brush = new SolidBrush(Color.Green);

StringFormat x_format = new StringFormat();
x_format.FormatFlags = StringFormatFlags.DirectionVertical;

x_graphics.DrawString(x_string, x_font, x_brush, 10.0F, 20.0F, x_format);
```

Table 18-7 details the arguments supplied to the *Graphics.DrawString* method.

Table 18-7 **Arguments for the *System.Drawing.Graphics.DrawString* Method**

Argument	Description
System.String	The character string to draw.
System.Drawing.Font	The font to use to draw the string.
System.Drawing.Brush	The details of the character fill settings and colors.
(float,float) *System.Drawing.PointF* *System.Drawing.RectangleF*	The location at which to draw the string. The location always refers to the upper left corner of the drawn text but can be expressed as a pair of floating-point numbers, a *PointF*, or a *RectangleF*.
System.Drawing.StringFormat	Optional argument that specifies the format of the drawn text, including spacing and alignment.

Drawing Images

The GDI+ managed classes support images through the abstract *System.Drawing.Image* class, equivalent to *java.awt.Image*. The .NET Framework provides two concrete implementations of the *Image* class, *System.Drawing.Bitmap* and *System.Drawing.Imaging.Metafile*.

The *Bitmap* class is responsible for managing bitmap images. GDI+ supports the following formats:

- Windows Bitmap Image Format (BMP)

- Graphics Interchange Format (GIF)

- Joint Photographic Experts Group (JPEG)

- Exchangeable Image File (EXIF)

- Portable Network Graphics (PNG)

- Tag Image File Format (TIFF)

The *Metafile* class is responsible for vector images, which are represented by a sequence of drawing commands. The *Metafile* class supports the following formats:

- Windows Metafile (WMF)

- Enhanced Metafile (EMF)

- Enhanced Metafile Plus (EMF+)

An image can be loaded from a file either by using the constructors of the *Bitmap* or *Metafile* class or by using the static *FromFile* method in the *Image* class.

Images are drawn onto a *Graphics* instance using the *DrawImage* method; this method provides extensive support for scaling and cropping images by providing 30 different overloaded forms. Consult the .NET documentation for details of these members.

The following example demonstrates loading and painting a bitmap, which is contained in the current working directory:

```
Graphics x_graphics = CreateGraphics();
Bitmap x_bitmap = new Bitmap("myImage.jpg");
x_graphics.DrawImage(x_bitmap, 0, 0);
```

Double Buffering

GDI+ causes the *Graphics* class to update the screen after every drawing operation, which can be seen by the user as screen *flicker*; this flickering can be eliminated by a technique known as *double buffering*, whereby the drawing operations are applied to a *Graphics* instance held in memory and then copied to the screen in a single operation.

Double buffering can be enabled by using the *SetStyle* method from the *System.Windows.Forms.Control* class; this method accepts an argument from the *System.Windows.Forms.ControlStyles* enumeration, as shown in the following code fragment:

```
SetStyle(ControlStyles.DoubleBuffer, true);
```

Flickering can also occur because the contents of a *Graphics* instance are cleared automatically before a component is asked to repaint itself. This feature can be disabled by specifying the *ControlStyles.UserPaint* and *ControlStyles.All-PaintingInWmPaint* values in the *SetStyle* method. The following statement demonstrates how to completely eliminate flicker:

```
SetStyle(ControlStyles.DoubleBuffer |
    ControlStyles.UserPaint |
    ControlStyles.AllPaintingInWmPaint, true);
```

Double buffering can also be performed programmatically by executing drawing operations on an in-memory bitmap, as shown in the following example:

```
protected override void OnPaint(PaintEventArgs p_event) {
    Bitmap x_bitmap = new Bitmap(Width, Height);
    Graphics x_offscreen = Graphics.FromImage(x_bitmap);
```

(continued)

```
// drawing operations

p_event.Graphics.DrawImage(x_bitmap, 0, 0);
x_bitmap.Dispose();
}
```

The *Bitmap* instance is created by specifying the dimensions of the area to draw; in the example, we use the *Width* and *Height* properties from the *Control* class. The off-screen *Graphics* instance is retrieved from the *Bitmap*, and the drawing operations are then applied without causing the screen to be updated. Finally, the contents of the *Bitmap* are drawn to the screen using the *Graphics.DrawImage* method; it's important to ensure that the *Dispose* method is called on the *Bitmap* to ensure that unmanaged resources are released.

The flicker caused by the automatic clearing of the contents of a specific component can be prevented by overriding the *Control.OnPaintBackground* method and providing an empty method body.

Summary

The Windows Forms toolkit has fewer features than Swing and can be more difficult to use but does have the advantage of producing applications that cannot be distinguished from native programs, something that can be difficult to do in a Java application. The GDI+ library allows for complex 2D operations, providing functionality similar to that of the Java 2D library.

Overall, graphics and UI programming with .NET follows a model similar to that for Java, but there is a good deal of opportunity for third-party developers to fill out the feature set with advanced components.

19

Introduction to XML Web Services

Microsoft .NET XML Web services are supported by Microsoft Internet Information Service (IIS) versions 5.0 and later. It's important that IIS be already installed on a machine before the .NET installation is performed: the .NET installer recognizes that IIS is installed and establishes the bindings that allow Microsoft ASP.NET and XML Web services to function. If IIS is installed later, the .NET Framework must be removed and reinstalled.

The XML Web service support in .NET is provided by ASP.NET, a component of .NET that is outside the scope of this book. ASP.NET is used by IIS to invoke XML Web services; however, the details and features of ASP.NET aren't required to write XML Web services.

Visual Studio .NET includes extensive support for working with XML Web services, including tight integration with IIS; for more information, consult the Visual Studio documentation. In this chapter, however, we demonstrate how to build and deploy XML Web services using the command-line tools included with the .NET SDK.

The .NET support for XML Web services abstracts building and deploying XML Web services from the underlying standards and protocols; however, for clarity, Table 19-1 includes simple definitions of the key technologies.

Table 19-1 Key Elements of the .NET Framework XML Web Services

Technology	Description
XML Web services	A component that exposes functionality through Internet protocols.
Simple Object Access Protocol (SOAP)	An XML-based protocol for exchanging structured and typed information on the Web. Messages between clients and XML Web services are usually encoded using SOAP.
Web Services Description Language (WSDL)	An XML-based contract language that defines the services offered by an XML Web service.
Universal Description, Discovery, and Integration (UDDI)	A protocol for advertising the existence, location, and features of XML Web services.
ASP.NET	An element of the .NET Framework used to build server-based Web applications.

Creating XML Web Services

XML Web services are created by using the *WebService* and *WebMethod* attributes defined in the *System.Web.Services* namespace. The following example demonstrates a simple class annotated to be an XML Web service, providing a method that adds two integers:

```
using System;
using System.Web.Services;

namespace SumService {

    [WebService(Namespace="http://mycompany.com")]
    public class Sum {

        [WebMethod]
        public int sumNumbers(int p_first_number,
            int p_second_number) {
            return p_first_number + p_second_number;
        }
    }
}
```

The *WebService* attribute is optional and is used to describe the service that will be offered to clients. The most important property of this attribute is *Namespace*, which is used to define a unique name for the XML Web service endpoints (the methods that are exposed). The *Namespace* property defaults to *http://tempuri.org* and should be changed before an XML Web service is released publicly; in our working example, we set the namespace to be *http://mycompany.com*.

The properties defined by the *WebService* attribute are listed in Table 19-2.

Table 19-2   The *WebService* **Properties**

Property	Description
Description	A descriptive message for the XML Web service
Name	The name of the XML Web service
Namespace	The default namespace for the XML Web service

The *WebMethod* attribute is applied to methods that should be made available as part of the XML Web service; only the methods that need to be available to XML Web service clients should be annotated. The *WebMethod* attribute can be applied only to instance methods; static methods, properties, and other members of a class cannot be exposed as part of an XML Web service.

Table 19-3 lists the properties available for use with the *WebMethod* attribute.

Table 19-3   The *WebMethod* **Properties**

Property	Description
BufferResponse	If set to *true*, the response to an XML Web service request will be buffered until complete and returned to the client all at once; responses are buffered by default.
CacheDuration	Defines the number of seconds that a response from an XML Web service method is cached in memory; the default is 0, meaning that responses are not cached. During the cache period, requests for the Web method that pass the same parameter values will return the cached response.
Description	A description of the XML Web service method. Defaults to an empty string.
EnableSession	See the "State Management" section later in this chapter for more information. *EnableSession* is disabled by default.
MessageName	The name that will be used to expose the method to clients. By default, the C# method name is used.

Building and Deploying XML Web Services

The following sections explain how an XML Web service is built and deployed, a process that's often called *publishing an XML Web service*. Although there seem to be a lot of steps to be performed, the process is simple and easily repeated.

Deployment Directory

A deployment directory must be created to house the XML Web service files. To make the XML Web service accessible, the deployment directory must be made available through IIS.

The easiest way to configure IIS is to use the IIS Server Management Wizard, which on Windows 2000 and Windows XP—consult the IIS documentation for other Windows operating systems—can be opened by right-clicking the My Computer icon, selecting Manage, expanding the Services And Applications tree, and selecting the IIS tree. This opens the IIS Server Management Wizard. To create a virtual directory, right-click the Default Web Site tree, select New, and then select Virtual Directory. For the working example, create a virtual directory named SumService that maps incoming requests to the underlying deployment directory—for example, C:\SumService.

Remember that the name of the virtual directory and the name of the actual directory don't need to match; we have made them match merely to keep things simple. The default settings for a virtual directory are suitable for an XML Web service; consult the IIS documentation for more details. Before continuing, a word of caution: using IIS safely and securely requires a thorough comprehension of the IIS documentation and vigilance in applying security patches.

Compiling

XML Web services are compiled in the same manner as normal C# source files; however, the target must be a library, not an application executable. To compile the example, save it using the filename Sum.cs. The following command will compile this example into a library that can be deployed to IIS:

```
csc /out:SumService.dll /target:library Sum.cs
```

> **More Info** For more information about using the C# compiler, see Chapter 4, "Language Syntax and Features."

The assembly that the compiler creates must be placed in a subdirectory named bin contained within the XML Web service deployment directory created earlier with the IIS Wizard—for example, C:\SumService\bin.

Creating the Directive

To deploy an XML Web service, a directive file must be created, acting as a bridge between ASP.NET and the assembly containing the XML Web service code. The file should have the same name as the XML Web service but with the .asmx extension, which for our example would be SumService.asmx. The complete contents of the file for our example service are shown here:

```
<%@ WebService Class="SumService.Sum" %>
```

The *Class* attribute defines the C# class that will be used for the XML Web service. This class must be contained within an assembly in the bin subdirectory of the deployment directory; the common laguage runtime (CLR) will search for an assembly that contains the specified class.

It's also possible to specify the assembly that the CLR should use, avoiding the need to perform a potentially time-consuming search; the assembly name is appended after the class name, as shown in the following example:

```
<%@ WebService Class="SumService.Sum, SumService" %>
```

The directive file must be placed in the root of the deployment directory.

The URL to access an XML Web service includes the name of the directive file, taking the following form:

```
http://<host name>/<virtual directory>/<directive file>.asmx
```

For our example, the URL would become:

```
http://localhost/SumService/SumService.asmx
```

Configuring XML Web Services

XML Web services can be configured using XML files, in much the same way that application configuration files are used; for more information, see Appendix C, "Configuring Applications." XML Web service configuration is contained in the *configuration/system.web/webservices* element. The allowed subelements are listed in Table19-4. XML Web services don't require a configuration file to operate; if a file isn't found, default values will be used.

Table 19-4   XML Web Service Configuration Subelements

Element	Description
<protocols>	See the "Protocols" section of this chapter for more information.
<serviceDescriptionFormatExtensionTypes>	Advanced SOAP settings. Consult the .NET documentation for more details.
<soapExtensionTypes>	
<soapExtensionReflectorTypes>	
<soapExtensionImporterTypes>	
<wsdlHelpGenerator>	Specifies a Web Forms page to display when the XML Web service is queried by a Web browser. Consult the .NET documentation for more information.

XML Web service configuration files are stored in the root of the deployment directory and are named Web.config; the .NET runtime automatically loads the configuration file.

Protocols

The only configuration element relevant to this chapter is *<protocols>*. This setting defines how an XML Web service can be used and accessed. The supported protocols are listed in Table 19-5.

Table 19-5   Supported XML Web Service Protocols

Protocol	Description
Documentation	A special protocol that allows XML Web services to be tested with a browser. See the section "Testing XML Web Services" coming up for more details.
HttpSoap	SOAP over HTTP protocol.
HttpGet	HTTP GET requests, where parameters for XML Web service methods are appended to the URL after a question mark (?).
HttpPost	HTTP POST requests, where the parameters for XML Web service methods are passed in the free-format section of the request.

The following configuration file demonstrates how to enable all four protocols:

```
<configuration>
  <system.web>
    <webServices>
      <protocols>
        <add name="Documentation"/>
```

```
        <add name="HttpSoap"/>
        <add name="HttpGet"/>
        <add name="HttpPost"/>
      </protocols>
    </webServices>
  </system.web>
</configuration>
```

Examples of how queries and responses for each of the protocols should be formatted can be obtained by using a Web browser to examine the XML Web service. See the "Testing XML Web Services" section coming up for more information.

The settings in the XML Web service configuration file are overridden by those in the machine configuration file. For more information, see Appendix C.

Testing XML Web Services

Once deployed, an XML Web service can be tested using a browser, such as Internet Explorer. The browser interface provides details of the SOAP messages that are required to invoke a Web method and allows the programmer to test Web methods by entering parameters and viewing the XML response.

To test an XML Web service, view the URL described in the preceding section. The XML Web service detects that the client is a browser, and an HTML interface for the XML Web service is displayed.

Appending the *?WDSL* suffix to the URL returns the WDSL document for the XML Web service.

Summary

Building and deploying an XML Web service is a simple task. However, it's important that the directive file and the code assembly be located correctly. For our example, the file locations are

```
<deployment directory>/SumService.asmx
<deployment directory>/bin/SumService.dll
```

State Management

The classes that an XML Web service comprises are instantiated for each request; instances aren't shared between clients or between requests from the same client, and no application state is maintained.

XML Web service classes that require state management must be derived from *System.Web.Services.WebService*. The *WebService* class provides two properties that are used for application-level and session-level state management.

Application State Management

The *WebService* class defines the *Application* property to provide state management; the property returns an instance of *System.Web.HttpApplicationState* that is shared across all requests to the XML Web service. The shared *HttpApplicationState* instance is created automatically the first time a request is made to the XML Web service.

HttpApplicationState is derived from *System.Collections.Specialized.NameObjectCollectionBase* and accepts key/value pairs. The following example demonstrates an XML Web service that keeps a running total of integer values using the *Application* property:

```
using System.Web.Services;

namespace RunningTotal {

    [WebService(Namespace="http://www.mycompany.com")]
    public class Total : WebService {

        [WebMethod]
        public int AddToTotal(int p_new_value) {
            if (Application["Total"] == null) {
                Application["Total"] = 0;
            }
            Application["Total"] = (int)Application["Total"]
                + p_new_value;
            return (int)Application["Total"];
        }
    }
}
```

The example demonstrates storing an integer value in the shared *Http_ApplicationState* instance using the *Application* property. When created, the *HttpApplicationState* object contains no values; the programmer must check to see that a key exists and, if not, provide a default value. Each invocation of the *AddToTotal* XML Web service method retrieves the value using the *Total* key and adds the argument value. The method returns the running total.

Session State Management

Setting the *EnableSession* property of the *WebMethod* attribute to *true* enables session-based state. When enabled, the *Session* property of the *WebService* class allows state information to be stored on a per-client basis. The *Session* property returns an instance of *System.Web.SessionState.HttpSessionState*; instances of this class are created automatically. Session-based state is illustrated in the following example:

```
using System.Web.Services;

namespace RunningTotal {

    [WebService(Namespace="http://www.mycompany.com")]
    public class Total : WebService {

        [WebMethod(EnableSession=true)]
        public int AddToTotal(int p_new_value) {
            if (Session["Total"] == null) {
                Session["Total"] = 0;
            }
            Session["Total"] = (int)Session["Total"] + p_new_value;
            return (int)Session["Total"];
        }
    }
}
```

The example demonstrates maintaining a running total for each client; the total is persistent between invocations from the same client but isn't shared between clients.

XML Web Service Clients

The .NET Framework allows the programmer to create a proxy class that represents an XML Web service. This proxy takes the form of a source file, which can be compiled and used as part of a client application; the class appears as a local type and accesses the XML Web service transparently.

Creating a Proxy Class

Proxy classes are generated using the wsdl.exe tool, included with the .NET Framework and located in the C:\Program Files\Microsoft Visual Studio .NET\FrameworkSDK\Bin folder. The wsdl tool provides the command-line options described in Table 19-6.

Table 19-6 Command-Line Options for the WSDL Tool

Option	Description
/language:<language>	Specifies the language to use when generating the source file. Languages are *CS* for C#, *VB* for Visual Basic, and *JS* for JScript. The default is C#.
/namespace:<namespace>	The namespace directive for the generated class. Defaults to the global namespace.
/out:<filename>	The name of the file to generate. The default name is generated from the WSDL definition.
/protocol:<protocol>	Specifies the protocol that will be used to communicate with the XML Web service. See the earlier section "Protocols" for more information.
/username:<username> */password:<password>* */domain:<domain>*	Specifies authentication details for password-protected XML Web services.
/proxy:<url> */proxyusername:<username>* */proxypassword:<password>* */proxydomain:<domain>*	Specifies the Internet proxy to be used. Defaults to the system proxy settings.

The following statement illustrates how to create a proxy for the example *SumService* XML Web service developed earlier in this chapter, accepting the default settings for the command-line options:

```
wsdl http://localhost/SumService/SumService.asmx
```

The statement generates a C# source file named Sum.cs containing a proxy class for the XML Web service.

Proxy classes can be created for XML Web services that haven't been created with .NET; the URL that is passed to the wsdl.exe tool must point to the WSDL document for the service.

Using a Proxy Class

Using a proxy class is no different from using any other class. The following example demonstrates a class that relies on the proxy just created, which we have saved in a source file named SumClient.cs:

```
public class SumClient {

    static void Main(string[] p_args) {
```

```
        Sum x_sum = new Sum();
        int x_result = x_sum.sumNumbers(10, 20);
        System.Console.WriteLine("Result: " + x_result);
    }
}
```

The statements related to the proxy class are marked in boldface. We create a new instance of the *Sum* proxy class and invoke the *sumNumbers* method. Each of the methods exposed by the XML Web service is represented by a C# method. The client class and the proxy are compiled using the following statement:

```
csc /out:SumClient.exe SumClient.cs Sum.cs
```

This statement creates an executable named SumClient.exe, which will automatically invoke the XML Web service as required.

> **More Info**   For more information about using the C# compiler, see Chapter 4.

Executing the SumClient application will generate the following output:

```
Result: 30
```

Asynchronous Programming

For each XML Web service method, three methods are automatically created in the proxy class, as described in Table 19-7.

Table 19-7   The XML Web Service Proxy Class Methods

Proxy Class Method	Description
<Web Service Method Name>	Sends a message to the XML Web service synchronously.
Begin<Web Service Method Name>	Begins the process of sending a message to the XML Web service asynchronously.
End<Web Service Method Name>	Ends the process of sending an asynchronous message.

Using the synchronous method is shown in the preceding section; this section deals with using XML Web services asynchronously, which follows the general model for all .NET asynchronous features.

The following example shows a client that makes asynchronous use of the example XML Web service:

```
using System;

public class AsyncSumClient {

    static void Main(string[] p_args) {
        Sum x_sum = new Sum();
        AsyncCallback x_callback =
            new AsyncCallback(AsyncSumClient.SumCallBack);
        x_sum.BeginsumNumbers(10, 20, x_callback, x_sum);

        Console.ReadLine();
    }

    static void SumCallBack(IAsyncResult p_callback) {
        Sum x_sum = (Sum)p_callback.AsyncState;
        int x_result = x_sum.EndsumNumbers(p_callback);
        System.Console.WriteLine("Result: " + x_result);
    }
}
```

The statements that relate to asynchronous support are marked in boldface. The request is started by calling the *BeginsumNumbers* method, passing in the arguments to the Web method, a delegate that references the *SumCallBack* method, and the instance of the proxy class that is being used. When the request has completed, the *SumCallBack* method is invoked, and we use the *AsyncState* property of the *IAsyncResult* to obtain the instance of the proxy class; the results of the request are obtained by calling the *EndsumNumbers* method.

Summary

XML Web services rely on IIS and tight integration with the underlying platform. However, creating and deploying XML Web services is a simple task, and the support for testing them with a Web browser makes debugging simple and quick.

Appendix A

Platform Integration

Java programmers who develop applications for the Microsoft Windows platform will be pleasantly surprised by the integration features provided by the Microsoft .NET Framework. In this appendix, we'll demonstrate the integration between .NET and some of the more commonly used Windows features, including the following:

- The operating system runtime environment
- System processes
- The Windows registry
- The event log
- Windows Services

All of these features are supported directly by .NET classes without intermediate mechanisms such as Java Native Interface (JNI), COM, or native DLLs; however, the behavior of these features depends on the version of Windows being used and could affect the future portability of an application's code.

The majority of the features described in this appendix require that the executing code or the current user have the necessary security permission to carry out the desired action. A full description of .NET Framework security is included in Chapter 17, "Security and Cryptography"; consult the Windows documentation for details of platform security.

Runtime Environment

The *System.Environment* class provides a set of static utility members that give access to the runtime environment of the current process; we explore some of the more commonly used features in the following sections.

Command-Line Arguments

The *Main* method of an application can optionally take a *String* array argument; on execution, the runtime passes any command-line arguments as members of this array. Alternatively, the *Environment.CommandLine* property returns a *String* containing the full command line used to start the current process, whereas the *Environment.GetCommandLineArgs* method returns a *String* array containing the individual command-line components. Key benefits of these members include the following:

- The program name used to launch the current application is included as the first component of the returned data; this isn't available via the arguments to the *Main* method.

- The command-line arguments are available irrespective of whether the *Main* method declares a *String* array argument.

- The command-line information is easily accessible from any component of an application.

Environment Variables

The *Environment.GetEnvironmentVariable* method returns a *String* containing the value of a specified environment variable, or *null* if the variable doesn't exist. The *GetEnvironmentVariables* method returns an *IDictionary* instance containing all environment variables; the variable names are the dictionary keys.

The *Environment.ExpandEnvironmentVariables* method takes a single *String* argument; any variable names enclosed by the percent (%) character are expanded in the return value. For example, the following statement uses *ExpandEnvironmentVariables* to formulate a string containing the values of the *OS* and *SystemRoot* environment variables:

```
System.Console.WriteLine(Environment.ExpandEnvironmentVariables(
    "OS Version = %OS% and SystemRoot = %SystemRoot%"));
```

On a Windows 2000 machine, the output will be similar to the following:

```
OS Version = Windows_NT and SystemRoot = C:\WINNT
```

Drives and Directories

Table A-1 summarizes four members of the *Environment* class that provide information about the configuration of drives and directories on the current machine.

Table A-1   Drive- and Directory-Related Members of the *Environment* Class

Member	Description
Properties	
CurrentDirectory	Gets or sets the fully qualified path of the current application directory; initially this property will return the directory from which the application was started.
SystemDirectory	Gets the fully qualified path of the system directory—for example, C:\WINNT\System32.
Methods	
GetFolderPath()	Returns the fully qualified path of a special system folder. The folder to return is identified using a value from the *Environment.SpecialFolder* enumeration. *SpecialFolder* includes values such as *System, Templates, Internet-Cache,* and *Recent*; consult the .NET documentation for full details.
GetLogicalDrives()	Returns a *String* array containing the names of all logical drives configured on the computer. For example, on most computers with a hard drive, the return value would include the logical drive name C:\.

Machine and Operating System Information

The *Environment* class provides properties that return information about the machine and the operating system; these are summarized in Table A-2.

Table A-2   Machine- and OS-Related Properties of the *Environment* Class

Property	Description
MachineName	Gets a *String* that is the name of the machine.
OSVersion	Gets a *System.OperatingSystem* instance that encapsulates platform and version information about the underlying operating system.
TickCount	Gets an *int* representing the number of milliseconds that have passed since the computer was started.
UserName	Gets a *String* that is the name of the user that started the current process.
Version	Gets a *System.Version* instance that contains version information about the currently running CLR. See the .NET documentation for details of *System.Version*.
WorkingSet	Gets a *long* value indicating the amount of physical memory mapped to the current process.

Process Control

The .NET Framework provides extensive capabilities to manipulate processes on both the local and remote machines. The *Process* class of the *System.Diagnostics* namespace provides an association through which to query and control an underlying system process.

Creating New Processes

There are two approaches for creating new system processes using the *Process* class. Both approaches work only on the local machine; processes cannot be created on remote machines. The first approach is to instantiate a *Process* object, set the necessary configuring information via the *StartInfo* property, and call *Start* on the *Process* instance. The *StartInfo* property takes a *System.Diagnostics.ProcessStartInfo* instance that encapsulates configuration information for the process to be created. This includes details such as

- The name of the file to execute
- Command-line arguments to pass to the application
- Whether the standard error, input, and output streams should be redirected, allowing them to be obtained via the *StandardError*, *StandardInput*, and *StandardOutput* properties of the *Process* instance (discussed later in this section)
- Whether an application with a UI should be started minimized or maximized
- The initial directory where the process should be started

> **More Info**   Consult the .NET documentation for complete details of all the properties that can be configured using the *ProcessStartInfo* class.

The following code fragment demonstrates starting a new process using a *ProcessStartInfo* instance as an argument to a *Process* constructor:

```
// Create a ProcessStartInfo instance
ProcessStartInfo psi = new ProcessStartInfo();
psi.FileName = "MyApplication.exe";
psi.Arguments = "arg1 arg2";
```

```
psi.WorkingDirectory = @"C:\Temp";

// Create and start a Process using the ProcessStartInfo instance
Process proc1 = new Process();
proc1.StartInfo = psi;
proc1.Start();
```

Alternatively, *Process* provides three static overloads of the *Start* method that take configuration information as arguments, start a process, and return a *Process* instance. The following statements demonstrate the use of the static methods to execute an application named MyApplication.exe:

```
// Create a new process from a file name
Process proc2 = Process.Start("MyApplication.exe");

// Create a new process from a file name with arguments
Process proc3 = Process.Start("MyApplication.exe", "arg1 arg2");

// Create a new process from a ProcessStartInfo
ProcessStartInfo psi = null;
psi = new ProcessStartInfo("MyApplication.exe", "arg1 arg2");
psi.WorkingDirectory = @"C:\Temp";
Process proc4 = Process.Start(psi);
```

The file name passed to the *Process* doesn't have to represent an executable file; any file for which the operating system has an extension to application mapping is valid. For example, if passed a file name with the .doc extension, the application associated with .doc files will be launched (for example, Microsoft Word) and the specified document opened.

When finished with a *Process* instance, the *Close* method should be called to correctly release the resources consumed by the object; this doesn't affect the underlying system process.

Obtaining a Reference to an Existing Process

Table A-3 summarizes four static methods provided by the *Process* class used to obtain references to running processes. With the exception of the *GetCurrent-Process* method, all of the methods provide overloaded forms to access processes running on a remote Windows machine.

Table A-3 *Process* **Class Static Methods for Obtaining References to Existing Processes**

Static Method	Description
GetCurrentProcess()	Returns a *Process* instance that is associated with the current application
GetProcessById()	Returns a *Process* instance associated with the specified ID
GetProcesses()	Returns a *Process* array containing all of the processes currently running
GetProcessesByName()	Same as *GetProcesses* but returns only those processes with a given name

Terminating Processes

The *Process* methods summarized in Table A-4 terminate the associated local process; termination of remote processes is not supported.

Table A-4 *Process* **Methods for Terminating Local Processes**

Method	Description
CloseMainWindow()	Sends a *Close* message to the main window of a GUI application to request termination; the target application can choose to ignore the message. The *CloseMainWindow* method returns *true* if the message was successfully sent and *false* if the target process doesn't have a main window, or if the main window is currently disabled.
Kill()	Causes the immediate termination of a running process. For GUI applications, *CloseMainWindow* is a better alternative because it allows the application to close down gracefully; however, *Kill* is the only way to terminate non-GUI applications.

Instances of the *Process* class remain valid after the system process they represent has been terminated; the *HasExited*, *ExitCode,* and *ExitTime* properties contain information relating to the terminated process.

Information About Existing Processes

The properties of the *Process* class provide information about the underlying system processes. The first call to a *Process* property populates the instance with information about the system process, representing a snapshot of the process at the time the property was accessed; this information is cached in the *Process* instance and won't be updated until the *Refresh* method is called.

Table A-5 provides a summary of the commonly used *Process* properties. Other properties provide details about the resources that the system process is using; consult the .NET documentation for complete details.

Table A-5 *Process* **Properties**

Property	Description
BasePriority	Gets the base priority of the system process; individual threads of the process can be prioritized independently but use the base priority initially.
Id	Gets the unique ID of the system process.
MachineName	Gets the name of the machine the system process is running on.
MainWindowHandle	Gets the handle to the main window for processes running on the local machine; if the process doesn't have a main window, 0 (zero) is returned.
ProcessName	Gets the name of the system process.
ProcessorAffinity	On multiprocessor machines, *ProcessorAffinity* gets or sets the processors on which threads of the associated process will be scheduled to run; a bit mask is used to specify the processors that can be used.
Responding	Returns *true* if the UI of the associated process is capable of responding to user input; if the UI is unresponsive, *false* is returned.
StandardError	Gets a *System.IO.StreamReader* through which the standard error output can be read from the associated process. The process must be configured to redirect error messages when it is created or an exception is thrown; see "Creating New Processes" earlier in this section for details.
StandardInput	Similar to *StandardError* but provides a *System.IO.StreamWriter* for writing standard input to the system process.
StandardOutput	Similar to *StandardError* but provides access to the standard output of a process.
StartInfo	Returns a *System.Diagnostics.ProcessStartInfo* instance that contains the information used to create the system process; the "Creating New Processes" topic earlier in this section contains an overview of the *ProcessStartInfo* class.
StartTime	Gets a *System.DateTime* instance containing the time the system process was started.

Process Synchronization and Events

Two methods of the *Process* class allow the current thread to synchronize with the state of a given process. The *WaitForExit* method blocks the current thread indefinitely until the associated process terminates. For processes that have user interfaces, the *WaitForInputIdle* method blocks the current thread until the process enters an idle state. Both methods provide overloads where a timeout period is specified, after which the method returns *false* and the blocked thread continues.

The *Process* class also provides an event mechanism to notify listeners of process termination. To enable events, the *Process.EnableRaisingEvents* property must be set to *true*. An event handler can then be registered with the *Process.Exited* event that will be called when the associated process is terminated.

Windows Registry

The Windows registry provides a centralized repository where the operating system and applications can store information. The registry is structured hierarchically, with the registry key being the base unit of organization. Registry keys can hold both typed data and subkeys.

Given the changes implemented with .NET, including self-describing assemblies, configuration files, and isolated storage, the importance of the registry is diminished. However, the registry is still a useful service, and the .NET Framework provides direct access to it through a simple set of classes in the *Microsoft.Win32* namespace.

The *Registry* Class

Despite having a hierarchical structure, the registry doesn't derive from a single root key. *Microsoft.Win32.Registry* is a utility class that contains seven static read-only *RegistryKey* fields (discussed next); these fields represent the primary entry points into the registry.

The registry classes don't support direct random access to named registry keys; entry points must be obtained through the *Registry* class. The members of *Microsoft.Win32.RegistryKey* are used to navigate to the required registry key.

Table A-6 lists the seven static fields, indicates the area they map to in the registry, and summarizes the information contained in that area.

Table A-6   Static *RegistryKey* Fields of the *Registry* Class

Field	Description
ClassesRoot	Maps to HKEY_CLASSES_ROOT. Contains information about extension to application mappings and OLE objects.
CurrentConfig	Maps to HKEY_CURENT_CONFIG. Contains current non-user-specific hardware configuration information.
CurrentUser	Maps to HKEY_CURRENT_USER. Contains information about current user preferences.
DynData	Maps to HKEY_DYN_DATA. Contains dynamic registry data.
LocalMachine	Maps to HKEY_LOCAL_MACHINE. Contains local machine configuration data.
PerformanceData	Maps to HKEY_PERFORMANCE_DATA. Contains performance information.
Users	Maps to HKEY_USERS. Contains information about user accounts and default user information.

The *RegistryKey* Class

The *RegistryKey* class represents a key node within the *Registry* hierarchy. Table A-7 details the members of the *RegistryKey* class that provide access to information about a particular key as well as the values and child keys it contains. All get, set, and delete methods are case preserving but not case sensitive with regard to the registry key and value names.

Table A-7   Members of the *RegistryKey* Class

Member	Description
Properties	
Name	Gets the name of the *RegistryKey*.
SubkeyCount	Gets the number of subkeys in the *RegistryKey*.
ValueCount	Gets the number of values in the *RegistryKey*.
Methods	
Close()	Closes an open *RegistryKey* and flushes any changes to disk.
CreateSubKey()	Creates a new subkey with the specified name and returns a *RegistryKey* instance. If the subkey already exists, the existing subkey is returned.
DeleteSubKey()	Deletes the specified empty subkey.
DeleteSubKeyTree()	Deletes the subkey and all child subkeys recursively.
DeleteValue()	Deletes the specified value from the *RegistryKey*.
Flush()	Causes the registry write buffers to be flushed.
GetSubKeyNames()	Gets a *String* array containing the names of all subkeys contained in the key.
GetValue()	Gets the contained value with the specified name. The value is returned as an *Object* that must be cast to the correct data type. Details of the types returned are included in the .NET documentation.
GetValueNames()	Gets a *String* array containing the names of all values contained in the *RegistryKey*.
OpenSubKey()	Returns an instance of *RegistryKey* representing the named subkey; *null* is returned if the subkey doesn't exist. An overload to this method allows the programmer to request write access to the opened key.
SetValue()	Creates or updates the specified value. Despite the fact that the registry supports different data types, it isn't possible to choose what type will be used to store the value; the most appropriate type is chosen automatically based on the data provided.

Remote Registry Access

The registry of a remote machine can be accessed using the static *RegistryKey.OpenRemoteBaseKey* and providing two arguments:

- A value from the *Microsoft.Win32.RegistryHive* enumeration that identifies which root key to open. The valid values map to the static fields of the *Registry* class discussed earlier; they are *ClassesRoot*, *CurrentConfig*, *CurrentUser*, *DynData*, *LocalMachine*, *PerformanceData*, and *Users*.

- A *String* containing the name of the machine on which the registry to be opened is located. If *String.Empty* is used, the registry on the local machine is opened.

  OpenRemoteBaseKey returns a *RegistryKey* instance representing the opened key on the remote machine and can subsequently be used as described in the preceding section.

Windows Event Log

The Windows event log provides a centralized, remotely accessible mechanism for the operating system and applications to log events. By default, the event log contains three separate logs: Application, System, and Security.

Access to the event log is exposed through the *System.Diagnostics.EventLog* class. *EventLog* provides a mixture of static and instance members used to read from and write to the event log as well as create, delete, and clear individual logs.

Writing to the Event Log

Registering an Event Source

Before an application can write to the event log, an event *source* must be configured and registered against a particular log; a source is a string that uniquely identifies a component and is usually the application name.

A source can be registered with only one log at a time; attempting to register a source against multiple logs results in a *System.ArgumentException* being thrown.

Sources can be registered using the static *EventLog.CreateEventSource* method, which offers the following two overloads:

```
void CreateEventSource(String source, String log);
void CreateEventSource(String source, String log, String machine);
```

The first overload takes a source name and the name of the log to register the source against. If *null* or an empty string is provided, the *log* argument defaults to Application.

The second overload takes a computer name; this permits events to be written to the event log of a remote machine. Specifying a dot () as the computer name uses the local event log and is equivalent to using the first overload. The following statements demonstrate the use of the *CreateEventSource* method:

```
// Register the "myApp" source against the local
// "Application" log
EventLog.CreateEventSource("myApp", "Application");

// Equivalent to the above statement; "." is the local machine
// and the "Application" log is the default log.
EventLog.CreateEventSource("myApp",null,".");

// Register against "SomeLog" log of a
// remote machine called "myMachine"
EventLog.CreateEventSource("myApp","SomeLog","myMachine");
```

Event sources are manually deregistered using the static *EventLog.Delete-EventSource* method or automatically if a log is deleted; deleting logs is discussed later in this section.

Writing Events

Entries are written to the event log using the *EventLog.WriteEntry* method; *Write-Entry* offers a choice of ten instance and static overloads. The static methods of *EventLog* mirror the instance methods but take an extra argument that identifies the event source. Instance methods use the source specified in the *Event-Log.Source* property; an exception is thrown if the *Source* property isn't set when *WriteEntry* is called.

When *WriteEntry* is called, an entry is made to the log that the source is registered against. If the source of a *WriteEntry* call isn't already registered against a log, it's automatically registered; static *WriteEntry* overloads register the source against the Application log, whereas instance overloads use the log specified by the *EventLog.Log* property. If the *Source* and *Log* properties don't match the configured source/log registration settings when *WriteEntry* is called, an *ArgumentException* is thrown.

The arguments that can be passed to the various overloaded versions of *WriteEntry* are summarized in Table A-8.

Table A-8   Arguments of the *EventLog.WriteEntry()* Overloaded Method

Argument	Comments
message	The text of the event to write to the event log.
type	A value from the *EventLogEntryType* enumeration identifying the type of event. Valid values include *Error, Warning, Information, SuccessAudit,* and *FailureAudit.*
	The *SuccessAudit* and *FailureAudit* values are used only for security events.
eventID	An application-specific event identifier.
category	An application-specific category identifier.
rawData	A *byte* array that holds binary data associated with the event.

The following example program periodically writes an entry to the Application log with the source name MyApp:

```
using System;
using System.Diagnostics;
using System.Threading;

public class EventLogWriter {

    public static void Main(String[] args) {

        // Create the EventLog instance and open the
        // "Application" log
        EventLog log = new EventLog("Application", ".", "MyApp");

        // Loop and write an entry every 5 seconds
        while (true) {
            log.WriteEntry("Test Message",
                EventLogEntryType.Error, 200);
            Thread.Sleep(5000);
        }
    }
}
```

Reading from the Event Log

Although applications are more likely to write to than read the event log, sometimes an application will read the event log. The *EventLog.Entries* property returns an *EventLogEntryCollection* containing *EventLogEntry* instances. Each *EventLogEntry* represents a single event log record and provides the properties detailed in Table A-9 to access the details of the event.

Table A-9   *EventLogEntry* Properties

Property	Description
Category	Gets the text associated with the *CategoryNumber* of the entry.
CategoryNumber	Gets the category number of the entry.
Data	Gets the binary data associated with the entry.
EntryType	Gets the event type of the entry. The returned value is a member of the *Event-LogEntryType* enumeration; valid values are *Error, Warning, Information, SuccessAudit,* and *FailureAudit.*
EventID	Gets the application-specific event ID for the entry.
Index	Gets the index of the entry in the event log.
MachineName	Gets the name of the machine on which the entry was generated.
Message	Gets the message associated with the entry.
Source	Gets the source associated with the entry.
TimeGenerated	Gets the local time at which the entry was generated.
TimeWritten	Gets the local time at which the entry was written.
UserName	Gets the name of the user responsible for logging the entry.

When an application reads from a log, the *Source* doesn't need to be specified; only the *Log* and *MachineName* properties are required. Changing the *Log* and *MachineName* properties of an existing *EventLog* instance provides access to the newly specified log.

The following example opens the Application log on the local machine and counts the events generated by the source MyApp:

```
using System;
using System.Diagnostics;

public class EventLogReader {

    public static void Main() {

        // Create the EventLog instance and open the
        // "Application" log
        EventLog log = new EventLog("Application");

        // Get the collection of log entries
        EventLogEntryCollection entries = log.Entries;

        // Declare a counter
        int count = 0;
```

(continued)

```
            // Loop through the entries and count occurrences for
            // the "MyApp" source
            foreach (EventLogEntry entry in entries) {
                if (entry.Source == "MyApp") count++;
            }

            // Display count information for the source to the console
            Console.WriteLine("Logged events for MyApp = {0}", count);
        }
    }
```

Creating and Deleting Custom Logs

There is no method to explicitly create a new log; if a source is registered against a log that doesn't exist, calls to the *WriteEntry* method will cause the log to be created automatically. The following statements show two distinct approaches to creating the MyApplicationLog log using a source named MySrc (assuming the log doesn't already exist):

```
// Using an EventLog instance
EventLog e = new EventLog("MyApplicationLog", ".", "MySrc");
e.WriteEntry("A test message");

// Using EventLog static methods
EventLog.CreateEventSource("MySrc", "MyApplicationLog");
EventLog.WriteEntry("MySrc", "A test message");
```

The existence of a log is determined using the static *EventLog.Exists* method, passing it a *String* argument containing the name of the log to test for. An overloaded version also accepts a machine name for testing the existence of a log on a remote machine.

The static *EventLog.Delete* method accepts the same arguments as *Exists* but deletes the specified log if it exists; if the log doesn't exist, a *System.System-Exception* is thrown.

Event Log Notifications

Applications can use the *EventLog.EntryWritten* event to be notified when entries are written to the event log of the local computer; notifications from remote computers are not supported.

First an *EventLog* instance is created and mapped to a specific log. Second the *EnableRaisingEvents* property is set to *true*; this enables event notifications on the *EventLog* instance. Finally the *EventLog.EntryWritten* event is provided with an event handler delegate to be notified when event log entries are written. The delegate that defines the *EntryWritten* event handler has the following signature:

```
public delegate void EntryWrittenEventHandler(object sender,
    EntryWrittenEventArgs e);
```

The *sender* argument is the *EventLog* instance that raised the event, and *e* is a *System.Diagnostics.EntryWrittenEventArgs* instance; *EntryWrittenEventArgs* contains an *Entry* property that gets an *EventLogEntry* representing the event log entry that caused the event to be raised.

The following example program listens to the Application event log and displays summary details to the console each time an entry is written:

```
using System;
using System.Diagnostics;

public class EventLog1Listener {

    public static void Main() {

        // Create the EventLog instance and open the
        // "Application" log
        EventLog log = new EventLog("Application",
            ".", "testapp");

        // Enable event notifications
        log.EnableRaisingEvents = true;

        // Create the event handler
        log.EntryWritten +=
            new EntryWrittenEventHandler(EventLogEventHandler);

        // Make sure the process does not terminate
        Console.ReadLine();
    }

    public static void EventLogEventHandler(object sender,
            EntryWrittenEventArgs arg) {
        // Get the EventLogEntry that triggered the event
        EventLogEntry entry = arg.Entry;

        // Display summary information for the event to
        // the console
        Console.WriteLine(
            "{0}:Category {1} event triggered by {2}",
            entry.TimeWritten, entry.CategoryNumber,
            entry.Source);
    }
}
```

If we run the previous *EventLogWriter* example while the *EventLogListener* example is running, we get output similar to the following:[*]

```
02/04/2002 15:04:06:Category 0 event triggered by MyApp
02/04/2002 15:04:11:Category 0 event triggered by MyApp
02/04/2002 15:04:16:Category 0 event triggered by MyApp
02/04/2002 15:04:21:Category 0 event triggered by MyApp
```

Windows Services

A Windows Service is an application that runs as a background process independent of the currently logged on user. Services are supported on Windows NT, Windows 2000, and Windows XP.

The life cycle and runtime configuration of a service is controlled by a component of Windows called the Service Control Manager (SCM) based on configuration information held in the Windows registry. The SCM also controls how other programs can interact with the service.

Service development and deployment are straightforward but lack the elegant simplicity of many aspects of .NET. The complexity stems from the necessity to install the service instead of simply running it like a normal assembly.

The creation of a service involves the development of the following three components: the service application, an installer, and a service controller. We discuss each component individually in the following sections.

The Service Application

Development of the service application involves the following steps:

1. Derive a class from *System.ServiceProcess.ServiceBase* that will contain the functionality for the service.

2. Implement an instance constructor that configures the service and sets the inherited properties of *ServiceBase* to the correct initial values.

3. Override the methods inherited from *ServiceBase* that process life cycle messages from the SCM; all services should override the *OnStart* method.

4. Implement a *Main* method that calls the static *ServiceBase.Run* method, passing an instance of the service class as an argument.

Despite having a *Main* method, service code cannot be executed directly; the *ServiceBase.Run* call causes a Windows Service Start Failure dialog to appear. The service must be installed before it can execute; we cover installation in the next section.

No lengthy processing should be carried out in the *Main* method or the instance constructor, nor should the service functionality be started until instructed by the SCM.

The creation of a service is best explained by example, so we'll develop two simple services that exist in a single assembly. Despite being defined in a single assembly, each service is independently controlled via the SCM. We have called one service *LogBeacon1* and the other *LogBeacon2*.

Both the *LogBeacon1* and *LogBeacon2* services are instances of the *Beacon-Service* class that derives from *ServiceBase*. When instantiated, the *BeaconService* class creates a thread that periodically writes entries to the Application event log; the activity of the logging thread is controlled by commands from the SCM. The *BeaconService* code is listed here; a discussion of the code follows.

```
using System;
using System.Threading;
using System.ServiceProcess;

public class BeaconService : ServiceBase {

    private Thread BeaconThread = null;
    private int Interval = 5000;

    public BeaconService(String name) {
        ServiceName = name;
        CanStop = true;
        CanPauseAndContinue = true;
        BeaconThread = new Thread(new ThreadStart(Beacon));
    }

    protected override void OnStart(String[] args) {
        if (BeaconThread != null) {
            BeaconThread.Start();
        }
    }

    protected override void OnStop() {
        if (BeaconThread != null) {
            BeaconThread.Abort();
        }
    }

    protected override void OnPause() {
        if (BeaconThread != null) {
            BeaconThread.Suspend();
        }
    }
```

(continued)

```
        protected override void OnContinue() {
            if (BeaconThread != null) {
                BeaconThread.Resume();
            }
        }

        private void Beacon() {
            while (true) {
                EventLog.WriteEntry(ServiceName + " active at "
                    + DateTime.Now);
                Thread.Sleep(Interval);
            }
        }

        public static void Main() {

            // Create an array to hold instances of each
            // Windows Service
            ServiceBase [] ServiceList = new ServiceBase [2];

            ServiceList[0] = new BeaconService("LogBeacon1");
            ServiceList[1] = new BeaconService("LogBeacon2");

            ServiceBase.Run(ServiceList);
        }
    }
```

The *Main* method creates two *BeaconService* instances, one for each of the services. We pass the service name as an argument to the *BeaconService* constructor; this is used to set the value of the inherited *ServiceName* property. *ServiceName* is the name the SCM uses internally to identify the service.

In the *BeaconService* constructor, we have set the value of the inherited *CanStop* and *CanPauseAndContinue* properties to *true*. The SCM uses these properties to determine the life cycle control messages that the service can process. These properties as well as the *CanShutdown* and *CanHandlePower-Event* properties are summarized in Table A-10.

Table A-10 Life Cycle Control Properties of the *ServiceBase* Class

Property	Description
CanHandlePowerEvent	Defines whether the service can handle notifications of changes to the computer power status via the *OnPowerEvent* method.
CanPauseAndContinue	Defines whether the service can be paused and resumed via the *OnPause* and *OnContinue* methods.

Table A-10   Life Cycle Control Properties of the *ServiceBase* Class   *(continued)*

Property	Description
CanShutdown	Defines whether the service should be notified prior to system shutdown via the *OnShutdown* method. This is useful if the service needs to store data or state before being terminated.
CanStop	Defines whether the service can be stopped via the *OnStop* method once it has been started.

The SCM controls the operation of a service via a set of methods inherited from *ServiceBase*. However, the SCM will call only those methods that the service has indicated it supports via the properties just discussed. Each of these methods is summarized in Table A-11.

Table A-11   Life Cycle Control Methods of the *ServiceBase* Class

Member	Descirption
OnContinue()	Method called by the SCM to make the service resume processing after being paused. Invoked only if the *CanPauseAndContinue* property is *true*.
OnCustomCommand()	Allows the SCM control mechanisms to be extended to support custom commands. *OnCustomCommand* takes an integer argument that can be used by the service to determine the appropriate action to take.
OnPause()	Method called by the SCM to make the service pause any processing. Invoked only if the *CanPauseAndContinue* property is *true*.
OnPowerEvent()	Method called when a system-level power status change occurs, such as a laptop going into suspend mode.
OnShutdown()	Method called when the system is being shut down. Invoked only if the *OnShutdown* property is *true*.
OnStart()	Method called by the SCM to start the service. Receives a *String* array of arguments. All services should override the *OnStart* method. No lengthy processing should be carried out in the *OnStart* method; the SCM expects it to return within 30 seconds.
OnStop()	Method called by the SCM to halt the service. Invoked only when the *CanStop* property is *true*.

We override the *OnStart* method to initiate the functionality of the service; we also override the *OnStop*, *OnPause*, and *OnContinue* methods because the *CanStop* and *CanPauseAndContinue* properties are set to *true*. In the example, we use methods of the *Thread* class to start, abort, suspend, or resume the operation of the logging thread in response to each SCM message.

Finally, in the *Main* method, references to the new *BeaconService* instances are placed in a *ServiceBase* array and passed as an argument to the static *ServiceBase.Run* method. The *Run* method calls the SCM and passes it the references to the two services.

Event Logging

The *ServiceBase* class provides support for automated event logging. If the inherited *AutoLog* property is set to *true* (the default value), the *ServiceBase* constructor creates a *System.Diagnostics.EventLog*. The *EventLog.Source* property is set to the *ServiceName* of the service and is registered against the Application log. See the "Windows Event Log" section earlier in this appendix for details.

The service will automatically log events when the *OnStart*, *OnStop*, *OnPause*, or *OnContinue* method of the service is invoked.

The *EventLog* instance can be obtained using the inherited *EventLog* property and can be used to write additional entries to the event log; however, if there is a need to write to a log other than the Application log, the *AutoLog* property should be set to *false* and the service itself should implement the necessary event-logging functionality.

Service Installer

Services cannot be executed like other assemblies; the tight integration with the operating system and the configuration information held in the Windows registry requires that they be explicitly installed.

A service installer class must be developed and compiled into the assembly containing the service class. Once the installer class is compiled, the Installer Tool (installutil.exe) provided with the .NET SDK is used to install the service.

An installer class must

■ Derive from the *System.Configuration.Install.Installer* class.

■ Be annotated with the *RunInstaller(true)* attribute.

■ Create and configure a *System.ServiceProcess.ServiceProcessInstaller* instance to describe the service application.

■ Create and configure *System.ServiceProcess.ServiceInstaller* instances to describe each of the individual contained services.

■ Add the *ServiceProcessInstaller* and *ServiceInstaller* instances to the *InstallerCollection* exposed through the inherited *Installers* property.

Note that a *Main* method is not required; the installutil tool instantiates the installer, so all logic should be contained in the instance constructor.

The following code provides an installer for the *BeaconService* service:

```
using System.ServiceProcess;
using System.Configuration.Install;
using System.ComponentModel;

[RunInstaller(true)]
public class BeaconServiceInstaller : Installer {

    // Create a ServiceProcessInstaller for each application
    private ServiceProcessInstaller BeaconProcess = null;

    // Create a ServiceInstaller instance for each
    // service contained in the application
    private ServiceInstaller BeaconLogService1 = null;
    private ServiceInstaller BeaconLogService2 = null;

    public BeaconServiceInstaller() {

        // Instantiate and configure the ServiceProcessInstaller
        BeaconProcess = new ServiceProcessInstaller();
        BeaconProcess.Account = ServiceAccount.LocalSystem;

        // Instantiate and configure the ServiceInstaller for the
        // First Event Log Beacon
        BeaconLogService1 = new ServiceInstaller();
        BeaconLogService1.DisplayName = "Log Beacon 1";
        BeaconLogService1.ServiceName = "LogBeacon1";
        BeaconLogService1.StartType = ServiceStartMode.Automatic;


        // Instantiate and configure the ServiceInstaller for the
        // Second Event Log Beacon
        BeaconLogService2 = new ServiceInstaller();
        BeaconLogService2.DisplayName = "Log Beacon 2";
        BeaconLogService2.ServiceName = "LogBeacon2";
        BeaconLogService2.StartType = ServiceStartMode.Automatic;


        // Add the installers to the Installers collection
        Installers.Add(BeaconLogService1);
        Installers.Add(BeaconLogService2);
        Installers.Add(BeaconProcess);
    }
}
```

ServiceProcessInstaller

One *System.ServiceProcess.ServiceProcessInstaller* instance is required per assembly that contains one or more services. The properties of the *ServiceProcess-Installer* instance are used to provide configuration information common to all services contained in the assembly. The important properties of the *Service-ProcessInstaller* class are summarized in Table A-12.

Table A-12   Properties of the *ServiceProcessInstaller* Class

Property	Description
Account	Controls the account under which the service will run. Specified using a value from the *System.ServiceProcess.ServiceAccount* enumeration; valid values include *User*, *LocalService*, *LocalSystem*, and *NetworkService*. These values are described in Table A-13; the default is *User*.
Username	If the *Account* property is set to *User*, this property must contain the name of the user account to run the service as.
Password	If the *Account* property is set to *User*, this property must contain the password for the user account.

If the *Account* property is set to *User* and the *Username* and *Password* properties don't have values, a dialog box will appear during installation asking for *Username* and *Password* values.

Table A-13   Members of the *ServiceAccount* Enumeration

Value	Description
LocalService	A predefined account that has limited privileges on the local system and that presents anonymous credentials to remote servers during network operations. Available only on Windows XP.
LocalSystem	A predefined account that has extensive privileges on the local system and that presents the computer's credentials to remote servers during network operations.
NetworkService	A predefined account that has limited privileges on the local system and that presents the computer's credentials to remote servers during network operations. Available only on Windows XP.
User	The service will run in the context of a specified user.

ServiceInstaller

One *System.ServiceProcess.ServiceInstaller* instance is required for each service contained in the assembly. The *ServiceInstaller* properties listed in Table A-14 are used to configure the service.

Table A-14 *ServiceInstaller* **Properties**

Property	Description
ServiceName	Specifies the name used to identify the service; this must be the same as the *ServiceBase.ServiceName* specified in the service application. In the example, we use *LogBeacon1* and *LogBeacon2*.
DisplayName	A user-friendly name to identify the service.
StartType	A value from the *System.ServiceProcess.ServicesStartMode* enumeration that defines how the service will be started; valid values are *Automatic*, *Disabled*, and *Manual*.
ServicesDependedOn	A *String* array containing the service names of all services that must be started before the service being defined.

Installer Compilation and Service Installation

Assuming the *BeaconService* class is in a file named BeaconService.cs and the *BeaconServiceInstaller* class is in a file named BeaconInstaller.cs, we compile them into an installable assembly named Beacon.exe using the following command:

```
csc /out:Beacon.exe BeaconService.cs BeaconInstaller.cs
```

To execute the assembly and install the *LogBeacon1* and *LogBeacon2* services, use the installutil.exe tool as follows:

```
installutil Beacon.exe
```

Using the Services utility available from Administrative Tools in Control Panel, the two services can be seen listed as Log Beacon 1 and Log Beacon 2. Using the Services tool, they can be started, paused, and stopped. The effect of changing the state can be seen as the events are written to the Application event log.

The *Beacon* services can be uninstalled using the installutil.exe tool with the */u* option as follows:

```
installutil /u Beacon.exe
```

Service Controller

Various tools included with Microsoft Windows provide basic service configuration and life cycle control. However, services can also be controlled programmatically, often via a service-specific management interface. Implementation of a service controller is the only way to send custom commands to a service via the *ServiceBase.OnCustomCommand* method described earlier.

The *System.ServiceProcess.ServiceController* class provides the functionality to query and control installed services on both local and remote machines.

Instances of the *ServiceController* class represent installed services. The *ServiceController* instance can be bound to a specified local or remote service during construction or by changing the *ServiceName* and *MachineName* properties after instantiation. Changing the *MachineName* and *ServiceName* of a bound instance will bind to the newly specified service.

ServiceController also provides the static *GetServices* method that returns a *ServiceController* array representing all the services installed on a local or remote machine.

Once a *ServiceController* is instantiated and bound to an installed service, the members detailed in Table A-15 can be used to control and query the service.

Table A-15 *ServiceController* **Members**

Member	Description
Property	
CanPauseAndContinue	Returns the value of the *CanPauseAndContinue* property of the service.
CanShutdown	Returns the value of the *CanShutdown* property of the service.
CanStop	Returns the value of the *CanStop* property of the service.
DependentServices	Gets a *ServiceController* array containing the services that depend on this service.
DisplayName	Gets or sets the value of the *DisplayName* property of the service.
MachineName	Gets or sets the name of the machine where the service is located.
ServiceName	Returns the value of the *ServiceName* property of the service.
ServicesDependedOn	Gets a *ServiceController* array containing the services that this service depends on.
Status	Gets the status of the service represented by a value from the *System.ServiceProcess.ServiceControllerStatus* enumeration.
Method	
Close()	Closes the *ServiceController* instance and frees used resources.
Continue()	Executes the *OnContinue* method of the service; throws *InvalidOperationException* if the *CanPauseAndContinue* property of the service isn't *true*. Works only if the service *Status* property is *Paused*.
ExecuteCommand()	Executes the *OnCustomCommand* method of the service; an application-specific *int* argument identifies the command to perform.

Table A-15   *ServiceController* **Members**   *(continued)*

Member	Description
Pause()	Executes the *OnPause* method of the service; throws *InvalidOperation-Exception* if the *CanPauseAndContinue* property of the service isn't *true*. Works only if the service has a *Status* of *Running*.
Start()	Executes the *OnStart* method of the service. Optionally takes a *String* array to pass to the service as an argument. Works only if the service *Status* property is *Stopped*.
Stop()	Executes the *OnStop* method of the service; throws *InvalidOperation-Exception* if the *CanStop* property of the service isn't *true*. Works only if the service *Status* property is *Running*.

Appendix B

Shared Assemblies

Assemblies can be *private* or *shared*. Private assemblies can be used by only one application, and the assemblies that the application comprises are stored together. Shared assemblies are available for use by many applications and can be stored in a shared directory, a network server, or a managed assembly store known as the global assembly cache (GAC). This appendix explains how to create a shared assembly and illustrates the benefits of providing common functionality in this manner. Private assemblies are discussed in Chapter 3, "Creating Assemblies."

Creating a Shared Assembly

Assembly names affect how an assembly can be used. Private assemblies have a name that is unique among the assemblies that make up the application. Shared assemblies have a *strong* name, which consists of the assembly name, the version, and culture information and relies on public key cryptography to ensure that the strong name is globally unique.

Strong names incorporate a digital signature to ensure that the contents of an assembly cannot be modified after creation. When an application loads an assembly, the common language runtime (CLR) checks the contents of the file to ensure that no changes have occurred.

Creating a strong name is a simple process; the first step is to create a file containing a key pair that will be used to sign the assembly. (Existing key files can be used if available.) The following command uses the Strong Name Tool (sn.exe) to generate a key file named myKey.snk in the local directory:

```
sn -k myKey.snk
```

In the following example, we'll use the C# compiler to build a single-file assembly, so we'll create a file named AssemblyInfo.cs that contains the global attributes required to generate the strong name. The contents of the file are listed here:

```
using System.Reflection;
using System.Runtime.CompilerServices;
```

(continued)

```
[assembly: AssemblyCulture("")]
[assembly: AssemblyVersion("1.0.0.0")]
[assembly: AssemblyKeyFile("myKey.snk")]
```

Our metadata specifies that the assembly can be used by any culture (the assembly is said to be *culture-neutral*), that this is version 1.0.0.0 of the assembly, and that the key pair can be found in the myKey.snk file. Our shared assembly will contain the *StringPrinter* class, stored in a file named String-Printer.cs, the contents of which are listed here:

```
public class StringPrinter {
    public void printString(string messageString) {
        System.Console.WriteLine("Message: " + messageString);
    }
}
```

We compile the classes into an assembly, using the following command:

```
csc /out:StringPrinter.dll /target:library
    AssemblyInfo.cs StringPrinter.cs
```

When a key file is specified in the global attributes, the compiler automatically generates a strong name and includes it in the assembly metadata. We can inspect the signature of the assembly by using the Strong Name Tool (sn.exe), as follows:

```
sn -T StringPrinter.dll
```

The Strong Name Tool prints the following. (Note that your public key token will be different.)

```
Microsoft (R) .NET Framework Strong Name Utility  Version 1.0.3705.0
Copyright (C) Microsoft Corporation 1998-2001. All rights reserved.

Public key token is 539a6301c167d487
```

The Global Assembly Cache

The GAC is a storage area where the CLR can locate shared assemblies; shared assemblies don't have to be installed in the GAC to be used by applications, but doing so can ease the burden of system administration; see the "Assembly Versions" section later in this appendix for more details of how the GAC can be used.

The Global Assembly Cache Tool (gacutil.exe) is used to install shared assemblies in the GAC; the following command installs the *StringPrinter* assembly:

```
gacutil -i StringPrinter.dll
```

The .NET Framework includes a Windows Explorer extension that is used to view the GAC. Navigate to the assembly subdirectory of the Windows directory (usually either C:\WINNT\assembly or C:\Windows\assembly). The list of shared assemblies should include *StringPrinter*.

To remove the shared assembly, use the following command:

```
gacutil -u StringPrinter
```

Unfortunately, shared assemblies installed in the GAC can't be referenced when source files are compiled. The GAC is intended as a deployment tool and not an aid to development; a local copy of a shared assembly must be available during development.

The following example demonstrates how to make use of a GAC shared assembly; the file HelloWorld.cs contains the following statements:

```
class HelloWorld {
    public static void Main(string[] args) {
        StringPrinter myPrinter = new StringPrinter();
        myPrinter.printString("Hello World!");
    }
}
```

This class depends on the *StringPrinter* type that we have installed in the GAC. To compile this class, a copy of the StringPrinter.dll file needs to be in the same directory as the HelloWorld.cs file. We compile the application with the following command:

```
csc /target:exe HelloWorld.cs /reference:StringPrinter.dll
```

Once the application has been compiled, deleting the StringPrinter.dll file won't affect the execution of the program because a copy of the assembly has been installed in the GAC. (Before you try this, you'll need to reinstall String-Printer.dll in the GAC if you've already uninstalled it.) Executing the program produces the following output:

```
Message: Hello World!
```

Assembly Versions

Assembly versioning is a solution to the *DLL Hell* problem, wherein applications relied on a shared copy of a DLL; installing a new version of a DLL that wasn't backward-compatible often caused problems with older applications.

When a .NET application uses a shared assembly, part of the reference stored in the metadata specifies the version required; by default, the .NET Framework won't execute an application if the correct versions of shared assemblies can't be located.

Side-by-Side Execution

One of the most interesting assembly features is the support for different versions of an assembly being used by different applications. Part of the identity for an assembly with a strong name is the version number, and the GAC can store multiple versions of an assembly without conflict. When an application depends on a strong-named assembly, the reference in the metadata specifies which version of the assembly is required. To demonstrate this, we'll create a new version of the *StringPrinter* assembly and a new application that depends on it.

Assuming that the first version of StringPrinter.dll is installed in the GAC, we'll update the source files to include slightly different functionality and a new version number. The contents of the AssemblyInfo.cs file are as follows:

```
using System.Reflection;
using System.Runtime.CompilerServices;

[assembly: AssemblyCulture("")]
[assembly: AssemblyVersion("2.0.0.0")]
[assembly: AssemblyKeyFile("myKey.snk")]
```

The changed statement, shown in boldface, indicates that the new assembly will be version 2.0.0.0. The StringPrinter.cs file is now as follows:

```
public class StringPrinter {
    public void printString(string messageString) {
        System.Console.WriteLine("Message version 2.0: "
            + messageString);
    }
}
```

We'll define a new client application in a file named NewClient.cs with the following statements:

```
class NewClient {
    public static void Main(string[] args) {
        StringPrinter myPrinter = new StringPrinter();
        myPrinter.printString("Hello World!");
    }
}
```

The following statements build the new version of the shared assembly, install it in the GAC, build the new client, and delete the local copy of String-Printer.dll:

```
csc /target:library StringPrinter.cs AssemblyInfo.cs
gacutil -i StringPrinter.dll
csc /target:exe NewClient.cs /reference:StringPrinter.dll
del StringPrinter.dll
```

The build directory should now contain the application from the previous section (HelloWorld.exe) and the new application (NewClient.exe). Executing HelloWorld.exe produces the following output:

```
Message: Hello World!
```

Executing NewClient.exe results in the following:

```
Message version 2.0: Hello World!
```

Assembly Version Policies

Although multiple versions of an assembly can coexist, the .NET Framework provides a mechanism for forcing applications built using one version of an assembly to use another version, in effect forcing an upgrade.

The publisher of an assembly can issue a *policy file* that, when installed in the GAC, causes requests for one version of an assembly to be satisfied with another version. It's important that the newer version of the assembly be compatible with the older version; if it isn't, applications might not function as expected (reintroducing the DLL Hell problem).

Creating a publisher policy file   A policy file contains the strong name details of the original assembly version and the version of the new assembly to use. The following file shows a policy file that states that version 1.0.0.0 of the *String-Printer* assembly, shown earlier, should be satisfied by version 2.0.0.0:

```
<configuration>
    <runtime>
        <assemblyBinding xmlns="urn:schemas-microsoft-com:asm.v1">
            <dependentAssembly>
                <assemblyIdentity name="StringPrinter"
                    publicKeyToken="539a6301c167d487"
                    culture="" />
                <!-- Redirect to version 2.0.0.0 of the assembly -->
                <bindingRedirect oldVersion="1.0.0.0"
                    newVersion="2.0.0.0"/>
            </dependentAssembly>
        </assemblyBinding>
    </runtime>
</configuration>
```

The *assemblyIdentity* element specifies the name, key signature, and culture of the assembly that the policy relates to. The *bindingRedirect* element specifies the old and new versions of the assembly that will be used to redirect requests. The details of the strong name can be obtained either from the GAC or by using the Strong Name Tool (sn.exe).

Creating and installing a publisher policy assembly   The policy file must be linked into an assembly before it can be used. The following statement demonstrates the usage form of the Assembly Linker Tool (al.exe) to achieve this; Table B-1 provides details of the command options.

```
al /link:publisherPolicyFile /out:publisherPolicyAssemblyFile
    /keyfile:keyPairFile
```

Table B-1   Assembly Linker Options for Creating Policy Assemblies

Assembly Linker Switch	Description
/link:publisherPolicyFile	The policy file containing the assembly version information.
/out:publisherPolicyAssemblyFile	The name of the output file.
/keyfile:keyPairFile	The key file, created using the sn.exe tool. This must be the same key that was used to sign the assemblies.

The name of the assembly is based on the assembly version being redirected and must adhere to the following form:

```
policy.majorNumber.minorNumber.mainAssemblyName.dll
```

For the example just shown, the name would be

```
policy.1.0.StringPrinter.dll
```

Assuming that the policy file was named policyfile.xml, the command to assemble the example is

```
al /link:policyfile.xml /keyfile:myKey.snk
    /out:policy.1.0.StringPrinter.dll
```

The policy assembly must be installed in the GAC before the policy will take effect. Policy assemblies are installed the same way as code assemblies, using the gacutil.exe tool. The following command demonstrates how to install the sample assembly:

```
gacutil /i policy.1.0.StringPrinter.dll
```

Assembly Probing

Shared assemblies don't have to be installed in the GAC; as an alternative, *assembly probing* specifies a set of application subdirectories to search when attempting to locate an assembly. The probing information is included in the application configuration file.

> **More Info**   For more general information about configuration files, consult Appendix C, "Configuring Applications."

The following configuration file demonstrates the use of probing:

```
<configuration>
    <runtime>
        <assemblyBinding xmlns="urn:schemas-microsoft-com:asm.v1">
            <probing privatePath="dir1;dir2\subdirectory;dir3"/>
        </assemblyBinding>
    </runtime>
</configuration>
```

This example specifies that assemblies should be searched for in the *dir1*, *dir2\subdirectory*, and *dir3* directories, relative to the location of the application; the shared assemblies that an application uses must be included in the distribution that is installed on the system. Including shared assemblies with an application distribution means that a single copy cannot be shared among multiple applications unless applications share the same installation directory. The techniques that are described in the "Assembly Version Policies" section earlier in this appendix cannot be applied to applications that rely on assembly probing but can be used to locate private, as well as shared, assemblies.

Codebase Probing

Assembly probing can be used only to locate assemblies in subdirectories relative to the location of the application. The .NET Framework provides another alternative to the GAC that can be used to locate assemblies anywhere on the local system as well as on remote Internet servers; this alternative is available through the *codebase* element of an application configuration file. The following example demonstrates how to look for version 1.0.0.0 of the *StringPrinter* assembly in the C:\temp directory of the local system:

```
<configuration>
    <runtime>
        <assemblyBinding xmlns="urn:schemas-microsoft-com:asm.v1">
            <dependentAssembly>
                <assemblyIdentity name="StringPrinter"
                    publicKeyToken="539a6301c167d487"
                    culture="" />
```

(continued)

```
        <codeBase version="1.0.0.0"
            href="file://c:\temp\StringPrinter.dll"/>
      </dependentAssembly>
    </assemblyBinding>
  </runtime>
</configuration>
```

The details for specifying an assembly are the same as for a version policy file. This example specifies a local directory, but the *href* attribute can also be used to specify any valid URL. This can be used to locate assemblies on remote servers; for example, the URL *http://www.mycompany.com/StringPrinter.dll* would cause the assembly to be downloaded using HTTP.

> **Caution** The *codebase* attribute is subject to version policy files installed in the GAC. For example, if there is a policy that redirects version 1.0.0.0 to version 2.0.0.0, the technique shown in our example won't be able to locate the desired assembly.

Summary

Shared assemblies confer a number of benefits on the programmer:

- A single copy of an assembly stored in the GAC can be used by multiple applications. Each application doesn't require a local copy of the assembly.

- The contents of shared assemblies can't be maliciously altered. The CLR checks the contents of the assembly files against the signature and will generate an error if a change has occurred.

Shared assemblies installed in the GAC are contained in a single location. Administering shared assemblies is a simple task, and system managers can easily inspect the contents of the GAC.

Appendix C

Configuring Applications

The Microsoft .NET Framework includes support for configuring applications by using XML configuration files; this appendix demonstrates how to make use of these.

Application Configuration Files

An application configuration file is stored in the same directory as the application it relates to. The file name is the name of the application with a .config extension. For example, an application named MyApplication.exe would have a configuration file named MyApplication.exe.config. For multifile assemblies, the configuration file should be named after the file that contains the manifest.

When an application requests configuration information, the common language runtime (CLR) tries to satisfy the request from the global machine configuration file before the application file; that is to say that the machine configuration file overrides the application file. This approach allows machine administrators to redefine the settings for an application after it has been installed; this should not be done lightly and can result in unexpected application behavior. The machine configuration file is named Machine.config and can be found in the Config subdirectory of the .NET Framework installation.

The CLR ensures that configuration files are loaded automatically; thus, no action is required by the programmer. Configuration files must contain the root XML node <configuration>, as shown here:

```
<configuration>
    <!-- configuration statements -->
</configuration>
```

The following sections detail the uses of application configuration files.

Specifying a CLR Version

Applications that require a specific version of the CLR can use the *<startup><requiredruntime>* declaration, as shown in the following example:

```
<configuration>
    <startup>
        <requiredRuntime version="v1.0.3706.000" safemode="false"/>
    </startup>
</configuration>
```

An application with this configuration file requires version 1.0.3706.000 of the CLR to operate properly. The *safemode* attribute specifies whether the application will accept versions that might be compatible; setting the attribute to *true* ensures that only the specified version will be used, while the value *false* indicates that a suitable substitute can be used. Substitutes are required to have the same major and minor versions (in this case, 1 and 0) but can have different build and revision versions (3706 and 000 respectively); the expectation is that releases with similar version numbers are likely to be interchangeable.

Using Concurrent Garbage Collection

By default, the CLR assigns a separate thread for the garbage collector (GC); this is known as *concurrent* garbage collection because the GC thread runs alongside application threads. Applications that are heavily multithreaded can gain performance benefits from disabling GC concurrency, as shown here:

```
<configuration>
    <runtime>
        <gcConcurrent enabled="false"/>
    </runtime>
</configuration>
```

The *enabled* attribute specifies whether the GC should operate concurrently. The advantage of GC concurrency is that user interfaces tend to be more responsive and won't freeze during a collection run.

Disabling GC concurrency causes memory management to be performed using the same threads that execute the application code. The application will be less responsive, but the performance of GC tasks is greatly increased. Server-side applications typically benefit from disabling GC concurrency.

> **More Info**   For more information about garbage collection, consult Appendix D, "Garbage Collection."

Managing Assembly Versions and Locations

Application configuration files can be used to manage assemblies. See Appendix B, "Shared Assemblies," for more details.

Registering Remote Objects

Objects can be registered with the .NET remoting system with configuration files. See Chapter 15, "Remoting," for details.

Application Settings

Configuration files also allow the programmer to define settings that can be read from within an application. The *System.Configuration* namespace contains the classes that provide access to these settings.

Simple Settings

The *<appSettings>* section of a configuration file can be used to define key/value pairs, as shown in the following example:

```
<configuration>
    <appSettings>
        <add key="MyFirstKey" value="MyFirstValue"/>
        <add key="MySecondKey" value="MySecondValue"/>
        <add key="MyThirdKey" value="MyThirdValue"/>
    </appSettings>
</configuration>
```

These key/value pairs are accessible independently or as a collection through the *AppSettings* property of the *System.Configuration.ConfigurationSettings* class, as shown in the following example:

```
// Access values independantly
Console.WriteLine("First Value: " +
    ConfigurationSettings.AppSettings["MyFirstKey"]);
Console.WriteLine("Second Value: " +
    ConfigurationSettings.AppSettings["MySecondKey"]);
```

(continued)

```
// Access key/values as a collection
System.Collections.Specialized.NameValueCollection x_coll =
    ConfigurationSettings.AppSettings;

foreach (string x_key in x_coll.AllKeys) {
    Console.WriteLine("KEY {0}, Value {1}",
        x_key, x_coll[x_key]);
}
```

The *AppSettings* property returns an instance of *System.Collections.Specialized.NameValueCollection*, which can be used to iterate through the keys and values or to access a key by name or index. See Chapter 9, "Collections," for more information about the *NameValueCollection* class. The preceding example writes out the following statements:

```
First Value: MyFirstValue
Second Value: MySecondValue
KEY MyFirstKey, Value MyFirstValue
KEY MySecondKey, Value MySecondValue
KEY MyThirdKey, Value MyThirdValue
```

Complex Settings

Configuration files allow the programmer to specify more complex settings, grouped into sections. Three types of section can be used, but all must be declared in the same manner. The declaration of a configuration section includes the section name and the type from the *System.Configuration* namespace that will be used to parse the section.

Declarations of sections are included in the *configSections* configuration file element, but the contents of the section are declared as an element of the *configuration* element, as shown here:

```
<configuration>
    <configSections>
        <section name="sectionname" type="section parser"/>
    </configSections>

    <!-- specification of section values -->
</configuration>
```

The section values are accessible through the *GetConfig* method of the *System.Configuration.ConfigurationSettings* class; the method takes the name of the section as an argument and returns an *Object* that can be cast to a collection type in order to access the keys and values.

Single Tag Sections

Single tag sections allow key/value pairs to be defined as the attributes of an XML element. The following example demonstrates the declaration and specification of a single tag section:

```
<configuration>
    <configSections>
        <section name="MySingleSection"
            type="System.Configuration.SingleTagSectionHandler"/>
    </configSections>

    <MySingleSection
        MyFirstKey="MyFirstValue"
        MySecondKey="MySecondValue"
        MyThirdKey="MyThirdValue"/>

</configuration>
```

The following code fragment demonstrates how to access the values in a single tag section:

```
IDictionary x_dict =
    (IDictionary)ConfigurationSettings.GetConfig(
        "MySingleSection");

Console.WriteLine("First Value: "  + x_dict["MyFirstKey"]);
Console.WriteLine("Second Value: " + x_dict["MySecondKey"]);

foreach (string x_key in x_dict.Keys) {
    Console.WriteLine("KEY {0}, Value {1}",
        x_key, x_dict[x_key]);
}
```

Name/Value Sections

Name/value sections are defined in the same way as the simple application settings just shown. The following configuration file demonstrates this type of section:

```
<configuration>
    <configSections>
        <section name="nameValueSection"
            type="System.Configuration.NameValueSectionHandler"/>
    </configSections>
```

(continued)

```
    <nameValueSection>
        <add key="MyFirstKey"      value="MyFirstValue"/>
        <add key="MySecondKey"     value="MySecondValue"/>
        <add key="MyThirdKey"      value="MyThirdValue"/>
    </nameValueSection>
</configuration>
```

When accessing name/value sections, the *GetConfig* method returns an instance of the *System.Collections.Specialized.NameValueCollection* class. The following code fragment demonstrates the use of a name/value section:

```
NameValueCollection x_dict = (NameValueCollection)
    ConfigurationSettings.GetConfig("nameValueSection");

Console.WriteLine("First Value: "  + x_dict["MyFirstKey"]);
Console.WriteLine("Second Value: " + x_dict["MySecondKey"]);

foreach (string x_key in x_dict.Keys) {
    Console.WriteLine("KEY {0}, Value {1}",
        x_key, x_dict[x_key]);
}
```

Dictionary Sections

Dictionary sections are declared in the same way as name/value sections, but the return type from the *GetConfig* method is a *System.Collections.Hashtable*. The following configuration file demonstrates a dictionary section:

```
<configuration>
    <configSections>
        <section name="nameValueSection"
            type="System.Configuration.DictionarySectionHandler"
            />
    </configSections>

    <nameValueSection>
        <add key="MyFirstKey"      value="MyFirstValue"/>
        <add key="MySecondKey"     value="MySecondValue"/>
        <add key="MyThirdKey"      value="MyThirdValue"/>
    </nameValueSection>
</configuration>
```

Ignore Sections

Ignore sections are included in the configuration file system to allow sections of a file to be skipped by the parser. This is useful if a configuration file contains information that will be processed by another system.

The following section demonstrates an ignore section:

```
<configuration>
    <configSections>
        <section name="nameValueSection"
            type="System.Configuration.IgnoreSectionHandler"/>
    </configSections>

    <nameValueSection>
        <add key="MyFirstKey"    value="MyFirstValue"/>
        <add key="MySecondKey"   value="MySecondValue"/>
        <add key="MyThirdKey"    value="MyThirdValue"/>
    </nameValueSection>
</configuration>
```

Declaring the type to be *System.Configuration.IgnoreSectionHandler* (shown in boldface) causes calls to the *ConfigurationSettings.GetContent* method to always return *null*, irrespective of the section contents.

Summary

The .NET support for configuration files provides a flexible mechanism for configuring applications without relying on hard-coded settings. During the development process, configuration files allow for settings to be changed and tested without requiring recompilation. When an application is deployed, the files can be used to provide tailored support to different groups of users without the need to build multiple versions of the same application.

Appendix D

Garbage Collection

As is the case with Java, a Microsoft .NET programmer will usually not take an interest in the operational details of garbage collection and can safely assume that unreferenced objects will be collected as required. This appendix, however, covers some of the features that are available when the default behavior of the garbage collector (GC) doesn't meet the demands of an application; we expect the reader to be familiar with the principles of garbage collection.

Controlling the Garbage Collector

The *System.GC* class provides methods to directly control the execution of the garbage collector. The garbage collector is designed to determine the best time to perform a collection; however, in some situations forcing a collection can improve performance, typically when the memory requirement of an application significantly decreases at a defined point in the code.

Forcing a Collection

The static *System.GC.Collect* method is called to request a collection. The garbage collector will suspend active threads and compact the heap.

> **Important** The Java collector doesn't guarantee that explicit collection requests will be honored. The common language runtime (CLR) does guarantee that requests will be performed but doesn't promise to release all of the memory held by unreferenced objects.

Generations

The CLR includes a performance enhancement known as *generations*. A generational collector—also known as an *ephemeral collector*—works on the following assumptions:

- It's faster to compact part of the heap than the whole heap.

- The older an object is, the longer its lifetime will be.

- New objects tend to be short lived, and groups of newly allocated objects tend to be accessed at the same time and have strong relationships.

Although these assumptions aren't universally true, empirical testing has shown that they are valid for the majority of common business applications.

When an application starts, no objects are on the heap. As objects are allocated, they are considered to be in generation 0 (zero), which is the set of heap references that have yet to be examined by the garbage collector. When the collector runs, any objects that aren't collected are promoted to generation 1 (one). New object allocations will be assigned to generation 0, and when the collector runs again, surviving generation 0 objects are promoted to generation 1 and generation 1 objects are promoted to generation 2. The CLR GC supports three generations (0, 1, and 2).

In normal operation, the GC will attempt a collection if there is insufficient memory in the heap to make a new object allocation. The generational approach allows the GC to attempt to satisfy an allocation request by reclaiming memory from the areas of the heap that are most likely to yield a return. Given the assumption that newly allocated objects tend to be short lived, it's likely that a memory requirement can be satisfied by the references in generation 0. If the request cannot be satisfied, the GC can elect to move on to older generations, potentially minimizing the amount of time spent clearing the heap.

The GC class provides a method to allow explicit requests for generations to be collected. Calls to the *GC.Collect(int)* method will cause the indicated generation and all lesser generations to be collected, so a call to collect generation 1 will also cause collection of generation 0. The following GC methods determine which generation an object belongs to:

```
Int32 GetGeneration(Object obj)
Int32 GetGeneration(WeakReference wr)
```

The *WeakReference* class in the second method is discussed in the "Weak References" section later in this appendix.

Concurrent Collection

By default, the CLR assigns a separate thread for the Garbage Collector (GC), which allows the garbage collector to operate concurrently with application code. Disabling GC concurrency causes memory management to be performed using the same threads that execute the application code. The application will be less responsive, but the performance of GC tasks is greatly increased. Server-side applications typically benefit from disabling GC concurrency.

GC concurrency can be controlled by using the .NET application configuration file. For more details about configuration files and an example of disabling GC concurrency, see Appendix C, "Configuring Applications."

Finalizing and Disposing

Finalization allows an object to release unmanaged resources it's using before it's collected. The .NET *Object* class defines the following method signature for this purpose:

```
protected override void Finalize();
```

During a collection run, the GC places all unreferenced objects in a *finalize queue*. This queue is then scanned, and the memory occupied by classes that don't define a *Finalize* method is released. Objects that do define a *Finalize* method are placed on the *freachable* (pronounced F-Reachable) queue. A dedicated thread responsible for calling *Finalize* methods sleeps when no objects are in the freachable queue. When objects are added to the queue, the thread is awakened and calls the *Finalize* method.

Caution   A dedicated thread calls the *Finalize* method. Code in the *Finalize* method can't make assumptions about the state of the thread. For example, local *Thread* variables won't be available.

Destructors

While the .NET Framework defines the *Finalize* method, C# doesn't allow classes to override it. Instead, classes that need to clean up resources before collection must implement a destructor. Here's a simple example of a class that defines a destructor:

```
public class Destructor {

    public Destructor() {
        Console.WriteLine("Instantiated");
    }

    ~Destructor() {
        Console.WriteLine("Destructor called");
    }
}
```

The destructor is marked in boldface and takes the form of a constructor with a tilde (~) prepended; destructors take no arguments and return no value. The destructor is implicitly translated to the following code:

```
protected override void Finalize() {
    try {
        Console.WriteLine("Destructor called");
    } finally {
        base.Finalize();
    }
}
```

For the following reasons, it's advisable to avoid destructors when designing classes:

- Objects with a destructor get promoted to older generations, increasing the pressure on memory allocation and preventing the memory held by the object from being released immediately. Generations are discussed in the "Controlling the Garbage Collector" section earlier in this appendix.

- Calling a destructor on an object takes time. Forcing the GC to call the destructors for a large number of objects can affect performance.

- The garbage collector doesn't guarantee when a destructor will be called; objects will hold resources until the method is called, which can put pressure on system memory.

- A destructor might not be called when an application exits. To allow a process to terminate quickly, destructors aren't called on unreachable objects, and objects that are used by background threads or were created during the termination phase won't be finalized.

- The garbage collector doesn't guarantee the order in which objects will be finalized. References with destructors that refer to inner objects with destructors can cause unpredictable results.

When using destructors, all exceptions must be caught. If an exception is propagated outside the destructor, the finalizer thread assumes that finalization has completed and not all resources will be freed.

Resurrection

The freachable queue gets it name because objects contained in the queue are considered to be reachable (and the *f* stands for finalization). The queue is a root, and objects referenced by the queue aren't garbage-collected; objects remain in the queue until the destructor is called, at which point they are removed from the queue and are available for garbage collection.

There is a technique called *resurrection*, whereby a reference to an object is created from within the object's destructor, preventing it from being garbage-collected. Here's an example of how to resurrect an object:

```
public class MyObject {

    ~MyObject() {
        Holder.s_holder = this;
        GC.ReRegisterForFinalize(this);
    }
}

class Holder {
    public static object s_holder;
}
```

In the destructor, a reference to *MyObject* is created from the static object in the *Holder* class. When the finalizer thread has called this method, the object is placed on the finalizer queue, but because there's a valid reference from the *Holder* class, it won't be collected.

Calling *GC.ReRegisterForFinalize* ensures that the destructor will be called again if the reference in *Holder* is set to *null* and the object is collected. Resurrection rarely represents good practice and should be used with caution.

Weak References

C# and Java both define weak references. If the only reference to an object is a weak reference, the object can be collected as garbage. Weak references are useful for referencing data that can easily be re-created and that should be freed if there is pressure for memory. Weak references are frequently used for cached data, where there is a performance improvement when the data is read from the cache but the data can be re-created if the cached information is collected.

The *System.WeakReference* class is used to create a weak reference. A weak reference is said to *track* an object, which is to say, maintain a weak association. There are two forms of weak reference, short-lived and long-lived. The difference is that long-lived weak references continue to track an object if it's resurrected during garbage collection. (See the "Resurrection" section earlier in this appendix.) The *WeakReference* class takes the *Object* to track as a constructor argument.

■ The *IsAlive* property will return *true* if the object tracked by the *WeakReference* hasn't been garbage-collected.

■ The *TrackResurrection* property can be used to determine and control whether the *WeakReference* is short-lived or long-lived.

■ The *Target* property returns the *Object* that's being tracked, or *null* if the object has been garbage-collected.

Summary

The garbage collector is one of the most important elements of a modern programming environment, one that's used by both .NET and Java. For the majority of applications, the programmer can rely on the default behavior to offer the best performance; on the rare occasions when this isn't the case, the .NET Framework provides a range of features that allow the programmer to take a more active role in the management of system memory.

Appendix E

Cross-Language Code Interoperability

An important feature of Microsoft .NET is the common language runtime (CLR) support for multiple languages. As well as enabling applications written in different languages to run, CLR support for cross-language integration allows components developed in one language to be used and extended by components developed in other languages. Specifically, this allows

- Classes defined in one language to be inherited and extended by classes defined in another language, including support for overriding virtual methods.

- Interfaces defined in one language to be implemented by types defined in another language.

- The instantiation and use of types written in other languages, including the passing of types defined in another language as parameters.

- The handling of exceptions thrown by components written in another language.

  Cross-language integration is possible because

- Assemblies contain metadata that describes the characteristics and requirements of the contained types.

- All languages compile to a common intermediate language (IL).

- All applications execute in the context of a shared, managed execution environment (the CLR) and share a *Common Type System* (CTS).

The Common Type System

The CTS defines how types are declared, used, and managed within the CLR. The CTS defines a rich set of types and operations, enough to support the complete implementation of many different languages. The CTS provides the basis for cross-language integration. However, every programming language offers different capabilities, and not all languages support every feature of the CTS. A subset of the CTS necessary to support cross-language integration has been defined as the *Common Language Specification* (CLS). Any .NET language that implements the features defined by the CLS can be used to produce components that support cross-language integration.

The Common Language Specification

The CLS is a set of 41 rules that define the baseline for language interoperability; they are formalized in the *Common Language Infrastructure* (CLI) specification. CLS compliance is achieved by writing code that adheres to the rules and conventions of the CLS. However, an important point to remember is that only elements that are accessible or visible outside the defining assembly need to be CLS-compliant; this includes elements such as public classes and interfaces as well as public and protected members. Private code elements, which aren't visible outside the defining assembly, can use any language features without affecting the CLS compliance of the component.

Writing CLS-Compliant Code in C#

The syntax of C# ensures that many CLS rules can't be broken. For example, C# doesn't permit the declaration of global static fields or non-zero-based arrays, both requirements of CLS compliance. However, some CLS rules can't be enforced by the language, and guaranteeing that they're followed is the responsibility of the programmer. The following list highlights some key requirements of writing CLS-compliant code in C#:

- Case must not be used to differentiate between program element identifiers such as member names.

- All member parameter and return types must be CLS-compliant; this means the following simple types cannot be used: *sbyte, ushort, uint,* and *ulong.*

- Pointer types and function pointers aren't CLS-compliant.

- The underlying type of an array must be CLS-compliant.

- The underlying type of an enumeration must be one of *byte*, *short*, *int*, or *long*.

- A comparable CLS-compliant element should be provided for a non-compliant element.

- CLS-compliant program elements and their non-CLS-compliant members must be identified using the *CLSCompliant* attribute (discussed in the next section).

> **Note**   The CLS specifies that variable parameter lists cannot be used. This doesn't apply to C# parameter arrays (identified with the *param* keyword) because the C# compiler maps these to fixed-size arrays.

> **More Info**   For a complete list of CLS rules, consult the Common Language Infrastructure, which is available as standard ECMA-335 from the ECMA Web site, *http://www.ecma.ch*.

The *CLSCompliant* Attribute

The *System.CLSCompliantAttribute* attribute is applied to program elements to indicate CLS compliance. An assembly that is CLS-compliant must specify the following global attribute:

```
[assembly:CLSCompliant(true)]
```

An assembly that doesn't explicitly declare CLS compliance is assumed to be noncompliant. For multifile assemblies, CLS compliance needs to be declared only once. If the *CLSCompliantAttribute* attribute is specified multiple times with different values, a compile-time error is generated.

There is no need to specify the *CLSCompliant* attribute on every program element. A program element is assumed to have the same CLS compliance as its containing element. For example, a class defined within a compliant assembly is assumed to be compliant, as is a member of a compliant class. An element cannot be marked as CLS-compliant if its enclosing element isn't compliant.

Noncompliant elements contained within compliant elements must be marked as such using the *CLSCompliant* attribute with a *false* argument—for example:

```
[CLSCompliant(false)]
```

A compiler error is raised if the compiler determines that a program element marked as CLS-compliant is actually not compliant.

The following example demonstrates the use of the *CLSCompliant* attribute to identify various CLS-compliant program elements:

```
using System;

[assembly:CLSCompliant(true)]

public class MyClass {

    [CLSCompliant(true)]
    protected void MethodA(int a, params int[] b) {
        // method implementation code
    }

    [CLSCompliant(false)]
    protected void MethodB(uint a) {
        // method implementation code
    }

    [CLSCompliant(false)]
    protected void methodC(byte a) {
        // method implementation code
    }

    [CLSCompliant(false)]
    protected void MethodC(byte a) {
        // method implementation code
    }

    private ushort MethodD(sbyte a) {
        // method implementation code
        return 0;
    }

    public static int Main(String[] args) {
        // Main method implementation code
        return 0;
    }
}
```

The assembly resulting from the compilation of this code is identified as CLS-compliant using the global attribute *assembly:CLSCompliant(true)*. The *MyClass* type doesn't have a *CLSCompliant* attribute specified; it's assumed to be compliant because it's a member of a compliant assembly. *MethodA* is CLS-compliant, while *MethodB* is not; it takes a *uint* argument that is non-CLS-compliant.

At least one version of *MethodC* must be marked as noncompliant, or a compiler error will occur. However, we have marked both versions noncompliant because the CLS specifies that case must not be used to differentiate between program elements. *MethodD* takes a non-CLS-compliant argument; however, it's *private* and so is not bound by the CLS rules. Finally, the *Main* method has no *CLSCompliant* attribute but is assumed to be compliant because it's contained within the compliant *MyClass* type.

Summary

The multiple-language support provided by the .NET platform is a powerful and useful feature. However, as we have discussed, writing software components that can be used across multiple languages isn't straightforward and imposes limitations on the functionality exposed by the component. In some situations, the benefits of cross-language support may warrant the limitations and additional development complexity, but often this will not be the case.

Appendix F

Java to .NET API Reference

When viewed as a whole, the Java and .NET class libraries provide comparable functionality. However, as this book has shown, the implementation specifics and structure can often be quite different. This appendix provides a quick reference to Java-to-.NET class library functionality.

We structure the cross-reference at the class level; we exclude interfaces unless they're essential to understanding the relationship between Java and the Microsoft .NET Framework. Each commonly used Java type from the major packages is listed. We map each Java type to one or more .NET types that provide the same or similar functionality.

The *java.awt* Package

The .NET Windows Forms system provides a smaller class set than the Abstract Window Toolkit (AWT) for constructing client applications. See Chapter 18, "Graphics and UI," for more information about the Windows Forms system. The mapping between the Java *java.awt* package and the corresponding .NET classes is provided in Table F-1.

Table F-1   The Java to .NET Mapping for the *java.awt* Package

Java	.NET
AlphaComposite	N/A
AWTEvent	*System.EventArgs*
AWTEventMulticaster	N/A
AWTKeyStroke	*System.Windows.Forms.KeyPressEventArgs*
AWTPermission	*System.Security.Permissions.UIPermission*
BasicStroke	*System.Drawing.Pen*
BorderLayout	N/A
BufferCapabilities	N/A

(continued)

Table F-1 **The Java to .NET Mapping for the *java.awt* Package** *(continued)*

Java	.NET
Button	*System.Windows.Forms.Button*
Canvas	*System.Windows.Forms.Control*
CardLayout	N/A
Checkbox	*System.Windows.Forms.RadioButton*
CheckboxGroup	N/A (All *RadioButton* objects in a .NET control are mutually exclusive within a control.)
CheckboxMenuItem	N/A
Choice	*System.Windows.Forms.ComboBox*
Color	*System.Drawing.Color*
Component	*System.Windows.Forms.Control*
ComponentOrientation	N/A
Container	*System.Windows.Forms.Control*
Cursor	*System.Windows.Forms.Cursor*
Dialog	*System.Windows.Forms.CommonDialog*
Dimension	*System.Drawing.Size*
DisplayMode	N/A
Event	*System.EventArgs*
EventQueue	N/A
FileDialog	*System.Windows.Forms.FileDialog*
	System.Windows.Forms.OpenFileDialog
	System.Windows.Forms.SaveFileDialog
FlowLayout	N/A
FocusTraversalPolicy	N/A
Font	*System.Drawing.Font*
FontMetrics	N/A
Frame	*System.Windows.Forms.Form*
GradientPaint	*System.Drawing.Drawing2D.LinearGradientBrush*
Graphics	*System.Drawing.Graphics*
Graphics2D	*System.Drawing.Graphics*
GraphicsConfigTemplate	N/A
GraphicsConfiguration	N/A
GraphicsDevice	N/A
GraphicsEnvironment	N/A

Table F-1   The Java to .NET Mapping for the *java.awt* Package   *(continued)*

Java	.NET
GridBagConstraints	N/A
GridBagLayout	N/A
GridLayout	N/A
Image	*System.Drawing.Image*
ImageCapabilities	N/A
Insets	N/A
JobAttributes	*System.Drawing.Printing.PageSettings*
	System.Drawing.Printing.PrinterSettings
KeyboardFocusManager	N/A
Label	*System.Windows.Forms.Label*
List	*System.Windows.Forms.ListBox*
MediaTracker	N/A
Menu	*System.Windows.Forms.MainMenu*
MenuBar	N/A
MenuComponent	N/A
MenuItem	*System.Windows.Forms.MenuItem*
MenuShortcut	N/A
PageAttributes	*System.Drawing.Printing.PageSettings*
Panel	*System.Windows.Forms.Panel*
Point	*System.Drawing.Point*
Polygon	N/A
PopupMenu	*System.Windows.Forms.ContextMenu*
PrintJob	*System.Drawing.Printing.PrintDocument*
Rectangle	*System.Drawing.Rectangle*
RenderingHints	N/A
RenderingHints.Key	N/A
Robot	N/A
Scrollbar	*System.Windows.Forms.HScrollBar*
	System.Windows.Forms.VScrollBar
ScrollPane	*System.Windows.Forms.Panel*
ScrollPaneAdjustable	N/A
SystemColor	N/A

(continued)

Table F-1   **The Java to .NET Mapping for the *java.awt* Package**   *(continued)*

Java	.NET
TextArea	*System.Windows.Forms.TextBox*
	System.Windows.Forms.RichTextBox
TextComponent	N/A
TextField	*System.Windows.Forms.TextBox*
TexturePaint	*System.Drawing.TextureBrush*
Toolkit	N/A
Window	N/A

The *java.awt.color* Package

The .NET Framework doesn't provide equivalent functionality for this package.

The *java.awt.datatransfer* Package

The .NET Framework doesn't provide equivalent functionality for this package.

The *java.awt.dnd* Package

The *System.Windows.Forms.Clipboard* class provides equivalent functionality for this package. Consult the .NET Framework documentation for more information.

The *java.awt.event* Package

The .NET Windows Forms system uses fewer events than the AWT. Consult the documentation for details of events defined by Windows Forms components. The mapping between the Java *java.awt.event* package and the corresponding .NET classes is provided in Table F-2.

Table F-2   The Java to .NET Mapping for the *java.awt.event* Package

Java	.NET
ActionEvent	*System.EventArgs*
AdjustmentEvent	*System.Windows.Forms.ScrollEventArgs*
AWTEventListenerProxy	N/A
ComponentAdapter	N/A
ComponentEvent	*System.EventArgs*
ContainerAdapter	N/A
ContainerEvent	*System.Windows.Forms.ControlEventArgs*
FocusAdapter	N/A
FocusEvent	*System.EventArgs*
HierarchyBoundsAdapter	N/A
HierarchyEvent	N/A
InputEvent	N/A
InputMethodEvent	N/A
InvocationEvent	N/A
ItemEvent	*System.EventArgs*
KeyAdapter	N/A
KeyEvent	*System.Windows.Forms.KeyPressEventArgs*
	System.Windows.Forms.KeyEventArgs
MouseAdapter	N/A
MouseEvent	*System.Windows.Forms.MouseEventArgs*
MouseMotionAdapter	N/A
MouseWheelEvent	*System.Windows.Forms.MouseEventArgs*
PaintEvent	*System.Windows.Forms.PaintEventArgs*
TextEvent	*System.EventArgs*
WindowAdapter	N/A
WindowEvent	*System.EventArgs*

The *java.awt.font* Package

The .NET Framework doesn't provide equivalent functionality for this package.

The *java.awt.geom* Package

The .NET Framework offers support for drawing shapes through the methods of the *System.Drawing* namespace. For more information, see Chapter 18.

The *java.awt.im* Package

The .NET Framework doesn't provide equivalent functionality for this package.

The *java.awt.im.spi* Package

The .NET Framework doesn't provide equivalent functionality for this package.

The *java.awt.image* Package

The .NET Framework doesn't provide equivalent functionality for this package.

The *java.awt.image.renderable* Package

The .NET Framework doesn't provide equivalent functionality for this package.

The *java.awt.print* Package

The mapping between the Java *java.awt.print* package and the corresponding .NET types is provided in Table F-3.

Table F-3   The Java to .NET Mapping for the *java.awt.print* Package

Java	.NET
Book	N/A
PageFormat	*System.Drawing.Printing.PageSettings*
Paper	*System.Drawing.Printing.PaperSize*
PrinterJob	*System.Drawing.Printing.PrintDocument*

The *java.io* Package

See Chapter 10, "Streams, Files, and I/O," for details of the .NET types listed in Table F-4, which displays the mapping between the Java *java.io* package and the corresponding .NET types.

Table F-4   The Java to .NET Mapping for the *java.io* Package

Java	.NET
BufferedInputStream	*System.IO.BufferedStream*
BufferedOutputStream	*System.IO.BufferedStream*
BufferedReader	*System.IO.StreamReader*
BufferedWriter	*System.IO.StreamWriter*
ByteArrayInputStream	*System.IO.MemoryStream*
ByteArrayOutputStream	*System.IO.MemoryStream*
CharArrayReader	*System.IO.StreamReader*
CharArrayWriter	*System.IO.StreamWriter*
DataInputStream	*System.IO.BinaryReader*
DataOutputStream	*System.IO.BinaryWriter*
File	*System.IO.File*
FileInputStream	*System.IO.FileStream*
FileOutputStream	*System.IO.FileStream*
FilePermission	N/A
FileReader	*System.IO.StreamReader*
FileWriter	*System.IO.StreamReader*
FilterInputStream	N/A
FilterOutputStream	N/A
FilterReader	N/A
FilterWriter	N/A
InputStream	*System.IO.Stream*
InputStreamReader	N/A
LineNumberInputStream	N/A
LineNumberReader	N/A
ObjectInputStream	No direct equivalent; consult the "Object Serialization" section in Chapter 10 for details of .NET object serialization.
ObjectOutputStream	No direct equivalent; consult Chapter 10 for details of .NET object serialization.

(continued)

Table F-4   The Java to .NET Mapping for the *java.io* Package   *(continued)*

Java	.NET
OutputStream	System.IO.Stream
OutputStreamWriter	N/A
PipedInputStream	N/A
PipedOutputStream	N/A
PipedReader	N/A
PipedWriter	N/A
PrintStream	System.IO.StreamWriter
PrintWriter	System.IO.StreamWriter
PushbackInputStream	System.IO.StreamReader
PushbackReader	System.IO.StreamReader
RandomAccessFile	System.IO.FileStream
Reader	N/A
SequenceInputStream	N/A
StreamTokenizer	N/A
StringBufferInputStream	System.IO.StringReader
StringReader	System.IO.StringReader
StringWriter	System.IO.StringWriter
Writer	N/A

The *java.lang* Package

The mapping between the Java *java.lang* package and the corresponding .NET types is provided in Table F-5. For details of these .NET types, consult the following chapters wherever relevant:

- Chapter 5, "Data Types"
- Chapter 7, "Strings and Regular Expressions"
- Chapter 13, "Threading and Synchronization"
- Appendix A, "Platform Integration"

Table F-5   **The Java to .NET Mapping for the *java.lang* Package**

Java	.NET
Boolean	*System.Boolean*
Byte	*System.Byte*
Character	*System.Char*
Class	*System.Type*
ClassLoader	N/A
Compiler	N/A
Double	*System.Double*
Float	*System.Single*
InheritableThreadLocal	N/A
Integer	*System.Int32*
Long	*System.Int64*
Math	*System.Math*
Number	N/A
Object	*System.Object*
Package	N/A
Process	*System.Diagnostics.Process*
Runtime	*System.Diagnostics.Process*
SecurityManager	N/A
Short	*System.Int16*
StackTraceElement	N/A
StrictMath	*System.Math*
String	*System.String*
StringBuffer	*System.Text.StringBuilder*
System	N/A
Thread	*System.Threading.Thread*
ThreadGroup	N/A
ThreadLocal	*System.LocalDataStoreSlot*
Throwable	*System.Exception*
Void	*System.Void*

The *java.lang.ref* Package

The mapping between the Java *java.lang.ref* package and the corresponding .NET types is provided in Table F-6. See Appendix D, "Garbage Collection," for details of these .NET types.

Table F-6   The Java to .NET Mapping for the *java.lang.ref* Package

Java	.NET
PhantomReference	N/A
Reference	N/A
ReferenceQueue	N/A
SoftReference	N/A
WeakReference	*System.WeakReference*

The *java.lang.reflect* Package

The mapping between the Java *java.lang.reflect* package and the corresponding .NET types is provided in Table F-7. See Chapter 12, "Reflection," for details of these .NET types.

Table F-7   The Java to .NET Mapping for the *java.lang.reflect* Package

Java	.NET
AccessibleObject	*System.Reflection.MemberInfo*
Array	*System.Array*
Constructor	*System.Reflection.ConstructorInfo*
Field	*System.Reflection.FieldInfo*
Method	*System.Reflection.MethodInfo*
Modifier	*System.Reflection.MethodAttributes*
Proxy	N/A
ReflectPermission	*System.Security.Permissions.ReflectionPermission*

The *java.math* Package

The mapping between the Java *java.math* package and the corresponding .NET types is provided in Table F-8.

Table F-8   The Java to .NET Mapping for the *java.math* Package

Java	.NET
BigDecimal	*System.Decimal*
BigInteger	N/A

The *java.net* Package

The mapping between the Java *java.lang.reflect* package and the corresponding .NET types is provided in Table F-9. See Chapter 14, "Networking," for details of these .NET types.

Table F-9   The Java to .NET Mapping for the *java.net* Package

Java	.NET
Authenticator	*System.Net.AuthenticationManager*
ContentHandler	N/A
DatagramPacket	N/A
DatagramSocket	*System.Net.Sockets.UdpClient*
DatagramSocketImpl	N/A
HttpURLConnection	*System.Net.WebClient*
	System.Web.WebRequest
	System.Web.WebResponse
Inet4Address	*System.Net.IPAddress*
Inet6Address	*System.Net.IPAddress*
InetAddress	*System.Net.IPAddress*
InetSocketAddress	*System.Net.IPEndPoint*
JarURLConnection	N/A
MulticastSocket	*System.Net.Sockets.UdpClient*
NetPermission	*System.Net.SocketPermission*
	System.Net.WebPermission
NetworkInterface	N/A
PasswordAuthentication	*System.Net.NetworkCredential*
ServerSocket	*System.Net.Sockets.TcpListener*
Socket	*System.Net.Sockets.TcpClient*
SocketAddress	*System.Net.SocketAddress*

(continued)

Table F-9 **The Java to .NET Mapping for the *java.net* Package**   *(continued)*

Java	.NET
SocketImpl	N/A
SocketPermission	*System.Net.SocketPermission*
	System.Net.WebPermission
URI	*System.Uri*
URL	*System.Uri*
URLClassLoader	N/A
URLConnection	*System.Net.WebClient*
	System.Web.WebRequest
	System.Web.WebResponse
URLDecoder	*System.Uri*
URLEncoder	*System.Uri*
URLStreamHandler	N/A

The *java.nio* Package

There are no direct class mappings for the *java.nio* package; consult the section "Asynchronous I/O" in Chapter 10 for details of .NET asynchronous I/O.

The *java.rmi* Package

There are no direct class mappings for the *java.rmi* package; consult Chapter 15, "Remoting," for details of the .NET remoting systems, which can be used as a replacements for Remote Method Invocation (RMI).

The *java.security* Package

Java and .NET take a different approach to enforcing security. For more information, consult Chapter 17, "Security and Cryptography."

The *java.sql* Package

The mapping between the Java *java.sql* package and the corresponding .NET types is provided in Table F-10. See Chapter 16, "Database Connectivity," for details of these .NET types.

Table F-10   The Java to .NET Mapping for the *java.sql* Package

Java	.NET
Interfaces	
Array	N/A
Blob	*Blob* objects are read through a *DataReader*; see the following types:
	System.Data.IDbDataReader
	System.Data.SqlClient.SqlDataReader
	System.Data.OleDb.OleDbDataReader
CallableStatement	*System.Data.IDbCommand*
	System.Data.SqlClient.SqlCommand
	System.Data.OleDb.OleDbCommand
Clob	*Clob* objects are read through a *DataReader*; see the following types:
	System.Data.IDbDataReader
	System.Data.SqlClient.SqlDataReader
	System.Data.OleDb.OleDbDataReader
Connection	*System.Data.IDb*
	System.Data.SqlClient.Sql
	System.Data.OleDb.OleDb
DatabaseMetaData	N/A
Driver	N/A
ParameterMetaData	*System.Data.IDataParameter*
	System.Data.IDbDataParameter
	System.Data.IDataParameterCollection
	System.Data.SqlClient.SqlParameter
	System.Data.SqlClient.SqlParameterCollection
	System.Data.OleDb.OleDbParameter
	System.Data.OleDb.OleDbParameterCollection
PreparedStatement	*System.Data.IDbCommand*
	System.Data.SqlClient.SqlCommand
	System.Data.OleDb.OleDbCommand
Ref	N/A

(continued)

Table F-10 **The Java to .NET Mapping for the *java.sql* Package** *(continued)*

Java	.NET
ResultSet	System.Data.IDbDataReader
	System.Data.SqlClient.SqlDataReader
	System.Data.OleDb.OleDbDataReader
	System.Data.DataSet
ResultSetMetaData	System.Data.IDbDataReader
	System.Data.SqlClient.SqlDataReader
	System.Data.OleDb.OleDbDataReader
	System.Data.DataSet
Savepoint	System.Data.SqlClient.SqlTransaction
SQLData	N/A
SQLInput	N/A
SQLOutput	N/A
Statement	System.Data.IDbCommand
	System.Data.SqlClient.SqlCommand
	System.Data.OleDb.OleDbCommand
Struct	N/A
Classes	
Date	System.Data.SqlTypes.SqlDateTime
DriverManager	N/A
DriverPropertyInfo	N/A
SQLPermission	System.Data.Common.DBDataPermission
	System.Data.Common.DBDataPermissionAttribute
	System.Data.SqlClient.SqlClientPermission
	System.Data.SqlClient.SqlClientPermissionAttribute
	System.Data.OleDb.OleDbPermission
	System.Data.OleDb.OleDbPermissionAttribute
Time	System.Data.SqlTypes.SqlDateTime
TimeStamp	N/A
Types	System.Data.DbTypes

The *java.text* Package

The mapping between the Java *java.text* package and the corresponding .NET types is provided in Table F-11.

Table F-11   The Java to .NET Mapping for the *java.text* Package

Java	.NET
ChoiceFormat	N/A
DateFormat	*System.DateTime*
	System.Globalization.DateTimeFormatInfo
DateFormatSymbols	*System.Globalization.DateTimeFormatInfo*
FieldPosition	N/A
MessageFormat	N/A (Formatting is built into classes that implement the *System.IFormattable* interface.)
NumberFormat	*System.Convert*
	System.Globalization.NumberFormatInfo
	Formatting is built into classes that implement the *System.IFormattable* interface.
ParsePosition	N/A
RuleBasedCollator	N/A
SimpleDateFormat	*System.DateTime*
	System.Globalization.DateTimeFormatInfo
StringCharacterIterator	*System.IEnumerator* obtained via *System.String*

The *java.util* Package

The mapping between the Java *java.util* package and the corresponding .NET types is provided in Table F-12. See Chapter 9, "Collections," for details of these .NET types.

Table F-12   The Java to .NET Mapping for the *java.util* Package

Java	.NET
AbstractCollection	*System.Collections.CollectionsBase*
AbstractList	N/A
AbstractMap	N/A

(continued)

Table F-12 The Java to .NET Mapping for the *java.util* Package *(continued)*

Java	.NET
AbstractSequentialList	N/A
AbstractSet	N/A
ArrayList	*System.Collections.ArrayList*
Arrays	*System.Array*
BitSet	N/A
Calendar	*System.Globalization.Calendar*
Collections	N/A
Currency	*System.Globalization.RegionInfo*
Date	*System.DateTime*
Dictionary	*System.Collections.DictionaryBase*
EventListenerProxy	N/A
EventObject	*System.EventArgs*
GregorianCalendar	*System.Globalization.GregorianCalendar*
HashMap	*System.Collections.Hashtable*
HashSet	N/A
Hashtable	*System.Collections.Hashtable*
IdentityHashMap	N/A
LinkedHashMap	N/A
LinkedHashSet	N/A
LinkedList	N/A
ListResourceBundle	*System.Resources.ResourceManager*
	System.Resources.ResourceSet
Locale	*System.Globalization.RegionInfo*
	System.Globalization.CultureInfo
Observable	N/A
Properties	N/A
PropertyPermission	N/A
PropertyResourceBundle	N/A
Random	*System.Random*
ResourceBundle	*System.Resources.ResourceManager*
	System.Resources.ResourceSet
SimpleTimeZone	*System.DateTime*

Table F-12   The Java to .NET Mapping for the *java.util* Package *(continued)*

Java	.NET
Stack	*System.Collections.Stack*
StringTokenizer	N/A (See the "Regular Expressions" section of Chapter 7 for comparable functionality.)
Timer	*System.Threading.Timer*
	System.Timers.Timer
TimerTask	*System.Threading.TimerCallback*
	System.Timers.ElapsedEventHandler
TimeZone	*System.DateTime*
TreeMap	N/A
TreeSet	*System.Collections.SortedList*
Vector	*System.Collections.ArrayList*
WeakHashMap	N/A

The *java.util.jar* Package

The .NET Framework doesn't provide equivalent functionality for this package.

The *java.util.logging* Package

There are no direct class mappings for the *java.util.logging* package; consult Appendix A for details of writing to the Windows Event Log.

The *java.util.prefs* Package

.NET provides an alternative approach to storing preferences, called *isolated storage*. See the section "Isolated Storage" in Chapter 10 for more information.

The *java.util.regex* Package

The mapping between the Java *java.util.regex* package and the corresponding .NET types is provided in Table F-13. The *System.Text.RegularExpressions* classes are discussed in Chapter 7.

Table F-13   **The Java to .NET Mapping for the *java.util.regex* Package**

Java	.NET
Classes	
Matcher	*System.Text.RegularExpressions.Regex*
	System.Text.RegularExpressions.Match
	System.Text.RegularExpressions.MatchCollection
	System.Text.RegularExpressions.Group
	System.Text.RegularExpressions.GroupCollection
Pattern	*System.Text.RegularExpressions.Regex*
	System.Text.RegularExpressions.RegexCompilationInfo
	System.Text.RegularExpressions.RegexOptions
Exceptions	
PatternSyntaxException	*System.ArgumentException*

The *java.util.zip* Package

The .NET Framework doesn't provide equivalent functionality for this package.

The *javax.swing* Package

The mapping between the Java *javax.swing* package and the corresponding .NET types is provided in Table F-14. The .NET Windows Forms system provides a smaller class set than Swing for constructing client applications. See Chapter 18 for more information about the Windows Forms system.

Table F-14   **The Java to .NET Mapping for the *javax.swing* Package**

Java	.NET
AbstractAction	N/A
AbstractButton	*System.Windows.Forms.ButtonBase*
	System.Windows.Forms.Button
AbstractCellEditor	N/A
AbstractListModel	*System.Windows.Forms.ListControl*
AbstractSpinnerModel	*System.Windows.Forms.UpDownBase*
ActionMap	N/A

Table F-14   The Java to .NET Mapping for the *javax.swing* Package   *(continued)*

Java	.NET
BorderFactory	N/A
Box	N/A
BoxLayout	N/A
ButtonGroup	N/A
CellRendererPane	N/A
ComponentInputMap	N/A
DebugGraphics	N/A
DefaultBoundedRangeModel	N/A
DefaultButtonModel	N/A
DefaultCellEditor	N/A
DefaultComboBoxModel	N/A
DefaultDesktopManager	N/A
DefaultFocusManager	N/A
DefaultListCellRenderer	N/A
DefaultListModel	N/A
DefaultListSelectionModel	N/A
DefaultSingleSelectionModel	N/A
FocusManager	N/A
GrayFilter	N/A
ImageIcon	*System.Drawing.Image*
InputMap	N/A
InputVerifier	N/A
JApplet	N/A
JButton	*System.Windows.Forms.Button*
JCheckBox	*System.Windows.Forms.CheckBox*
JCheckBoxMenuItem	N/A
JColorChooser	*System.Windows.Forms.ColorDialog*
JComboBox	*System.Windows.Forms.ComboBox*
JComponent	*System.Windows.Forms.UserControl*
	System.Windows.Forms.Control
JDesktopPane	N/A
JDialog	*System.Windows.Forms.CommonDialog*

(continued)

Table F-14 **The Java to .NET Mapping for the *javax.swing* Package** *(continued)*

Java	.NET
JEditorPane	*System.Windows.Forms.TextBoxBase*
JFileChooser	*System.Windows.Forms.OpenFileDialog*
	System.Windows.Forms.SaveFileDialog
JFormattedTextField	*System.Windows.Forms.RichTextBox*
JFrame	*System.Windows.Forms.Form*
JInternalFrame	N/A
JLabel	*System.Windows.Forms.Label System.Windows.Forms.Link-Label*
JLayeredPane	N/A
JList	*System.Windows.Forms.ListBox*
JMenu	N/A
JMenuBar	*System.Windows.Forms.MainMenu*
JMenuItem	*System.Windows.Forms.MenuItem*
JOptionPane	N/A
JPanel	*System.Windows.Forms.Panel*
JPasswordField	*System.Windows.Forms.TextBox*
JPopupMenu	*System.Windows.Forms.ContextMenu*
JPopupMenu.Separator	N/A
JProgressBar	*System.Windows.Forms.StatusBar*
JRadioButton	*System.Windows.Forms.RadioButton*
JRadioButtonMenuItem	N/A
JRootPane	N/A
JScrollBar	*System.Windows.Forms.HScrollBar*
	System.Windows.Forms.VScrollBar
JScrollPane	*System.Windows.Forms.Panel*
JSeparator	N/A
JSlider	*System.Windows.Forms.Trackbar*
JSpinner	*System.Windows.Forms.DomainUpDown*
	System.Windows.Forms.NumericUpDown
JSplitPane	*System.Windows.Forms.Splitter*
JTabbedPane	*System.Windows.Forms.TabControl*
JTable	*System.Windows.Forms.ListView*
JTextArea	*System.Windows.Forms.TextBox*

Table F-14   The Java to .NET Mapping for the *javax.swing* Package   *(continued)*

Java	.NET
JTextField	*System.Windows.Forms.TextBox*
JTextPane	*System.Windows.Forms.RichTextBox*
JToggleButton	*System.Windows.Forms.ButtonBase*
JToolBar	*System.Windows.Forms.ToolBar*
JToolTip	*System.Windows.Forms.ToolTip*
JTree	*System.Windows.Forms.ListView*
JViewport	*N/A*
JWindow	*N/A*
KeyStroke	*N/A*
LayoutFocusTraversalPolicy	*N/A*
LookAndFeel	*N/A*
MenuSelectionManager	*N/A*
OverlayLayout	*N/A*
Popup	*System.Windows.Forms.ContextMenu*
PopupFactory	*N/A*
ProgressMonitor	*N/A*
ProgressMonitorInputStream	*N/A*
RepaintManager	*N/A*
ScrollPaneLayout	*N/A*
SizeRequirements	*N/A*
SizeSequence	*N/A*
SortingFocusTraversalPolicy	*N/A*
SpinnerDateModel	*N/A*
SpinnerListModel	*N/A*
SpinnerNumberModel	*N/A*
Spring	*N/A*
SpringLayout	*N/A*
SwingUtilities	*N/A*
Timer	*System.Windows.Forms.Timer*
ToolTipManager	*N/A*
TransferHandler	*N/A*
UIDefaults	*N/A*

(continued)

Table F-14 **The Java to .NET Mapping for the *javax.swing* Package** *(continued)*

Java	.NET
UIManager	N/A
ViewportLayout	N/A

The *javax.swing.border* Package

The .NET Framework doesn't provide equivalent functionality for this package.

The *javax.swing.colorchooser* Package

The .NET Framework doesn't provide equivalent functionality for this package. Colors can be selected by the user through the *System.Windows.Forms.Color-Dialog* class.

The *javax.swing.event* Package

The mapping between the Java *javax.swing.event* package and the corresponding .NET types is provided in Table F-15. The .NET Windows Forms system uses fewer events than Swing. Consult the documentation for details of events defined by Windows Forms components.

Table F-15 **The Java to .NET Mapping for the *javax.swing.event* Package**

Java	.NET
AncestorEvent	N/A
CaretEvent	*System.EventArgs*
ChangeEvent	N/A
EventListenerList	N/A
HyperlinkEvent	N/A
InternalFrameAdapter	N/A
InternalFrameEvent	N/A
ListDataEvent	*System.EventArgs*
ListSelectionEvent	*System.EventArgs*
MenuDragMouseEvent	N/A
MenuEvent	*System.EventArgs*

Table F-15   The Java to .NET Mapping for the *javax.swing.event* Package   *(continued)*

Java	.NET
MenuKeyEvent	N/A
MouseInputAdapter	N/A
PopupMenuEvent	*System.EventArgs*
SwingPropertyChangeSupport	N/A
TableColumnModelEvent	N/A
TableModelEvent	N/A
TreeExpansionEvent	N/A
TreeModelEvent	N/A
TreeSelectionEvent	N/A
UndoableEditEvent	N/A

The *javax.swing.filechooser* Package

The .NET Framework doesn't provide equivalent functionality for this package. Files can be selected by the user through the *System.Windows.Forms.OpenFile-Dialog* and *System.Windows.Forms.SaveFileDialog* classes.

The *javax.swing.plaf* Package

The .NET Framework doesn't provide equivalent functionality for this package.

The *javax.swing.table* Package

The Windows Forms class set doesn't provide a direct equivalent of the table support in Swing. Tables can be displayed by using the *System.Windows.Forms.ListBox* class, but this class doesn't offer the flexibility of the *javax.swing.JTable* class and doesn't provide access to the cell renderers that are contained in the *javax.swing.table* package.

The *javax.swing.text* Package

The .NET Framework doesn't provide equivalent functionality for this package. The *System.Windows.Forms.RichTextBox* class, however, does display text formatted with Rich Text Format (RTF).

The *javax.swing.tree* Package

The Windows Forms class set doesn't provide a direct equivalent of the tree support in Swing. Trees can be displayed by using the *System.Windows.Forms.ListBox* class, but this class doesn't offer the flexibility of the *javax.swing.JTree* class.

The *javax.swing.undo* Package

The .NET Framework doesn't provide equivalent functionality for this package.

The *javax.sql* Package

The .NET class libraries provide no directly comparable classes for those included in the *javax.sql* package. Connnection pooling and transaction functionality are incorporated into the ADO.NET Data Provider classes contained in the *System.Data* namespace. The Java *RowSet* classes have no directly equivalent .NET classes, although the *System.Data.DataSet* class provides some comparable functionality. Consult Chapter 16 for full details.

The *javax.xml.parsers* Package

.NET doesn't use a factory approach to create XML parsers. Consult Chapter 11, "XML Processing," for details of the instantiation of XML parsing classes.

The *javax.xml.transform* Package

The mapping between the Java *javax.xml.transform* package and the corresponding .NET types is provided in Table F-16. See Chapter 11 for details of these .NET types. The following subpackages of *javax.xml.transform* contain no direct class mappings within .NET:

- javax.xml.transform.dom
- javax.xml.transform.sax
- javax.xml.transform.stream

Table F-16   The Java to .NET Mapping for the *java.xml.transform* Package

Java	.NET
Interfaces	
ErrorListener	N/A
Result	N/A
Source	N/A
SourceLocator	N/A
Templates	N/A
URIResolver	*System.Xml.XmlResolver*
	System.Xml.XmlUrlResolver
Classes	
OutputKeys	N/A
Transformer	*System.Xml.Xsl.XslTransform*
TransformerFactory	N/A
Exceptions	
TransformerConfigurationException	*System.Xml.Xsl.XsltCompileException*
TransformerException	*System.Xml.Xsl.XsltException*
Errors	
TransformerFactoryConfigurationError	N/A

The *org.w3c.dom* Package

The mapping between the Java *org.w3c.dom* package and the corresponding .NET types is provided in Table F-17. See Chapter 11 for details of these .NET types.

Table F-17   The Java to .NET Mapping for the *org.w3c.dom* Package

Java	.NET
Interfaces	
Attr	*System.Xml.XmlAttribute*
CDATASection	*System.Xml.XmlCDataSection*
CharacterData	*System.Xml.XmlCharacterData*
Comment	*System.Xml.XmlComment*
Document	*System.Xml.XmlDocument*

(continued)

Table F-17   **The Java to .NET Mapping for the *org.w3c.dom* Package**   *(continued)*

Java	.NET
DocumentFragment	*System.Xml.XmlDocumentFragment*
DocumentType	*System.Xml.XmlDocumentType*
DOMImplementation	*System.Xml.XmlImplementation*
Element	*System.Xml.XmlElement*
Entity	*System.Xml.XmlEntity*
EntityReference	*System.Xml.XmlEntityReference*
NamedNodeMap	*System.Xml.XmlNamedNodeMap*
Node	*System.Xml.XmlNode*
	System.Xml.XmlNodeType
NodeList	*System.Xml.XmlNodeList*
Notation	*System.Xml.XmlNotation*
ProcessingInstruction	*System.Xml.XmlProcessingInstruction*
Text	*System.Xml.XmlText*
Exceptions	
DOMException	*System.ArgumentException*
	System.InvalidOperationException

The *org.xml.sax* Package

The .NET Type libraries don't include a SAX implementation. Consult Chapter 11 for details of the *System.Xml.XmlReader* class, which provides the .NET alternative to SAX.

Index

Symbols

& (address-of operator), 140
@ (at symbol), 48
@ (verbatim strings), 164–65
>>> (bitwise shift), 49
/// (code documentation indicator), 39
// (comment indicator), 39
+ (concatenation operator), 150
-- (decrement operator), 141
(digit placeholder), 180
$ (dollar sign) not permitted, 41
== (equals operator), 149
++ (increment operator), 141
!= (inequality operator), 149
-> (member access token), 140
* (pointer token), 139–40
~ (tilde), 97, 492

A

absolute numbers, 181
abstract classes, 53–54, 77
abstract keyword, 53–54
Abstract Window Toolkit (AWT), 20, 419, 501–6
access
    classes, modifiers for, 76–77
    code, security of. See CAS
    constants, table of modifiers, 92
    constructors modifiers, 96
    delegates, table of modifiers, 85
    enumeration modifiers, 75
    events modifiers, 103
    file system. See file system access
    indexer modifiers, 110
    method modifiers, 99
    modifier keywords, 45, 52
    property modifiers, 107
    protected internal, 52
accessors, event, 104
activation
    channel definition, 356–57
    client, 354, 358–60
    configuration files for, 356–60
    MarshalByRefObject, 355
    registration, client, 354–55, 358–59
    RemotingConfiguration class, 353
    server, 354–56, 357–58
    server vs. client, 353
    SingleCall, 355
    Singleton, 355
ad hoc regular expressions, 171
address-of operator (&), 140
ADO.NET
    connections, 372–74
    database access with. See Data Providers; DataSets
    JDBC API (Java 2). See JDBC API
    SQL with. See SQL commands

al.exe, 34–35
aliases, 57–58
anchoring controls, 425–26
anonymous classes, 78
APIs, Java 2 and .NET compared, 18–20. See also
    Java-to-.NET API reference
application configuration files. See configuration files
application entry points. See Main method
ArrayLists, 198–99, 203
arrays
    base class for, 82, 194
    CLS compliance rules, 496
    as collections, 194–96
    copying, 196
    declaring, 81–82
    elements, setting to default, 196
    elements as variables, 116
    foreach statements with, 82
    ICollection, 195
    IEnumerable, 195
    IList, 195
    initializing, 82
    memory streams, 220–21
    methods, table of, 195–96
    object nature of, 82, 195–96
    parameter arrays, 100
    searching, 196
    SortedLists, 201–2
    strings, copying to, 152
    syntax, 82
ASCII encoding, 158–59
ASP.NET, 435–36. See also Web services
assemblies
    Assembly Linker Tool, 478
    CLS compliance, 497
    codebase probing, 479–80
    configuration files, 481
    creating, 32–35
    culture-neutral, 474
    defined, 25
    elements of, 29–31
    formats for, table of, 29
    identification of, 30
    linker (al.exe), 34–35
    manifests. See assembly manifests
    metadata in. See assembly manifests
    modules, 30–31
    multifile. See multifile assemblies
    permission requests. See CAS
    policies for versioning, 477–78, 480
    probing, 478–80
    resources in, 31
    shared. See shared assemblies
    single-file, 31–33
    versioning, 475–78
    Web services, 439

527

Assembly Linker Tool, 478
assembly manifests
  culture information, 30
  defined, 25
  information defined in, 29–30
  metadata, defining, 32–33
  modules with, 31
  multifile assemblies, 34–35
  viewing, 33
assembly probing, 478–80
assertions (Java), 133
associativity of operators, 50–51
AsyncCallback delegate, 226–28
asynchronous I/O, 225–28
asynchronous sockets, 338
atomized strings, 240
attributes
  AttributeUsage, 130
  compile-time evaluation of, 131–33
  ConditionalAttribute, 131–32
  constructors, 131
  customizing, 129–31
  declaring custom, 129–30
  defined, 126
  elements used with, 127
  global, 128–29
  inspecting, 285
  named parameters, 128, 131
  naming conventions, 127, 131
  ObsoleteAttribute, 132–33
  parameters for, 128
  positional parameters, 128
  predefined, 126–27
  reflection, 285
  specifying predefined, 127–29
  syntax for specifying, 127
  target specifiers, 128–29
  XML, accessing with readers, 248–51
  XML, quotation mark selection, 259
AWT (Abstract Window Toolkit), 20, 419, 501–6

B

backing stores, 219
base keyword, 90, 95
base streams, 219–21
binary operator members, 113–14
BinaryReader class, 223
BinaryWriter class, 223
BindingFlags enumeration, 278
bitwise shift (>>>), 49
boxing, 67–68
break statements, 59–60, 61
BufferedStream class, 222
buttons
  adding to Windows Forms, 420
  event handling, 426–27
  positioning, 424–26
  table of, 422

C

caches, weak references with, 494
Calendar class, 183
callbacks
  thread pools, 303–4
  thread timers, 298–301
camel casing, 40
CAS (Code Access Security)
  caspol.exe command line tool, 406
  code groups, 405–6
  Configuration tool, 406
  declarative statements, 399–404
  defined, 397
  Demand method, 404–5
  denied permissions, 399
  Enterprise policy level, 406
  evidence-based security, 397–98
  exceptions, 397, 399, 402
  hard statements, 404–5
  imperative statements, 404–5
  Machine policy level, 406
  managing policies, 406
  membership conditions, 405–6
  minimum permissions, 399
  optional permissions, 399, 402
  permission classes, 398–99
  permission sets, 405–6
  Permission Viewer tool, 403–4
  permissions, 397–404
  policies, 405–6
  programming guidelines, 398
  purpose of, 397
  refusing permissions, 403
  run-time requests, 404–5
  scope of statements, 399–401
  security policies, 405–6
  SecurityAction enumeration, 400–401, 404–5
  soft statements, 399–404
  syntax for permissions, 400
  User policy level, 406
  viewing permissions, 403–4
  WebPermission class, 400–401
CAS security policies, 405–6
case, method for changing in strings, 151
case sensitivity
  camel casing, 40
  CLS compliance rules, 496
  language-neutrality considerations, 39
  naming conventions, 40
  Pascal casing, 40
casts, 85, 87–88
catching exceptions, 122–23
channels, remoting
  ChannelServices class, 351
  client class, 345
  configuration files with, 356–57
  constructors for, 350
  creating, 349–50
  default names, 353
  defined, 348

HttpChannel class, 349–53
interfaces for, 348–49
multiple channels, 351–53
multiple instances, 352–53
port property, 350
properties of, 350–51
registering, 351
server class, 342–43, 348
SOAP, 349, 351
TcpChannel class, 349–53
characters
casing. *See* case sensitivity
encoding, 157–62
literals, 51
manipulation methods, 151–52
Charset class (Java), 158, 160
checked keyword, 63–64
cipher support. *See* cryptography
class libraries
implicit importation of, 38
J2EE functionality, 18
naming conventions, 40
.NET Framework, 8–9
classes
abstract, 53–54, 77
anonymous, 78
constructors, default, 78
constructors for. *See* constructors
declaring, 76
destructors, 97–98, 492–93
instantiation, preventing, 78
members allowed, 77
modifiers of, 76–77
operators as members, 111–15
security. *See* role-based security
source files, multiple allowed in, 41
CLI (common language infrastructure), 6, 496
clients
remoting, creation of, 344–46
Web services, 443–46
CLR (common language runtime)
assembly manifests with, 25
code security. *See* CAS
defined, 8
language neutrality features. *See* language neutrality
version specification by configuration files, 482
CLS (Common Language Specification), 8, 496–97
CLSCompliant attribute, 497–99
code
security. *See* CAS
unsafe. *See* unsafe code
Code Access Security. *See* CAS
code documentation indicator (///), 39
codebase probing, 479–80
Collection Framework API (Java 2), 19
collections
abstract classes for, 205
ArrayLists, 198–99, 203
arrays as, 194–96
base interface, 190

case-insensitive implementations, 203
classes, 189
CollectionUtil class, 203
comparisons, 193
CopyTo method, 190
Count property, 190
Current property, 191
cursors, 190–92
customizing, 205
FIFO, 199–200
foreach statements, 60–61, 82, 190–92
GetEnumerator method, 190–92
Hashtables, 196–97, 201–3. *See also* Hashtables
HybridDictionary class, 203
ICollection, 190, 204
IComparable, 193
IComparer, 193
IDbDataParameter, 379–80
IEnumerable, 190–92
IEnumerator, 190–92
IList, 195, 198–99
indexers for. *See* indexers
interfaces for, 189–94
LIFO, 200–201
ListDictionary, 203
locking with ReadWriterLock, 307
LRU (least recently used) maps, 205
MoveNext method, 191
NameObjectCollectionBase, 202–3
namespace for, 189
NameValueCollection, 202–3
queues, 199–200
SortedLists, 201–2
sorting, 193
Specialized namespace, 202–3
stacks, 200–201
StringCollection, 203
StringDictionary, 203
string-typed, 202–3
strongly-typed, 202–3
Synchronized method, 204
thread safety, 190, 191, 204
writers, multiple concurrent, 204
color
colorchooser package, javax, 522
java.awt.color, 504
specifying in GDI+, 428–29
command line tools, 9
command-line arguments, 448, 450
comment indicator (//), 39
comment syntax, 39
common language runtime. *See* CLR
Common Language Specification. *See* CLS
common type system (CTS), 7–8, 496
CompareTo method, 174
comparisons
collections, sorting, 193
DateTime structs, 184
IComparable interface, 174
strings, 149–50, 240

compiling
  assembly creation, 32–35
  assembly formats, 29
  conditional compilation, 134–35
  csc command, 26
  csc.exe, 25
  DLLs, 346
  invoking the runtime, 26
  manifests, incorporating, 32–33
  modules, 31
  options, table of, 26–28
  preprocessor instructions. *See* preprocessor directives
  regular expressions, 164–66
  remoting applications, 346
  shared assemblies, 475
  syntax for, 26
  /unsafe flag, 138
  Web services, 438–39
  Windows Forms applications, 421
  Windows Services, 469
compliance, CLS, 496–99
concatenation of strings, 150–51
conditional statements, 46–47
ConditionalAttribute, 131–32
configuration files
  appSetting section, 483–84
  CLR version specification, 482
  .config extension, 481
  dictionary sections, 486
  garbage collection concurrency setting, 482
  GetConfig method, 484
  ignore sections, 486–87
  key/value pairs, 483–84
  loading, 481
  machine configuration files, 481
  multifile assemblies, 481
  name/value sections, 485–86
  naming, 481
  remoting, 356–60
  root node for, 481
  section declarations, 484–85
  settings, defining, 483–87
  shared assemblies, 478–80
  simple tag sections, 485
  System.configuration namespace, 483–84
  tag sections, 485
Configuration tool, .NET Framework, 406
connection strings, 372–73
connections, ADO.NET
  closing, 374
  Connection objects, 372
  connection strings, 372–73
  constructors, 372–73
  creating, 372
  database selection, 374
  IDbConnection interface, 372–73
  opening, 372–73
  pooling, 373–74
  security, 373
  SqlConnection class, 373–74
  state determination, 372

connections, HTTP
  accepting, 332–33
  setting, 319, 323–25
  sockets. *See* sockets
console
  advantages of using, 207
  changing streams, 209
  Error property, 208
  In property, 208–9
  log events, writing to, 461–62
  Out property, 208
  reading from, 209
  streams, Java vs. .NET, 207, 209–10
  System.Console class, 207–8
  TextReader streams, 208
  TextWriter streams, 208
constants, 91–92
constructors
  for attributes, 131
  base keyword with, 95
  classes, 78
  declaring, 95–96
  empty, 70
  modifiers with, 96
  parameters (Java), 117
  reflection, 280–82
  static, 96–97
  this keyword with, 95
containers, Windows Forms, 420, 422
continue statements, 59, 61
controls
  dialog box, 423
  PictureBox, 423
  text editing, 423
controls, Windows Forms
  adding, 420
  anchoring, 424–25
  buttons, 420, 422
  containers for, 420
  disposing of, 420
  docking, 425–26
  event handling, 426–27
  Location property, 424
  positioning, 424–26
  table of, 422–23
conversion of types
  boxing, 67–68
  Convert utility class, 86
  defined, 85–86
  enumerations, 86
  explicit, 85, 87–88
  IConvertible interface, 175
  implicit, 85–87
  numeric, 86, 177
  operators for, 115
  pointers, 141–42
  reference types, 86–87
  unboxing, 68
conversion operators, 115

cookies
  HttpWebResponse support for, 318
  WebClient, not supported by, 315
copying strings, 148, 150
CORBA, 20
Cosh function, 181
credentials, 315
cryptography
  asymmetrical encryption, 412–13
  classes, asymmetric encryption, 412
  classes, symmetric encryption, 410
  CryptoStream constructor, 410
  DES, 409–10
  digital signatures, 415–16
  DSA, 412
  hash codes, 413–14
  MD5, 413–16
  namespace for, 410
  RC2, 409–10
  Rijndael, 409–10
  RSA, 412–13, 415–16
  SHA, 413–14, 416
  signatures, 415–16
  symmetrical encryption, 409–11
  TripleDES, 409–11
.cs extension, 26
csc.exe, 25
CTS (common type system), 7–8, 496
culture information, assembly manifests, 30
currency format specifier, 179
cursors, collections using, 190–92
custom conversion, 112

D

daemon thread (Java), 295
Data Adapters
  defined, 366
  IDbDataAdapter members, 389–90
  populating DataSets with, 389–91
data members, 88
Data Providers
  Command elements, 366
  commands. *See* SQL commands
  Connection elements, 366
  connections, 372–74
  Data Adapters, 366, 389–91
  DataReaders, 366, 384–86
  DataSets with, 386–87. *See also* DataSets
  defined, 365, 366
  elements of, 366
  interfaces, 366–67
  namespace for interfaces, 366–67
  ODBC, 367
  OLE DB.NET Data Providers, 367
  result sets, 384–86
  sample code, 368–72
  SQL Server. *See* SQL Server.NET Data Providers
  transactions, 374–76

Data Readers, 366, 384–86
data sets. *See* DataSets
data slots, 297–98
data storage, safe. *See* isolated storage
databases
  ADO.NET, 365–66
  connections to, 372–74
  creation with SQL Server, 368
  Data Providers. *See* Data Providers
  DataSets. *See* DataSets
  JDBC API, 365–66
  result sets, 384–86
  ResultSet (Java), 384
DatagramSocket class (Java), 334
DataReaders, 366, 384–86
DataSets
  actions available, table of, 392
  Clone method, 389
  columns, 388, 392
  component classes, 387–88
  connectionless design, 386–87
  Copy method, 389
  creating, 388–89
  Data Adapters to populate, 389–91
  default name, 388
  defined, 365, 386
  DiffGrams, 393–94
  foreign key constraints, 388
  GetChanges method, 389
  GetXml method, 391
  manual management of, 391–92
  new keyword with, 388
  optimistic concurrency, 387
  populating, 389–91
  purpose of, 386–87
  ReadXml method, 393
  relationships, 388
  rows, 388, 392
  schemas, 393
  synchronizing data, 389, 394–95
  tables, 388, 392
  WriteXml method, 394
  XML support, 389–95
  XmlDataDocument synchronization, 394–95
DataTables, 388
dates. *See* DateTime struct
DateTime struct
  comparison operators, 184
  constructors, 184
  creating dates, 184–85
  current date and time, 185
  defined, 183
  formatting dates, 185
  immutability of, 184
  Java vs. .NET, 183–84
  manipulating dates, 185
  offset basis, 183
  offset span, 184
  parsing dates, 185
  System.Calendar association, 183

DateTime struct, *continued*
   ticks, 184
   TimeSpan struct, 184
   UTC time, conversion to, 185
DBDemo sample code, 368–72
Debug class, 133
debugging
   compiler options, 27
   conditional execution during, 132
decimal format strings, 179
decimal type, 72
declarative CAS statements, 399–404
declarative role-based statements, 407
decryption. *See* encryption
#define, 134
delegates
   adding (+ operator), 84
   declaring, 83
   defined, 83
   events with, 103
   instantiation of, 84
   invocation lists, 83
   invoking, 84
   modifiers for, 84–85
   purpose of, 83
   references to, 83–84
   remoting, 360
   removing references (- operator), 84
   thread-pool callbacks, 304
deployment directories, Web services, 438
deprecated keyword (Java), 132
deserialization, 234
destructors, 97–98, 492–93
development tools
   command line tools, 9
   IDEs, 9
   languages, programming, 10–12
   purpose of, 9
   Visual C# .NET, 10–11
   Visual Studio. *See* Visual Studio .NET
dialog box controls, 423
DiffGrams, 393–94
digit placeholder (#), 180
digital signatures, 415–16, 473–74
directories
   current, getting, 449
   Directory class, 212
   DirectoryInfo class, 212
   Environment class members returning, 449
   files, differentiating from, 212–13
   obtaining information about, 448–49
   Path class methods, 211
   system, getting, 449
   virtual, 438
disposal, value vs. reference types, 67
distributed applications. *See* remoting
DLLs (Dynamic Link Libraries)
   compiling, 346
   Hell, 475

DNS (Domain Name System), 324–28
docking controls, 424–25
Document Object Model. *See* DOM
document type definitions. *See* DTDs
DOM (Document Object Model), 260–62
double buffering images, 433–34
drawing. *See* GDI+
DTDs (document type definitions), 251

E

EJB (Enterprise Java Beans), 21
#elif, 134–35
#else, 134–35
empty statements, 58
Encoding class, 158–62
encryption
   asymmetrical, 412–13
   classes, asymmetric encryption, 412
   classes, symmetric, 410
   CryptoStream constructor, 410
   DES, 409–10
   DSA, 412
   initialization vectors (IVs), 410
   key generation, 410
   namespace for, 410
   RC2, 409–10
   Rijndael, 409–10
   RSA, 412–13
   symmetrical, 409–11
   TripleDES, 409–11
#endif, 134–35
#endregion, 136
Enterprise Java Beans, 21
enum keyword. *See* enumerations
enumerations
   advantages of, 73
   arguments of functions, as, 74
   assignment of integer values, 73–74
   base type, 73–74
   CLS compliance rules, 496
   data type nature of, 73–75
   declaring, 73–74
   members, listing, 73–74
   modifiers, 74–75
   strings, iterating through, 151
   System.Enum methods, 75
   thread safety, 204
   zeros, converting literal, 86
environment variables, 448
ephemeral collectors, 490
Equals method, 176
#error, 136–37
event handling
   OnPaint event handler, 427–28
   Windows Forms, 426–27
events
   accessors, 104
   add method, 104
   AWT, 504–5

declaring, 101
defined, 100
delegates with, 103
guidelines, 103
handling, 426–28
inspecting, 283
invoking, 101–3
java.awt, 504–5
listeners, declaring, 102–3
modifiers for, 103–4
Paint, 428
reflection, 283
registered listeners, removing, 101, 104
remove method, 104
resetting for threads, 309–10
security. *See* role-based security
Swing event equivalents, 522–23
ThreadPool class, 302–4
timers, thread, 298–301
triggering, 101
types, as, 100
Windows event log notifications, 460–62
evidence-based security, 397–98
exception handling
catching, 122–23
finally clauses, 123
keywords, table of, 47
performance issues, 123
throwing, 123
try keyword, 122
exception-handler parameters (Java), 117
exceptions
base class for, 124
chaining, 124
checked vs. unchecked, 124
declaring, 122
HelpLink, 125
inheritance hierarchy of, 124
InnerException, 125
members, table of, 125–26
Message, 125
SecurityExceptions, 397, 399, 402
Source, 125
StackTrace, 125
streams, 218
System.Exception class, 124–26
threading, 292, 296
throwing, 123
exe assembly format, 29
exit(int), 38
explicit conversion of types, 85, 87–88
explicit interface implementation, 80–81
Extensible Markup Language. *See* XML
extensions, returning, 211
extern keyword, 55
Externalizable (Java), 235

F

false keyword, 49, 112–13
fields
declaring, 92–93
defined, 92
inspecting, 284–85
modifiers, 93–94
read-only, 94
reflection, 284–85
structs, members of, 94
file requests and responses, networking, 320–23
file system access
access argument, 214–15
Attributes property, 213
buffer size, 215
creation time of files, 212
directories, 212–13
Exists method, 212–13
extensions, returning, 211
File class, 212, 215–16
file names, returning, 211
FileInfo class, 212, 215–16
FileStream. *See* FileStream class
Java vs. .NET classes, 216–18
modes of opening files, 214
Open methods, 216
paths, 210–12
sharing opened files, 215
streams for, 214–16. *See also* FileStream class
filechooser package, java.swing, 523
FileStream class
asynchronous I/O with, 226–28
backing stores using, 220
buffering, 222
creating streams with, 214–16
IsolatedStorageFileStream class, 231–32
FileWebRequest class, 320–23
FileWebResponse class, 320–23
final keyword (Java), 53, 55, 89
finalizers (Java). *See* destructors
finalizing objects, 491
finally blocks, 62, 123
fixed statements, 142–43
fixed-point numeric format strings, 179
flicker, eliminating, 433–34
flow control keywords, table of, 46–47
foreach statements
arrays with, 82
collections using, 190–92
using, 60–61
format specifications, 155
format strings, 156
formatters, serialization, 232–34
formatting
dates, 185
numbers, 177–81
strings, 154–57
forms, Windows. *See* Windows Forms

freachable queues, 491, 493
FTP protocol support lacking, 312
functional members, 88
functions
    math, table of, 181–82
    output parameters, 119
    reference parameters of, 118
    value parameters of, 117–18

G

GAC (Global Assembly Cache), 474–78
garbage collector (GC)
    concurrency, 482, 491
    destructors, 492–93
    finalization, 491
    fixed statements, 142–43
    forcing collection, 489–91
    freachable queues, 491, 493
    generations, 490–91
    names vs. unnamed slots, 297
    purpose of, 489
    resurrection, 493
    value vs. reference types, 67
    weak references, 494
GC. *See* garbage collector
GDI+
    Bézier curves, 430
    bitmaps, drawing, 432–33
    brush settings, specifying, 429
    color, specifying, 428–30
    defined, 427
    double buffering, 433–34
    drawing methods, table of, 430–31
    DrawString method, 431–32
    fill methods, table of, 431
    fill settings, specifying, 428–29
    flicker, eliminating, 433–34
    graphics instances, obtaining, 427–28
    images, drawing, 432–33
    in-memory bitmaps, 433–34
    OnPaint event handler, 427–28
    Paint events, 428
    pen settings, specifying, 428–30
    state maintenance, drawing, 428
    strings, drawing, 431–32
    System.Drawing.Graphics class, 427–28
    text, drawing, 431–32
    vector images, 432–33
generations, 490–91
get accessors, 106, 110
getter/setter pattern, 105–6
Global Assembly Cache (GAC), 474–78
global attributes, 128–29
goals of .NET initiative, 5–7
goto statements, 59–60, 62
graphics. *See* GDI+
groups, security, 406–9

H

hash codes, 413–14
Hashtables
    case-insensitive implementations, 203
    class for, 196–97
    dictionary sections of configuration files, 486
    HybridDictionary class, compared to, 203
    ListDictionary class, compared to, 203
    NameValueCollection, 202–3
Hello World! application, 25–26
HelpLink exceptions, 125
hexadecimal format strings, 180
hiding members, 90
history of Java, 3–4
HTTP (Hypertext Transfer Protocol)
    clients, 329–31
    connections, setting, 323–25
    header processing, 202–3
    HttpChannel class, 342–43, 345, 349–53
    HttpWebRequest class, 320–23
    HttpWebResponse class, 318, 320–23
    sockets, 329–31, 349–53
    Web service support, 440
HybridDictionary class, 203
hyperbolic functions, 181–82

I

ICollection interface, 190, 204
IComparable interface
    collections, 193
    number objects with, 174
IComparer collections, 193
IConvertible interface, 175
IDataReader, 384–86
IDbCommand interface, 376–79, 384
IDbConnection interface
    connections using, 372–73
    transactions using, 375
IDbDataAdapter, 389–91
IDbDataParameter, 379–83
identifiers
    keywords, using as, 48
    naming, 41
IDEs (integrated development environments), 10. *See also* Visual Studio .NET
IDictionary interface, 203
IDisposable interface, 64, 98
IEnumerable interface
    arrays using, 195
    collections with, 190–92
    foreach statements, 60–61
IEnumerator interface, 190–92
#if, 134–35
#ifdef, 131–32
IFormattable interface
    format strings with, 156–57
    numbers objects with, 175, 177–78

IFormatter interface, 232, 234
IIS (Microsoft Internet Information Services)
  binding requirement, 435
  deployment directories, 438
IL (intermediate language), 495
ILease interface, 360–64
IList interface
  ArrayLists, 198–99
  arrays using, 195
  StringCollection, 203
images. *See* GDI+
imperative role-based statements, 407
implicit boxing, 68
implicit conversion of types, 85–87
import keyword (Java). *See* using keyword
indexers
  declaring, 108–10
  defined, 108, 187
  explicit interface implementation, 80–81
  Hashtables with, 196–97
  interfaces with indexer members, 111
  modifiers for, 110
  overloading, 188–89
  strings with, 151–52
infinity, 176–77
information technology, recent changes in, 3–4
inheritance
  classes, modifiers for, 77
  constants, table of modifiers, 92
  constructor modifiers, 96
  delegates, table of modifiers, 85
  enumeration modifiers, 75
  event modifiers, 104
  hiding members, 90
  indexer modifiers, 110
  keywords for, 45, 53–54
  members, 89–90
  method modifiers, 99
  override keyword with, 90
  property modifiers, 107
InputStream class (Java), 218, 220
inspecting types. *See* reflection
instance variables, 116
instanceof operator (Java), 50
instantiation
  of classes, preventing, 78
  late binding, 285–87
  Mutexes with, 309
  of static members, 55
  of structs, 70
integer literals, 51
integrated development environments. *See* IDEs
interface types, boxing, 67–68
interfaces. *See also specific interfaces*
  access modifiers with, 81
  collections using. *See* collections, interfaces for
  conflicting member names, 80
  declaring, 78

exceptions with, 122
explicit implementation, 80–81
implementing, 80–81
indexers in, 80, 111
members allowed, 79
modifiers, 78–79
properties as members of, 107
syntax, 80
intermediate language (IL), 495
internal keyword, 52
Internet access. *See* networking
interoperability, cross-language. *See* language neutrality
invocation lists of delegates, 83
invoking the runtime, 26
I/O (input/output)
  asynchronous. *See* asynchronous I/O
  console. *See* console
  java.io package, 507–8
  streams. *See* streams
io package, 507–8
is operator, 50
isolated storage, 228–32
iteration
  enumerating. *See* enumerations
  foreach statements. *See* foreach statements
  looping keywords, 46–47
  strings, through, 151

J

J2EE (Java 2 Enterprise Edition), 17–18, 20–21
J2ME, 13
J2SDK (Java 2 software development kit), 5, 9
J2SE (Java 2 Standard Edition), 5, 6, 15, 18
Java
  advantages of, 4
  APIs, Java 2 and .NET compared, 18–20. *See also* Java-to-.NET API reference
  application servers, 13
  disadvantages of, 6
  EJB, 21
  history of, 3–4
  J2EE (Java 2 Enterprise Edition), 17–18, 20–21
  J2ME, 13
  J2SDK, 5, 9
  J2SE, 5, 6, 15, 18
  JNI (Java Native Interface), 6
  platform neutrality, 5–6
  security manager, 397
  XML support, 5, 19, 524–25
Java 2 Enterprise Edition (J2EE), 17–18, 20–21
Java 2 software development kit (J2SDK), 5, 9
Java 2 Standard Edition (J2SE), 5, 6, 15, 18
Java 2D API, 20, 427
Java API for XML Processing (JAXP), 19, 524–25
Java User Migration Path to Microsoft .NET (JUMP to .NET), 15
java.awt, 20, 419, 501–6

JavaBeans API (Java 2), 19
javadoc, 39
java.io package, 507–8
java.lang package, 38, 508–10
JavaMail, 21
java.math package, 510–11
java.net package, 511–12
java.nio package, 512
java.rmi package, 512
java.security package, 512
java.sql package, 512–14
java.text package, 515
Java-to-.NET API reference
    AWT, 501–6
    colorchooser package, 522
    events, java.awt, 504–5
    events, javax.swing, 522–23
    IO package, 507–8
    java.lang package, 508–10
    math package, 510–11
    net package, 511–12
    nio package, 512
    org.w3c.dom package, 525–26
    org.xml.sax package, 526
    overview, 501
    regex package, 517–18
    rmi package, 512
    security package, 512
    sql package, java, 512–14
    sql package, javax, 524
    swing package, 518–24
    text package, 515
    tree package, javax, 524
    util package, 515–17
    xml package, javax, 524–25
java.util package, 515–17
javax.swing package, 518–24
javax.xml package, 524–25
JAXP (Java API for XML Processing), 19, 524–25
JCA (Java Connector Architecture), 21
JCA (Microsoft Java Language Conversion Assistant), 15
JDBC API, 20, 365–66
JIT (just-in-time) compiling, 8
JMS (Java Message Service), 21
JNDI (Java Naming and Directory Interface), 20
JNI (Java Native Interface), 6, 19
JScript .NET, 11
JSP (Java Server Pages), 21
JTA (Java Transaction API), 21
jump statements, 59, 61–62
JUMP to .NET (Java User Migration Path to Microsoft
    .NET), 15

K

keys. *See also* cryptography
    foreign key constraints, DataSets, 388
    key file generation, 473
    key/value pairs in configuration files, 483–84

NameObjectCollectionBase, 202–3
    public/private pairs, 412–13
    SortedLists, 201–2
    strings as, 153
keywords. *See also specific keywords*
    @ symbol, 48
    access modifiers, 45, 52
    accessing members, 44
    complex type declarations, 43–44
    constants, 42–43
    exception handling, 47
    flow control, 46–47
    identifiers, using as, 48
    inheritance modifiers, 45, 53–54
    literals, table of, 51
    manipulating types, 44
    modifiers, 45–46
    namespaces, 41–42
    other modifiers, 55
    similarity with Java, 41
    simple types, 42–43
    unmanaged code, 48

L

labeled statements, 59, 62
Lang API, 18
lang package, 508–10
language neutrality
    benefits of, 495
    CLI (common language infrastructure), 496
    CLS (Common Language Specification), 496–97
    CTS (common type system), 496
    enabling architecture, 495
    goal of .NET initiative, 6–7
    intermediate language (IL), 495
    modules, 30–31
    multifile assemblies for, 31–32
    operator overloading, 115
languages, programming, for .NET, 10–12
late binding, 285
Lea, Doug, 289
leases, remote objects, 360–64
library assembly format, 29
#line, 137
linker (al.exe), 34–35
ListDictionary class, 203
literals, table of, 51
local classes, 78
local variables, 116
Locale Support API (Java 2), 19
localization string format specifications, 155
locks, 62, 305–7
logarithms, 181–82
Logging API (Java 2), 19
logical drives, obtaining information about, 448–49
logs. *See* Windows event log
looping keywords, 46–47
LRU (least recently used) maps, 205

M

machine properties, returning, 449
Machine.config, 481
Main method
    command-line arguments, 448
    entry point specification, 41
    parameters, 38
    purpose of, 38
    Windows Services, 462–63
managed types, 138
manifests. *See* assembly manifests
MapPoint .NET, 13
MarshalByRefObject, 342, 347–48, 355, 360–62
Math class, 181–82
math package, Java, 510–11
MaxValue field, 176
MBR. *See* MarshalByRefObject
MD5 hash codes, 413–16
members
    base class access, 90
    constants as, 91–92
    constructors as. *See* constructors
    events as, 100–104
    fields, 92–94
    hiding, 90
    indexers as, 108–11
    inheritance, 89–90
    MemberInfo class, reflection with, 277–79
    methods as. *See* methods
    operators as, 111–15
    override keyword with, 90
    overriding, 89–90
    properties as, 105–7
    sealed keyword with, 90
    static, 91
    table of types, 88–89
    variables as. *See* variables
    versioning, 89–90
    virtual, 89–90
memory allocation
    current process, 449
    garbage collections. *See* garbage collector
    sizeof operator, 139
    stackalloc command, 143
    value vs. reference types, 67
memory streams, 220–21
metadata. *See also* assembly manifests
    attributes for, 126
    multifile assemblies, setting for, 35
    strong names, 473–74
methods
    declaring, 98
    destructors, 97–98
    implicit overriding in Java, 89
    modifiers, 98–99
    naming conventions, 40
    parameter arrays, 100
    parameters of, 99–100

reflection, 280–82
remoting, 360
security. *See* role-based security
versioning issues, 89
virtual default in Java, 89
Microsoft intermediate language (MSIL), 8
Microsoft Java Language Conversion Assistant. *See* JCA
Microsoft Passport, 13
Microsoft SQL Server, 368
Microsoft Visual Studio .NET, 10, 435
Microsoft Windows
    forms. *See* Windows Forms
    registry. *See* Windows registry
    services. *See* Windows Services
    version effects on .NET, 447
migration issues
    basis for deciding to migrate, 14
    JUMP to .NET, 15
    open standards, 14
    skills transfer, 16
    Visual J# .NET, 15
MinValue field, 176
modifiers
    access, table of, 52
    classes, with, 76–77
    constants, table of modifiers, 92
    constructors with, 96
    delegates, with, 84–85
    enumerations, with, 74–75
    events with, 103–4
    fields with, 93–94
    indexers with, 110
    inheritance, table of, 53–54
    interfaces, with, 78–79
    methods with, 98–99
    other modifiers, table of, 55
    properties with, 107
    reflection, finding with, 282
    structs with, 69–70
    unsafe, 137–38
module assembly format, 29
modules
    features of, 30
    information in files, 31
    .netmodule extension, 31
    types, relying on other modules for, 31
MSIL (Microsoft intermediate language), 8
MSXML Schema, 251–52
MulticastSocket class (Java), 334
multifile assemblies
    CLS compliance, 497
    configuration files, 481
    creating, 34–35
    metadata, setting, 35
    purpose of, 31–32
Mutex class, 308–9

N

NameObjectCollectionBase, 202–3
names, computer, returning, 449
namespaces. *See also specific namespaces*
  accessibility of, 57
  aliases for, 57–58
  declaring, 56–57
  defined, 56
  elements allowed as members, 57
  keywords, 41–42
  nesting, 56–57
  syntax, 56–57
  using keyword to import, 57–58
NameValueCollection, 202–3
naming conventions
  @ symbol, 48
  $ not permitted, 41
  attributes, 127, 131
  casing, 40
  identifiers, 41
  method names, 40
native keyword (Java), 55
.NET Compact Framework, 13
.NET Framework
  class libraries, 8–9
  CLR, 8, 25, 482
  CLS, 8, 496–97
  CTS, 7–8, 496
  defined, 7–8
  JIT compiling, 8
  MSIL, 8
  tools, table of, 28
.NET initiative
  building block services, 13–14
  clients, 13
  development tools for, 9–12
  enterprise system support as goal, 5
  Framework. *See* .NET Framework
  goals of, 5–7
  JScript .NET, 11
  language neutrality, 6–7
  .NET Compact Framework, 13
  platform neutrality, 5–6
  programming languages for .NET, 10–12
  server products, 12–13
  shared source implementation, 6
  technology consolidation goal, 7
  Visual Basic .NET, 11
  Visual C++ .NET, 11
  Visual C# .NET, 10–11
  Visual J++ .NET, 11
  XML integration goal, 5
.NET SDK command line tools, 9
.netmodule extension, 31
network streams, 220
networking
  addressing, 323–28
  aliases, 326
  authorities, 313
  base addresses, 317–18
  byte arrays, downloading to, 316
  configuring hosts, 324–25
  configuring requests, 318–19
  connections, accepting, 332–33
  connections, database, 372–74
  connections, setting, 319, 323–25
  cookies, 315, 318
  creating requests, 318
  credentials, 315, 319–20
  DNS, 324–28
  downloading Web pages, 315–16, 321
  endpoints, application, 328, 333
  file requests and responses, 320–23
  FileWebRequest class, 320–23
  FileWebResponse class, 320–23
  FTP support lacking in .NET, 312
  GetResponse method, 320, 324
  headers, 317, 319, 320
  host names, 314, 315, 317, 323–28
  HTTP methods, 316
  HttpWebRequest class, 320–23
  HttpWebResponse class, 318, 320–23
  InetAddress class (Java), 326–28
  IP addressing, 323–28
  IPEndPoint class, 328
  Java vs. .NET classes for, 311–12
  local files, downloading to, 316
  methods, System.Uri, 313–15
  name resolution, 323–28
  pluggable protocol handlers, 312
  properties, WebRequest, 319
  properties, WebResponse, 320
  protocol-specific classes, 320–23
  proxies, 319
  requests, 318–20
  responses, 320–23
  ServicePoint class, 323–25
  sockets. *See* sockets
  SSL/TLS protocol, 321
  System.Uri class, 312–15
  TCP, 329–33
  tiers of service, 311
  timeouts, 323
  UDP, 334
  uploading data, 316–17
  URI class, 312–15
  UriBuilder class, 313
  URL class (Java), 312–13
  Web requests, performing, 315–23
  WebClient class, 315–17
  WebRequest class, 318–20
  WebResponse class, 318, 320–23
Networking API (Java 2), 19
New I/O APIs (Java 2), 18
new keyword
  hiding members, 90
  purpose of, 53
  strings created with, 148
  structs, 70

nodes, XML
content nodes, 247
DOM, Java vs. .NET, 261
Microsoft-specific node types, 244
names of, 244–45
navigating with XPath, 263–69
properties, table of, 246
returning content, methods for, 248
value, returning, 245
XmlTextReader class retrieval of, 244–48
XmlTextWriter to create, 257–58
noncompliance, CLS, 496–99
numbers
(digit placeholder), 180
CompareTo method, 174
converting, 86–87, 177
currency, 179
decimal format, 179
decimal members, 177
Equals method, 176
fixed-point format strings, 179
floating-point members, 176–77
formatting, 177–81
functions math, table of, 181–82
G strings, 179
hexadecimal format strings, 180
IComparable interface, 174
IConvertible interface, 175
IFormattable interface, 175, 177–78
infinity, 176–77
interfaces implemented by, 174–75
MaxValue field, 176
members implemented by types, 176–77
MinValue field, 176
N format strings, 179
numeric format strings, 179–81
objects, as, 173–77
operators on, 49
percentage format strings, 179
precision specifiers, 178–79
random, 182–83
rounding, 182
round-up format strings, 180
scientific notation, 178, 179, 181
standard numeric format strings, 179–80
ToString method, 175–78
WriteLine, formatting with, 178
numeric structs. *See* numbers
numeric types, 42–43, 72–73

O

object serialization. *See* serialization
object services. *See* remoting
object types, boxing, 67–68
observer pattern, 100
ObsoleteAttribute, 132–33
ODBC Data Providers, 367

OLE DB.NET Data Providers
defined, 367
direct SQL statements, 378
pooling connections, 373–74
OnPaint event handler, 427–28
operating system properties, returning, 449
operator members
binary, 113–14
conversion operators, 115
declaring, 112–15
defined, 111–12
implicit overloading, 114
language neutrality, 115
unary, 112–13
operator overloading
binary operators, 113–14
defined, 112
implicit, 114
indexers, 188–89
language neutrality, 115
unary operators, 112–13
operators
associativity, table of, 50–51
>>>(bitwise shift), 49
is, 50
Java compared to C#, table of, 49–50
pointer, 139–41
precedence, table of, 50–51
sizeof, 50
typeof, 50
optional permissions, CAS, 399, 402
options, C# compiler, table of, 26–28
org.w3c.dom package, 525–26
org.xml.sax package, 526
out keyword, 119
output parameters, 119
OutputStream class (Java), 218, 220
overflow, arithmetic, 63–64
overloading. *See* operator overloading
override keyword, 53, 90

P

packages. *See* namespaces
Paint events, 428
PAL (platform adaptation layer), 6
parameter arrays, 100
parameters
attributes with, 128
command-line arguments, 448
inspecting, 283–84
of methods, 99–100
output, of functions, 119
reference, 118
reflection, 283–84
SQL commands, 379–83
value, as variables, 117–18

parsing
  dates, 185
  Parse method for numbers, 176
  regular expressions, 164–65
  SAX parsers, 241
  strings, 153–54
  XML, 241–55. *See also* XmlReader class
Pascal casing, 40
Passport, Microsoft, 13
pass-through streams, 222
Path class, 210–12
PATH environment variable
  csc.exe not added, 25
  tools not added, 28
percentage format strings, 179
performance issues
  exception handling, 123
  implicit boxing, effect on, 68
  structs, 71–72
Permission Viewer tool, 403–4
permissions, CAS. *See* CAS, permissions
PictureBox controls, 423
PInvoke (Platform Invocation Service), 19
plaf package, java.swing, 523
Platform Invocation Service. *See* PInvoke
platform neutrality goal, 5–6
pluggable protocol handlers, 312
pointers
  & (address-of operator), 140
  -- (decrement operator), 141
  ++ (increment operator), 141
  -> (member access token), 140
  * (pointer token), 139–40
  addresses, displaying, 142
  arithmetic, 141
  comparison operators, 141
  conversions, 141–42
  declaring, 139–40
  defined, 139
  element access, 141
  fixed statements, 142–43
  indirection, 140
  member access, 140
  non-CLS compliant nature, 496
  to reference managed types, 138
  stackalloc command, 143
  strings with, 148–49
polymorphism, 89–90
portability
  hardware, 5–6
  programming languages. *See* language neutrality
  Windows, version effects of, 447
positioning controls, 424–26
precedence of operators, 50–51
Preferences API (Java 2), 19
preprocessor directives
  conditional directives, 134–35
  #define, 134
  defined, 133–34
  #elif, 134–35

#else, 134–35
#endif, 134–35
#endregion, 136
#error, 136–37
#if, 134–35
#ifdef, 131–32
#line, 137
operators, 135
#region, 136
#undef, 134
#warning, 136–37
primitive types (Java). *See* value types
printing, 506
process control
  closing objects, 451
  creating processes, 450–51
  events, 453
  Get methods, table of, 452
  Kill method, 452
  Mutex class, 308–9
  Process objects, 450–53
  ProcessStartInfo objects, 450–51
  properties of Process objects, 452–53
  references to existing processes, 451–52
  Start method, 450–51
  StartInfo property, 450
  synchronization, 308–9, 453
  System.Diagnostics namespace, 450
  terminating processes, 452
program structure, general, 37–38
programming languages for .NET, 10–12
properties
  declaring, 105–6
  get accessors with, 106
  inspecting, 282–83
  interfaces, as members of, 107
  modifiers with, 107
  purpose of, 105
  reflection, 282–83
  security. *See* role-based security
  set accessors with, 106
  types used for, 106
protected internal access, 52
protected keyword, 52
protocol handlers, 312
proxy classes, remoting, 347–48
public keyword, 38
publishing
  activation types, 353
  client activation, 354, 358–60
  client configuration, 358–60
  configuration files for, 356–60
  disconnecting instances, 356
  existing instances, 356
  limitations, 360
  scope, 360
  server activation, 354–56, 357–59
  server configuration, 357–58
  shared assemblies outside of GAC, 478–79
  Web services, 438–41

Q

queues, 199–200

R

random numbers, 182–83
Read method, 209
readers
    classes for, 222–25
    locking, 307–8
    XML, reading into, 242. *See also* XmlTextReader class
reading isolated data, 231–32
ReadLine method, 209
read-only fields, 94
readonly keyword, 55, 94
real literals, 51
ref keyword, 118
reference parameters, 118
reference types
    abstract classes, 77
    arrays, 81–82
    classes, 76–78
    conversion of, 86–87
    delegates, 83–85
    interfaces, 78–81
    memory allocation for, 67
references, weak, 494
reflection
    Activator class, 286–87
    Assembly class, 276–77
    attributes, 285
    BindingFlags enumeration, 278
    calling members using reflection classes, 286–87
    ConstructorInfo class, 280–82, 286
    constructors, 280–82
    defined, 275
    events, 283
    fields, 284–85
    foreign types, 276–77
    Get methods, 277–79
    instantiation, 286
    java.lang.reflect package equivalents, 510
    late binding, 285–87
    local types, 275–76
    MemberInfo class, 277–79
    MethodBase class, 280
    MethodInfo class, 287
    methods, 280–82, 286–87
    parameters, 283–84
    properties, 282–83
    representations of types, 277–79
    searching for members, 278
    system attributes, 285
    types, inspecting, 277–79
regex. *See* regular expressions
#region, 136
registry, Windows. *See* Windows registry

regular expressions
    @ (verbatim strings), 164–65
    ad hoc usage, 171
    compilation flags, table of, 165–66
    compiled flag, 166
    compiling, 164–66
    defined, 164
    IsMatch method, 166–69, 171
    matching input text, 166–69, 171
    parsing, 164–65
    Regex class, 164, 166–71
    regex package, .NET equivalents, 517–18
    Replace method, 169–70, 171
    replacing substrings in, 169–70
    splitting strings, 170–71
    text manipulation with, 166–71
Remote Method Invocation. *See* RMI
remoting
    activating services. *See* activation
    calling members, 347–48
    channels, 342–43, 345, 348–53
    client creation, 344–46
    compiling applications, 346
    configuration files for, 356–60
    copying classes via serialization, 347–48
    default lease values, 364
    defined, 341
    delegates, 360
    HttpChannel class, 342–43, 345
    ILease interface, 360–64
    instantiation, client activation, 354
    Java vs. .NET, 341
    leases, 360–64
    loading configuration files, 356–57
    MarshalByRefObject, 342, 347–48, 355, 360–62
    multithreaded environments with, 360
    namespace for, 342
    Object class methods, 360
    private methods, 360
    proxy classes, 347–48
    publishing services. *See* publishing
    referencing classes, 347–48
    referencing servers, 344–46
    registering for client activation, 354–55
    registering servers, 343–44
    Remote Method Invocation API (Java 2), 19
    renewing leases, 362–64
    scope of objects, 360
    server class creation, 342–44
    SOAP (Simple Object Access Protocol), 349, 351
    sponsors of objects, 363–64
    static members, 360
    System.Runtime.Remoting namespace, 342
    time before release, 360–64
    URLs, passing, 345
    well known requirement, 341
    Windows registry access, 456
requests, Internet, 318–20

resources, assemblies containing, 31
ResultSet (Java), 384
resurrection, 493
return statements, 61
RMI (Remote Method Invocation), 20, 341, 512
roaming users, isolated storage for, 229
role-based security, 406–9
rollbacks, 376
Rotor, 6
rounding numbers, 182
round-up format strings, 180
RowSet interface (Java), 365
RSA encryption, 412–13, 415–16
RTF (Rich Text Format), 523
Runnable interface (Java), 290
runtime environment, 447–49

S

SAX parsers, 241, 526
schemas
    DataSet, 393
    XML, 252
scientific notation, 178, 179, 181
SCM (Service Control Manager), 462, 465
sealed keyword, 53, 90
security
    code access. *See* CAS
    connections, setting, 373
    digital signatures, 415–16
    encryption. *See* cryptography
    evidence-based, 397–98
    role-based, 406–9
Security API (Java 2), 19
security manager, Java, 397
serialization
    AddValue method, 236–37
    custom, 235–37
    defined, 232
    deserialization, 234
    formatters, 232–34
    GetObjectData method, 235–37
    IFormatter interface, 232, 234
    ISerializable interface, 235–37
    remoting, class copying during, 347–48
    scope, setting, 236
    selective, 235
    Serializable attribute required, 233, 235
servers
    connections, setting, 323–25
    products, .NET integration of, 12–13
    remoting, class creation, 342–44
    TCP socket creation, 332–33
    XML services. *See* Web services
ServerSocket class (Java), 332
Service Control Manager (SCM), 462, 465
services, Web. *See* Web services
services, Windows. *See* Windows Services
Servlet API (J2EE), 21

set accessors, 106, 110
SHA hash codes, 413–14, 416
shared assemblies
    Assembly Linker Tool, 478
    assembly probing, 478–80
    codebase probing, 479–80
    compiling, 475
    creating, 473–74
    culture-neutral, 474
    defined, 473
    GAC, 474–78
    Global Assembly Cache Tool, 474–75
    key files, 474–75
    linker options for policies, 478
    naming, 473–74
    policies for versioning, 477–78, 480
    removing from GAC, 475
    side-by-side execution, 476–77
    storage of, 474
    strong names, 473–74, 476
    versioning, 475–78
    viewing list of, 475
signatures, digital, 415–16
simple types, table of, 42–43, 72–73
SingleCall activation, 355
single-file assemblies, 31–33
Singleton activation, 355
sizeof operator, 50, 139
smart devices, 13
SOAP (Simple Object Access Protocol)
    remoting channels with, 349, 351
    SoapFormatter, 232
    Web services with, 436, 440
sockets
    address families, 335
    asynchronous, 338
    byte arrays, 336
    client, 335–36
    closing, 333, 336
    configuring, 337–38
    connection options, setting, 337–38
    creating native, 335
    EndPoints, 336
    HTTP clients, 329–31
    IPv4, 335
    level elements, 337
    native, 335–38
    network streams, 220
    protocol specification, 335, 337
    server, 336–37
    shutting down, 336
    TCP client classes, 329–31
    TCP native, 335
    TCP server creation, 332–33
    type specification, 335, 337
    UDP, 334, 335
    WinSock32 API, 335
soft statements, 399–404

SortedLists, 201–2
sorting collections, 193
source files
    character sets, 40
    classes in, 41
    extension for, 26
    proxies, Web services, 443–44
sponsors of remote objects, 363–64
SQL commands
    configuring, 377–79
    CreateCommand method, 377
    Data Adapter methods for, 389
    DataReaders, 384–86
    DELETE command, 378
    direct SQL statements, 378–79
    execution methods, 383–84
    IDataReader, 384–86
    IDbCommand interface, 376–79, 384
    Java interfaces for, 376
    parameters, 379–83
    properties, table of, 377–78
    result sets, 384–86
    stored procedure execution, 379–83
    Transaction property, 378
    type, specifying, 377
    UPDATE command, 380–81
sql package, java, 512–14
sql package, javax.swing, 524
SQL Server database creation, 368
SQL Server.NET Data Providers
    commands. *See* SQL commands
    connections, 372–74
    defined, 367
    sample code, 368–72
    SqlConnection class, 373–74
    transactions, 374–76
SqlConnection class, 373–74
SSL/TLS protocol, 321
stack collection, 200–201
stackalloc command, 143
state maintenance
    GDI+ Graphics class, 428
    Web services, 441–43
statements
    empty, 58
    foreach statements, 60–61
    jump statements, 59, 61–62
    labeled, 59, 62
    lock statement, 62
    switch statements, 59–60
    syntax of, 58
    using statements, 64
static constructors, 96–97
static initialization blocks (Java). *See* static constructors
static keyword
    members with, 91
    purpose of, 55
    variables with, 116

storage, isolated, 228–32
stored procedure execution, 379–83
streams
    asynchronous, 225–28
    base streams, 219–21
    bidirectional support, 218
    BinaryReader class, 223
    BinaryWriter class, 223
    BufferedStream class, 222
    downloading Web pages, 315–16
    encrypted, 410–11
    exceptions, 218
    file access with, 214–16
    FileStream class, 214–16, 220, 222, 226–28
    isolated storage, 228–32
    memory streams, 220–21
    network streams, 220
    Null property, 219
    pass-through streams, 222
    random access, 218–19
    reader classes, 222–25
    serialization, 232–37
    Stream base class, 218
    StreamReader class, 224
    StreamWriter class, 224
    StringReader class, 225
    StringWriter class, 225
    synchronization support, 225
    TextReader class, 223–25
    TextWriter class, 223–25
    writer classes, 222–25
    XML, reading into, 242
    XmlTextWriter class with, 256
StreamWriter class, 224
strictfp keyword (Java), 46
string literals, 51
StringCollection class, 203
strings
    + (concatenation operator), 150
    == (equals operator), 149
    != (inequality operator), 149
    arrays, copying to, 152
    assignment operators, 148
    atomized, 240
    case, changing, 151
    character manipulation, 151–52
    comparing, 149–50
    comparisons with XML, 240
    concatenation, 150–51
    copying, 148, 150
    creating, constructors for, 148–49
    Decoder class, 160–61
    dynamically building, 162–63
    encoding characters, 157–62
    enumerating through, 151
    Equals method, 149
    format specifications, 155
    formatting, 154–57

strings, *continued*
    IFormattable interface, 156–57
    immutability of, 162
    importance of, 147
    indexers with, 151–52
    inserting substrings, 153, 163
    Join method, 150–51
    keys from, 153
    length of, obtaining, 150, 163
    new keyword with, 148
    objects, embedding in, 155
    padding characters, 152
    parsing, 153–54
    pointers with, 148–49
    regular expressions in. *See* regular expressions
    removing characters, 152, 163
    replacing characters, 152, 153, 163
    splitting, 153
    string keyword, 147
    StringBuilder class, 162–63
    StringReader class, 225, 241
    StringWriter class, 225
    substrings, 152–53
    System.String class, 147, 280–81
    trimming, 152
    WriteLine method with, 155
strong names, 473–74, 476
strongly-typed collections, 202–3
structs
    -> (member access token), 140
    assigning, 71
    defined, 69
    empty, 70
    field members, 94
    guidelines for using, 71–72
    instantiation, 70
    members allowed, 70
    modifiers for, 69–70
    new keyword, 70
    number objects as, 173
    operators as members, 111–15
    passing, 71
    performance issues, 71–72
    pointers, member access tokens, 140
    references, 71
    sizeof operator, 139
    value types implemented as, 68
structuring programs, 37–38
style sheets, XSL, 269–71
substrings, 152–53, 169–70
super keyword (Java), 90
Swing API (Java 2), 20, 419, 422–23, 518–24
switch statements, 59–60
synchronization
    AutoResetEvent class, 309–10
    defined, 305
    Enter method, 306–7
    Exit method, 306–7
    Interlocked class, 307–8

    locking, basic, 305–6
    locking, Monitor class, 306–7
    ManualResetEvent class, 309–10
    Monitor class methods, 306–7
    Mutex class, 308–9
    notifying, 306–7
    operating system, 308–10
    process control, 308–9, 453
    ReadWriterLock class, 307–8
    resetting events methods, 309–10
    Synchronized attribute, 305
    TryEnter method, 307
    variables, 307–8
    WaitHandle class, 308–10
    waiting, 306–7
synchronized keyword (Java), 55, 62, 305
Synchronized method for collections, 204
System.Environment class, 447–49
System.Net classes. *See* networking

T

table package, java.swing, 523
tables. *See* DataSets
TCP client classes, 329–31
TCP server creation, 332–33
TCP sockets, 349–53
termination status code, 38
text, XML, reading. *See* XmlTextReader class
TextReader class, 208, 223–25
TextWriter class
    console streams, 208
    methods, 223–25
    Write method, 208
    XmlTextWriter with, 256
this keyword
    constructors, 95
    indexer declarations with, 108
threading
    Abort method, 292–94
    advantages of .NET, 289
    annotated variables, 298
    asynchronous tasks, 302–4
    background threads, 295
    blocked threads, 295, 296–97, 306–7
    collections, safety, 204
    creating threads, 290–91
    daemon thread (Java), 295
    data slots, 297–98
    Enter method, 306–7
    enumerations, safety, 204
    exceptions, 292, 296
    Exit method, 306–7
    Forms.Timer class, 298–99
    Interlocked class, 307–8
    interrupting threads, 296–97
    IsAlive property, 295
    IsBackground property, 295
    Java, limitations of, 289
    local thread data, 297–98

locking threads, 305–7
members, table of, 301–2
metadata for local thread data, 298
Monitor class methods, 306–7
named slots, 297–98
new Thread method, 290–91
notifying, 306–7
operating system synchronization, 308–10
polling, 291–92
pools, 302–4
priorities, setting, 294
Process class control, 453
ReadWriterLock class, 307–8
ResetAbort method, 293–94
resuming threads, 291–92
safety, 204
starting threads, 290–91, 296
states of threads, 294–96
stopping threads, 292–94, 296
suspending threads, 291–92
synchronization of. *See* synchronization
System.Threading namespace, 290–91
System.Threading.Timer class, 299–300
System.Timers.Timer class, 300–301
Thread class, 301–2
ThreadAbortExceptions, 292–94
ThreadInterruptedExceptions, 296
ThreadPool class, 302–4
ThreadStart delegates, 290–91
ThreadState enumeration, 294–96
ThreadStateExceptions, 292
ThreadStatic attribute, 298
timers, 298–301
TryEnter method, 307
unnamed slots, 297–98
waiting, 306–7
yield method (Java), 294
throwing exceptions, 123
ticks, 184, 449
tilde (~), 97, 492
timers, thread, 298–301
times. *See* DateTime struct
TimeSpan struct, 184
tools, .NET Framework, table of, 28
ToString method, 175–78
Trace class, 133
tracking objects, 494
transactions
classes and methods, table of, 375
distributed, support for, 375
IDbCommand, Transaction property of, 378
IDbConnection.BeginTransaction method, 375
IDbTransaction interface, 375–76
inserting records, 375–76
isolation levels, 375
Java, 374–75
rollbacks, 376
transient keyword (Java), 46, 55

tree package, javax, 524
TripleDES, 409–11
true keyword, 49, 112–13
try keyword, 122
type members, 88–89
typeof operator, 50
types
base class, 66
boxing, 67–68
CLS compliance rules, 496
constants, 91–92
constructors. *See* constructors
conversion of, 85–88
declaring, keywords for, 43–44
events, 100–104
exposing information. *See* reflection
fields, 92–94
foreign, 276–77
implicit boxing, 68
inspecting, 277–79
interface types, 67
Java compared to C#, 65–66
keywords for manipulating, 43–44
kinds of, 65–66
late binding, 285–87
local, 275–76
members. *See* members
modules, relying on, 31
numeric, 42–43, 72–73
object capabilities, 66–68
reference. *See* reference types
reflection of. *See* reflection
simple, table of, 42–43, 72–73
structs, 68–69
System.Object base type, 66
System.Type, 275, 277–79
typeof operator, 50
unboxing, 68
unified type system, 66–68
unmanaged, 138
value. *See* value types
variables, 116–17
typography. *See* GDI+

U

UDDI (Universal Description, Discovery and
Integration), 436
UI toolkits, 20. *See also* Windows Forms
unary operator members, 112–13
unboxing, 68
unchecked keyword, 64
undo package, javax.swing, 524
Unicode
encoding characters, 157–62
identifiers with, 40
unified type system, 66–68. *See also* types
unmanaged code. *See* unsafe code

unsafe code
 defined, 137
 fixed statements, 142–43
 keywords, table of, 48
 pointers, 139–42
 sizeof operator for, 138
 stackalloc command, 143
 unmanaged types, 138
 /unsafe flag, 138
 unsafe modifier, 137–38
URI access
 methods, System.Uri, 313–15
 pluggable protocol handlers, 312
 System.Uri class, 312–15
 UriBuilder class, 313
URLConnection class (Java), 315
URLs
 access. *See* URI access
 remoting, specifying, 345
 Web services, for accessing, 439
users, current, identifying, 408, 449
users, security based on. *See* role-based security
using keyword, 38, 42, 57–58, 64
UTF-8, 158–62
Util API (Java 2), 18, 515–17

V
value parameters, 117–18
value types
 boxing, 67–68
 defined, 66–67
 implicit boxing, 68
 kinds of, 68
 object capabilities, 66–68
 simple types, table of, 72–73
 structs, 68–72
 unboxing, 68
variables
 environment, 448
 locking, Interlocked class, 307–8
 output parameters, 119
 reference parameters, 118
 strong typing of, 116
 types of, table of, 116–17
 value parameters as, 117–18
vector image support, 432–33
versioning
 assembly manifest information on, 30
 assembly probing, 478–79
 codebase probing, 479–80
 linker options for policies, 478
 of members, 89–90
 methods, polymorphism issues, 89
 policy files for applications, 477–78, 480
 shared assemblies, 475–78
 side-by-side execution, 476–77
virtual directories, 438

virtual keyword, 53, 89–90
Visual Basic .NET, 11
Visual C++ .NET, 11
Visual C# .NET, purpose of, 10–11
Visual J++ .NET, 11, 15
Visual J# .NET, 15
Visual Studio .NET
 purpose of, 10
 Web services support, 435
volatile keyword, 55

W
WaitHandle class, 308–10
#warning, 136–37
warning levels, compiler options, 27
weak references, 494
Web requests, performing, 315–23
Web services
 application state management, 442
 .asmx extension, 439
 ASP.NET basis for, 435–36
 assemblies, 439
 asynchronous programming of, 445–46
 CacheDuration property, 437
 clients, 443–46
 compiling, 438–39
 configuring, 439–41
 creating, 436–37
 defined, 436
 deployment directories, 438
 Description property, 437
 directive file creation, 439
 Documentation protocol, 440–41
 HTTP protocols, 440–41
 HttpApplicationState instances, 442–43
 IIS binding requirement, 435
 key technologies, table of, 436
 MapPoint .NET, 13
 Name property, 437
 namespaces for, 436–37
 Passport, Microsoft, 13
 protocols element, 440–41
 proxy classes, 443–45
 publishing, 438–41
 session state management, 442–43
 SOAP, 436, 440
 state management in, 441–43
 synchronous methods, 445
 system integration with, 14
 System.Web.Services namespace, 436
 testing, 441
 UDDI, 436
 URLs to access, 439
 virtual directories, 438
 Visual Studio .NET support for, 435
 WDSL, 441
 WebMethod attribute, 436–37, 442–43

WebService attribute, 436–37
WebService class, 441–42
WSDL, 436
wsdl.exe tool, 443–44
WebClient class, 315–17
WebRequest class, 318–20
WebResponse class, 318, 320–23
Windows event log
    Application logs, 456–58
    console, writing to, 461–62
    deleting logs, 460
    deregistration, 457
    EventLog class access, 456
    EventLogEntry properties, 458–60
    existence of logs, determining, 460
    new log creation, 460
    notifications, 460–62
    purpose of, 456
    reading logs, 458–60
    remote machine logs, 457
    service for automatic logging, 463–66
    source registration, 456–57
    writing entries, 457–58
Windows Forms
    adding controls, 420
    anchoring controls, 424–25
    base class for, 420
    buttons, adding, 420
    buttons, table of, 422
    compiling applications, 421
    containers for controls, 420, 422
    date controls, 423
    defined, 419
    dialog box controls, 423
    disposing of controls, 420
    docking controls, 425–26
    drawing. See GDI+
    event handling, 426–27
    exiting applications, 421
    Form class, 420
    graphics, 423. See also GDI+
    list controls, 422–23
    Location property, 424
    menu controls, 422
    PictureBox controls, 423
    positioning controls, 424–26
    scrollbar controls, 423
    starting applications, 421
    text display controls, 423
    text editing controls, 423
    value controls, 422
Windows registry
    keys, 454
    purpose of, 454
    Registry class, 454
    RegistryKey class, 454, 455
    remote access to, 456
Windows Services
    account control, 468

base class for, 462
compiling, 469
configuration information, 468
constructors, 462–64
controllers, 469–71
creating, 462–64
defined, 462
getting installed services, 470
Installer Tool, 466, 469
installers, 466–69
installuti.exe, 466, 469
life cycle control, 462, 464–65
Main method implementation, 462–63
name specification, 469
overriding base methods, 462
properties of installers, 468–69
SCM, 462, 465
service application component, 462–66
ServiceBase class, 462–66
ServiceController class, 469–71
ServiceInstaller, 468–69
ServiceProcessInstaller, 468
Services Utility, 469
Windows Users and Groups, security, 406–9
winexe assembly format, 29
Write method console streams, 208
write once, run anywhere slogan, 5–6
WriteLine methods
    console streams with, 208
    numeric formatting with, 178
    string formatting with, 154–55
writers
    classes, 222–25
    locking, 307–8
    XML. See XmlTextWriter class
writing isolated data, 231–32
WSDL (Web Services Description Language), 436
wsdl.exe tool, 443–44

X

XDR schemas, 251–52
XML (Extensible Markup Language)
    atomized strings, 240
    attributes, accessing, 248–51
    attributes, navigating with XPath, 264–66
    building block services, 13–14
    constructors, XmlTextReader class, 242
    content nodes, 247
    DataSet support for, 391–95
    DiffGrams, 393–94
    document nodes, 261
    DOM, 260–62
    DTDs. See DTDs
    extensibility, .NET approach to, 271
    features of .NET, table of, 240
    formatting output, 258–59
    integration as .NET goal, 5
    Java support for, 19, 239, 524–25

XML (Extensible Markup Language), *continued*
  namespace support, 260
  namespaces, navigating with XPath, 264–66
  NameTable class, 240
  nodes, readers working with, 244–48
  opening sources, 241–42
  org.w3c.dom package, 525–26
  parsing with XmlReader class, 241–55
  push vs. pull parsing models, 241
  query support, 267–69
  read operations, 246–48
  reader classes. *See* XmlReader class
  returning content, methods for, 248
  SAX parsers, 241
  serialization, 232
  SoapFormatter, 232, 234
  streams, reading, 242
  string comparison, 240
  text reader classes. *See* XmlTextReader class
  transformers, creating, 269–70
  validation. *See* XmlValidatingReader class
  Web services. *See* Web services
  writing. *See* XmlTextWriter class
  XmlDocument class, 261
  XmlNameTable base class, 240
  XmlNodeReader class, 255
  XmlReader class, 241–55
  XmlTextReader class, 241–51
  XmlTextWriter class, 254–60
  XmlWriter class, 255–60
  XSL Transformations, 269–71
XML Schema, 252
XML Web services. *See* Web services
XmlDataDocuments, 394–95
XmlDocument class, 261
XmlNodeReader class, 255
XmlReader class
  default method behaviors, 251
  validation with. *See* XmlValidatingReader class
  XmlNodeReader class, 255
  XmlTextReader. *See* XmlTextReader class
  XmlValidatingReader, 251–55
XmlSchemaCollection class, 253–54
XmlTextReader class
  attributes, accessing, 248–51
  closing, 251
  constructors, 242
  content nodes, 247
  cursor operations, 246–48
  IsStartElement method, 247
  MoveToAttribute method, 249
  MoveToContent method, 247
  names of nodes, returning, 244–45
  namespace support, 243
  node properties, table of, 246
  nodes, working with, 244–48
  opening sources, 241–42
  parsing behavior properties, 243

  properties, 242–43
  Read method, 247
  read operations, 246–48
  reader state, 242–43
  remainders, unparsed, 251
  resetting for multiple documents, 243
  returning content, methods for, 248
  Skip method, 247
  unimplemented default method behaviors, 251
  values of nodes, returning, 245
  white space, 243
  XmlResolver property, 243
  XmlValidatingReader class, compared to, 254–55
XmlTextWriter class
  closing, 260
  constructors for, 256
  creation, 256
  formatting output, 258–59
  namespace support, 260
  nodes, creating, 257–58
  noninherited members, 256
  status enumeration, 256–57
  streams with, 256
  writing with, 257–58
  XmlWriter class base for, 255
XmlValidatingReader class
  caching schemas, 253–54
  creating, 252
  errors, results of, 253
  Schemas property, 253
  specifying validation type, 252
  validators available, 251–52
  XmlSchemaCollection class with, 253–54
  XmlTextReader, compared to, 254–55
XPath
  attribute navigation, 264–66
  cache, providing, 263
  cursors, 263
  Evaluate method, 268
  expressions, access using, 262–63
  IXPathNavigable, 262
  Matches method, 268
  methods, navigation, table of, 264, 265
  namespace navigation, 264–66
  navigating nodes, 263–69
  node property information, 267
  node types, returning, 263–64
  optimized queries, 268–69
  query support, 267–69
  Select method, 268
  XPath namespace, 262
  XPathDocument class, 263
  XPathExpression class, 267–68
  XPathNavigator class, 263–69
XSD schemas, 393–94
XSL (Extensible Stylesheet Language), 269
XSLT (XSL Transformations), 269–71

Allen Jones

Allen Jones, a former Microsoft employee, has spent his career implementing corporate and financial solutions based on Microsoft enterprise products. One of the first MCSEs anywhere, he has developed Microsoft Windows–based solutions since 1990, has worked with Windows NT and Win32 since 1993, and has developed e-commerce and security systems with Java for years.

Adam Freeman

Adam Freeman has been developing in Java since before its public release and has written several best-selling Java books. He has developed some of the most complex and innovative Java projects in the world while working for companies such as Netscape, Sun Microsystems, and the NASDAQ stock exchange

Pipe Valves

Pipe valves come in a number of shapes, sizes, materials, and configurations, including ball, check, butterfly, diaphragm, gate, globe, and compressed-air valves. Some are made of metal; many these days, however, are made of polypropylene plastic, which is cheaper and lighter than most metals and can handle chemicals that metal valves cannot. Pipe valves are commonly used in residential, commercial, and industrial applications where pressurized liquid or air must be moved between two different pipes or containers. The pipe valve allows someone to start or shut off the flow of the liquid or gas.

At Microsoft Press, we use tools to illustrate our books for software developers and IT professionals. Tools very simply and powerfully symbolize human inventiveness. They're a metaphor for people extending their capabilities, precision, and reach. From simple calipers and pliers to digital micrometers and lasers, these stylized illustrations give each book a visual identity, and a personality to the series. With tools and knowledge, there's no limit to creativity and innovation. Our tagline says it all: *the tools you need to put technology to work.*

The manuscript for this book was prepared and galleyed using Microsoft Word. Pages were composed by Microsoft Press using Adobe FrameMaker+SGML for Windows, with text in Garamond and display type in Helvetica Condensed. Composed pages were delivered to the printer as electronic prepress files.

Cover Designer:	Methodologie, Inc.
Interior Graphic Designer:	James D. Kramer
Principal Compositor:	Dan Latimer
Interior Artist:	Joel Panchot
Principal Copy Editor:	Shawn Peck
Indexer:	Bill Meyers

Get a **Free**
e-mail newsletter, updates,
special offers, links to related books,
and more when you

register on line!

Register your Microsoft Press® title on our Web site and you'll get
a FREE subscription to our e-mail newsletter, *Microsoft Press Book
Connections.* You'll find out about newly released and upcoming books
and learning tools, online events, software downloads, special offers
and coupons for Microsoft Press customers, and information about
major Microsoft® product releases. You can also read useful additional
information about all the titles we publish, such as detailed book
descriptions, tables of contents and indexes, sample chapters, links to
related books and book series, author biographies, and reviews by other
customers.

Registration is easy. Just visit this Web page and fill in your information:

http://www.microsoft.com/mspress/register

Microsoft®

Proof of Purchase

Use this page as proof of purchase if participating in a promotion or rebate offer on
this title. Proof of purchase must be used in conjunction with other proof(s) of
payment such as your dated sales receipt—see offer details.

C# for Java Developers
0-7356-1779-1

CUSTOMER NAME

Microsoft Press, PO Box 97017, Redmond, WA 98073-9830